CLASSICS

FROM THE FILES OF

TODD WILBUR

Illustrated by the Author

A PLUME BOOK

PLUME
Published by the Penguin Group
Penguin Group (USA) Inc., 375 Hudson Street, New York, New York 10014, U.S.A.
Penguin Books Ltd, 80 Strand, London WC2R 0RL, England
Penguin Books Australia Ltd, 250 Camberwell Road, Camberwell, Victoria 3124, Australia
Penguin Books Canada Ltd, 10 Alcorn Avenue, Toronto, Ontario, Canada M4V 3B2
Penguin Books India (P) Ltd, 11 Community Centre, Panchsheel Park, New Delhi – 110 017, India
Penguin Books (N.Z.) Ltd, Cnr Rosedale and Airborne Roads, Albany, Auckland 1310, New Zealand
Penguin Books (South Africa) (Pty) Ltd, 24 Sturdee Avenue, Rosebank, Johannesburg 2196, South Africa

Penguin Books Ltd, Registered Offices: 80 Strand, London WC2R 0RL, England

First published by Plume, a member of Penguin Group (USA) Inc.

First Printing, October 2005
10 9 8 7 6 5 4 3 2 1

Most of the recipes in this edition are selected from *Top Secret Recipes, More Top Secret Recipes, Even More Top Secret Recipes, Top Secret Restaurant Recipes, Low-Fat Top Secret Recipes, Top Secret Recipes Lite!,* and *Top Secret Recipes: Sodas, Smoothies, Spirits, & Shakes,* all published by Plume.

ISBN: 0-452-28723-5

Manufactured in China.

CONTENTS

Conversions

A LITTLE FOREWORD

In the laboratory (my kitchen), each of these recipes was subjected to a battering array of bakings and mixings, batch after batch, until the closest representation of the actual commercial product was finally achieved. I did not swipe, heist, bribe, or otherwise obtain any formulas through coercion or illegal means. I'd like to think that many of these recipes are the actual formulas for their counterparts, but there's no way of knowing for sure. In such cases of closely guarded secret recipes, the closer one gets to matching a real product's contents, the less likely it is that the protective manufacturer will say so.

The objective here was to match the taste and texture of the products with everyday ingredients. In most cases, obtaining the exact ingredients for these mass-produced food products is nearly impossible. For the sake of security and convenience, many of the companies have contracted confidentially with vendors for the specialized production and packaging of each of their product's ingredients. These prepackaged mixes and ingredients are then sent directly to the company for final preparation.

Debbi Fields of Mrs. Fields Cookies, for example, arranged with several individual companies to custom manufacture many of her cookies' ingredients. Her vanilla alone is specially blended from a variety of beans grown in various places around the world. The other ingredients—the chocolate, the eggs, the sugars, the flour—all get specialized attention specifically for the Mrs. Fields company. The same holds true for McDonald's, Burger King, KFC, and most of the big-volume companies.

Even if you could bypass all the security measures and somehow get your hands on the secret formulas, you'd have a hard time executing the recipes without locating many ingredients usually impossible to find at the corner market. Therefore, with taste in mind, substitution of ingredients other than those that may be used in the actual products is necessary in many cases to achieve a closely cloned end result.

INTRODUCTION

THE QUESTIONS. THE ANSWERS.

After the first *Top Secret Recipes* came out, people had a lot of questions: "Why did you write this book?" "How did you write this book?" "Can I have a free book?" I started jotting the questions down in case I ever had an occasion to use them. This is that occasion. Here are several of the questions I've been asked most often along with their nearly spontaneous answers.

1. How did you learn to cook?

I started cooking when I was a kid, just because I was hyperactive and had to be doing something at all times. I made cookies. I cooked eggs. I made cookies in eggs. And, yes, I made a mess.

Eventually, I went off to college and was forced to learn a whole new culinary skill. The food in the dining halls was terrible, so those of us who wanted to eat something other than that prison food had to be resourceful. We were too broke to go out, so we designed a whole menu of cheap food that could be cooked in a toaster oven or hot pot. English muffin pizzas. Tuna melts. Top ramen. Kraft macaroni and cheese. Then we would invent new, creative dishes. Nacho popcorn (popcorn with sliced cheese melted over it.) Leftover pizza casserole (cut pizza slices into pan, add macaroni and cheese, bake). Ramen stew (top ramen mixed with bits of anything edible). These were staples of my college existence and my early culinary training.

Life after college was the real training ground. One of my many jobs was at a dinner theater called The Harlequin in Orange County, California. I was a waiter in the ritzy section of the theater, the balcony, where I had to learn to make Caesar salads at the table and flambé desserts without scorching any eyebrows. This is where my interest in gourmet cooking was piqued. And where, unfortunately, I was fired within a month for spending too much time backstage talking to the actresses.

But I kept cooking on my own, as anyone does out of the necessity to eat. It was in 1987 that I received in the mail the chain-letter recipe that was supposedly the "Secret Recipe" for Mrs. Fields Cookies. It wasn't actually the secret recipe, but it had become a very popular chain letter, one that had been distributed throughout the country by people who thought they had the real secret. I tried the recipe and the cookies were good, but I knew Mrs. Fields Cookies. I loved Mrs. Fields Cookies. These were *not* Mrs. Fields Cookies!

So I set out to improve the recipe. I went to the nearest Mrs. Fields outlet and got my hands on an ingredients list for her cookies, and went to work. Batch after batch, I experimented and eventually came up with a cookie that tasted like the real thing. I figured I'd see what else I could duplicate. How about a Big Mac? I went to McDonald's, bought the real thing, and took it apart. It wasn't hard to find a dressing like the "Special Sauce" (Kraft Thousand Island) and then to build a burger the same way McDonald's teaches it at Hamburger University.

I spent the next five years learning about cooking from the inside out. I cooked and baked and boiled to create clone recipes of famous foods. I learned the properties of different ingredients—which would thicken or sweeten, which would brown, when to fry. I learned from doing it over and over again, out of curiosity.

As I continued adding clone recipes to my growing list, I realized it would make a fun book. I did some line drawings of the products, put it all together, and eventually found a publisher who didn't think I was entirely nuts.

2. What have you heard from companies whose products you are copying?

Nothing. Not one of these companies has contacted me or my publisher to complain or otherwise comment about the book or any product that is represented.

I hope any company represented in a volume of *Top Secret Recipes* realizes that it is because its products are popular enough to warrant inclusion, and that imitation is the sincerest form of flattery.

3. How do you figure out the recipes for these products?

If it's a packaged product, I'll start with the ingredients list. Thanks to an FDA law, ingredients must be listed in descending order of their percentages in the product. Most of the main ingredients are easy to find at any supermarket. I just ignore the chemicals and preservatives that usually show up in small amounts at the end of the ingredients list, since we're going to eat the food fresh and don't have to worry about spoiling.

I then try to assemble the product in a test batch, which usually comes out tasting pretty horrible. From there it's just a matter of using more of some ingredients and less of others until the finished product tastes like the original. It may take only a couple of attempts to get it right, or it may take dozens.

Cooking times and preparation techniques can often be determined from recipes I've collected for products similar to the one I'm trying to clone. For example, if I want to make biscuits that taste like Popeye's Famous Biscuits, I may find a recipe for generic biscuits to give me a starting point and adjust it to match the brand-name original.

For products that don't have ingredients lists, like fast-food items, I use my own sense of taste. I take the product home and disassemble it, and then attempt to reassemble it with ingredients bought at a grocery store. Some products can't be duplicated because the basic ingredients aren't available.

Not only can the entire process be very time-consuming and frustrating, but it tends to get a bit expensive when I have to go through several versions of one recipe until I get it right. But I have to say, it's a thrill to finally come up with a recipe for a finished product that tastes exactly like the famous brand-name food.

4. Don't you have to do a lot of dishes?

Yes, I do. But I've learned that if you run really hot water at full blast over anything long enough it will eventually come clean.

5. What do you do with all that food you make?

Most of the rejects that don't come out like the original are still perfectly tasty. I give those to friends or neighbors, even my dog, just as I do most of the recipes that finally come out perfect. I like to get a little feedback from time to time to see if someone other than me thinks the recipe is a good one.

6. After testing all these recipes, aren't you a huge, fat pig?

I'm not huge, and I'm not fat. I'm 6' 1" and weigh 190 pounds. Although, yes, I am a pig.

7. When you're not working on one of these books, do you eat all this stuff anyway?

You bet. The books originated out of my true passion for "convenience food." And I know there are a lot of other people out there who get secret cravings for the items featured in my books, whether they'll admit it or not. America loves this food. It's all around us, and fast-food chains are still opening stores at a rate of nine or ten a week. Somebody's buying it.

Yes, I eat this stuff. But not all the time. I do think it's important to balance your diet with healthful, low-fat meals. I just eat this type of food when I get irresistible cravings. Like I did yesterday. And the day before that. And the day before that.

8. What if I make a recipe and it doesn't taste like the real thing?

Gosh, I don't know what to say. Maybe you made it wrong. Maybe you made a mistake. Maybe you scorched your taste buds on hot coffee one too many times and need expensive experimental microsurgery to restore those fragile sensors to their normal state. I'm just throwing out ideas here.

9. Why would people want to make these recipes at home if they can just as easily go out and buy the real thing?

This is a good question that I get asked all the time. And there are several possible answers.

1. *Cost.* It is actually less expensive to clone most of these products at home in your kitchen than it is to buy the originals.
2. *Taste.* Most of these goodies taste better fresh than they do after sitting on a store shelf for days, sometimes weeks.
3. *Availability.* Some of these brand-name products are only available

in very limited regions of the country. Now you can enjoy anything in this book, anytime, anywhere.

4. *Customization.* Now you can cook your McDonald's hamburger the way *you* want to, or you can use dark chocolate on a candy bar that is only available with milk chocolate.
5. *Fun.* This is a cheap, fun, and harmless thrill.
6. *Curiosity.* You too can find out if it's really possible to make an Oreo at home. (It really is. Try it.)

SOME COOKING TIPS FROM A GUY WHO CARES

Sometimes I can be a real idiot in the kitchen. I've wasted as many as four eggs when separating the whites by accidentally dropping in specks of yolk. I've often burned chocolate when melting it for dipping candy, and I've squandered hours on making dough for a simple recipe just because I forgot to look at the date on the package of yeast.

It was on these days that I determined there is a hard way to pick up little cooking hints, and there's an easy way. The hard way is by doing what I did—screwing up, then having to throw away your mistakes and run to the store in the pouring rain with a fistful of change to buy more ingredients so you can start the whole thing over again.

Then there is the easy way, which is to get cooking tips from somebody who learned the hard way.

SOME WORDS ABOUT CHOCOLATE

First off, some words about that delicate substance we call chocolate. Everybody's eaten it, but if you've cooked with it, you know it can be a pain—especially when the recipe requires that you melt it, as some of the recipes in this book do.

There are several different types of chocolate: sweet, semisweet, bittersweet, unsweetened, milk chocolate, and white chocolate (which actually isn't chocolate at all).

You will be using only semisweet and milk chocolate. Both are called for in the form of chocolate chips, which you buy by the bag. The most common are Nestlé and Hershey. Each company makes both milk chocolate and semisweet, and each works equally well.

I have found that the best place to melt chocolate is in the microwave. Semisweet chocolate is much easier to work with than milk chocolate, because it contains more chocolate liquor and no milk solids. Semisweet will melt to a much smoother, thinner consistency, and will not scorch as easily. This means that semisweet lends itself much more readily to dipping.

When melting either type of chocolate, use a microwave-safe glass or ceramic bowl that will retain heat. Set your microwave on half power and melt the chips for 1 minute. Stir. Rotate the bowl and microwave for another minute. Stir again. After 2 minutes, if the chocolate needs to melt more, heat it in 30-second intervals.

With milk chocolate, you have to find a delicate balance between microwaving and stirring. If you heat the chips too much, the chocolate will scorch. If you stir too much, the chocolate won't set up properly when you dip. Perfectly melted milk chocolate should set nearly as firm as it was in its original form at room temperature (68 to 70°F).

If you can't use a microwave to melt your chocolate, use a double boiler. You want to set the heat very low so that the water in the double boiler is only simmering and not boiling. Boiling water will scorch chocolate. Grease the inside of your double boiler lightly before you put the chocolate in and you'll be able to get practically all melted chocolate out of the pan.

For some of the recipes in this book, you may feel like substituting dark, semisweet chocolate instead of milk chocolate or even using white chocolate. It may be worth a try. How about a white-chocolate–covered Milky Way? Hmm.

And here's another tip to remember when making anything with chocolate. You can intensify the chocolate flavor by adding some vanilla to the recipe. You'll notice that this is what I've done with the recipes in the book for chocolate icings.

SOME WORDS ABOUT YEAST DOUGH

There are some recipes in this book that call for yeast dough, and I thought it was important to supply you with some pointers that will help you here and in the rest of your dough-making life.

The only yeast you'll need to use with this book is Fleischmann's—the type that comes in the three-envelope packages. That's the only kind I ever use. Always check to be sure the yeast you're using has not expired. Every package of yeast is stamped with an expiration date—usually eight to twelve months from the date you purchased it. Store your unopened yeast packages in the refrigerator.

When kneading dough, use your hands. This is much better than a wooden or plastic spoon because the warmth of your hands will help the yeast start rising (and it brings you back to those carefree Play-Doh days). When the dough pulls away from your hands easily, it has been kneaded enough.

One good way to get the dough rising is to put it in its bowl, uncovered, in the oven (the oven should be off) with a pan of boiling water. The hot water will start the dough rising right away, and the moisture from the water will keep the dough's surface from getting hard and dry.

You can tell when the dough has risen enough by sticking your finger into it up to the first knuckle. If the dough does not bounce back, it's ready. If it giggles, you're in a Pillsbury commercial.

SOME WORDS ABOUT SEPARATING EGGS

For the recipes that require egg whites, I've found that one of the easiest ways to separate the white from the yolk is to crack the egg with one hand into the other hand cupped over a small bowl. The egg whites will run out between your fingers, and you will be holding just the yolk in your hand. You can also use a small funnel. Just crack the egg into the funnel, and the egg white will run through, leaving the yolk. Use a container other than the bowl you will be beating the whites in. You don't want to risk ruining all the whites if some yolk should fall through.

If an accident should happen and you do get some yolk into the whites, use one of the egg shells to scoop out the yolk. Strangely, the shells act like a magnet for the specks of stray yolk.

To save your yolks for another recipe, slide them into a small bowl or cup, pour some cold water over them, and store them in the refrigerator. When you want to use the yolks, just pour off the water and slide the yolks into your recipe.

By the way, as a general rule in this book and any other cookbook, when a recipe calls for eggs and does not specify size, always use large eggs. Medium or extra-large eggs could throw off your measurements.

SOME WORDS ABOUT BAKING

Every once in a while, you should check your oven thermostat with an oven thermometer. I did and found out that my oven was off by twenty-five degrees. That's normal. It can be off by twenty-five degrees in either direction, but if it's any more than that, you should make adjustments when cooking, and get it fixed.

When baking, allow at least fifteen minutes for your oven to preheat. This is especially important if you do not have an indicator light that tells you when your oven is ready.

Several recipes in this book call for baking on cookie sheets. I highly recommend using two cookie sheets and alternating them, putting one sheet in the oven at a time. This will allow you to let one sheet cool before loading it up for the next run. If you don't let the sheet cool, your cooking time may be inaccurate because the dough will start to heat before you put the sheet into the oven.

If you absolutely must bake more than one cookie sheet at a time, you'll have to extend the cooking time. It will take the oven longer to reach the proper temperature with more dough to heat.

If you're baking cookies, you can very easily make them all uniform in size by rolling the dough into a tube with the diameter you need, then slicing it with a very sharp knife.

Keep in mind, especially with cookies, that baked goods will continue to cook for a while even after they've come out of the oven unless you remove them to a rack. The cookie sheet or baking pan will still be hot, and the sugar in the recipe will retain heat. This is why many people tend to overcook their cookies. I know the feeling. When you follow suggested cooking times, it sometimes seems as though the cookies aren't done when they come out of the oven—and they probably aren't. But they'll be fine after sitting for some time on the cookie sheet.

SOME WORDS ABOUT HAMBURGER PATTIES

Just about every backyard hamburger cookout I've attended included hamburger patties that tipped the scale in size and weight. Most homemade burgers are way too thick to cook properly, and the added thickness doesn't add anything to the taste of the sandwich. In fact, if we cut the amount of beef we use in the hamburger patties, we're cutting out excess fat and calories, decreasing the chance that the burgers may not cook thoroughly, while not compromising anything in overall taste. At the same time, thicker patties tend to shrink up as they cook into unmanageable mutant forms, bulging in the middle, and stacking poorly onto buns and lettuce.

You'll notice that every hamburger recipe in this book requires a very thin patty. This is the way the experts in the business do it—the Dave Thomases, the Carl Karchers, the McDonald Brothers—for concerns over cost, taste and a thorough, bacteria-free cooking process. But just how do we get our patties so thin like the big boys, and still make them easy to cook without breaking? We freeze 'em, folks.

Plan ahead. Hours, even days, before you expect to make your hamburgers, pat the patties out onto wax paper on a cookie sheet with a diameter slightly larger than the buns you are using, and about 1/8 to 1/4 inch thick (with consistent thickness from center to edge). Thickness depends on the burger: If you're making a small hamburger, like the one at McDonald's, which is only about 1/8 ounce before cooking, make the patties 1/8 inch thick. If you're going for the Quarter Pounder, make your patty 1/4 inch thick—never more than that. Lay wax paper over the top of your patties and put them in the freezer.

When your patties are completely frozen, it's time to cook. You can cook them straight out of the freezer on a hot grill or frying pan for 3 to 7 minutes per side, without worrying about thorough cooking. And the patties will flip easily without falling apart.

INTRODUCTION TO *TOP SECRET RECIPES®* *CLASSICS*

Just about every person with taste buds wonders on some occasion after savoring a delicious restaurant dish or an addictive mass-produced convenience food if it's possible to re-create the taste in a home kitchen. I call it "kitchen cloning," and with this book, not only will you see that it is possible, but you'll also find out, first-hand, what a kick it is to duplicate the most famous brand-name foods in your own home using common ingredients.

My mission over the last decade—as I have chosen to accept it—is to develop secret formulas and simple techniques to help you produce home versions of the food on which America most loves to nosh. Throughout the previous *Top Secret Recipes* books are hundreds of kitchen clones for famous brand-name foods, often with deep histories and cult followings. These are foods that have made millionaires of their creators, and that trigger a reaction in our salivary glands upon a mere mention. These are foods that have satiated generations before us, and will continue to satisfy long after we are gone.

The mission is not often a simple one, since reverse-engineering foods can be a tedious and time-consuming task. Trial and error is the play of the day, and many of the results take a fateful trip into the garbage disposal or into the super-fat Chow Chow dog, Zebu. But when the finished product hits the mark, all the work is rewarded, and the successful results are passed along to you.

Here is a collection of my favorite recipes culled from all of my books produced over the last decade, arranged in one easy-to-use volume. These are my all-time favorites—my go-to recipes when I'm cooking from the *Top Secret Recipes* books, and the recipes I recommend when a friend asks, "What should I make?"

Special in this book are 22 new recipes that have never been available in stores. These recipes are truly special since they come from hundreds of reader requests, and have been on the *Top Secret* back burner for a long time. I'm talking about recipes such as Burger King Onion Rings, Carnegie Deli Classic New York City Cheesecake, and Popeyes Buttermilk Biscuits. Oh, there go the salivary glands.

So have fun with this unique collection. And beware of other so-called copycat recipes floating around out there. My culinary assignment guarantees these *Top Secret Recipes* to be original creations that are thoroughly tested before I share them with you. That's the only way I can consider this a "mission accomplished."

—Todd Wilbur

TOP SECRET RECIPES VERSION OF

ARBY'S BRONCO BERRY SAUCE

☆ ✌ 💣 ✏ ☯ ✂ ☞

This sweet and spicy jelly sauce comes on the side, in little 1.5-ounce containers, with Arby's battered jalapeño and cheese Side Kickers. But, you know, you just never get enough of the tasty gelatinous goo in those little dipping packs to use later with your own home-cooked delicacies. And isn't it odd that the sauce is called "Bronco Berry" when there's not a berry to be found in there? Sure, the sauce is bright red and sugary, but you won't find a speck of fruit on the ingredients list. Nevertheless, the sweet and spicy flavors make this a delicious jelly sauce that has many uses beyond dipping quick service finger foods. For one, use it as a side sauce for your next batch of lamb chops rather than mint jelly. It would take more than just a few blister packs to perk up that meal.

¾ cup water
⅓ cup sugar
¼ cup corn syrup
3 tablespoons pectin
2 teaspoons cornstarch
1 teaspoon vinegar
50 drops or ¼ teaspoon red food coloring
⅛ teaspoon onion powder
dash cayenne pepper
dash garlic powder
dash paprika
¼ cup minced red bell pepper
½ teaspoon minced canned jalapeño peppers

1. Combine all the ingredients except the bell and minced jalapeño peppers in a small saucepan. Whisk well.
2. Set saucepan over medium/high heat, uncovered. Add peppers and bring mixture to a full boil, stirring often.

3. Reduce heat and simmer sauce for 5 to 7 minutes, or until thick. Remove from heat and let sauce sit for about 10 minutes. Stir and cover.
4. Use sauce when it reaches room temperature or cover and chill until needed.

• MAKES 1 CUP.

• • • •

TOP SECRET RECIPES VERSION OF

BEN & JERRY'S HEATH BAR CRUNCH ICE CREAM

When Ben Cohen and Jerry Greenfield first met in their seventh-grade gym class, they quickly became good friends. After college, the two decided they wanted to try their hand at selling ice cream. With $12,000 to invest, they moved from New York to Burlington, Vermont, where they purchased an abandoned gas station as the first location for their ice cream store.

After passing a five-dollar correspondence course on ice cream making from Pennsylvania State University and spending their life savings on renovating the gas station, the two were officially in the ice cream business. Ben and Jerry opened the doors to their first ice cream parlor in 1978. The pair's ice cream was such a big hit that they soon moved to a much larger facility. Today, just fifteen years after opening day, they produce more than 500,000 gallons of ice cream each month.

Heath Bar Crunch was one of the earliest flavors on the menu and is still the most popular of the thirty original chunky ice cream creations that made them famous.

5 Heath candy bars
3 eggs
1 cup granulated sugar
3 cups whipping cream
1 ½ cups half-and-half
3 teaspoons vanilla extract

1. Freeze the candy bars.
2. Beat the eggs by hand until fluffy.
3. Slowly beat in the sugar.
4. Add the cream, half-and-half, and vanilla and mix well.

5. Pour the mixture into an ice cream maker and freeze.
6. While the ice cream is freezing, place the frozen candy bars in a plastic bag and break them into small pieces with a knife handle.
7. When the ice cream is done, remove it from the ice cream maker and add the candy pieces. Mix well with a large spoon and store in the freezer.

• MAKES 1 QUART.

TIDBITS

The real secret to Ben & Jerry's ice cream is its consistency. It is a thick and creamy ice cream developed with special equipment that keeps a great deal of air out of the mixture. The less air in the ice cream, the thicker the consistency. Therefore, you may find the above recipe fills your ice cream maker a little more than other ice cream recipes.

It's also important to get the right consistency of Heath bar chunks. Most of the candy bar should be crushed into crumbs, but stop breaking the candy when there are still several 1- and ½-inch chunks remaining.

I hope you enjoy experimenting with this recipe and that you try substituting other ingredients for the Heath bar chunks, just as Ben and Jerry have. Try Reese's Peanut Butter Cups, Oreo cookies, Kit Kat bars, Rollo cups, M&Ms, and chunks of raw cookie dough.

TOP SECRET RECIPES VERSION OF

BURGER KING BIG KING

The Burger Wars have become the biggest food fight since that cafeteria scene from the movie *Animal House*. The two burger giants, McDonald's and Burger King, have each been cloning the other's top products in the bloody battle for the big burger buck. Burger King stepped up first with the Big King—Burger King's version of McDonald's Big Mac. Yes, it had two all-beef patties, special sauce, lettuce, cheese, pickles, onions on a sesame seed bun; although everything was arranged a bit differently, and there's no middle bun in there. Then McDonald's rolled out the Big 'N Tasty, which bore a striking resemblance to Burger King's Whopper, with fresh lettuce, tomato, and onion on top of a huge beef patty. Who's winning this fight by leveraging the popularity of the other company's product? Nobody, really. McDonald's chose to alter its Big 'N Tasty recipe by making it smaller 'n cheaper, then changed the name to BigXtra!, while Burger King limited sale of the Big King. But this food fight is far from over. More recently Burger King tweaked its french fry formula in an unsuccessful attempt to steal away fans of McDonald's winning fried spuds recipe. And McDonald's has added more breakfast sandwiches to compete with Burger King's wider wake-up selection. So the war continues. And the battlefield is splattered with ketchup.

1 ½ pounds ground beef
dash salt
dash pepper
4 sesame seed hamburger buns
1 ⅓ cups chopped lettuce
8 slices American cheese
1 to 2 slices white onion, separated
8 dill pickle slices

SPREAD
¼ cup mayonnaise
2 teaspoons French dressing
2 teaspoons sweet pickle relish
1 teaspoon white vinegar
½ teaspoon sugar
¼ teaspoon lemon juice
⅛ teaspoon paprika

1. Prepare the spread by combining the ingredients in a small bowl. Set this aside until you are ready to use it.
2. Preheat your barbecue or indoor grill to high heat.
3. Divide the ground beef into eight even portions (3 ounces each). Roll each portion into a ball, then press each ball flat to form a patty about the same diameter as the bun.
4. Grill the beef patties for 2 to 3 minutes per side, or until done. Lightly salt and pepper each side of the patties.
5. As the meat cooks, brown the faces of the buns in a hot skillet, toaster oven, or facedown on the grill. Watch the buns closely so that they do not burn.
6. Build each burger by first spreading a tablespoon of the spread on the face of the top bun. Arrange about ⅓ cup of lettuce evenly over the spread.
7. On the bottom bun stack a patty, then a slice of American cheese, another patty, and another slice of cheese.
8. On the top slice of cheese arrange 2 to 3 separated onion slices (rings), then 2 pickle slices.
9. Turn the top part of the burger over onto the bottom and serve. You may also want to zap the sandwiches in the microwave, individually, for 15 to 20 seconds each.

- SERVES 4.

• • • •

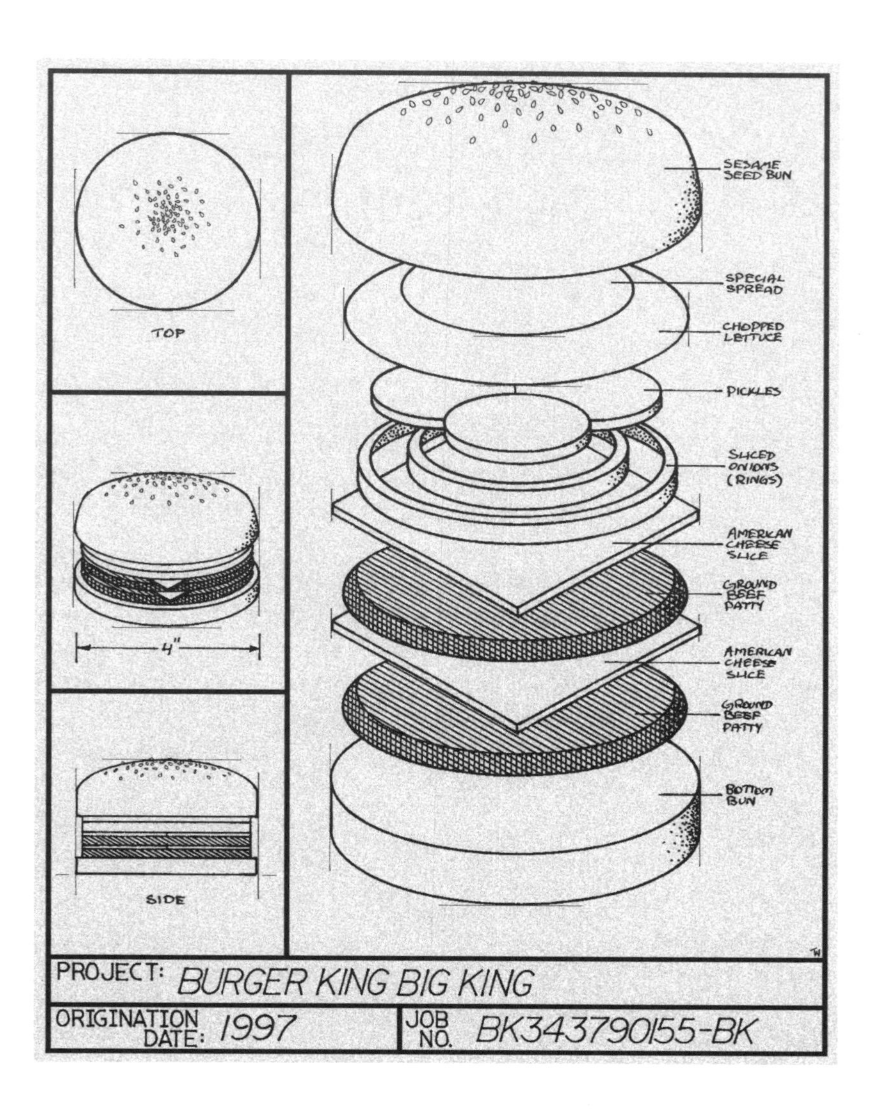
TOP
4"
SIDE
SESAME SEED BUN
SPECIAL SPREAD
CHOPPED LETTUCE
PICKLES
SLICED ONIONS (RINGS)
AMERICAN CHEESE SLICE
GROUND BEEF PATTY
AMERICAN CHEESE SLICE
GROUND BEEF PATTY
BOTTOM BUN
PROJECT: BURGER KING BIG KING
ORIGINATION DATE: 1997
JOB NO. BK343790155-BK

BURGER KING BK BROILER

This grilled chicken sandwich was introduced by America's number-two burger chain in 1990, and soon after the launch the BK Broiler was selling at a rate of over a million a day. Not good news for chickens.

This one's easy to duplicate at home. To clone the shape of the chicken served at the burger giant, you'll simply slice the chicken breasts in half, and pound each piece flat with a mallet. Pounding things is fun. Let the chicken marinate and then fire up the grill. The recipe makes four sandwiches and can be easily doubled if necessary for a king-size munch-fest.

MARINADE

¾ cup water
2 teaspoons ketchup
1 teaspoon salt
¼ teaspoon liquid smoke
⅛ teaspoon pepper
⅛ teaspoon oregano
dash onion powder
dash parsley

2 skinless chicken breast fillets
4 sesame seed hamburger buns
1 ⅓ cups chopped lettuce
¼ cup mayonnaise
8 tomato slices

1. Make the marinade by combining the ingredients in a medium bowl.
2. Prepare the chicken by cutting each breast in half. Fold a piece of plastic wrap around each piece of chicken and pound the meat with a tenderizing mallet until it is about ¼-inch thick and

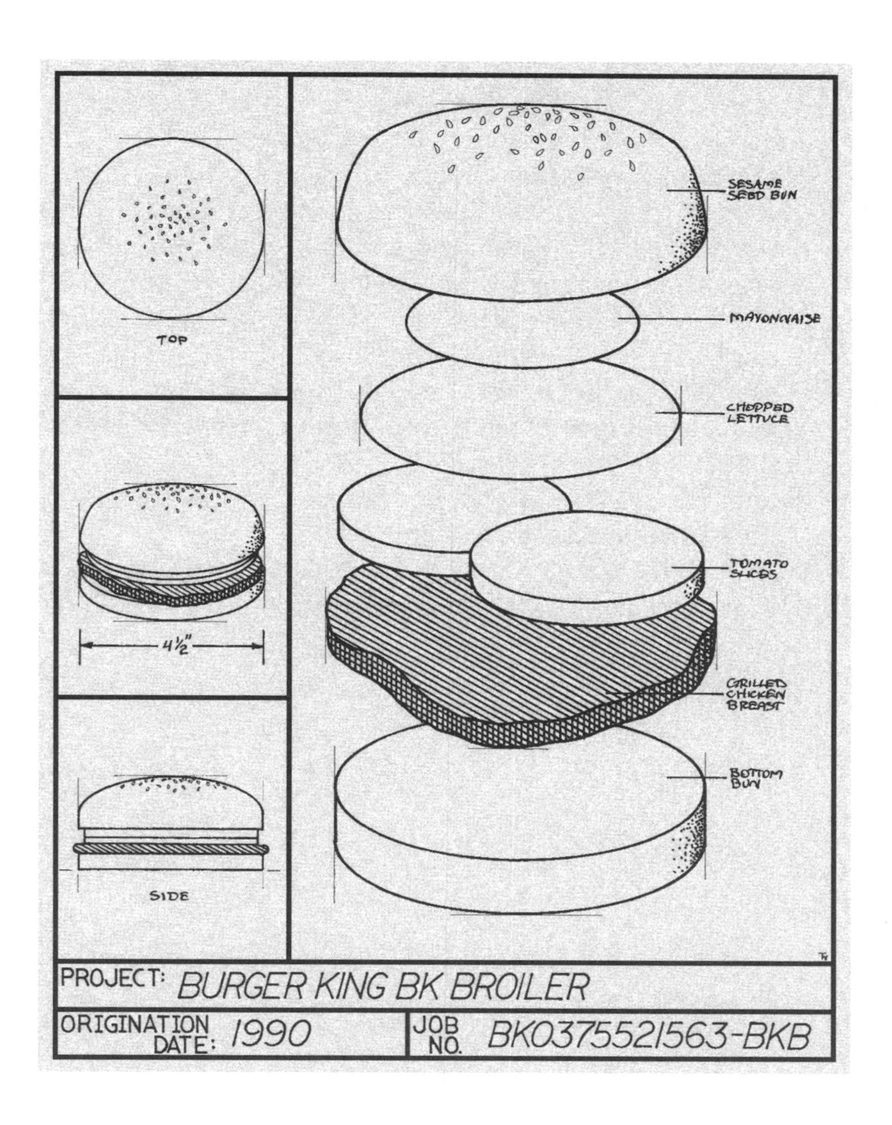
TOP
4½"
SIDE
SESAME SEED BUN
MAYONNAISE
CHOPPED LETTUCE
TOMATO SLICES
GRILLED CHICKEN BREAST
BOTTOM BUN
PROJECT: BURGER KING BK BROILER
ORIGINATION DATE: 1990
JOB NO. BK0375521563-BKB

about the same diameter as the hamburger buns. Place the chicken into the marinade, cover it, and chill for at least 4 hours. Overnight is even better.

3. Preheat your barbecue or indoor grill to high heat. Grill the chicken for 3 to 4 minutes per side or until done.
4. Toast the faces of the hamburger buns in a pan or griddle, in a toaster oven, or facedown on the grill. Watch the buns closely to be certain that the faces turn only light brown and do not burn.
5. Build each sandwich from the top down by first spreading about a tablespoon of the mayonnaise on the toasted face of a top bun.
6. Spread about ⅓ cup of chopped lettuce over the mayonnaise.
7. Arrange two tomato slices on the lettuce.
8. Place a chicken breast on the toasted face of the bottom bun.
9. Flip the top part of the sandwich over onto the bottom and scarf out.

• SERVES 4.

• • • •

TOP SECRET RECIPES VERSION OF

BURGER KING BREAKFAST SANDWICHES

Get vertical with these top secret breakfasts-in-sandwich from the world's number-two fast food chain. A great way to make the eggs for these breakfast sandwiches is to pour the beaten egg into a well-greased mold made from an empty pineapple can. Just cut both ends off an 8-ounce pineapple can—you know, the short cans that have the crushed or sliced pineapple inside. Oh, and take the pineapple out. Then, before you know it, you'll be making perfectly round eggs like the fast food pros.

BISCUIT SANDWICH

1 small can (5 biscuits) Pillsbury Grands Buttermilk Biscuits
melted butter
non-stick cooking spray
5 eggs
salt
ground black pepper
10 ounces ground breakfast sausage (such as Jimmy Dean) or 10 slices of bacon
5 slices American cheese

1. Prepare biscuits following instructions on the can (bake at 350ºF for 15 to 18 minutes). When you remove the biscuits from the oven brush the top of each with melted butter.
2. Spray a skillet over medium heat with non-stick cooking spray. Open both ends of a clean, small, sliced pineapple can. Spray the inside of the empty can with the non-stick spray, and then place the can in the pan to heat up. Use more than one can if you'd like to speed up the cooking process.
3. Beat an egg, then pour it into the empty can mold, add a bit of salt and pepper, and cover with a saucepan lid. Cook for a

couple minutes, then scrape a knife around the edge of the egg to release it. Remove the can, then turn the egg over and cook it for another minute or 2. Repeat with the remaining eggs.

4. If using sausage, form 2-ounce portions of sausage into patties with the same diameter as the biscuits. Cook the sausage in another hot skillet over medium heat until brown. If using bacon, cook the bacon and drain on paper towels.
5. Slice a biscuit in half through the middle. Build each sandwich by first stacking egg on the bottom half of the biscuit. Next arrange sausage (or 2 slices of bacon) on the egg, then a slice of American cheese. Top off each sandwich with the top biscuit half, and then zap it in the microwave for 15 to 20 seconds to help melt the cheese. Repeat with the remaining ingredients.

- MAKES 5 SANDWICHES.

CROISSAN'WICH

1 8-ounce can Pillsbury Original Crescent Rolls
4 eggs
salt
ground black pepper
8 ounces ground breakfast sausage (such as Jimmy Dean) or 8 slices bacon
4 slices American cheese

1. Prepare the rolls by first unrolling the dough out of the can. Separate the dough into four sections, each made up of two triangles. Detach the triangles by tearing along the diagonal perforation, then reattach the dough along the outside parallel edges, pinching the dough together along the middle. This will make one bigger triangle. Loosely roll the dough, starting from the wide end, all the way up. Now, bring the ends around so that they overlap and the roll is in the shape of a circle. Press the ends together and place the roll onto a baking sheet. Repeat with the remaining dough, then bake following the directions on the package (bake at 375°F for 11 to 13 minutes).
2. When the rolls are done baking build the sandwich using steps 2 through 5 in the recipe for the biscuit sandwich clone.

- MAKES 4 SANDWICHES.

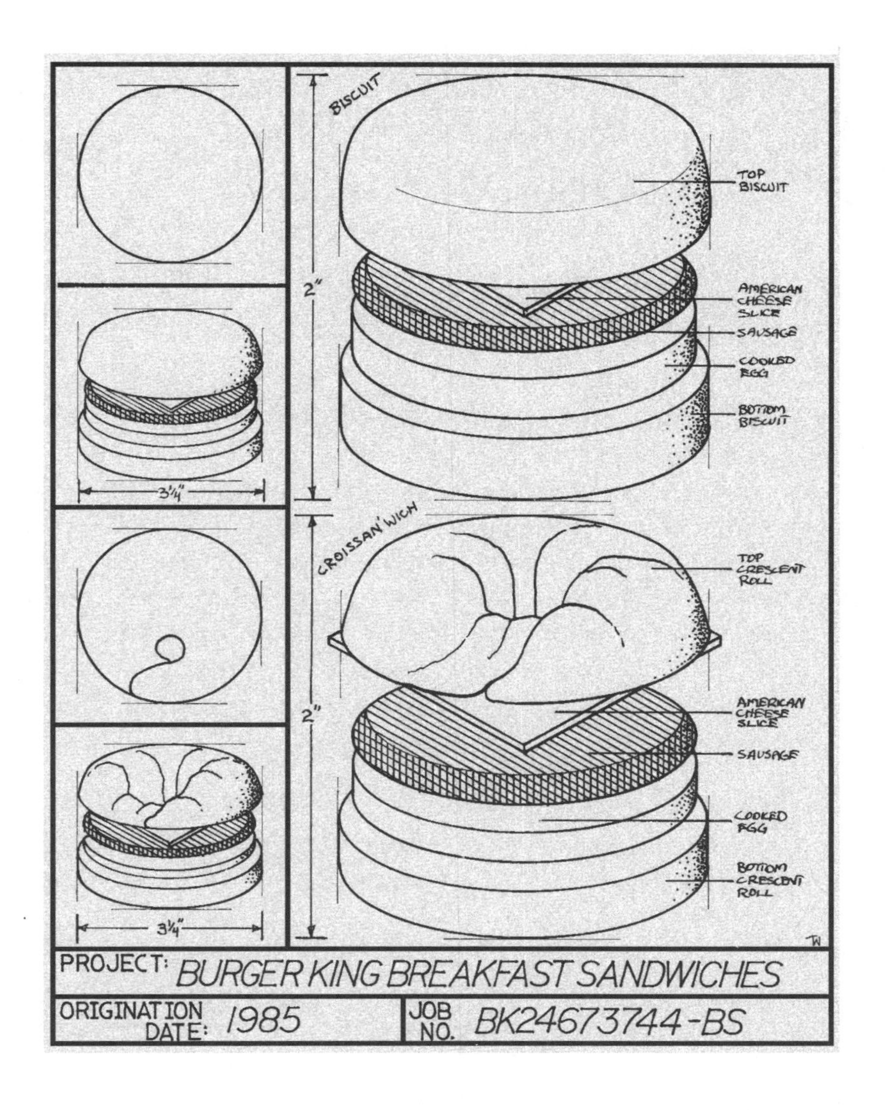
BISCUIT
TOP BISCUIT
AMERICAN CHEESE SLICE
SAUSAGE
COOKED EGG
BOTTOM BISCUIT
2"
3¼"
CROISSAN'WICH
TOP CRESCENT ROLL
AMERICAN CHEESE SLICE
SAUSAGE
COOKED EGG
BOTTOM CRESCENT ROLL
2"
3¼"
TW
PROJECT: BURGER KING BREAKFAST SANDWICHES
ORIGINATION DATE: 1985
JOB NO. BK24673744-BS

BURGER KING ONION RINGS

Since McDonald's doesn't sell onion rings, these crunchy, golden hoops from the world's number two restaurant chain are the most popular onion rings in the world. There's more than 11,400 Burger Kings in 58 countries these days and, after french fries, onion rings are the second-most popular companion to the chain's signature Whopper sandwich. Now check out how simple it is to clone a whopping 4 dozen onion rings from one onion using this triple-breading process. When frying, vegetable shortening makes the best clone here, but you can get by fine using vegetable oil if that's the way you want to go.

6 to 10 cups vegetable shortening (or vegetable oil)
1 medium white onion
2 cups milk
2 cups all-purpose flour
2 cups Progresso plain bread crumbs
salt

1. In a fryer, heat up 6 to 10 cups of vegetable shortening or oil (use the amount required by your fryer) to 350ºF.
2. Cut the onion into ¼-inch-thick slices, then separate the slices into rings.
3. Pour the milk into a large shallow bowl, dump flour into another large shallow bowl and pour bread crumbs into a third large shallow bowl. The large shallow bowls will make breading easier. Easy is good.
4. While the shortening is heating up, bread all of the onion rings: First, dip an onion ring into the milk, then into the flour. Dip it

back into the milk, then into the bread crumbs; and once more into the milk and into the bread crumbs. This will give each of the rings a nice, thick breading. Arrange the breaded rings on a plate until all of them are breaded.

5. When the oil is hot, fry the rings, a handful at a time, in the oil for 1 ½ to 3 minutes or until golden brown. Remove rings from the oil to a rack or paper towels to drain. Lightly salt the onion rings and serve 'em up hot.

- MAKES 5 DOZEN ONION RINGS.

• • • •

TOP SECRET RECIPES VERSION OF

BURGER KING ZESTY ONION RING SAUCE

If you're a big fan of onion rings from Burger King, you probably already know about the spicy dipping sauce offered from the world's number two burger chain. It's not necessarily on the menu, and you usually have to request it. The creamy, mayo-based sauce is obviously inspired by the dipping sauce served with Outback's signature Bloomin' Onion appetizer, since both sauces contain similar ingredients, among them horseradish and cayenne pepper. If you're giving the previous clone for Burger King Onion Rings a try, whip up some of this sauce and go for a dip. It's just as good with low-fat mayonnaise if you're into that. And the stuff works really well as a spread for burgers and sandwiches, or for dipping artichokes.

½ cup mayonnaise
1 ½ teaspoons ketchup
1 ½ teaspoons horseradish
½ teaspoon granulated sugar
½ teaspoon lemon juice
¼ teaspoon cayenne pepper

1. Combine all ingredients in a small bowl. Cover and chill for at least an hour before using.

- MAKES ½ CUP.

• • • •

TOP SECRET RECIPES VERSION OF

CARL'S JR. FAMOUS STAR

It was in Los Angeles in 1941 that Carl Karcher and his wife, Margaret, found a hot-dog cart on Florence and Central for sale for $326. They borrowed $311 on their Plymouth, added $15 of their own, and bought the brightly colored stand. Although the sign on this first stand read HUGO'S HOT DOGS, Karcher began purchasing more carts, painting on them CARL'S HOT DOGS. In 1945 Karcher opened his first drive-thru restaurant, which he named Carl's Drive-In Barbecue. In 1956 he opened two smaller restaurants in Anaheim and Brea, California, and used the Carl's Jr. name for the first time.

With 642 units as of 1993, the chain's trademark smiling star can be seen throughout the West and Southwestern United States, as well as in Mexico, Japan, and Malaysia. The chain has come a long way from the days when Karcher used to mix the secret sauce in twenty-gallon batches on his back porch. Carl's Jr. takes credit for introducing salad bars to fast-food restaurants back in 1977. Today, salads are regular fare at most of the major chains.

Carl's top-of-the-line hamburger is still the flame-broiled Famous Star, one of several products that has made Carl's Jr. famous.

1 sesame-seed hamburger bun
2 onion rings
½ teaspoon sweet pickle relish
1 ½ teaspoons catsup
¼ pound ground beef
dash salt
2 teaspoons mayonnaise
3 dill pickle slices
¼ cup coarsely chopped lettuce
2 tomato slices

1. Preheat a clean barbecue grill on high. (The cleaner the barbecue, the less likely the beef patty will pick up other flavors left on the grill.)
2. Toast both halves of the bun, face down, in a skillet over medium heat. Set aside.
3. Cut each of the 2 onion rings into quarters.
4. Mix the catsup and relish together. This is your "secret sauce."
5. Form the ground beef into a thin patty slightly larger than the bun.
6. Grill the meat for 2 or 3 minutes per side. Salt lightly.
7. Build the burger in the following stacking order from the bottom up:

   bottom bun
   half of the mayonnaise
   pickles
   lettuce
   tomato slices
   onion
   beef patty
   remainder of mayonnaise
   special sauce (catsup and relish)
   top bun

• MAKES 1 HAMBURGER.

• • • •

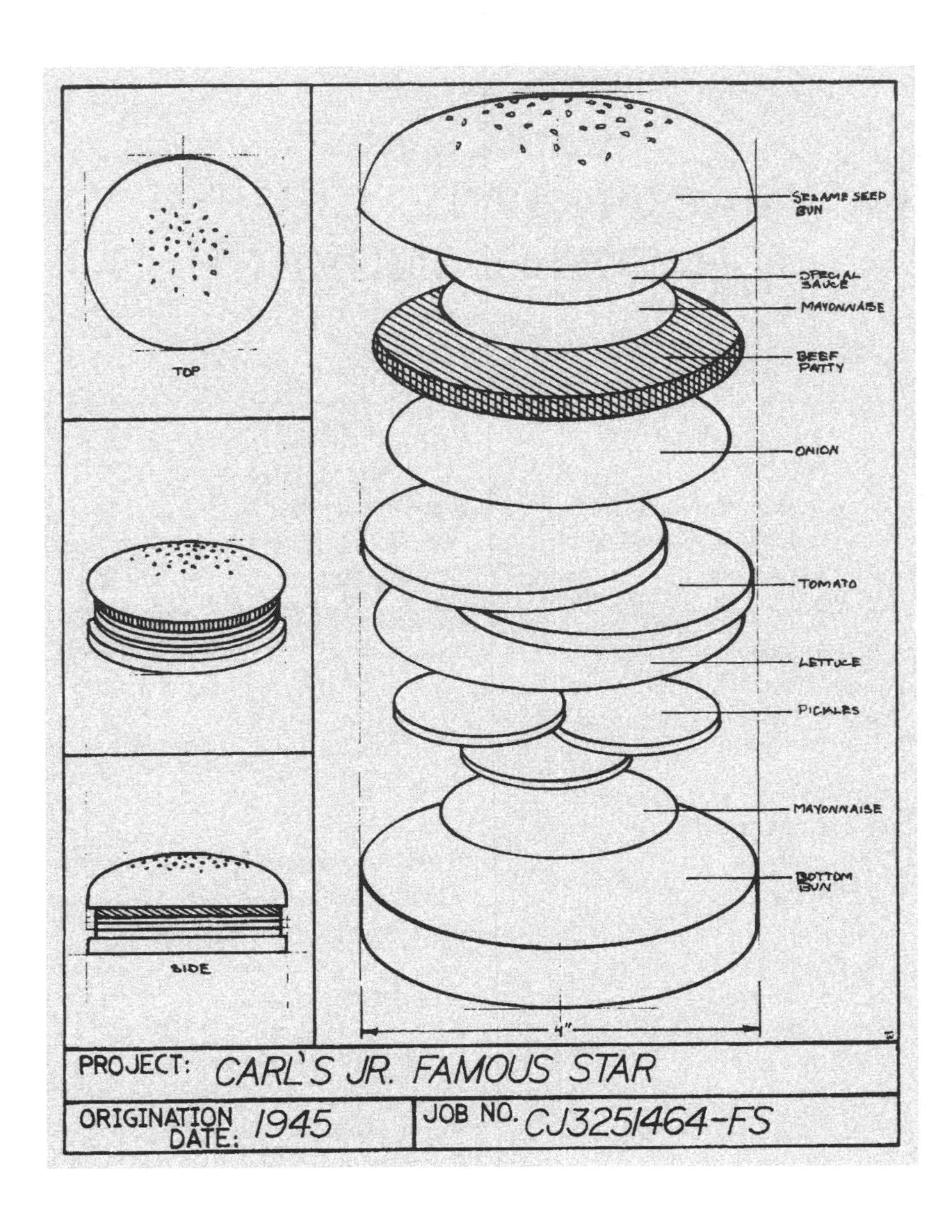
TOP
SIDE
SESAME SEED BUN
SPECIAL SAUCE
MAYONNAISE
BEEF PATTY
ONION
TOMATO
LETTUCE
PICKLES
MAYONNAISE
BOTTOM BUN
4"
PROJECT: CARL'S JR. FAMOUS STAR
ORIGINATION DATE: 1945
JOB NO. CJ3251464-FS

TOP SECRET RECIPES VERSION OF

CARL'S JR. BACON SWISS CRISPY CHICKEN SANDWICH

☆ ✌ 💣 ✎ ☯ ✂ ☞

If you love crispy chicken sandwiches—and especially if you don't live in the West—you'll want to try out this clone of the tasty Carl's Jr. creation. The recipe makes four of the addicting chicken sandwiches from the California-based chain, but will also come in handy for making a delicious homemade ranch dressing. Try using some lean turkey bacon, fat-free Swiss cheese, and light mayonnaise if you feel like cutting back on the fat. Then you can eat two.

RANCH DRESSING

1/3 cup mayonnaise
2 tablespoons sour cream
1 tablespoon buttermilk
1 1/2 teaspoons white vinegar
1 teaspoon sugar
1/4 teaspoon lemon juice
1/8 teaspoon salt
1/8 teaspoon parsley
1/8 teaspoon onion powder
dash dill weed
dash garlic powder
dash ground black pepper
2 teaspoons hot water
1/2 teaspoon unflavored gelatin

6 to 8 cups vegetable shortening
1 egg
1 cup water
1 cup all-purpose flour
2 1/2 teaspoons salt
1 teaspoon paprika
1 teaspoon onion powder
1/8 teaspoon garlic powder
4 skinless chicken breast fillets
4 sesame seed hamburger buns
4 lettuce leaves
4 tomato slices
Kraft Singles Swiss cheese
8 slices bacon, cooked

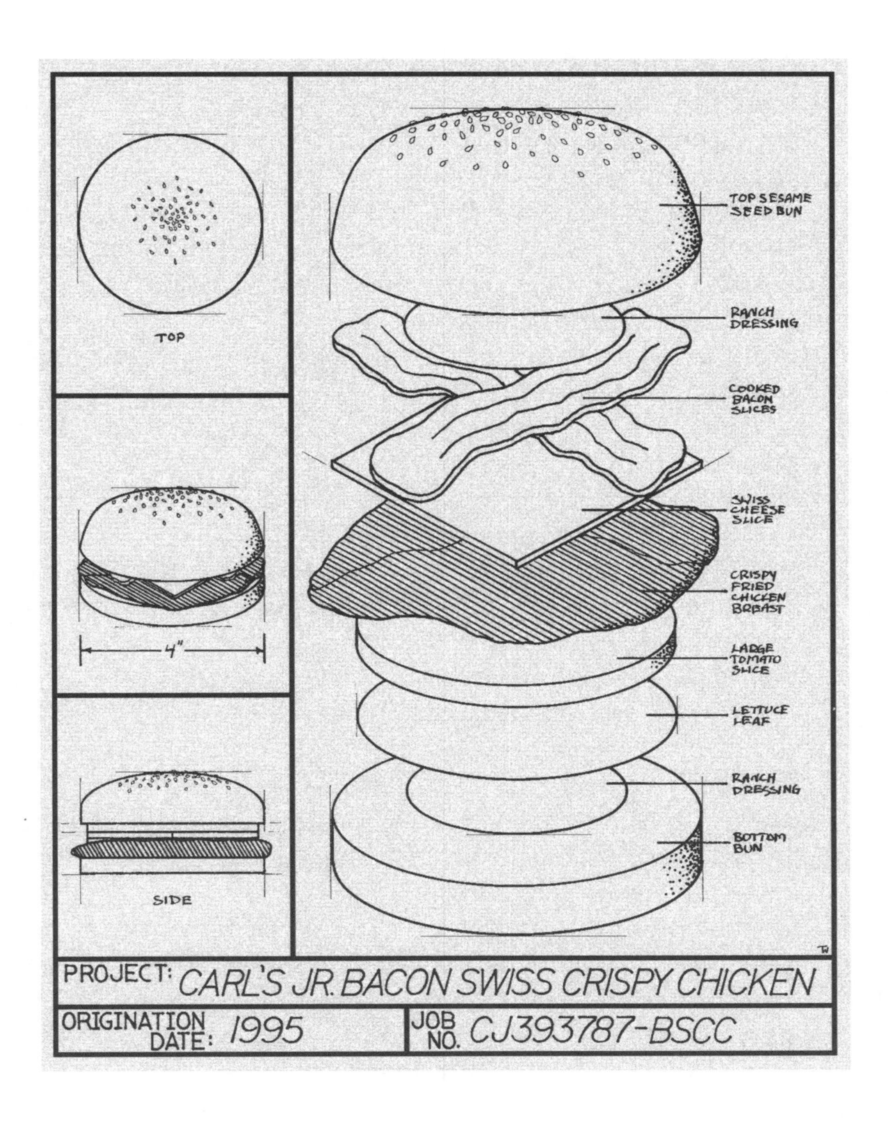
TOP
4"
SIDE
TOP SESAME SEED BUN
RANCH DRESSING
COOKED BACON SLICES
SWISS CHEESE SLICE
CRISPY FRIED CHICKEN BREAST
LARGE TOMATO SLICE
LETTUCE LEAF
RANCH DRESSING
BOTTOM BUN
PROJECT: CARL'S JR. BACON SWISS CRISPY CHICKEN
ORIGINATION DATE: 1995
JOB NO. CJ393787-BSCC

1. Preheat 6 to 8 cups of shortening in a deep fryer to 350°F. If you don't have a deep fryer, you can also pan fry using a large frying pan and just a couple cups of shortening.
2. To prepare the ranch dressing, combine all of the ingredients except the water and gelatin in a small bowl. Mix the water with the gelatin in a small cup until all of the gelatin is dissolved. Add this gelatin solution to the other ingredients and stir. Cover and chill the dressing until it's needed.
3. Beat the egg and then combine with 1 cup of water in a small, shallow bowl. Stir.
4. Combine the flour, salt, paprika, onion powder, and garlic powder in another shallow bowl.
5. Pound each of the breast fillets with a mallet until about ¼-inch thick. Trim each breast fillet until it is round.
6. Working with one fillet at a time, first coat each fillet with the flour, then dredge it in the egg and water mixture. Coat the chicken once again in the flour and set it aside until all of the fillets have been coated.
7. Fry the chicken fillets for 8 to 12 minutes or until light brown and crispy.
8. As chicken is frying, prepare each sandwich by grilling the face of the hamburger buns on a hot skillet over medium heat. Spread about 1½ teaspoons of the ranch dressing on the face of the top and bottom buns.
9. On the bottom bun, stack a leaf of lettuce and a tomato slice.
10. When the chicken is done frying, remove the fillets from the fryer and drain them on paper towels or a rack for a couple minutes.
11. Stack one fillet on the bottom of the sandwich (on top of the tomato), then stack a slice of the Swiss cheese onto the chicken.
12. Arrange the bacon, crosswise, on top of the Swiss cheese, then top off the sandwich with the top bun. Repeat the stacking process for each of the remaining sandwiches.

- MAKES 4 SANDWICHES.

• • • •

TOP SECRET RECIPES VERSION OF

CARL'S JR. RANCH CRISPY CHICKEN SANDWICH

☆ ✌ 💣 ✎ ☯ ✂ ☞

We'll use elements of the previous recipe to whip up another one of Carl's Jr.'s crispy chicken sandwiches, because I always say you can never have too much crispy chicken. This fried chicken breast sandwich includes lettuce and tomato, and is slathered with a clone of Carl's tasty ranch dressing. Use the recipes together and you can easily serve up two different sandwich clones for different tastes, with little extra effort. And your diners will be so impressed.

RANCH DRESSING

1/3 cup mayonnaise
2 tablespoons sour cream
1 tablespoon buttermilk
1 1/2 teaspoons white vinegar
1 teaspoon sugar
1/4 teaspoon lemon juice
1/8 teaspoon salt
1/8 teaspoon parsley
1/8 teaspoon onion powder
dash dill weed
dash garlic powder
dash ground black pepper
2 teaspoons hot water

1/2 teaspoon unflavored gelatin
6 to 8 cups vegetable shortening
1 egg
1 cup water
1 cup all-purpose flour
2 1/2 teaspoons salt
1 teaspoon paprika
1 teaspoon onion powder
1/8 teaspoon garlic powder
4 skinless chicken breast fillets
4 sesame seed hamburger buns
4 lettuce leaves
4 tomato slices

1. Preheat 6 to 8 cups of oil in a deep fryer to 350°F. If you don't have a deep fryer, you can also pan fry using a large frying pan, and just a couple cups of shortening.
2. To prepare the ranch dressing, combine all of the ingredients except the water and gelatin in a small bowl. Mix the water with the gelatin in a small cup until all of the gelatin is dissolved. Add this gelatin solution to the other ingredients and stir. Cover and chill the dressing until it's needed.
3. Beat the egg and then combine with 1 cup of water in a small, shallow bowl. Stir.
4. Combine the flour, salt, paprika, onion powder, and garlic powder in another shallow bowl.
5. Pound each of the breast fillets with a mallet until about ¼-inch thick. Trim each breast fillet until it is round.
6. Working with one fillet at a time, first coat each fillet with the flour, then dredge it in the egg and water mixture. Coat the chicken once again in the flour and set it aside until all of the fillets have been coated.
7. Fry the chicken fillets for 8 to 12 minutes or until light brown and crispy.
8. As the chicken is frying, prepare each sandwich by grilling the face of the hamburger buns on a hot skillet over medium heat. Spread about 1½ teaspoons of the ranch dressing on the face of the top and bottom buns.
9. On the bottom bun, stack a leaf of lettuce and a tomato slice.
10. When the chicken is done frying, remove the fillets from the fryer and drain on paper towels or a rack for a couple minutes.
11. Stack one fillet on the bottom of the sandwich (on top of the tomato), then top it off with the top bun. Repeat the stacking process for each of the sandwiches.

- MAKES 4 SANDWICHES.

• • • •

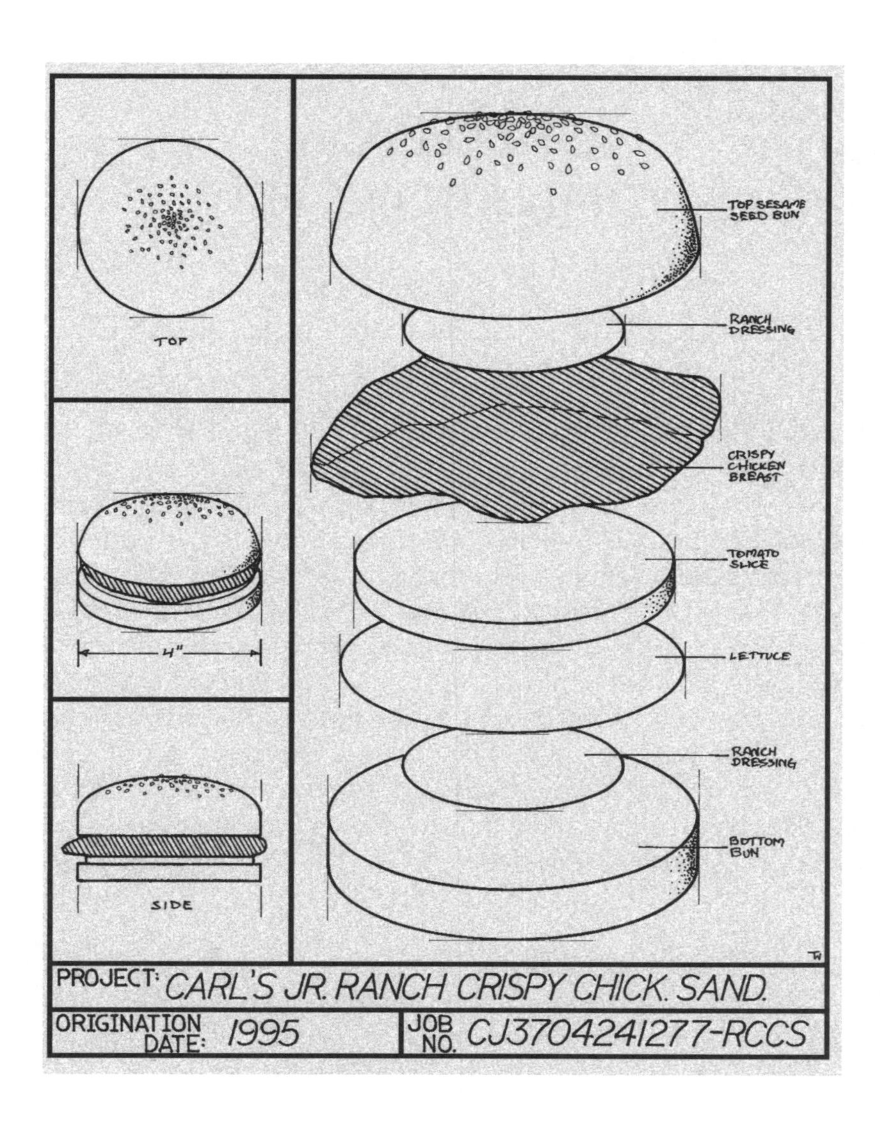
TOP
4"
SIDE
TOP SESAME SEED BUN
RANCH DRESSING
CRISPY CHICKEN BREAST
TOMATO SLICE
LETTUCE
RANCH DRESSING
BOTTOM BUN
PROJECT: CARL'S JR. RANCH CRISPY CHICK. SAND.
ORIGINATION DATE: 1995
JOB NO. CJ3704241277-RCCS

TOP SECRET RECIPES VERSION OF

CINNABON CINNABONSTIX

Cinnabon product development guys were looking for a new baked cinnamon product that customers could eat on the go while carrying bags and scurrying about. In June of 2000, they found it. Bakers brushed Danish dough with a flavored cinnamon butter, and then rolled the dough in a generous cinnamon sugar coating. These golden brown little sticks of cinnamony delight are sold in bags of five or ten from the company's famous cinnamon roll outlets, most likely found in a mall or airport near you. Now you can create your own version of the tasty pastries at home, and you won't even have to make the dough from scratch. Just grab yourself a tube of Pillsbury crescents and all you have to do is fold and roll up the dough, and then coat it. Run around the house in a hurry while eating these to further re-create the experience.

1 tube Pillsbury crescent dinner rolls (8)
1 stick (½ cup) margarine, melted
2 teaspoons granulated sugar
¼ teaspoon cinnamon
¼ teaspoon vanilla
non-stick cooking spray

COATING

½ cup granulated sugar
1 tablespoon cinnamon

1. Preheat oven to 400°F.
2. Separate the dough into eight portions. Fold over two of the corners of the triangular dough piece so that it forms a rectangle. Roll the dough on a flat surface to make a tube, then twist the tube a couple of times, and stretch it a little longer. Repeat for all the dough triangles.

3. Combine the melted margarine, 2 teaspoons sugar, ¼ teaspoon cinnamon, and ¼ teaspoon vanilla in a small bowl.
4. Combine ½ cup sugar and 1 tablespoon cinnamon for the coating in another small bowl.
5. Brush the melted margarine mixture over the top and bottom of the dough sticks. Toss the dough into the sugar and cinnamon coating mixture. Roll the dough around with your fingers so that it is well coated. Place the coated dough sticks on a cookie sheet that has been sprayed with non-stick cooking spray. Spray the top of the sticks with a light coating of the spray.
6. Bake for 8 minutes or until the sticks are golden brown. Serve the sticks right out of the oven or reheat them in the microwave for just a bit before serving if they have cooled. These puppies are best served hot!

- MAKES 8 STICKS.

• • • •

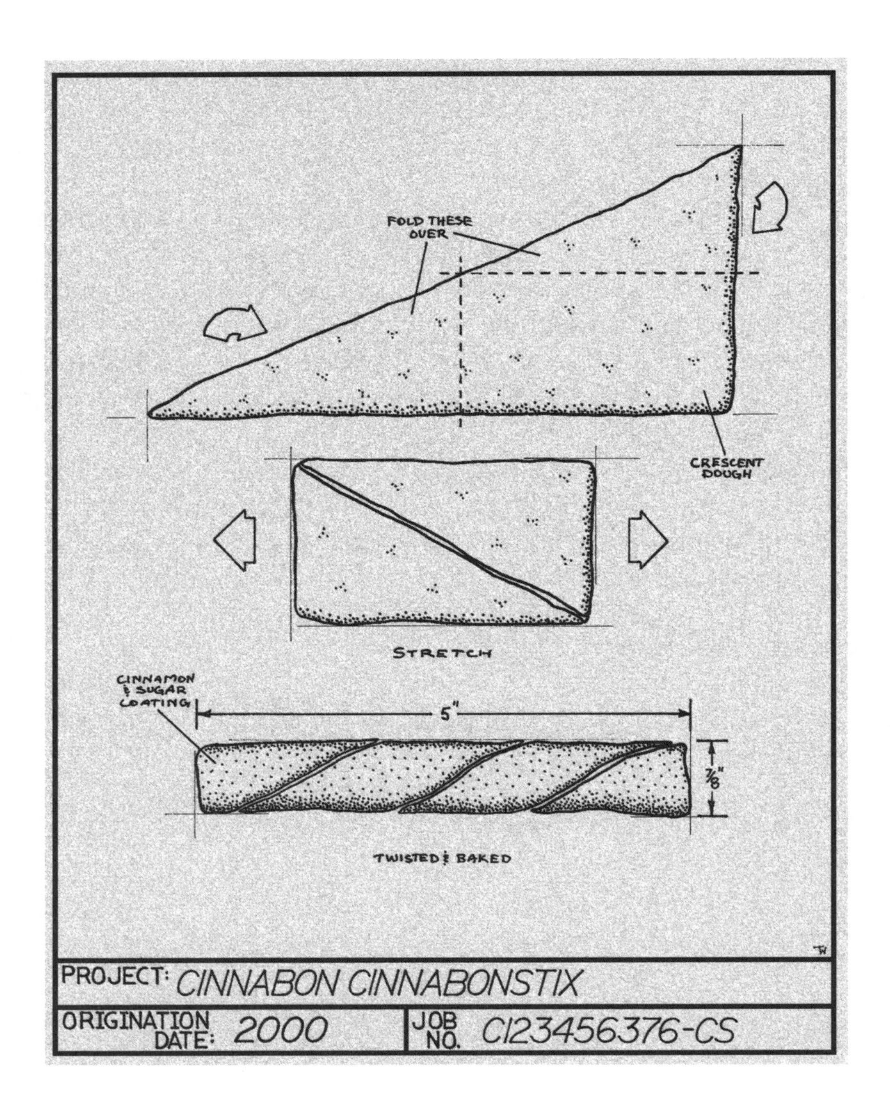
FOLD THESE OVER
CRESCENT DOUGH
STRETCH
CINNAMON & SUGAR COATING
5"
7/8"
TWISTED & BAKED
PROJECT: CINNABON CINNABONSTIX
ORIGINATION DATE: 2000
JOB NO. CI23456376-CS

TOP SECRET RECIPES VERSION OF

CINNABON CINNAMON ROLLS

In early 1985, restaurateur Rich Komen decided there was a specialty niche in convenience-food service just waiting to be filled. His idea was to create an efficient outlet that could serve freshly made cinnamon rolls in shopping malls throughout the country. It took nine months for Komen and his staff to develop a cinnamon roll he knew customers would consider the "freshest, gooiest, and most mouthwatering cinnamon roll ever tasted." The concept was tested for the first time in Seattle's Sea-Tac mall later that year, with workers mixing, proofing, rolling, and baking the rolls in full view of the customers. Now, more than 200 outlets later, Cinnabon has become the fastest-growing cinnamon roll bakery in the country.

ROLLS

1 package active dry yeast (1/4-ounce size)
1 cup warm milk (105 to 110°F)
1/2 cup granulated sugar
1/3 cup margarine, melted
1 teaspoon salt
2 eggs
4 cups all-purpose flour

FILLING

1 cup packed brown sugar
2 1/2 tablespoons cinnamon
1/3 cup margarine, softened

ICING

8 tablespoons (1 stick) margarine, softened
1 1/2 cups powdered sugar
1/4 cup (2 ounces) cream cheese
1/2 teaspoon vanilla extract
1/8 teaspoon salt

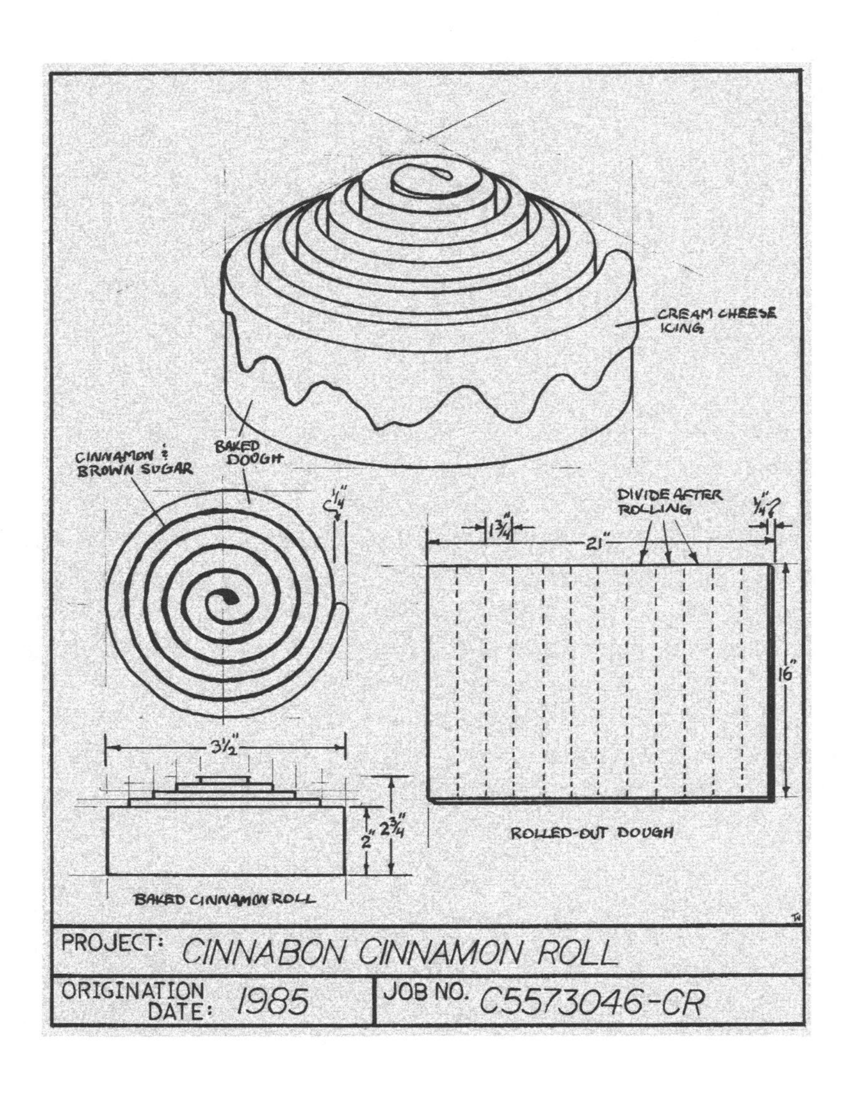
CREAM CHEESE ICING
CINNAMON & BROWN SUGAR
BAKED DOUGH
¼"
DIVIDE AFTER ROLLING
1¾"
21"
¼"
16"
3½"
2"
2¾"
ROLLED-OUT DOUGH
BAKED CINNAMON ROLL
PROJECT: CINNABON CINNAMON ROLL
ORIGINATION DATE: 1985
JOB NO. C5573046-CR

1. For the rolls, dissolve the yeast in the warm milk in a large bowl.
2. Mix together the sugar, margarine, salt, and eggs. Add flour, and mix well.
3. Knead the dough into a large ball, using your hands dusted lightly with flour. Put in a bowl, cover, and let rise in a warm place about 1 hour, or until the dough has doubled in size.
4. Roll the dough out on a lightly floured surface. Roll the dough flat until it is approximately 21 inches long and 16 inches wide. It should be about 1/4 inch thick.
5. Preheat oven to 400°F.
6. For the filling, combine the brown sugar and cinnamon in a bowl. Spread the softened margarine evenly over the surface of the dough, and then sprinkle the cinnamon and sugar evenly over the surface.
7. Working carefully from the top (a 21-inch side), roll the dough down to the bottom edge.
8. Cut the rolled dough into 1 3/4-inch slices and place 6 at a time, evenly spaced, in a lightly greased baking pan. Let the rolls rise again until double in size (about 30 minutes). Bake for 10 minutes, or until light brown on top.
9. While the rolls bake, combine the icing ingredients. Beat well with an electric mixer until fluffy.
10. When the rolls come out of the oven, coat each generously with icing.

• MAKES 12 ROLLS.

TIDBITS

These rolls can be frozen after baking. Just pop one into the microwave for 20–30 seconds to reheat.

• • • •

TOP SECRET RECIPES VERSION OF

EINSTEIN BROS. BAGELS SANTA FE EGGS 4 WAYS SANDWICH

This way is by far the most creative and tasty of the four ways you can have your bagel breakfast sandwich at Einstein Bagels. The salsa and jalapeño salsa cream cheese make for a slightly spicy affair that anyone who goes for Southwestern-style tastes will thoroughly dig. The sausage used here is a turkey breakfast sausage that you can find in most supermarkets (Wampler makes a good version that comes in a 1-pound tube and is sometimes found in the freezer section). You can also use small uncooked turkey breakfast links. Just squeeze the sausage out of the casing and form your patties, then toss out the casings. In a pinch you can also use good old pork sausage. Either way you go, you're in for a tasty way to rev up your day.

JALAPEÑO SALSA CREAM CHEESE

8 ounces cream cheese
¼ cup Ortega medium salsa
2 tablespoons minced jalapeño slices (canned)
⅛ teaspoon chili powder

6 ounces turkey breakfast sausage
3 large eggs, beaten (about ⅔ cup)
2 bagels, sliced in half and lightly toasted
2 slices pepper jack Kraft Singles cheese
2 tablespoons Ortega medium salsa

1. First make your jalapeño salsa cream cheese by mixing all ingredients together in a small bowl. Cover and chill cream cheese until it's needed.
2. Make the turkey sausage patties by forming sausage into 2 3-ounce patties that are about 4½ inches in diameter. If you have time, form the patties on wax paper and freeze them to make handling easier. They will shrink when cooking to just the right size.
3. Beat the eggs in a bowl, then measure half (about ⅓ cup) into a bowl with the same approximate diameter as the bagels. Microwave each bowl (separately) for 1 to 1½ minutes on high, or until the egg is completely cooked.
4. Lightly toast all of the bagel halves.
5. Spread about 2 teaspoons of the jalapeño salsa cream cheese on the toasted face of the bottom half of the bagel.
6. When the eggs are cooked, arrange them on the cream cheese on each bagel bottom.
7. Lay a slice of pepper jack cheese on each of the egg layers.
8. Arrange a sausage patty on top of the cheese on each sandwich.
9. Spread about 2 teaspoons of salsa on the toasted face of each of the top bagel halves.
10. Top off the sandwiches with the top bagel halves, slice each sandwich in half, and serve while hot.

- MAKES 2 SANDWICHES.

• • • •

TOP SECRET RECIPES VERSION OF

HARDEE'S FRENCH FRIES

☆ ✌ 💣 ✏ ☯ ✂ ☞

Led by CEO Leonard Rawls, the Hardee's Company opened its first hamburger restaurant in 1961 at the corner of Church Street and Falls Road in Rocky Mount, North Carolina. Hardee's has grown steadily through the years, with a number of well-planned acquisitions: first, the purchase of the 200-unit Sandy's chain in 1972, then the buyout of the 650-unit Burger Chef chain in 1983. The company's latest acquisition was the 1990 buyout of the 648 Roy Rogers restaurants. This latest purchase made Hardee's the third largest hamburger chain in the world, just behind McDonald's and Burger King. With that acquisition, the company claimed to be operating close to 3,800 restaurants in forty-one states and nine foreign countries.

Hardee's was the first major hamburger chain to switch to all-vegetable oil to cook its fried products. One of those products is french fries, the most popular item on the Hardee's menu.

6 cups vegetable oil
⅓ cup granulated sugar
2 cups warm water
2 large russet potatoes, peeled
Salt

1. Heat the oil in a deep saucepan over low-medium heat for about 20 minutes.
2. In a medium bowl, mix the sugar into the water until dissolved.
3. Cut the potatoes in half lengthwise, and then into ¼-inch strips.

4. Put the potatoes into the sugar solution and soak for 15 minutes.
5. Remove the potatoes and dry them thoroughly on paper towels.
6. The right oil temperature is crucial here. To test the oil, fry a couple of potato slices for 6 minutes. Remove and cool, then taste. The fries should not get too dark too soon and should be soft in the middle. If the oil is too hot, turn it down and test again. The fries should not be undercooked, either. If they are, turn up the heat.
7. When the oil temperature is just right, put all the potato slices in the oil for 1 minute. This is the blanching stage.
8. Take the fries out of the oil and let them cool.
9. When the fries have cooled, place them into the oil again for 5 minutes, or until golden brown.
10. Remove from the oil and place on a paper towel–covered plate.
11. Salt to taste.

- MAKES 4 TO 5 DOZEN FRENCH FRIES.

TIDBITS

Oil temperature is crucial in cooking these french fries. Be sure to test the oil on several potato slices before cooking massive portions. And keep in mind that the more you cook at once, the longer your cooking time may be.

The blanching stage may seem to be a nuisance, but it is crucial if you want your fries to come out right. Blanching allows the fries to soak up a little oil while cooling, and will make them crispy when done.

• • • •

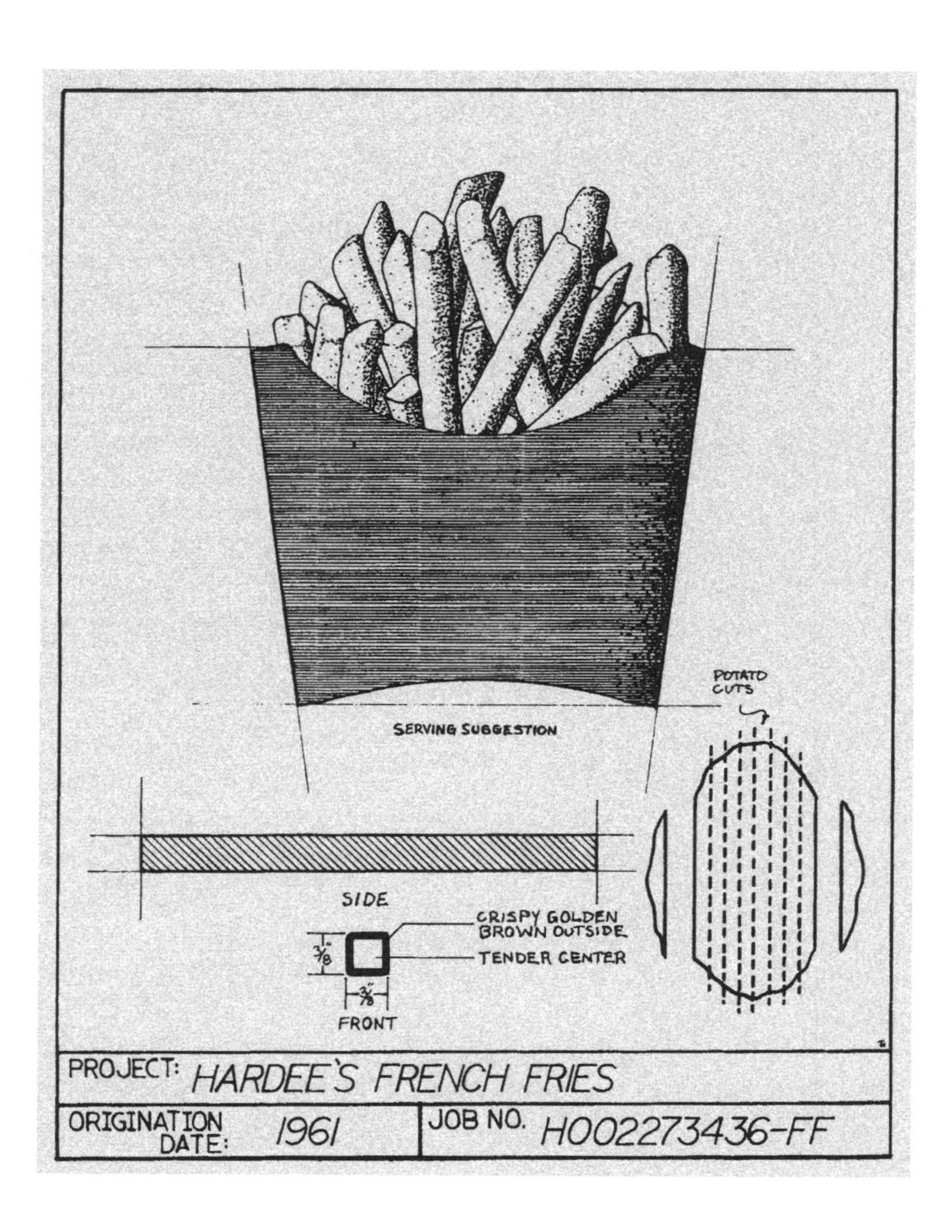
POTATO CUTS
SERVING SUGGESTION
SIDE
CRISPY GOLDEN BROWN OUTSIDE
TENDER CENTER
3/8"
3/8"
FRONT
PROJECT: HARDEE'S FRENCH FRIES
ORIGINATION DATE: 1961
JOB NO. H002273436-FF

TOP SECRET RECIPES VERSION OF

HARDEE'S 1/4-POUND HAMBURGER

☆ ✌ 💣 ✏ ☯ ✂ ☞

In 1975 Hardee's opened its 1,000th restaurant. The 2,000th unit was opened in 1983, and shortly after that, in 1988, the 3,000th unit opened its doors. This pattern of expansion has continued: A new Hardee's restaurant now opens on the average of one each workday. With the acquisition of the Roy Rogers chain in 1990, Hardee's neared the 4,000-unit mark, racking up systemwide sales of more than $3 billion. This is a chain that has come a long way since its first menu in 1961, which contained only eight items, including fifteen-cent hamburgers and ten-cent soft drinks.

As part of its continuing effort to offer nutrition-conscious customers a range of menu choices, Hardee's was one of the first of the "Big Four" burger chains to switch to low-calorie mayonnaise for its sandwiches.

1 sesame-seed hamburger bun
1/4 pound ground beef
dash salt
2 onion rings
3 sliced dill pickles
1 large tomato slice
1 leaf lettuce
1 teaspoon low-calorie mayonnaise
1 teaspoon catsup

1. Preheat a griddle or frying pan to medium temperature.
2. Toast both halves of the hamburger bun, face down. Set aside.
3. Form the ground beef into a patty slightly larger than the bun. Salt it lightly.
4. Cook the patty for 2 to 3 minutes on each side.

5. Build the burger in the following stacking order from the bottom up:

   bottom bun   lettuce leaf   beef patty   mayonnaise
   onion rings   catsup   pickles   top bun
   tomato slice

- MAKES 1 HAMBURGER.

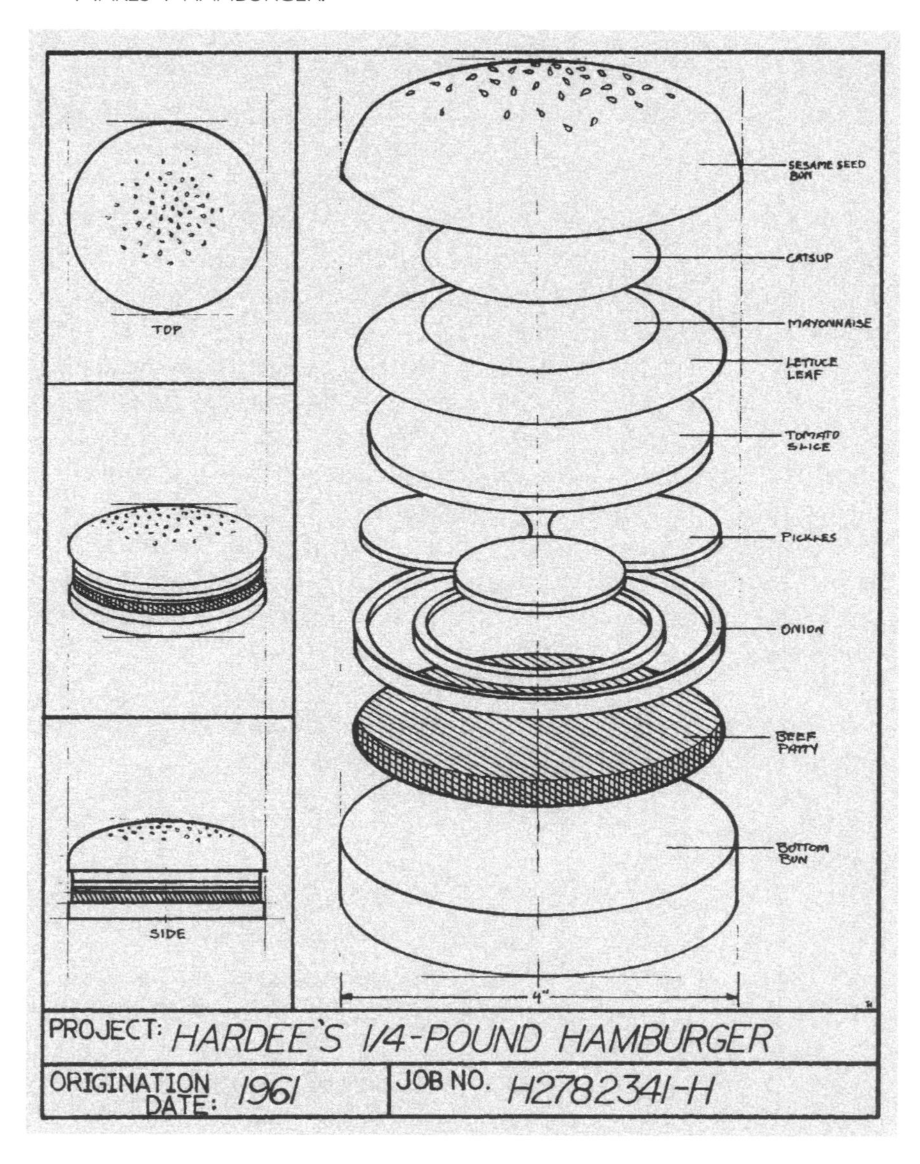

TOP SECRET RECIPES VERSION OF

PANCAKES FROM INTERNATIONAL HOUSE OF PANCAKES

Al Lupin opened the first International House of Pancakes in Toluca Lake, California, in 1958. Now, more than thirty years later, the company has added 490 restaurants, which together serve more than 400,000 pancakes on an average day. That's enough pancakes to make a stack 8,000 feet tall! For comparison, the huge stack of flapjacks would dwarf Chicago's Sears Tower, the world's tallest building, which rises a mere 1,454 feet.

nonstick spray
1 ¼ cups all-purpose flour
1 egg
1 ½ cups buttermilk
¼ cup granulated sugar
1 heaping teaspoon baking powder
1 teaspoon baking soda
¼ cup cooking oil
¼ teaspoon salt

1. Preheat a skillet over medium heat. Use a pan with a nonstick surface or apply a little nonstick spray.
2. In a blender or with a mixer, combine all of the remaining ingredients until smooth.
3. Pour the batter by spoonfuls into the hot pan, forming 5-inch circles.
4. When the edges appear to harden, flip the pancakes. They should be light brown.
5. Cook on the other side for same amount of time, until light brown.

- MAKES 8 TO 10 PANCAKES.

JACK-IN-THE-BOX JUMBO JACK

In 1950 a man named Robert O'Petersen built the first Jack-in-the-Box restaurant at El Cahon and 63rd streets in San Diego, California. The restaurant was originally built for drive-thru and walk-up service only—customers would speak into a clown's mouth to order their food. The clown was blasted to smithereens with explosives in a 1980 advertising campaign, however, signifying a shift toward a more diverse adult menu.

The Jumbo Jack hamburger has been on the menu since 1974.

1 sesame-seed hamburger bun
1/5 pound ground beef
dash salt
2 teaspoons mayonnaise
2 tomato slices
1 large lettuce leaf
2 dill pickle slices
1 tablespoon chopped onion

1. Preheat a frying pan over medium heat.
2. Lightly toast both halves of the hamburger bun, face down. Set aside.
3. Form the ground beef into a thin patty slightly larger than the hamburger bun.
4. Cook the patty in the hot pan for 2 to 3 minutes per side. Lightly salt.
5. Build the burger in the following stacking order from the bottom up:
   bottom bun
   half of mayonnaise
   beef patty
   onion
   remainder of mayonnaise
   tomatoes
   lettuce leaf
   pickles
   top bun

• MAKES 1 HAMBURGER.

TIDBITS

If you want to add a slice of American cheese, it should go on top of the beef patty.

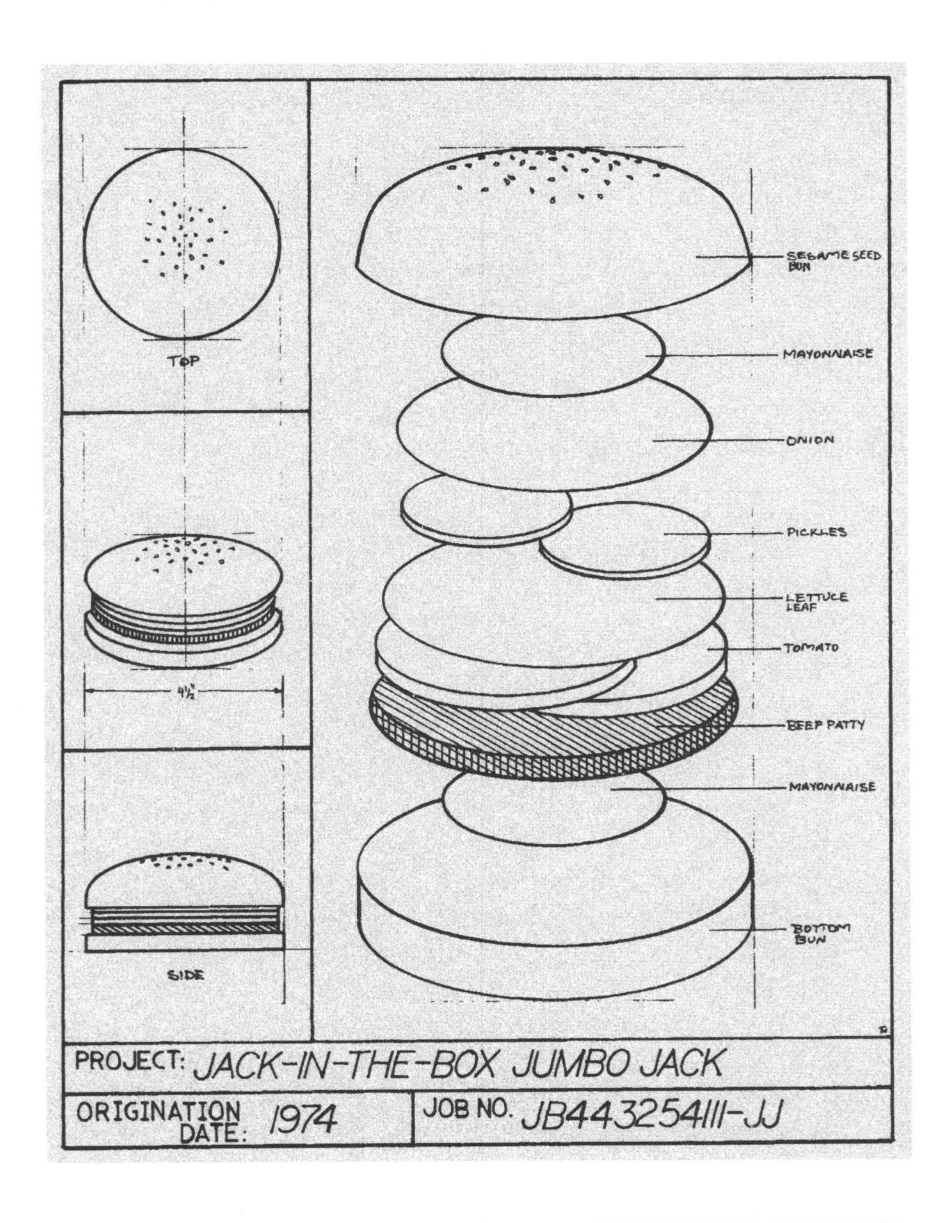

JACK-IN-THE-BOX TACO

Older than both McDonald's and Burger King, Jack-in-the-Box is the world's fifth-largest hamburger chain, with 1,089 outlets (by the end of 1991) in thirteen states throughout the West and Southwest. The restaurant, headquartered in San Diego, boasts one of the largest menus in the fast-food world—a whopping forty-five items.

Now taste for yourself the homemade version of Jack's most popular item. The Jack-in-the-Box Taco has been served since the inception of the chain, with very few changes over the years.

1 pound ground beef
1/3 cup refried beans
1/4 teaspoon salt
2 tablespoons chili powder
1/4 cup Ortega or Pico Pica brand mild taco sauce
3 cups cooking oil (Crisco brand preferred)
12 soft corn tortillas
6 slices American cheese
1 head finely chopped lettuce

1. Slowly brown the ground beef over low heat, using a wooden spoon to chop and stir the meat, keeping it very fine and smooth.
2. When the beef is brown, drain the fat.
3. Add the refried beans and use the wooden spoon to smash the whole beans into the mixture, creating a smooth texture.
4. Add the salt, chili powder, and 2 tablespoons of the taco sauce to the mixture. Remove from the heat.
5. In another skillet, heat 1/4 inch of oil until hot. (Test with a small piece of tortilla—it should bubble when dropped into the oil.) Crisco oil will give the food a taste closest to the original.

6. Spread ½ of the beef mixture on the center of each corn tortilla.
7. Fold the tortillas over and press so that the beef filling acts as an adhesive and holds the sides together.
8. Drop each taco into the pan of hot oil and fry on both sides until crispy.
9. When cooked, remove the tacos from the oil and place them on a rack or some paper towels until they are a little cooler.
10. Pry open each taco slightly. Add ½ slice of American cheese (cut diagonally) and some lettuce. Top with about 1½ teaspoons of the remaining taco sauce.

- MAKES 12 TACOS.

TIDBITS

Try to use very thin tortillas for this recipe so that they won't crack when you fold the filled tacos in half before frying. It's best to use warm tortillas and even moisten them along the middle where you will be folding, for additional flexibility.

• • • •

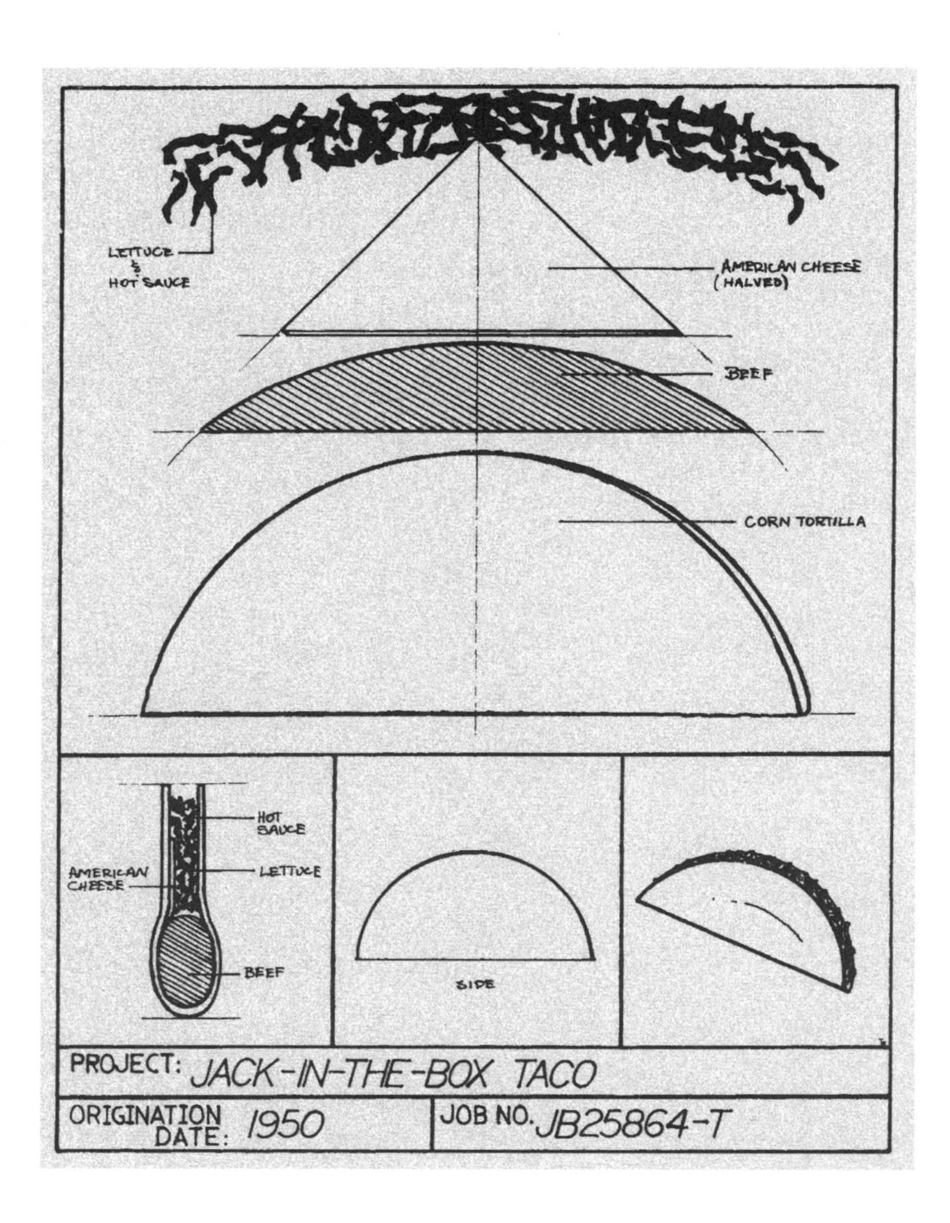
LETTUCE
&
HOT SAUCE
AMERICAN CHEESE
(HALVED)
BEEF
CORN TORTILLA
HOT
SAUCE
AMERICAN
CHEESE
LETTUCE
BEEF
SIDE
PROJECT: JACK-IN-THE-BOX TACO
ORIGINATION DATE: 1950
JOB NO. JB25864-T

TOP SECRET RECIPES VERSION OF

KFC BUTTERMILK BISCUITS

☆ ✌ 💣 ✏ ☯ ✂ ☞

In 1991 Kentucky Fried Chicken bigwigs decided to improve the image of America's third-largest fast-food chain. As a more health-conscious society began to affect sales of fried chicken, the company changed its name to KFC and introduced a lighter fare of skinless chicken. The company is now working hard on developing a new line of baked and roasted chicken.

In the last forty years KFC has experienced extraordinary growth. Five years after first franchising the business, Colonel Harland Sanders had 400 outlets in the United States and Canada. Four years later there were more than 600 franchises, including one in England, the first overseas outlet. In 1964 John Y. Brown, Jr., twenty-nine, a young Louisville lawyer, and Jack Massey, sixty, a Nashville financier, bought the Colonel's business for $2 million. Only seven years later, in 1971, Heublein, Inc., bought the KFC Corporation for $275 million. Then in 1986, for a whopping $840 million, PepsiCo added KFC to its conglomerate, which now includes Pizza Hut and Taco Bell. That means PepsiCo owns more fast-food outlets than any other company including McDonald's—totaling over 20,000.

At each KFC restaurant, workers blend real buttermilk with a flour mixture to create the well-known buttermilk biscuits that have been a popular menu item since their introduction in 1982.

½ cup (1 stick) butter
2½ tablespoons granulated sugar
1 beaten egg
¾ cup buttermilk
¼ cup club soda
1 teaspoon salt
5 cups Bisquick biscuit mix

1. Preheat the oven to 450°F.
2. Combine all of the ingredients. Knead the dough by hand until smooth.
3. Flour your hands. Pat the dough flat to ¾-inch thickness on waxed paper and punch out biscuits with a biscuit cutter.
4. Bake on a greased baking sheet for 12 minutes, or until golden brown.

• MAKES 18 BISCUITS.

TIDBITS

To produce biscuits that most closely resemble the KFC variety, it is best to use a biscuit cutter for this recipe, as specified above. If you don't have a biscuit cutter, the lid of an aerosol can will suffice—just be sure it's not from a product that is toxic. A lid from a can of nonstick cooking spray, for example, works great.

If all you have is a lid from a can of Raid bug. spray, I would say that you should form the biscuits as best you can with your bare hands.

• • • •

TOP SECRET RECIPES VERSION OF

KFC ORIGINAL RECIPE FRIED CHICKEN

Since 1952, when Colonel Harland Sanders opened his first franchise, only a select few have been privy to the secret "herbs and spices" contained in the billion-dollar blend. To protect the top-secret recipe, the company claims, portions of the secret blend are premixed at two confidential spice companies and then distributed to KFC's offices, where they are combined. In 1983, in his book *Big Secrets*, author William Poundstone hired a laboratory to analyze a dry sampling of the spice mixture. The surprising discovery was that instead of identifying "eleven herbs and spices," the analysis showed only four ingredients: flour, salt, pepper, and monosodium glutamate, a flavor enhancer.

The cooking procedure is believed to be the other half of the secret. Colonel Sanders became famous for using a pressure cooker shortly after its invention in 1939. He discovered that hungry travelers greatly appreciated the ten-minute pressure-cooking process (compared to the half hour it used to take for frying chicken), and the new process made the chicken juicy and moist inside.

KFC is the third-largest fast-food chain in the country, and uses around 500 million chickens every year.

6 cups Crisco cooking oil
1 egg, beaten
2 cups milk
2 cups all-purpose flour
4 tablespoons salt
2 teaspoons black pepper
1 teaspoon MSG (monosodium glutamate—you can use Accent Flavor Enhancer)
2 frying chickens with skin, each cut into 8 pieces

1. Pour the oil into the pressure cooker and heat over medium heat to about 400°F.
2. In a small bowl, combine the egg and milk.
3. In a separate bowl, combine the remaining four dry ingredients.
4. Dip each piece of chicken into the milk until fully moistened.
5. Roll the moistened chicken in the flour mixture until completely coated.
6. In groups of four or five, drop the covered chicken pieces into the oil and lock the lid in place.
7. When steam begins shooting through the pressure release, set the timer for 10 minutes.
8. After 10 minutes, release the pressure according to manufacturer's instructions, and remove the chicken to paper towels or a metal rack to drain. Repeat with the remaining chicken.

- MAKES 16 PIECES.

TIDBITS

If you prefer not to use MSG, you may substitute an additional ½ tablespoon of salt. Be aware, however, that using MSG produces the best clone of KFC's Fried Chicken.

Since my recipe was created, most manufacturers of pressure cookers have discouraged frying in their products, and warn that doing so could be hazardous. For that reason you should NEVER use a pressure cooker to fry anything unless the manufacturer has specifically designed the cooker for this use. I understand that there are now only a few cookers available that you can fry in, and finding one may now be difficult. The alternative is to pan fry or deep fry the chicken for roughly double the specified cooking time, until the chicken is golden brown.

• • • •

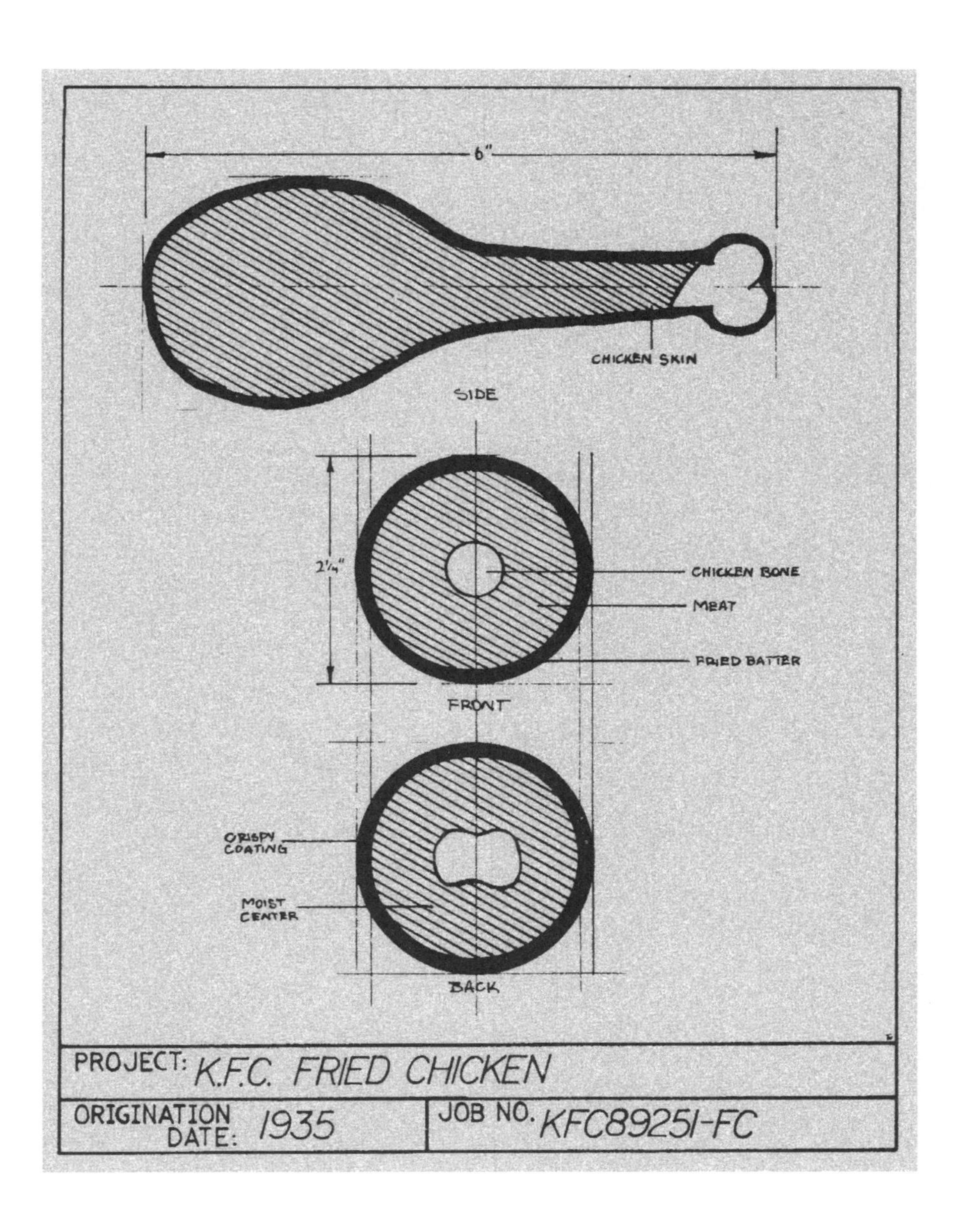
6"
CHICKEN SKIN
SIDE
2¼"
CHICKEN BONE
MEAT
FRIED BATTER
FRONT
CRISPY COATING
MOIST CENTER
BACK
PROJECT: K.F.C. FRIED CHICKEN
ORIGINATION DATE: 1935
JOB NO. KFC89251-FC

TOP SECRET RECIPES VERSION OF

KFC BBQ BAKED BEANS

☆ ✌ 💣 ✎ ☯ ✂ ☞

Here's a clone recipe to add to the table for your next picnic, cookout, or all-purpose pig-out. Just find yourself a couple cans of the small white beans (be sure they're not pinto beans or great northern beans), and the rest is easy. Throw all of the ingredients into a casserole dish and let the sucker bake. While you get on with the party.

2 15-ounce cans small white beans (with liquid)
2 tablespoons water
1 tablespoon cornstarch
½ cup ketchup
½ cup dark brown sugar
2 tablespoons white vinegar
4 teaspoons minced fresh onion
2 pieces cooked bacon, crumbled
½ teaspoon dry mustard
¼ teaspoon salt
dash pepper
dash garlic powder

1. Preheat oven to 350°F.
2. Pour entire contents of two 15-ounce cans of beans into a covered casserole dish.
3. Combine the water with the cornstarch in a small bowl until cornstarch dissolves. Stir mixture into the beans.
4. Stir the remaining ingredients into the beans and cover the dish.
5. Bake for 90 minutes or until sauce thickens. Stir every 30 minutes. Let the beans sit for 5 to 10 minutes after removing them from the oven before serving.

- SERVES 4 TO 6.

TOP SECRET RECIPES VERSION OF

KFC EXTRA CRISPY CHICKEN

☆ ✌ ● ✎ ☯ ✂ ☞

In 1971, with KFC now out of his control, the new owners, the Heublein Company, approached Colonel Harland Sanders with a recipe for a crispier version of the famous fried chicken. The marketing department decided they wanted to call the product "Colonel Sanders' New Recipe" but the Colonel would have nothing to do with it. The stern and opinionated founder of the company, who had publicly criticized the changes to his secret formulas (in a newspaper interview he called the revised mashed potatoes "wallpaper paste"), refused to allow the use of his name on the product. Since the Colonel was an important component of the company's marketing plan, KFC appeased him. The new chicken was then appropriately dubbed "Extra Crispy," and sales were finger-licking good. Now you can reproduce the taste and crunchy breaded texture of the real thing with a brining process similar to that used by the huge fast food chain, followed by a double-dipped coating. Make sure you thoroughly toss the chicken around in the breading so that you get lots of crispy bits on each piece. Unlike the Original Recipe chicken clone, which is pressure-cooked, this version is deep fried. Find the smallest chicken you can for this clone since small cluckers will fry much better and will create the closest clone to the real deal. This recipe is a tweaked version of the recipe found in "Even More Top Secret Recipes".

1 whole frying chicken, cut up (smaller the better)
8 to 12 cups vegetable shortening (amount required by your fryer

BRINE SOLUTION
5 cups cold water
¼ cup salt
2 teaspoon MSG (see Tidbits)

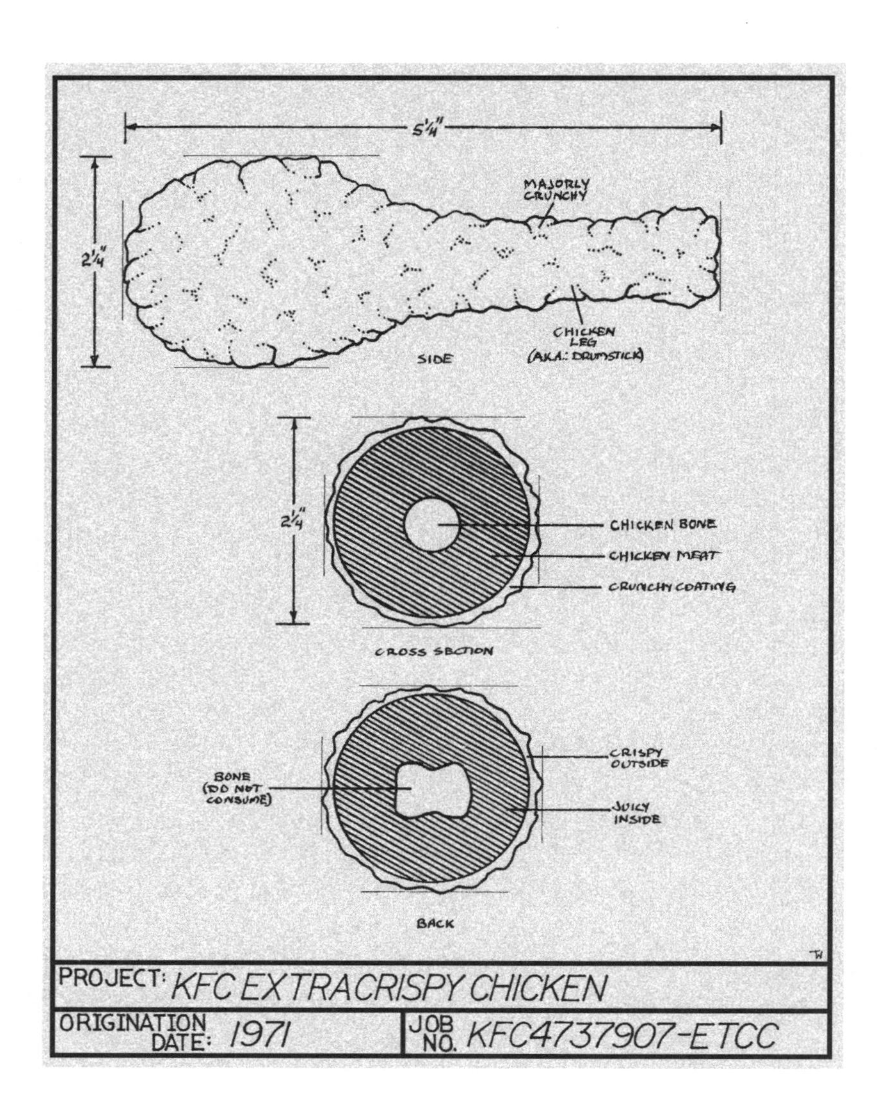
5¼"
2¼"
MAJORLY CRUNCHY
CHICKEN LEG (A.K.A.: DRUMSTICK)
SIDE
2¼"
CHICKEN BONE
CHICKEN MEAT
CRUNCHY COATING
CROSS SECTION
BONE (DO NOT CONSUME)
CRISPY OUTSIDE
JUICY INSIDE
BACK
PROJECT: KFC EXTRACRISPY CHICKEN
ORIGINATION DATE: 1971
JOB NO. KFC4737907-ETCC

COATING

1 egg, beaten
1 cup milk
2 cups all-purpose flour
2½ tablespoons salt
1 teaspoon ground black pepper
1 teaspoon paprika
¾ teaspoon MSG (see Tidbits)
½ teaspoon poultry seasoning

1. Trim any excess skin and fat from the chicken pieces. Preheat the shortening in a deep fryer to 350°F.
2. Combine the water, salt, and 2 teaspoons MSG for the brine in a large bowl and let it sit for 2 hours. Turn the chicken a couple times as it marinates.
3. Combine the beaten egg and milk in a medium bowl. In another medium bowl, combine the remaining coating ingredients (flour, salt, pepper, paprika, ¾ teaspoon MSG, and poultry seasoning).
4. When the chicken has marinated in the brine, transfer each piece to paper towels so that excess liquid can drain off. Working with one piece at a time, first coat the chicken with the dry flour mixture, then the egg and milk mixture, and then back into the flour. Toss the chicken around in the coating to build up a heavy coating on each piece. Stack the chicken on a plate or cookie sheet until each piece has been coated.
5. Drop the chicken, one piece at a time, into the hot shortening. Fry half of the chicken at a time (4 pieces) for 7 to 10 minutes, or until it's golden brown. You should be sure to stir the chicken around halfway through the cooking time so that each piece cooks evenly.
6. Remove the chicken to a rack to drain for about 5 minutes before eating.

- SERVES 3 TO 4 (8 PIECES OF CHICKEN).

TIDBITS

MSG is monosodium glutamate, the solid form of a natural amino acid found in many vegetables. It can be found in stores in the spice sections, and as the brand name Accent Flavor Enhancer. MSG is an important component of many KFC items.

TOP SECRET RECIPES VERSION OF

KFC HONEY BBQ WINGS

☆ ✌ 💣 ✎ ☯ ✂ ☞

Once a regular menu item, these sweet, saucy wings are now added to the KFC menu on a "limited-time-only" basis in many markets. So how are we to get that sticky sauce all over our faces and hands during those months when we're cruelly denied our Honey BBQ Wings? Now it's as easy as whipping up a clone that re-creates a crispy breading on the chicken wings, and then slathering those puppies with a tasty knock-off of the sweet, tangy honey BBQ sauce. "Limited-time-only" signs—we laugh at you!

SAUCE

1 1/4 cups ketchup
1/3 cup white vinegar
1/4 cup molasses
1/4 cup honey
1 teaspoon liquid smoke (see Tidbits)
1/2 teaspoon salt
1/4 teaspoon onion powder
1/4 teaspoon chili powder

6 to 8 cups vegetable shortening
1 egg, beaten
1 cup milk
2 cups all-purpose flour
2 1/2 teaspoons salt
3/4 teaspoon pepper
3/4 teaspoon MSG (see Tidbits)
20 chicken wing pieces

1. Combine the sauce ingredients in a small saucepan over medium heat. Stir until ingredients are well combined and bring to a boil. Then reduce heat and simmer uncovered for 15 to 20 minutes.
2. As sauce is simmering, heat up 6 to 8 cups of shortening in a deep fryer set to 350 degrees.
3. Combine the beaten egg with the milk in a small bowl.

4. In another small bowl, combine the flour, salt, pepper, and MSG.
5. When the shortening is hot, dip each wing first in the flour mixture, then into the milk and egg mixture, and back into the flour. Arrange wings on a plate until each one is coated with batter.
6. Fry the wings for 9 to 12 minutes or until light golden brown. If you have a small fryer, you may wish to fry 10 of the wings at a time. Drain on a rack.
7. When the sauce is done, brush the entire surface of each wing with a light coating of sauce. Serve immediately.

• MAKES 2 TO 4 SERVINGS (20 WINGS).

TIDBITS

Liquid smoke is a flavoring found in the store near the barbecue sauces and marinades. Use hickory-flavored liquid smoke if you have a choice.

MSG is monosodium glutamate, the solid form of a natural amino acid found in many vegetables. It can be found in stores in the spice sections and as the brand name Accent Flavor Enhancer. MSG is an important component of several KFC items.

• • • •

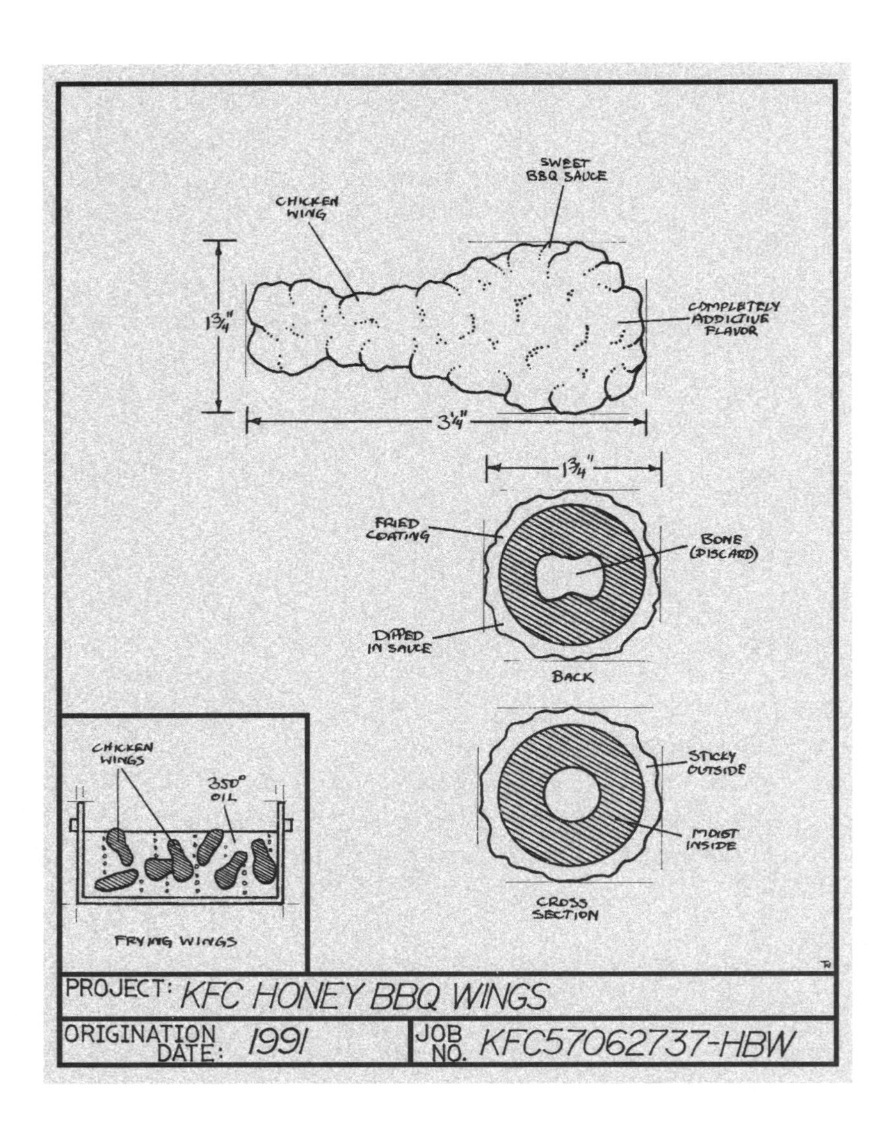
SWEET BBQ SAUCE
CHICKEN WING
1¾"
COMPLETELY ADDICTIVE FLAVOR
3¼"
1¾"
FRIED COATING
BONE (DISCARD)
DIPPED IN SAUCE
BACK
CHICKEN WINGS
350° OIL
STICKY OUTSIDE
MOIST INSIDE
CROSS SECTION
FRYING WINGS
PROJECT: KFC HONEY BBQ WINGS
ORIGINATION DATE: 1991
JOB NO. KFC57062737-HBW

TOP SECRET RECIPES VERSION OF

KFC MACARONI & CHEESE

☆ ✌ 💣 ✎ ☯ ✂ ☞

Here's a clone for another of KFC's famous side dishes. We'll use easy-to-melt Velveeta, with its very smooth texture, as the main ingredient for the cheese sauce. Then a bit of cheddar cheese is added to give the sauce a sharp cheddary zing like the original. It's a very simple recipe that will take only 15 minutes to prepare. That's great news for impatient cooks who want to dig right into the tasty vittles. Weeell doggies!

6 cups water
1 1/3 cups elbow macaroni
4 ounces Velveeta cheese
1/2 cup shredded cheddar cheese
2 tablespoons whole milk
1/4 teaspoon salt

1. Bring water to a boil over high heat in a medium saucepan. Add elbow macaroni to the water and cook it for 10 to 12 minutes or until tender, stirring occasionally.
2. While the macaroni is boiling, prepare the cheese sauce by combining the remaining ingredients in a small saucepan over low heat. Stir often as the cheese melts into a smooth consistency.
3. When the macaroni is done, strain it and then pour it back into the same pan, without the water.
4. Add the cheese sauce to the pan and stir gently until the macaroni is well coated with the cheese. Serve immediately while hot.

- MAKES ABOUT 3 SERVINGS.

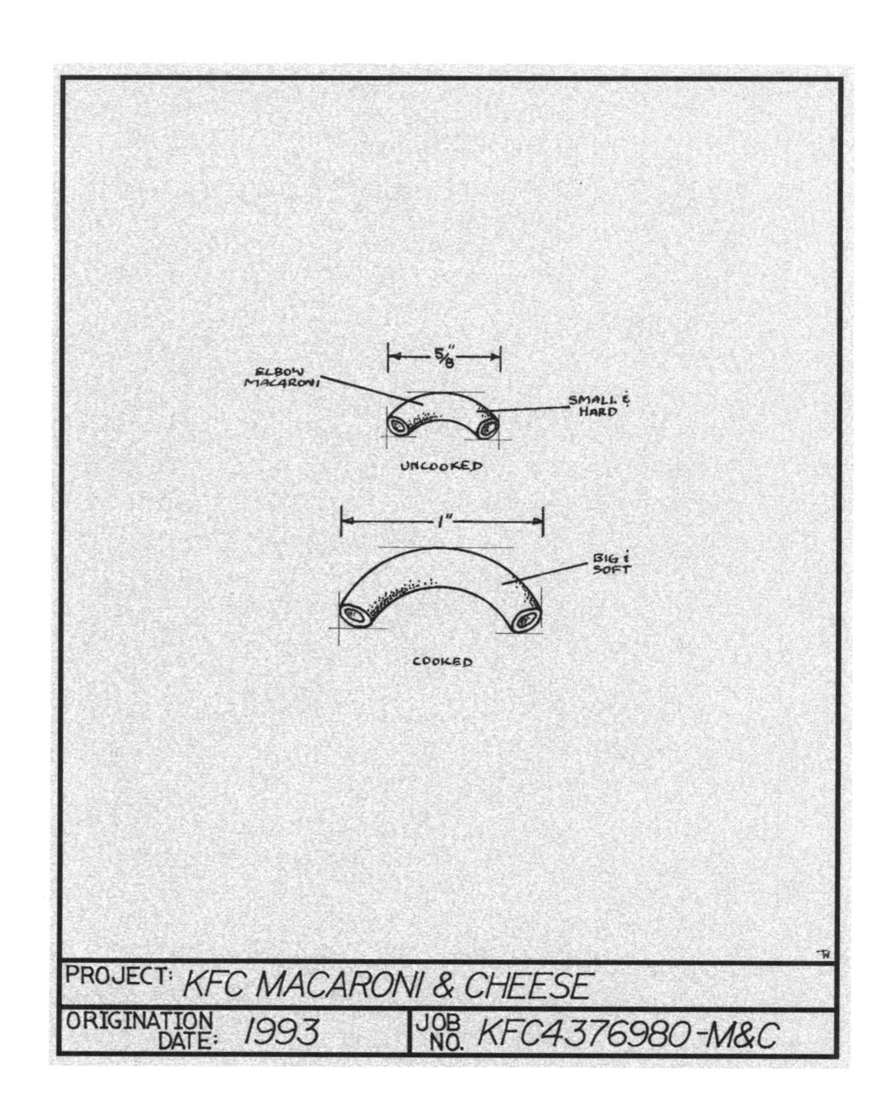
5/8"
ELBOW MACARONI
SMALL & HARD
UNCOOKED
1"
BIG & SOFT
COOKED
PROJECT: KFC MACARONI & CHEESE
ORIGINATION DATE: 1993
JOB NO. KFC4376980-M&C

TOP SECRET RECIPES VERSION OF

KFC MASHED POTATOES & GRAVY

☆ ✌ 💣 ✎ ☯ ✂ ☞

This gravy recipe should come very close to that tasty tan stuff that's poured over the fluffy mashed potatoes at the Colonel's chain of restaurants. And since the original recipe contains MSG (as does their chicken), this clone was designed with that "secret" ingredient. You may choose to leave out the MSG, which is a natural amino acid found in vegetables and seaweed. But your clone won't taste exactly like the real thing without it.

GRAVY

1 tablespoon vegetable oil
4½ tablespoons all-purpose flour
1 can Campbell's chicken broth (plus 1 can water) (see Tidbits)
¼ teaspoon salt
⅛ teaspoon MSG or Accent Flavor Enhancer
⅛ teaspoon ground black pepper

MASHED POTATOES

1½ cups water
⅓ cup milk
3 tablespoons butter
½ teaspoon salt
1½ cups instant mashed potato flakes (Potato Buds)

1. First make a roux by combining the oil with 1½ tablespoons of flour in a medium saucepan over low to medium heat. Heat the mixture for 20 to 30 minutes, stirring often, until it is a chocolate color.
2. Remove the roux from the heat, add the remaining ingredients to the saucepan, and stir.

3. Put the saucepan back over the heat, turn it up to medium, and bring the gravy to a boil. Reduce heat and simmer for 10 to 15 minutes, or until thick.
4. As the gravy is reducing, prepare the potatoes by combining 1½ cups of water, ⅓ cup of milk, butter, and ½ teaspoon of salt in a medium saucepan over medium heat. Bring to a boil, then remove the pan from heat. Add the potato flakes, and whip with a fork until fluffy.
5. Serve the mashed potatoes with gravy poured over the top. As if you didn't know.

• MAKES 3 TO 4 SERVINGS.

TIDBITS

If Campbell's chicken broth is not available you can use 2½ cups of any chicken stock.

• • • •

TOP SECRET RECIPES VERSION OF

KFC POTATO SALAD

Here's a simple clone for the scrumptious potato salad that you get as a side dish from America's largest fast food chicken chain. Some of the skin is left on the potatoes in the real thing, so you don't have to peel them too thoroughly. Just be sure to chop your potatoes into cubes that are approximately ½ inch thick, and then let the salad marinate for at least 4 hours so that the flavors can properly develop. If you let the salad chill overnight, it tastes even better.

2 pounds russet potatoes
1 cup mayonnaise
4 teaspoons sweet pickle relish
4 teaspoons sugar
2 teaspoons minced white onion
2 teaspoons prepared mustard
1 teaspoon vinegar
1 teaspoon minced celery
1 teaspoon diced pimentos
½ teaspoon shredded carrot
¼ teaspoon dried parsley
¼ teaspoon pepper
dash salt

1. Lightly peel the potatoes (leave a little skin on), then chop them into bite-size pieces and boil in 6 cups of boiling, salted water for 7 to 10 minutes. The potato chunks should be tender, yet slightly tough in the middle when done. Drain and rinse potatoes with cold water.
2. In a medium bowl, combine remaining ingredients and whisk until smooth.
3. Pour drained potatoes into a large bowl. Pour the dressing over the potatoes and mix until well combined.
4. Cover and chill for at least 4 hours. Overnight is best.

- Makes 6 cups (about 8 servings).

TOP SECRET RECIPES VERSION OF

KFC CAJUN HONEY WINGS

When the "Limited-time only" signs came down for this one, I just smiled. Because now we've got a clone recipe to last forever that'll closely duplicate the sweet and spicy sauce on these amazing chicken wings. The Colonel's people coat the wings with a KFC-style breading before frying them up and adding the Cajun sauce. But you don't need wings to put this sauce to work. This recipe makes 1 cup of the sauce that you can use to coat beef, pork, or other chicken parts. This recipe requires the meat variety of Paul Prudhomme's Magic Seasoning Blends, but it will also work with other Cajun seasoning blends, which are available in most markets.

SAUCE

¼ cup ketchup
1 cup water
¾ cup white vinegar
1 tablespoon vegetable oil
⅓ cup honey
4 teaspoons Chef Paul Prudhomme's Meat Magic
1 tablespoon canned green chilies, minced
1 ¼ teaspoons chili powder
1 teaspoon minced garlic
½ teaspoon liquid smoke (hickory flavor)
⅛ teaspoon dried thyme

6 to 12 cups vegetable shortening
1 egg, beaten
1 cup milk
2 cups all-purpose flour
2½ teaspoons salt
¾ teaspoon pepper
¾ teaspoon MSG (such as Accent)
20 chicken wing pieces

1. Combine the sauce ingredients in a small saucepan over medium heat. Stir until ingredients are well combined, and bring to a boil. Then reduce heat and simmer sauce uncovered for 20 to 25 minutes or until it has thickened.
2. As sauce is simmering, heat up 6 to 12 cups of shortening in a deep fryer set to 350°F.
3. Combine the beaten egg with the milk in a small bowl.
4. In another small bowl, combine the flour, salt, pepper, and MSG.
5. When shortening is hot, dip each wing first in the flour mixture, then into the milk-and-egg mixture, and back into the flour. Arrange wings on a plate until each one is coated with batter.
6. Fry the wings in the shortening for 9 to 12 minutes or until light golden brown. If you have a small fryer, you may wish to fry 10 of the wings at a time. Drain on paper towels or a rack.
7. When the sauce is done, brush the entire surface of each wing with a coating of sauce. Serve immediately.

- MAKES 2 TO 4 SERVINGS (20 WINGS).

• • • •

LONG JOHN SILVER'S BATTER-DIPPED FISH

Jerrico, Inc., the parent company for Long John Silver's Seafood Shoppes, got its start in 1929 as a six-stool hamburger stand called the White Tavern Shoppe. Jerrico was started by a man named Jerome Lederer, who watched Long John Silver's thirteen units dwindle in the shadow of World War II to just three units. Then, with determination, he began rebuilding.

In 1946 Jerome launched a new restaurant called Jerry's, and it was a booming success, with a growth across the country. Then he took a chance on what would be his most successful venture in 1969, with the opening of the first Long John Silver's Fish 'n' Chips. The name was inspired by Robert Louis Stevenson's Treasure Island.

In 1991 there were 1,450 Long John Silver Seafood Shoppes in thirty-seven states, Canada, and Singapore, with annual sales of more than $781 million. That means the company holds about 65 percent of the $1.2-billion quick-service seafood business.

3 cups soybean oil
2 pounds fresh cod fillets
1 ⅓ cups self-rising flour
1 cup water
1 egg
2 teaspoons granulated sugar
2 teaspoons salt

1. Heat the oil in a deep pan to about 400°F.
2. Cut the fish into approximately 7 × 2-inch wedges.
3. With a mixer, blend the flour, water, egg, sugar, and salt.

4. Dip each fillet into the batter, coating generously, and quickly drop into the oil.
5. Fry each fillet until dark golden brown, about 5 minutes.
6. Remove from the oil and place on paper towels or a metal rack to drain.

• Makes 4 to 6 fillets.

TIDBITS

Soybean oil is what your local Long John Silver's uses to fry their fish, and you will best duplicate the real thing by using the same oil. But any other oil may be substituted. You might want to try canola oil. It is the oil lowest in saturated fat, and the taste difference is only slight.

It's crucial that your oil be hot before frying the fish. To test the temperature, drip some batter into the oil. It should bubble rapidly. After 5 minutes, the test batter should become golden brown. If so, fry away, fish fiends.

• • • •

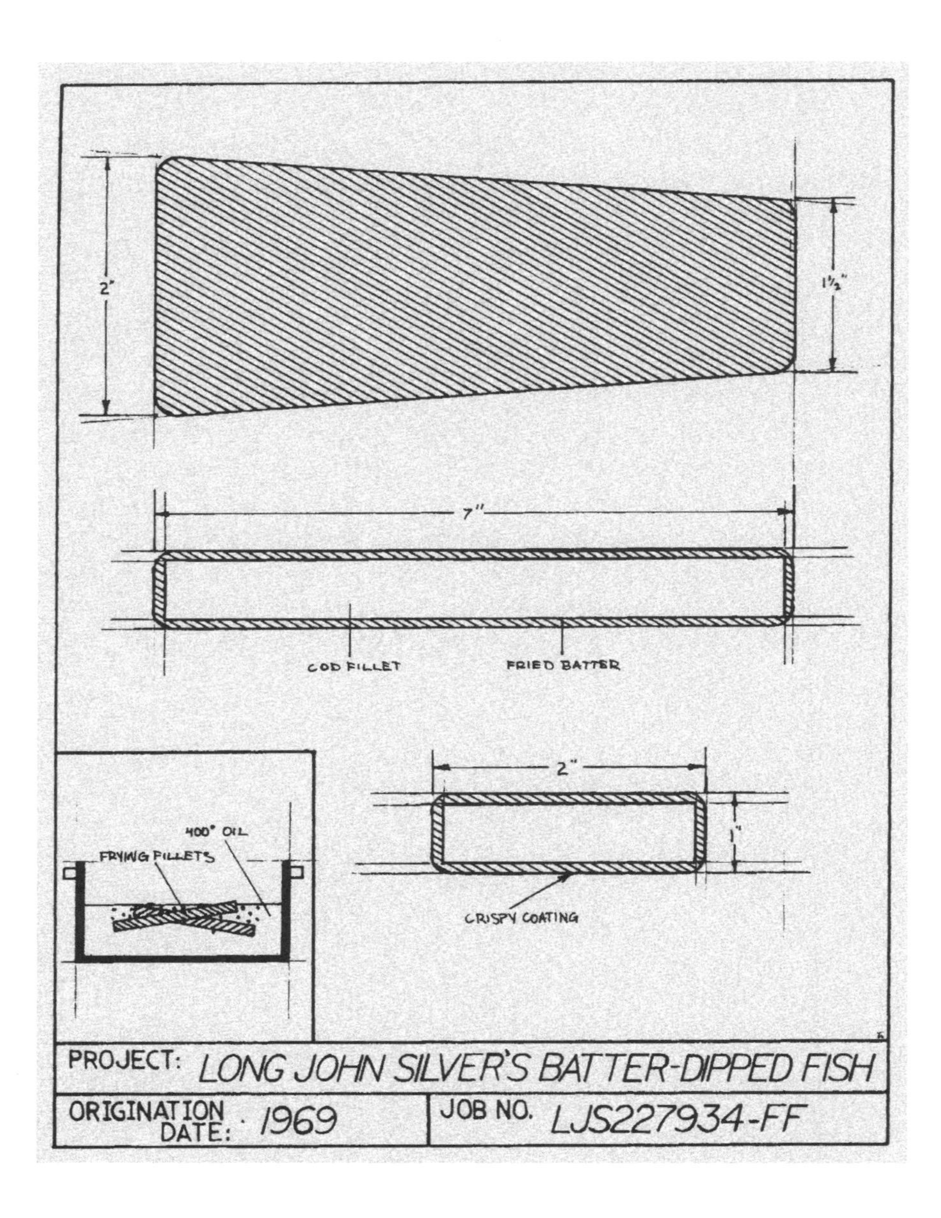
2"
1½"
7"
COD FILLET
FRIED BATTER
400° OIL
FRYING FILLETS
2"
1"
CRISPY COATING
PROJECT: LONG JOHN SILVER'S BATTER-DIPPED FISH
ORIGINATION DATE: 1969
JOB NO. LJS227934-FF

TOP SECRET RECIPES VERSION OF

MAID-RITE LOOSE MEAT SANDWICH

☆ ✌ 💣 ✏ ☯ ✂ ☞

It's been an Iowa tradition since 1926, and one of our longtime requested items at TSR. Even ex-comedienne Roseanne and her Iowa native ex-husband Tom Arnold spoke many salivating praises of Maid-Rites when they shared a home together in the state. There are now 83 Maid-Rite stores located throughout Iowa and seven other Midwestern states. Although the sandwich is not much more than a traditional hamburger with the ground beef arranged uncompressed on a white bun, the product has a huge cult following. And since the meat is loose, the sandwich is served with a spoon for scooping up the ground beef that will inevitably fall out.

The nice thing about having a popular Web site (www.TopSecretRecipes.com) is the instant feedback that comes with each posted weekly recipe. This recipe was certainly no exception. In fact, the clone for Maid-Rite elicited more e-mail than any recipe in the site's history. Numerous Midwesterners were keyboard-ready to insist that the clone was far from accurate without inclusion of a few bizarre ingredients, the most common of which was good old Coca-Cola. One letter states: "You evidently have not ever had a Maid-Rite. The secret to the Maid-Rite is coke syrup. Without it, you cannot come close to the taste." Another e-mail reads; "'Having lived in the Midwest all of my life and knowing not only owners of a Maid-Rite restaurant, but also many people who worked there, I can tell you that one of the things you left out of your recipe is Coca-Cola. Not a lot, just enough to keep the meat moist."

Then, on the flip side, I received comments such as this one from a fan who lived in Iowa, the state where Don Taylor's original

Maid-Rite franchise was located: "The secret to the best Maid-Rite is the whole beef. Don had a butcher shop in his basement where he cut and ground all his beef. Some people still swear they added seasoning, but that is just not true. Not even pepper. They do add water, which steams the meat."

To create this clone, I did, of course, consume many a Maid-Rite sandwich. Obviously, there's no way I could create a clone recipe for a product I haven't tasted. In fact, I arranged for Maid-Rites to be shipped in dry ice directly from Don Taylor's original store in Marshalltown. As I write this, I still have a few of those puppies in the freezer, and after a couple minutes in the microwave, they're almost as good as fresh.

Upon receiving all the e-mails, I went back to the freezer and back to the drawing board to see if the cloning work on this famous Top Secret Recipe could be bettered. But no matter how hard I examined the meat, I could not detect Coca-Cola in there. There's no sweetness to the meat at all, although the buns themselves seem to include some sugar (when the buns are chewed with the meat, the sandwich does taste mildly sweet). I finally concluded that Coca-Cola is an absolutely unnecessary ingredient for cloning this sandwich. If it's being added to the meat in the Maid-Rite stores, it's an insignificant amount that does not have any noticeable effect on the flavor. Perhaps beef broth is being mistaken as Coca-Cola? Or this could simply be one of those crazy urban food legends that spread so easily on the Web. So there's still no Coke in the ingredients list, but I've made a few other small changes that improve the recipe.

While my original clone recipe included a dash of black pepper, I have now concluded that there is no such ingredient in the real thing. Black pepper specks would show easily against the white, flour, hamburger bun, and I have not found any after examining several sandwiches. Also, the texture is important, so adding more liquid to the simmering meat is crucial. This revised recipe requires a cup of water in addition to a 1/4 cup of beef broth. By simmering the ground beef in this liquid for an hour or so, we can maintain a temperature over 140 degrees that breaks down the collagen in the meat. This makes the final product tender, just like the real thing. The beef broth, plus a little salt, adds all the flavor you'll need. Try it, and you'll see for yourself. And, yes, that's without any Coca-Cola. It also helps to use good quality ground beef. You'll get out of the recipe what you put in.

When building your sandwich, firmly press the beef into a 1⁄2-cup measuring cup. Dump the meat onto the bottom of a plain hamburger bun; add your choice of mustard, onions, and pickles; ready a spoon, and dig in. Adding ketchup is up to you, although it's not an ingredient found in Maid-Rite stores. Many say that back in the early days, "hobos" would swipe the ketchup and mix it with water to make tomato soup. Free ketchup was nixed from the restaurants way back then, and the custom has been in place ever since.

1 pound lean ground beef (15% fat is best)
1 cup water
1⁄4 cup beef broth
1⁄4 teaspoon salt
4 plain hamburger buns
yellow mustard
minced onion
dill pickle slices

1. Brown ground beef in a large skillet over medium-low heat. Use a potato masher to help get the ground beef into small pieces. Drain any excess fat. If you use lean meat (15% fat or less) you won't need to drain the fat. As soon as all the pink in the meat is gone, add 1 cup of water and 1⁄4 cup beef broth plus 1⁄4 teaspoon salt. Simmer the meat uncovered for one hour or until all the liquid is gone, stirring every 10 minutes or so.
2. Build each sandwich by pressing the hot ground beef into a 1⁄2 cup measuring cup. Dump the meat onto the bottom of a plain hamburger bun. Add mustard on the top bun, along with pickles and minced onion if desired. Put the sandwich to-

gether, and heat it up in your microwave oven for 10 to 15 seconds to warm the buns. Serve with a spoon as they do in the restaurants.

- MAKES 4 SANDWICHES.

• • • •

TOP SECRET RECIPES VERSION OF

MCDONALD'S MCD.L.T.

☆ ✌ 💣 ✎ ☯ ✂ ☞

And how about this . . . ?

In 1963 the busiest clown in America, Ronald McDonald, made his debut in Washington, D.C. But beneath that red wig and 14½-inch shoes was someone who would later become the portly weatherman on NBC's "Today" show. You got it, Willard Scott.

Future Ronald McDonald wanna-bes get their training at McDonald's so-called college, just as many of the chain's managers and franchise owners do. It is a surprisingly busy institution. By 1991 the 40,000th student was granted a Hamburgerology Degree from McDonald's Hamburger University in Oak Brook, Illinois. (Hamburger University was set up to provide instruction for McDonald's personnel in the various aspects of their business—equipment, controls, human relations skills, and management skills.)

Nearly 3,000 students pass through the halls of the school each year as they continue to grow in their McDonald's careers. And the American Council on Education has approved eighteen of the university's courses for college credit.

One more chapter in the studies of H.U. graduates came in 1985, when the "hot side" and "cool side" of the McD.L.T. found their way onto McDonald's menu. It lives on only in this book, for five years after it was introduced, the McD.L.T. was dropped and replaced with the McLean Deluxe.

1 sesame-seed hamburger bun
⅛ teaspoon prepared mustard
1 teaspoon catsup
2 medium onion rings, chopped
3 dill pickle slices
¼ cup chopped lettuce
1 tablespoon mayonnaise
1 slice American cheese
2 tomato slices
¼ pound ground beef
dash salt

1. Lightly brown both halves of the hamburger bun, face down, in a hot pan. Set aside; keep the pan hot.
2. Build the "cool side" of the McD.L.T. in the following stacking order from the bottom up:

   bottom bun
   mustard
   catsup
   chopped onion
   pickle slices
   chopped lettuce
   mayonnaise
   American cheese slice
   tomato slices
3. With your hands, form the ground beef into a thin patty slightly larger in diameter than the bun.
4. Cook the patty in the hot pan for 2 to 3 minutes per side. Salt lightly.
5. Build the "hot side" in the following stacking order from the bottom up:

   top bun
   beef patty
6. When you are ready to eat, slap the "cool side" and the "hot side" together.

• MAKES 1 HAMBURGER.

• • • •

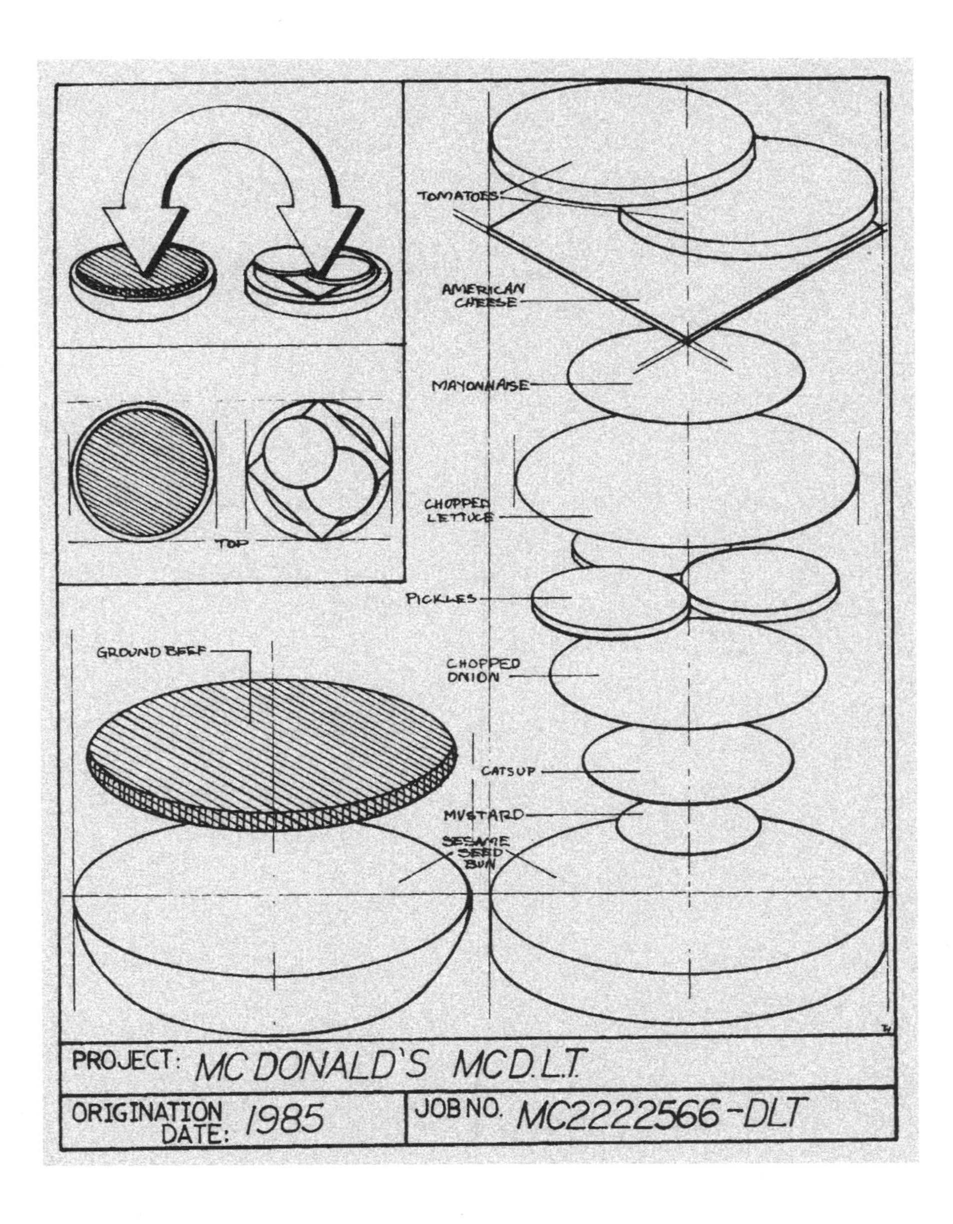
TOMATOES
AMERICAN CHEESE
MAYONNAISE
CHOPPED LETTUCE
PICKLES
CHOPPED ONION
CATSUP
MUSTARD
SESAME SEED BUN
GROUND BEEF
TOP
PROJECT: MC DONALD'S MCD.L.T.
ORIGINATION DATE: 1985
JOB NO. MC2222566-DLT

TOP SECRET RECIPES VERSION OF

MCDONALD'S BREAKFAST BAGEL SANDWICHES

☆ ✌ 💣 ✎ ☯ ✂ ☞

Hold an entire breakfast in two hands and bring it right up to your face for a bite. Here are clones for all three varieties of the newest breakfast sandwiches from the Golden Arches. The only requirement is that you have a small 6-inch skillet to make the omelette for each sandwich. Take your pick.

HAM & EGG BAGEL

SAUCE
2 tablespoons mayonnaise
1 teaspoon creamy dill mustard

4 eggs
salt
ground black pepper
1 teaspoon butter
8 ounces deli-sliced ham (2 to 3 slices per sandwich)
4 plain bagels
8 slices Kraft Singles American cheese

1. First prepare the sauce by combining the mayonnaise with the dill mustard in a small bowl. Set this aside until you are ready to use it.
2. To prepare the eggs it's best to make one at a time in a small 6-inch skillet. If you have more than one of these small pans, you can save a little time.
3. Beat an egg in a small bowl with a whisk until it is smooth, but not foamy. Add a pinch of salt and pepper to the egg. Heat a small 6-inch skillet over low heat. Add ¼ teaspoon of butter to

the pan. When the butter has melted add the egg to the pan. Swirl the pan so that the egg spreads evenly. As the egg begins to cook, use a spatula to pull in a couple of the edges so that raw egg flows from the top onto the hot pan. Cook for 2 to 3 minutes, then fold over one of the edges of the egg using a spoon or fork. Fold it down about an inch. Fold the opposite end over as well. Then fold the remaining two edges over, creating a small rectangular or square mini-omelette. Flip the little omelette over and turn off the heat.

4. Heat up the ham in a covered dish in the microwave for 1 minute. This will make it hot, and keep it from drying.
5. Slice a bagel in half and place it with the faces up on a baking sheet. Grill the faces of the bagel halves in your oven, set on broil, until golden brown. You may also use a toaster oven for this step, but be sure to place the sliced bagel halves onto a small baking sheet or on aluminum foil so that only the faces are toasted.
6. When the bagels are toasted, spread about ½ tablespoon of the sauce onto the face of the top bagel half.
7. Place a slice of cheese onto the face of each bagel half.
8. Place the finished omelette onto the cheese on the bottom half of the sandwich.
9. Place the ham onto the egg.
10. Finish by flipping the top half of the sandwich over onto the bottom. Heat for 15 seconds in microwave if needed to warm.

- MAKES 4 SERVINGS.

• • • •

STEAK & EGG BAGEL

SAUCE
2 tablespoons mayonnaise
1 teaspoon creamy dill mustard

1 teaspoon vegetable oil
1 slice white onion, quartered
One 14-ounce package Steak-Umm chopped steak (7 steaks)
4 eggs
1 teaspoon butter
salt
ground black pepper
4 plain bagels
8 slices Kraft Singles American cheese

1. First prepare the sauce by combining the mayonnaise with the dill mustard in a small bowl. Set this aside until you are ready to use it.
2. Heat 1 teaspoon of vegetable oil in a medium skillet over medium heat. Separate the onion slices and sauté in the oil until light brown.
3. Heat a large skillet over medium high heat. Break up the sandwich steak into the hot pan and cook until brown. Drain off fat. Add the grilled onions to the meat and stir.
4. To make the eggs it's best to make one at a time in a small 6-inch skillet. If you have more than one of these small pans, you can save a little time.
5. Beat an egg in a small bowl with a whisk until it is smooth, but not foamy. Add a pinch of salt and pepper to the egg. Heat a small 6-inch skillet over low heat. Add ¼ teaspoon of butter to the pan. When the butter has melted add the egg to the pan. Swirl the pan so that the egg spreads evenly. As the egg begins to cook, use a spatula to pull in a couple of the edges so that raw egg flows from the top onto the hot pan. Cook for 2 to 3 minutes, then fold over one of the edges of the egg using a spoon or fork. Fold it down about an inch. Fold the opposite end over as well. Then fold the remaining two edges over, creating a small rectangular or square mini-omelette. Flip the little omelette over and turn off the heat.
6. Slice a bagel in half and place it with the faces up on a baking sheet. Grill the faces of the bagel halves in your oven, set on broil, until golden brown. You may also use a toaster oven for

this step, but be sure to place the sliced bagel halves onto a small baking sheet or on aluminum foil so that only the faces are toasted.

7. When the bagels are toasted, spread about ½ tablespoon of the sauce onto the face of the top bagel half.
8. Place a slice of cheese onto the face of each bagel half.
9. Divide the meat into four portions and stack one portion onto the cheese on the bottom bagel half.
10. Place the finished omelette onto the meat on the bottom half of the sandwich.
11. Finish by flipping the top half of the sandwich over onto the bottom. Heat for 15 seconds in microwave if needed to warm.

• MAKES 4 SERVINGS.

SPANISH OMELET BAGEL

SAUCE
2 tablespoons mayonnaise
1 teaspoon creamy dill mustard
2 teaspoons minced green pepper
2 teaspoons minced white onion
4 eggs
1 teaspoon butter
salt
ground black pepper
8 ounces breakfast sausage

4 plain bagels
4 slices Kraft Singles American cheese
4 slices Kraft Singles Monterey Jack cheese

1. First prepare the sauce by combining the mayonnaise with the dill mustard in a small bowl. Set this aside until you are ready to use it.
2. To prepare the eggs it's best to make one at a time in a small 6-inch skillet. If you have more than one of these small pans, you can save a little time.
3. First preheat pan over low heat. Add ¼ teaspoon of butter. Add ½ teaspoon of minced green pepper along with ½ teaspoon of minced white onion to the pan and sauté for a couple minutes, or until soft.
4. Beat an egg in a small bowl with a whisk until it is smooth, but

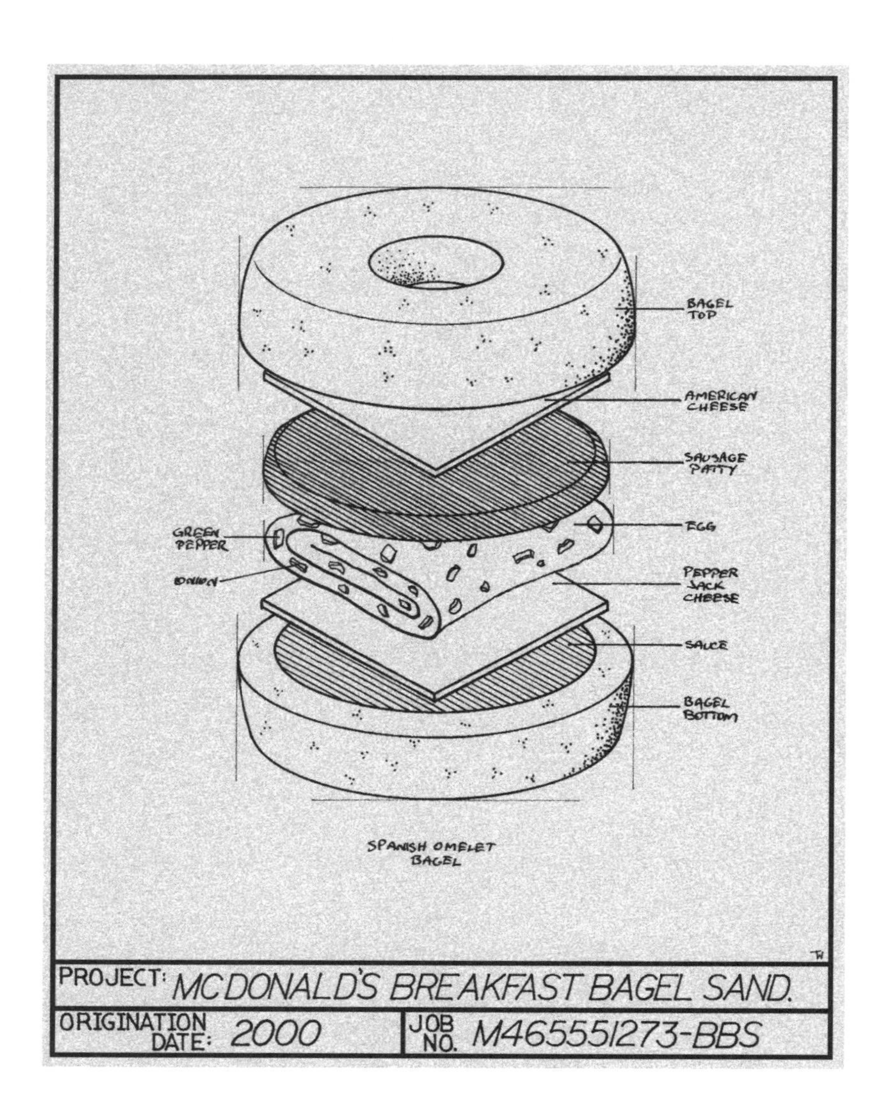
BAGEL TOP
AMERICAN CHEESE
SAUSAGE PATTY
GREEN PEPPER
EGG
ONION
PEPPER JACK CHEESE
SAUCE
BAGEL BOTTOM
SPANISH OMELET BAGEL
PROJECT: MCDONALD'S BREAKFAST BAGEL SAND.
ORIGINATION DATE: 2000
JOB NO. M465551273-BBS

not foamy. Add a pinch of salt and pepper to the egg. Add the egg to the pan with the vegetables. Swirl the pan so that the egg spreads out. As the egg begins to cook, use a spatula to pull in a couple of the edges so that raw egg flows from the top onto the hot pan. Cook for 2 to 3 minutes, then fold over one of the edges of the egg using a spoon or fork. Fold it down about an inch. Fold the opposite end over as well. Then fold the remaining two edges over, creating a small rectangular or square mini-omelette. Flip the little omelette over and turn off the heat.

5. Press the sausage into four 2-ounce patties approximately the size of the bagel. Cook the sausage in a large skillet over medium heat until brown. Drain when done.
6. Slice a bagel in half and place it with the faces up on a baking sheet. Grill the faces of the bagel halves in your oven, set on broil, until golden brown. You may also use a toaster oven for this step, but be sure to place the sliced bagel halves onto a small baking sheet or on aluminum foil so that only the faces are toasted.
7. When the bagels are toasted, spread about ½ tablespoon of the sauce onto the face of the bottom bagel half.
8. Place a slice of Monterey Jack cheese on the face of the bottom bagel half.
9. Place a sausage patty on the Jack cheese.
10. Place the finished omelette onto the sausage and then place the American cheese on the omelette.
11. Finish the sandwich with the bagel top and heat for 15 seconds in microwave if needed to warm. Repeat for remaining servings.

- Makes 4 servings.

• • • •

TOP SECRET RECIPES VERSION OF

MCDONALD'S BREAKFAST BURRITO

It was in the late seventies, shortly after McDonald's had introduced the Egg McMuffin, that the food giant realized the potential of a quick, drive-thru breakfast. Soon, the company had developed several breakfast selections, including the Big Breakfast with eggs, hash browns, and sausage, and this morning meal in a tortilla, first offered on the menu in 1991.

4 ounces breakfast sausage
1 tablespoon minced white onion
½ tablespoon minced mild green chilies (canned)
4 eggs, beaten
salt
pepper
4 8-inch flour tortillas
4 slices American cheese

ON THE SIDE
salsa

1. Preheat a skillet over medium heat. Crumble the sausage into the pan, then add the onion. Sauté the sausage and onion for 3 to 4 minutes or until the sausage is browned.
2. Add the mild green chilies and continue to sauté for 1 minute.
3. Pour the beaten eggs into the pan and scramble the eggs with the sausage and vegetables. Add a dash of salt and pepper.
4. Heat up the tortillas by steaming them in the microwave in moist paper towels or a tortilla steamer for 20 to 30 seconds.
5. Break each slice of cheese in half and position two halves end-to-end in the middle of each tortilla.
6. To make the burrito, spoon ¼ of the egg filling onto the cheese in a tortilla. Fold one side of the tortilla over the filling, then fold up about 2 inches of one end. Fold over the other side of the

tortilla to complete the burrito (one end should remain open). Serve hot with salsa on the side, if desired.

- MAKES 4 BURRITOS.

• • • •

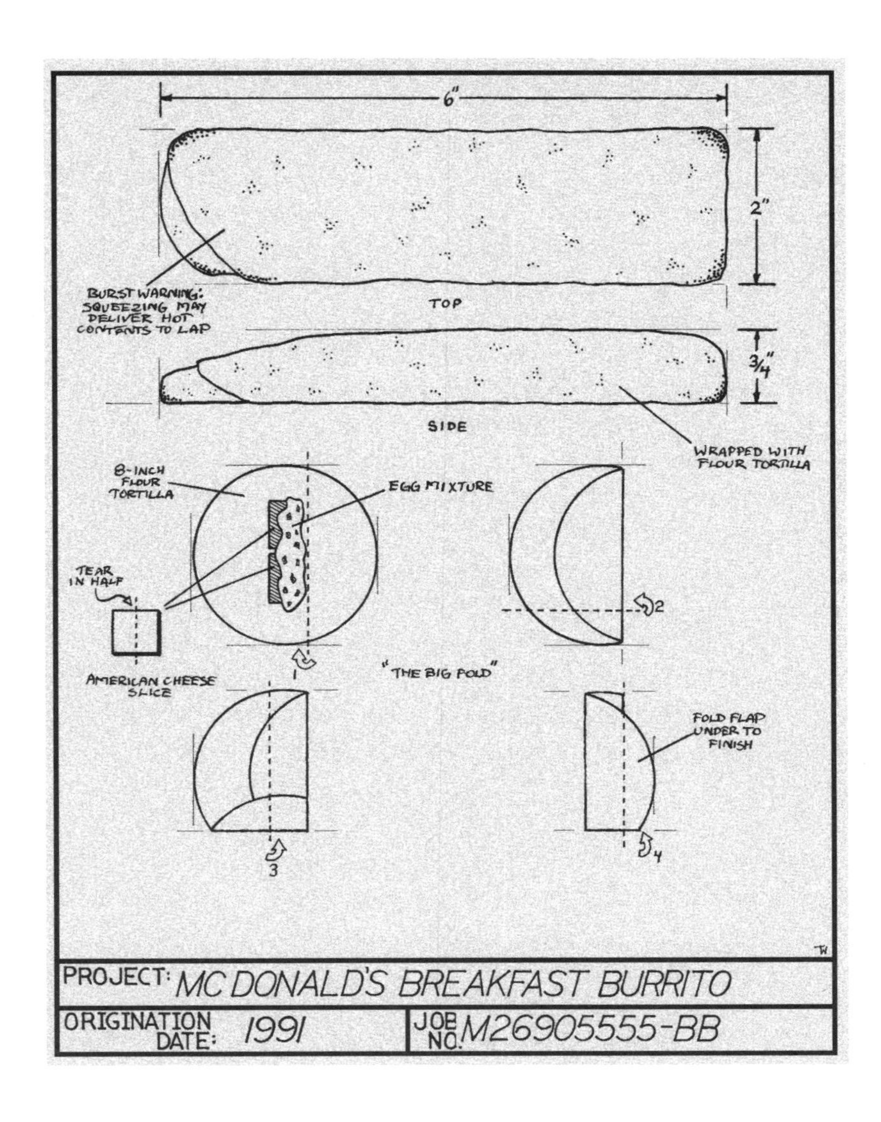

TOP SECRET RECIPES VERSION OF

MCDONALD'S FRENCH FRIES

☆ ✌ 💣 ✏ ☯ ✂ ☞

They're the world's most famous french fries, responsible for one-third of all U.S. french fry sales, and many would say they're the best. These fried spud strips are so popular that Burger King even changed its own recipe to better compete with the secret formula from Mickey D's. One quarter of all meals served today in American restaurants come with fries; a fact that thrills restaurateurs since fries are the most profitable menu item in the food industry. Proper preparation steps were developed by McDonald's to minimize in-store preparation time, while producing a fry that is soft on the inside and crispy on the outside. To achieve this same level of texture and taste our clone requires a two-step frying technique: Once before the fries are frozen, and then once afterward before serving. Be sure to use a slicer to cut the fries for a consistent thickness (¼ inch is perfect) and for a cooking result that will make them just like the real thing. McDonald's uses a minuscule amount of beef fat in the blanching stage when preparing the french fries. But we can still get away with a great-tasting clone without having to add lard to our recipe. In the stores the chain uses only vegetable fat for the final frying step.

2 large russet potatoes
One 48-ounce can shortening
salt

RECOMMENDED
Potato slicer

1. Peel the potatoes, dry them, and slice using a mandolin or other slicer with a setting as close to ¼-inch-square strips as you've got. If your fries are a little thicker than ¼ inch the recipe

will still work, but you definitely don't want super thick steak fries here.

2. Rinse the fries in a large bowl filled with around 8 cups of cold water. The water should become milky. Dump the water out and add another 8 cups of cold water plus some ice and let the fries sit for an hour.
3. Spoon the shortening into your deep fryer and turn to 375°F. On many fryers this is the highest setting.
4. Remove the fries from the water and spread them out on a paper towel to dry for 10 to 15 minutes. Don't let them sit much longer than this or they will begin to turn brown.
5. The shortening should now be hot enough for the blanching stage. Add bunches of the fries to the shortening for 1½ minutes at a time. Watch them carefully to be sure they don't begin to brown. If they start to brown on the edges, take 'em out. Remove the fries to a paper towel or metal rack to drain and cool. When the fries have cooled, put them into a resealable bag or covered container and freeze for 4 to 5 hours or until the potatoes are completely frozen. As the fries freeze you can turn off the fryer, but turn it back on and give it plenty of time to heat up before the final frying stage.
6. Split up the frozen fries and add one half at a time to the hot shortening. Fry for 4½ to 6 minutes or until the fries have become a golden brown color and are crispy on the outside when cool. The second batch may take a tad longer than the first, since the shortening may have cooled. Drain the fries to paper towels or a metal rack and salt generously.

- MAKES 4 SERVINGS.

• • • •

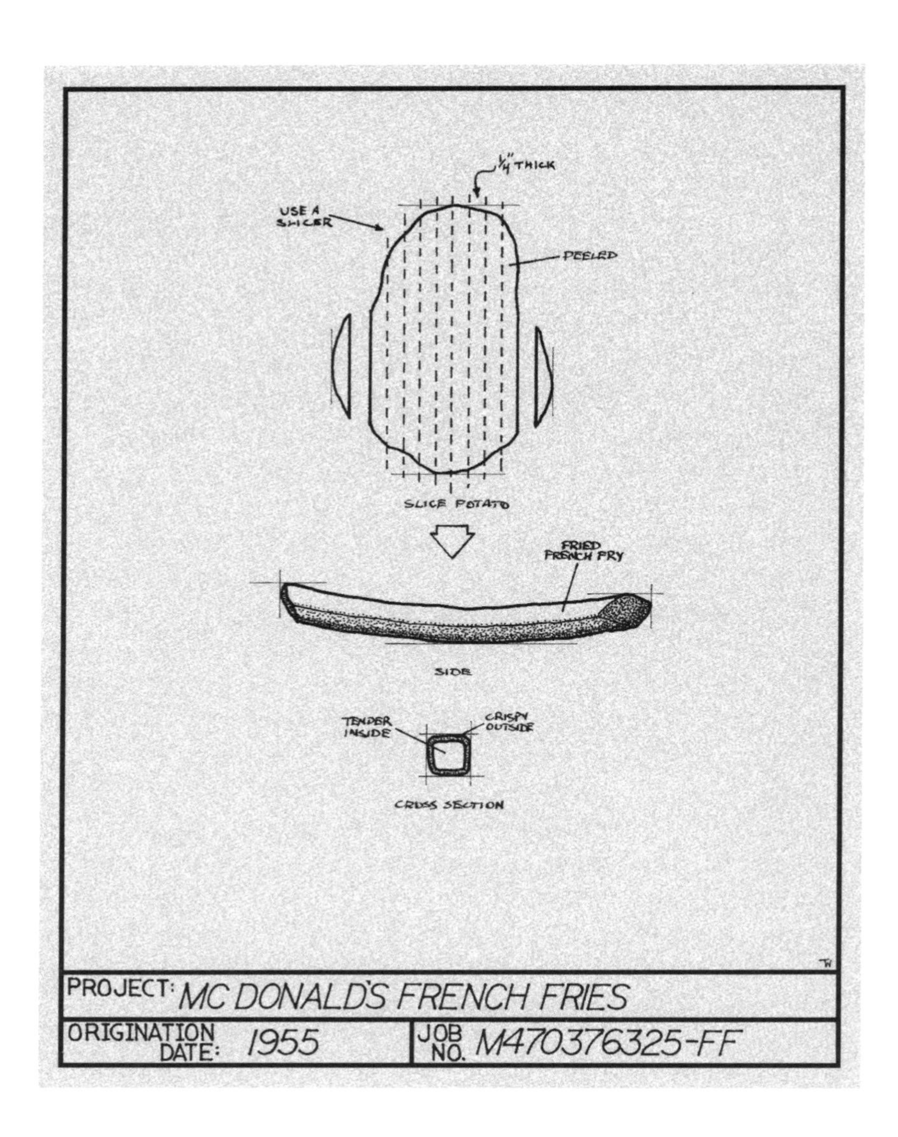
1/4" THICK
USE A SLICER
PEELED
SLICE POTATO
FRIED FRENCH FRY
SIDE
TENDER INSIDE
CRISPY OUTSIDE
CROSS SECTION
PROJECT: MC DONALD'S FRENCH FRIES
ORIGINATION DATE: 1955
JOB NO. M470376325-FF

TOP SECRET RECIPES VERSION OF

MCDONALD'S HOT MUSTARD SAUCE

☆ ✌ 💣 ✎ ☯ ✂ ☞

I finally got on the case to bring you the definitive kitchen clone for this one—and it's a cinch! Tie one hand behind your back and witness plain old ground dried mustard mixing it up with sweet and sour flavors in a saucepan over medium heat. The cornstarch wrangles around in there to thicken and stabilize while Captain Habanero pops in for the perfect spicy punch. Use it for dipping, use it for spreading . . . use it again and again, since you'll make about a cup of the stuff. And McDonald's will be glad that we no longer need to hoard the little blister packs from the restaurants.

½ cup water
½ cup corn syrup
⅓ cup plus 1 tablespoon white vinegar
2 tablespoons ground dried mustard
4 teaspoons cornstarch
1 tablespoon granulated sugar
1 tablespoon vegetable oil
½ teaspoon turmeric
½ teaspoon salt
10 to 14 drops habanero hot sauce

1. Combine all ingredients in a small uncovered saucepan. Whisk until smooth.
2. Turn heat to medium and bring mixture to a boil, stirring often. Sauce should thicken in 2 to 3 minutes after it begins to boil. Remove sauce from heat and chill in refrigerator in a covered container.

• MAKES 1 CUP.

TOP SECRET RECIPES VERSION OF

MCDONALD'S SPECIAL SAUCE

If you like Big Macs, it's probably because of that tasty "secret" spread that is plopped onto both decks of the world's most popular double-decker hamburger. So what's so special about this sauce? After all, it's basically just thousand island dressing, right? Pretty much. But this sauce has a bit more sweet pickle relish in it than a typical thousand island salad slather. Also, I found that this clone comes close to the original with the inclusion of French dressing. It's an important ingredient—ketchup just won't do it. That, along with a sweet & sour flavor that comes from vinegar and sugar, makes this sauce go well on any of your home burger creations, whether they're Big Mac clones or not. This is the closest "special sauce" clone you'll find . . . anywhere.

½ cup mayonnaise
2 tablespoons French dressing
4 teaspoons sweet pickle relish
1 tablespoon finely minced white onion
1 teaspoon white vinegar
1 teaspoon sugar
⅛ teaspoon salt

1. Combine all of the ingredients in a small bowl. Stir well.
2. Place sauce in a covered container and refrigerate for several hours, or overnight, so that the flavors blend. Stir the sauce a couple of times as it chills.

• MAKES ABOUT ¾ CUP.

TOP SECRET RECIPES VERSION OF

MCDONALD'S SWEET & SOUR DIPPING SAUCE

This recipe clones one of those sauces you get with your order of McNuggets at the world's largest hamburger outlet. Now, instead of shoving a fistful of the little green packs into your backpack, you can make up a batch of your own to use as a dip for store-bought nuggets, chicken fingers, fried shrimp, and tempura. It's a simple recipe that requires a food processor or a blender, and the sauce will keep well for some time in the fridge.

¼ cup peach preserves
¼ cup apricot preserves
2 tablespoons light corn syrup
5 teaspoons white vinegar
1 ½ teaspoons cornstarch
½ teaspoon soy sauce
½ teaspoon yellow mustard
¼ teaspoon salt
⅛ teaspoon garlic powder
2 tablespoons water

1. Combine all ingredients except the water in a food processor or a blender and puree until the mixture is smooth.
2. Pour mixture into a small saucepan over medium heat. Add water, stir, and bring mixture to a boil. Allow it to boil for 5 minutes, stirring often. When the sauce has thickened, remove it from the heat and let it cool. Store sauce in a covered container in the refrigerator.

- MAKES ABOUT ¾ CUP.

TOP SECRET RECIPES VERSION OF

MCDONALD'S YOGURT PARFAIT

☆ ✌ 💣 ✏ ☯ ✂ ☞

This one's super easy to make, plus it's low fat and delicious. The yogurt in the original is very sweet and creamy, like Yoplait. So that's the brand that you should use, although any brand of vanilla yogurt will work fine. If you use Yoplait, you'll need two 6-ounce containers of the stuff per serving. For the granola, just look for one that contains mostly oats. It should be crunchy and sweet (such as "maple" flavor) and can also include puffed rice bits. You can even make these a day or two ahead of time. Keep them covered in the fridge, and hold off on the granola topping until you serve 'em up or it'll get mighty soggy.

4 cups vanilla-flavored low-fat yogurt (or eight 6-ounce containers Yoplait)
Two 10-ounce boxes sliced frozen strawberries with sugar added, thawed
⅓ cup frozen blueberries, thawed
½ cup crunchy, sweet granola

1. Pour ½ cup of yogurt into a parfait cup or tall glass.
2. Add ½ cup of strawberries into the glass on top of the yogurt.
3. Add 1 tablespoon of blueberries to the glass.
4. Pour ½ cup of yogurt over the fruit.
5. Sprinkle granola over the top and serve. Repeat for remaining 3 servings.

- MAKES 4 SERVINGS.

GRANOLA
VANILLA YOGURT
BLUEBERRIES
STRAWBERRIES
VANILLA YOGURT
PRESENTATION
PROJECT: MCDONALD'S FRUIT 'N YOGURT PARFAIT
ORIGINATION DATE: 1998
JOB NO. M99766-FNYP

TOP SECRET RECIPES VERSION OF

PANDA EXPRESS MANDARIN CHICKEN

☆ ✌ 💣 ✎ ☯ ✂ ☞

Here's a dish from a rapidly growing Chinese food chain that should satisfy anyone who loves the famous marinated bourbon chicken found in food courts across America. The sauce is the whole thing here, and it's quick to make right on your own stovetop. Just fire up the barbecue or indoor grill for the chicken and whip up a little white rice to serve on the side. Panda Express—now 370 restaurants strong—is the fastest-growing Asian food chain in the world. You'll find these tasty little quick-service food outlets in supermarkets, casinos, sports arenas, college campuses, and malls across the country passing out free samples for the asking.

⅔ cup sugar
¼ cup soy sauce
1 tablespoon lemon juice
1 teaspoon vegetable oil
1 teaspoon minced fresh garlic
½ teaspoon minced fresh ginger
¼ cup water
4 teaspoons arrowroot
6 skinless chicken thigh fillets

ON THE SIDE
steamed white rice

1. Combine sugar, soy sauce, lemon juice, oil, garlic, and ginger in a small saucepan. Combine water with arrowroot in a small bowl and stir until arrowroot is dissolved. Add to saucepan and turn heat to high. Stir often while bringing mixture to a boil, then reduce heat and simmer for 4 to 6 minutes or until sauce is thick.
2. Preheat your grill on high for the chicken.
3. When the grill is hot, rub each chicken piece with oil and cook

the chicken for 4 to 6 minutes per side or until completely cooked. Chicken should have browned in spots.

4. When chicken is done, chop it into bite-size pieces. Pour the chicken pieces into a large frying pan over medium heat. Heat until chicken sizzles then reduce heat and cover chicken until ready to serve. Spoon chicken into a medium bowl, then pour all the sauce over the chicken and stir until well coated. Serve with steamed white rice.

- SERVES 4.

• • • •

TOP SECRET RECIPES VERSION OF

PANDA EXPRESS ORANGE FLAVORED CHICKEN

☆ ✌ 💣 ✏ ☯ ✂ ☞

As far as Chinese food goes, I think the stuff these guys throw together in sizzling woks is surprisingly tasty for a takeout chain. This dish is something of a twist on the traditional sweet and sour chicken commonly found at Chinese restaurants over the years. This popular menu item has a delicious, citrus-laced, tangy-sweet sauce with a spicy nip the regulars find truly addictive. The chain claims to cook all of its food in woks, including the sauces. But this homegrown version will work fine—whether you go for a wok, or not.

SAUCE

1 ½ cups water
2 tablespoons orange juice
1 cup packed dark brown sugar
⅓ cup rice vinegar
2½ tablespoons soy sauce
¼ cup plus 1 teaspoon lemon juice
1 teaspoon minced water chestnuts
½ teaspoon minced fresh ginger
¼ teaspoon minced garlic
1 rounded teaspoon chopped green onion
¼ teaspoon crushed red pepper flakes
5 teaspoons cornstarch
2 teaspoons arrowroot
3 tablespoons water

CHICKEN

4 skinless chicken breast fillets
1 cup ice water
1 egg
¼ teaspoon baking soda
¼ teaspoon salt
1 ½ cups unsifted cake flour

2 to 4 cups vegetable oil

1. Combine all of the sauce ingredients except the cornstarch, arrowroot, and 3 tablespoons of water in a small saucepan over

high heat. Stir often while bringing mixture to a boil. When sauce reaches a boil, remove it from heat and allow it to cool a bit, uncovered.

2. Slice chicken breasts into bite-size chunks. Remove exactly 1 cup of the marinade from the pan and pour it over the chicken in a large resealable plastic bag or another container that allows the chicken to be completely covered with the marinade. The chicken should marinate for at least a couple hours. Cover the remaining sauce and leave it to cool until the chicken is ready.
3. When chicken has marinated, preheat 2 inches of vegetable oil in a wok or skillet to 350°F.
4. Combine cornstarch with arrowroot in a small bowl, then add 3 tablespoons of water. Stir until cornstarch and arrowroot have dissolved. Pour this mixture into the sauce and set the pan over high heat. When sauce begins to bubble and thicken, cover and remove it from heat.
5. Beat together the ice water and egg in a medium bowl. Add baking soda and salt.
6. Add ¾ cup of the flour and stir with a fork just until the flour is blended into the mixture. The batter should still be lumpy.
7. Sprinkle another ¼ cup of flour on top of the batter and mix it up with only one or two strokes. Most of the new flour will still be floating on top of the mixture. Put the remaining flour (½ cup) into a separate medium bowl.
8. Dip each piece of chicken first into the flour, then into the batter. Let some of the batter drip off and then slide the chicken into the oil. Fry up to ½ of the chicken pieces at a time for 3 to 4 minutes, or until golden brown. Flip the chicken over halfway through cooking time. Remove the chicken to a rack or paper towels to drain.
9. As the chicken cooks, reheat the sauce left covered on the stove. Stir occasionally.
10. When all of the chicken is done, pour it into a large bowl, and cover with the thickened sauce. Stir gently until all of the pieces are well coated.

- SERVES 4.

TOP SECRET RECIPES VERSION OF

POPEYES BUTTERMILK BISCUITS

☆ ✌ 💣 ✏ ☯ ✂ ☞

In 2001, the number one Cajun-style restaurant celebrated its 30th birthday with 1,620 stores worldwide. But Popeyes didn't start out with the name that most people associate with a certain spinach-eating cartoon character. When Al Copeland opened his first Southern-fried-chicken stand in New Orleans in 1972, it was called Chicken on the Run. The name was later changed to "Popeyes" after Gene Hackman's character in the movie "The French Connection." In addition to great, spicy fried chicken, Popeyes serves up wonderful biscuits that we can now easily duplicate at home. The secret is to cut cold butter into the mix with a pastry knife so that the biscuits turn out flaky and tender like the real deal.

2 cups all-purpose flour
1 tablespoon sugar
1 ½ teaspoons salt
1 ½ teaspoons baking powder
½ teaspoon baking soda
½ cup butter, cold (1 stick)
½ cup buttermilk
¼ cup milk

TO BRUSH ON TOP
2 tablespoons butter, melted

1. Preheat oven to 400°F.
2. Mix together flour, sugar, salt, baking powder, and baking soda in a medium bowl.
3. Slice cold butter into cubes and use a pastry knife or potato masher to cut butter into dry mixture until no large chunks of butter remain.

4. Add buttermilk and milk and stir with a spoon until dough forms. Roll out to ½-inch thick on a floured surface.
5. Cut biscuits with a 3-inch biscuit cutter and arrange on a lightly greased or parchment paper–lined baking sheet. Bake for 22 to 24 minutes or until tops begin to turn light brown. Remove biscuits from the oven and cool for a couple of minutes, then brush each biscuit top with melted butter.

- Makes 10 biscuits.

• • • •

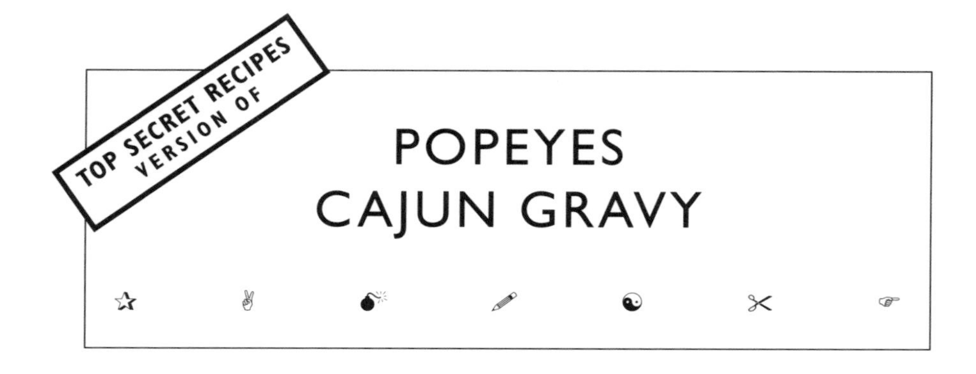

POPEYES CAJUN GRAVY

Chicken gizzard. It took more than ten years to get around to cloning a recipe that absolutely requires chicken gizzard. I've seen the official ingredients list for the Cajun gravy from Popeyes, and if we're gonna do this one right there's just got to be some gizzard in there. Pour this delicious creamy stuff over the Popeyes Buttermilk Biscuits clone that precedes this one, or onto whatever begs to be swimming in pure flavor. Cajun or not, get ready for some of the best gravy that's ever come off your stovetop.

1 tablespoon vegetable oil
1 chicken gizzard
2½ ounces ground beef (¼ cup)
2½ ounces ground pork (¼ cup)
2 tablespoons minced green bell pepper
2 cups water
14-ounce can Swanson beef broth
2 tablespoons cornstarch
1 tablespoon flour
2 teaspoons milk
2 teaspoons distilled white vinegar
1 teaspoon sugar
1 teaspoon salt
½ teaspoon coarse ground black pepper
¼ teaspoon cayenne pepper
⅛ teaspoon garlic powder
⅛ teaspoon onion powder
dash dried parsley flakes

1. Heat 1 tablespoon vegetable oil in a large saucepan over medium heat. Sauté chicken gizzard in the oil for 4 to 5 minutes until cooked. Remove gizzard from the pan and let it cool so that you can handle it. Finely mince the chicken gizzard.
2. Combine ground beef and ground pork in a small bowl.

Smash the meat together with your hands until it's well-mixed. Add bell pepper to the saucepan and sauté it for 1 minute. Add ground beef and pork to the pan and cook it until it's brown. Use a potato masher to smash meat into tiny rice-size pieces as it browns.

3. Add water and beef broth to the pan. Immediately whisk in cornstarch and flour.
4. Add remaining ingredients and bring the mixture to a boil. Reduce heat and simmer gravy for 30 to 35 minutes or until thick.

- MAKES 3 CUPS.

• • • •

TOP SECRET RECIPES VERSION OF

POPEYES RED BEANS & RICE (IMPROVED)

☆ ✌ 💣 ✏ ☯ ✂ ☞

I created the clone for this recipe back in 1994 for the second TSR book, *More Top Secret Recipes,* but I've never been absolutely pleased with the end result, and vowed to one day rework it. After recently convincing a Popeyes manager to show me the ingredients written on the box of red bean mixture, I determined that the best way to clone this one accurately is to include an important ingredient omitted from the first version: pork fat. Emeril screams "pork fat rules" on his cooking show all the time, and now we get to play with the stuff here at TSR. After some work, I found a good way to get the best flavor from the right type of fat is to render it from smoked ham hocks. Ham hocks, which are pretty cheap at most markets, are placed in the oven for several hours so that the fat drains out. There's your rendering. If you don't feel like waiting around for four or five hours while ham hocks render, you can also use ¼ cup of the bacon grease that's left over from breakfast. As for the beans, find red beans (they're smaller than kidney beans) in two 15-ounce cans. If you're having trouble tracking down red beans, red kidney beans will substitute splendidly.

BEANS
2 pounds smoked ham hocks
2 15-ounce cans red beans
½ cup water
½ teaspoon brown sugar
⅛ teaspoon salt
dash garlic powder
dash onion powder

RICE

2¼ cups water
¼ cup butter
¼ teaspoon salt
1 cup converted rice

1. First you must render the fat from the smoked ham hocks. Preheat oven to 375°F and place the ham hocks in a deep pan. Cover pan with foil and bake for 4 to 5 hours or until ¼ cup of fat has rendered from the hocks (you may substitute with ¼ cup of bacon grease).
2. Combine ¼ cup pork fat with one 15-ounce can red beans plus liquid in a medium saucepan. Add ½ cup water, brown sugar, ⅛ teaspoon salt, garlic powder, and onion powder. Bring mixture to a boil, then reduce heat and simmer for 20 minutes. Use a potato masher to smash beans into a pastelike consistency. Add entire contents of remaining can of beans to the mixture and cook for an additional 10 minutes or until thick.
3. Prepare rice for 4 servings. For Uncle Ben's converted rice you bring 2¼ cups water to a boil. Add ¼ cup butter and ¼ teaspoon salt. Add 1 cup of rice, reduce heat to low, and simmer rice for 20 minutes or until tender.
4. To prepare each serving, scoop ½ cup of beans into a bowl. Add ½ cup of rice on top of the beans and serve.

- MAKES 4 REGULAR-SIZE SERVINGS.

• • • •

TOP SECRET RECIPES VERSION OF

"THE SOUP NAZI"'S CRAB BISQUE

☆ ✌ 💣 ✎ ☯ ✂ ☞

New Yorkers have lined up around the block for years now to get a hot cup of Al Yeganeh's delicious soup at Soup Kitchen International. Many are familiar with the demands: "Pick the soup you want!", "Have your money ready!", and "Move to the *extreme* left after ordering!" Customers know if they don't stick to the rules, they'll be quickly scolded and may not get served; even after waiting for as long as two hours to get to the front of the line. This is precisely how the nonsmiling Yeganeh was portrayed by actor Larry Thomas in *Seinfeld* episode number 115, when he forever became known as "The Soup Nazi."

4 pounds snow crab clusters (legs)
4 quarts water (16 cups)
1 small onion, chopped
1 ½ stalks celery, chopped
2 cloves garlic, quartered
2 potatoes, peeled and chopped
¼ cup fresh chopped Italian parsley
2 teaspoons mustard seed
1 tablespoon chopped pimento
½ teaspoon coarse ground pepper
2 bay leaves
⅓ cup tomato sauce
2 tablespoons half-and-half
¼ cup unsalted butter
¼ teaspoon thyme
⅛ teaspoon basil
⅛ teaspoon marjoram

1. Remove all the crab meat from the shells and set it aside.
2. Put half the shells into a large pot with 4 quarts of water over high heat. Add onion, 1 stalk of chopped celery, and garlic, then bring mixture to a boil. Continue to boil for 1 hour, stirring occasionally (the white part of the shells will start to

become transparent), then strain stock. Discard the shells, onion, celery, and garlic, keeping only the stock.

3. Measure 3 quarts (12 cups) of the stock into a large saucepan or cooking pot. If you don't have enough stock, add enough water to make 3 quarts.
4. Add potatoes, bring mixture to a boil, then add ½ of the crab and the remaining ingredients to the pot and bring it back to boiling. Reduce heat and simmer for 4 hours, uncovered, until it reduces by about half and starts to thicken. Add the remaining crab and simmer for another hour until the soup is very thick.

- MAKES 4–6 SERVINGS.

• • • •

TOP SECRET RECIPES VERSION OF

"THE SOUP NAZI"'S CREAM OF SWEET POTATO SOUP

Posted above the counter of the take-out-only Soup Kitchen International in New York City is a sign laying out the important three steps to properly buying soup: "Pick the soup you want!", "Have your money ready!", and "Move to the *extreme* left after ordering!" Knowing that to violate the rules is to risk being refused service, I decided to ask owner Al Yeganeh a few questions about the November 1995 *Seinfeld* episode that made him famous. Needless to say, the interview was very brief:

TW: How do you feel about all the publicity that followed the *Seinfeld* episode?
AY: I didn't need it. I was known well enough before that. I don't need it.

TW: But it must have been good for business, right?
AY: He [Seinfeld] used me. He used me. I didn't use him, he used me.

TW: How many people do you serve in a day?
AY: I cannot talk to you. If I talk, I cannot work.

TW: How many different soups do you serve?
AY: (getting very upset) I cannot talk (pointing to sign). Move to the left. Next!

I felt truly honored to have been yelled at by the Soup Nazi himself. Here now is a clone of one of Al's popular selections, Cream of Sweet Potato Soup.

4 sweet potatoes
(about 1 pound each)
8 cups water
⅓ cup butter
½ cup tomato sauce
2 tablespoons half-and-half
2 teaspoons salt
⅛ teaspoon pepper
dash thyme
1 cup cashews (split in half)

1. Preheat oven to 400°F. Bake the sweet potatoes for 45 minutes or until they are soft. Cool the potatoes until they can be handled.
2. Peel away the skin, then put the potatoes into a large bowl. Mash the potatoes for 15–20 seconds, but you don't need to mash them until they are entirely smooth.
3. Spoon the mashed sweet potato into a large saucepan over medium/high heat, add the remaining ingredients and stir to combine.
4. When the soup begins to boil, reduce the heat and simmer for 50–60 minutes. Cashews should be soft. Serve hot with attitude.

- MAKES 6–8 SERVINGS.

• • • •

TOP SECRET RECIPES VERSION OF

"THE SOUP NAZI"'S INDIAN MULLIGATAWNY

☆ ✌ 💣 ✏ ☯ ✂ ☞

Elaine: "Do you need anything?"
Kramer: "Oh, a hot bowl of Mulligatawny would hit the spot."
Elaine: "Mulligatawny?"
Kramer: "Yeah, it's an Indian soup. Simmered to perfection by one of the great soup artisans in the modem era."
Elaine: "Oh. Who, the Soup Nazi?"
Kramer: "He's not a Nazi. He just happens to be a little eccentric. You know, most geniuses are."

Kramer was right. Al Yeganeh—otherwise known as the Soup Nazi from the *Seinfeld* episode that aired in 1995—is a master at the soup kettle. His popular soup creations have inspired many inferior copycats in the Big Apple, including The Soup Nutsy, only 10 blocks away. Yeganeh's mastery shows when he combines sometimes unusual ingredients to create unique and delicious flavors in his much-raved-about soups. In this one, you may be surprised when you discover pistachios and cashews among the many vegetables. But it's a combination that works.

A few years back, I took a trip to New York and tasted around a dozen of the Soup Nazi's creations. The Mulligatawny was among my faves. After each daily trip to Soup Nazi headquarters, I immediately headed back to the hotel and poured samples of the soups into labeled, sealed containers that were then chilled for the trip back home. There, in the "lab," portions of the soup were rinsed through a sieve and ingredients were identified. After that, it was a matter of trial and error figuring out the measurements for those ingredients. The result was a successful clone that I can now share with you. Just be sure when you make this soup that you simmer it for at least four hours or until the soup reduces by more than half. The soup will darken as the flavors intensify, the potatoes will begin to fall apart, and the nuts will soften. If you follow these directions, you should end up with a clone that would fool even Cosmo himself.

4 quarts water (16 cups)
6 cups chicken stock
2 potatoes, peeled and sliced
2 carrots, peeled and sliced
2 stalks celery, with tops
2 cups peeled and diced eggplant (about ½ of an eggplant)
1 medium onion, chopped
1 cup frozen yellow corn
⅔ cup canned roasted red pepper, diced
½ cup tomato sauce
½ cup shelled pistachios
½ cup roasted cashews
½ cup chopped fresh Italian parsley
¼ cup lemon juice
¼ cup butter
3 tablespoons sugar
½ teaspoon curry powder
½ teaspoon pepper
¼ teaspoon thyme
1 bay leaf
dash marjoram
dash nutmeg

1. Combine all ingredients in a large pot over high heat.
2. Bring to a boil, then reduce heat and simmer for 4–5 hours or until soup has reduced by more than half, and is thick and brownish in color. It should have the consistency of chili. Stir occasionally for the first few hours, but stir often in the last hour. The edges of the potatoes should become more rounded, and the nuts will soften. Serve hot.

- MAKES 4–6 SERVINGS.

TIDBITS

Because of the extreme reduction, I found that the salt in the chicken stock was enough for the recipe. However, if you use a stock that isn't so salty, you may find you need to add extra salt to the soup.

TOP SECRET RECIPES VERSION OF

"THE SOUP NAZI"'S MEXICAN CHICKEN CHILI

☆ ✌ 💣 ✎ ☯ ✂ ☞

In Zagat's New York City Restaurant Survey, Le Cirque 2000, one of the city's most upscale restaurants, received a 25 rating out of a possible 30. In the same guide, Al "The Soup Nazi" Yeganeh's International Soup Kitchen scored a whopping 27. That puts the Soup Nazi's eatery in 14th place among the city's best restaurants!

It's common to see lines stretching around the corner and down the block as hungry patrons wait for their cup of one of five daily hot-soup selections. Most of the selections change every day, but of the three days that I was there doing research, the Mexican Chicken Chili was always on the menu. The first two days it was sold out before I got to the front of the line. But on the last day, I got lucky, "One extra-large Mexican Chicken Chili, please." Hand over money, move to the extreme left.

So here now is a clone for what has apparently become one of the Soup Nazi's most popular culinary masterpieces. The secret to this soup, as with many of his creations, seems to be the long simmering time. If you like, you can substitute turkey breast for the chicken to make turkey chili, which was the soup George Costanza ordered on the show.

1 pound chicken breast fillets (4 fillets)
1 tablespoon olive oil
10 cups water
2 cups chicken stock
½ cup tomato sauce
1 potato, peeled and chopped
1 small onion, diced
1 cup frozen yellow corn
½ carrot, sliced
1 celery stalk, diced
1 cup canned diced tomatoes
1 15-ounce can red kidney beans, plus liquid
¼ cup diced canned pimento
1 jalapeño, diced
¼ cup chopped Italian parsley
1 clove garlic, minced
1½ teaspoons chili powder
1 teaspoon cumin
¼ teaspoon salt
dash cayenne pepper
dash basil
dash oregano

ON THE SIDE
sour cream
pinch chopped Italian parsley

1. Sauté the chicken breasts in the olive oil in a large pot over medium/high heat. Cook the chicken on both sides until done—about 7–10 minutes per side. Cool the chicken until it can be handled. Do not rinse the pot.
2. Shred the chicken by hand into bite-size pieces and place the pieces back into the pot.
3. Add the remaining ingredients to the pot and turn heat to high. Bring mixture to a boil, then reduce heat and simmer for 4–5 hours. Stir mixture often so that many of the chicken pieces shred into much smaller bits. Chili should reduce substantially to thicken and darken (less orange, more brown) when done.
4. Combine some chopped Italian parsley with sour cream and serve it on the side for topping the chili, if desired.

• MAKES 4–6 SERVINGS.

• • • •

TACO BELL ENCHIRITO

An enterprising young man named Glen Bell was fresh out of the Marines in 1946 and was looking for something to do. He worked at a couple of odd jobs, then eventually scraped together $400 in 1947 to buy a hot-dog stand in San Bernardino, California. By 1952 business was so good at Bell's Drive-In that he decided to add hamburgers, just as two brothers named McDonald were starting their own hamburger business in the same city.

Bell soon realized that he needed to expand his menu to differentiate his restaurant from the McDonald brothers'. A fan of Mexican food, Bell devised a way to make tacos and other Mexican specialties quickly and inexpensively. The business grew rapidly, and the name Taco Bell was officially established in 1962, when Bell sold forty company shares to family members at $100 apiece. In 1969, to take his corporation public, he split those original stocks 30,000 to 1.

There are now more than 3,600 Taco Bell units dotting the globe, with total sales in 1991 of $2.8 billion. The company, owned by PepsiCo, Inc., plans to have more than 10,000 outlets by the year 2001.

Today this is the only place you will find the Enchirito. When the product's popularity waned in early 1992, the company said adios.

1 pound ground beef
1/4 teaspoon salt
1 teaspoon chili powder
1/2 tablespoon dried minced onion
One 30-ounce can refried beans
1 package 10- or 12-inch flour tortillas
1/4 onion, diced
One 10-ounce can La Victoria enchilada sauce
2 1/2 cups shredded cheddar cheese
One 2-ounce can sliced black olives

1. Slowly brown the ground beef in a skillet, using a wooden spoon or spatula to separate the beef into pea-size pieces.
2. Add the salt, chili powder, and minced onion.
3. With a mixer or a potato masher, beat the refried beans until smooth.
4. Heat the refried beans in a small saucepan or in a microwave oven.
5. Warm the tortillas all at once in a covered container, or wrapped in moist towel in microwave. Set on high for 40 seconds, or warm individually in a skillet over low heat for 2 to 3 minutes each side.
6. Spoon 3 tablespoons of beef into the center of each tortilla. Sprinkle on ½ teaspoon diced fresh onion. Add ⅓ cup refried beans.
7. Fold the sides of each tortilla over the beans and meat. Flip the tortilla over onto a plate.
8. Spoon 3 tablespoons of enchilada sauce over the top of the tortilla.
9. Sprinkle on ¼ cup shredded cheese.
10. Top with 3 olive slices.

- Makes 10

• • • •

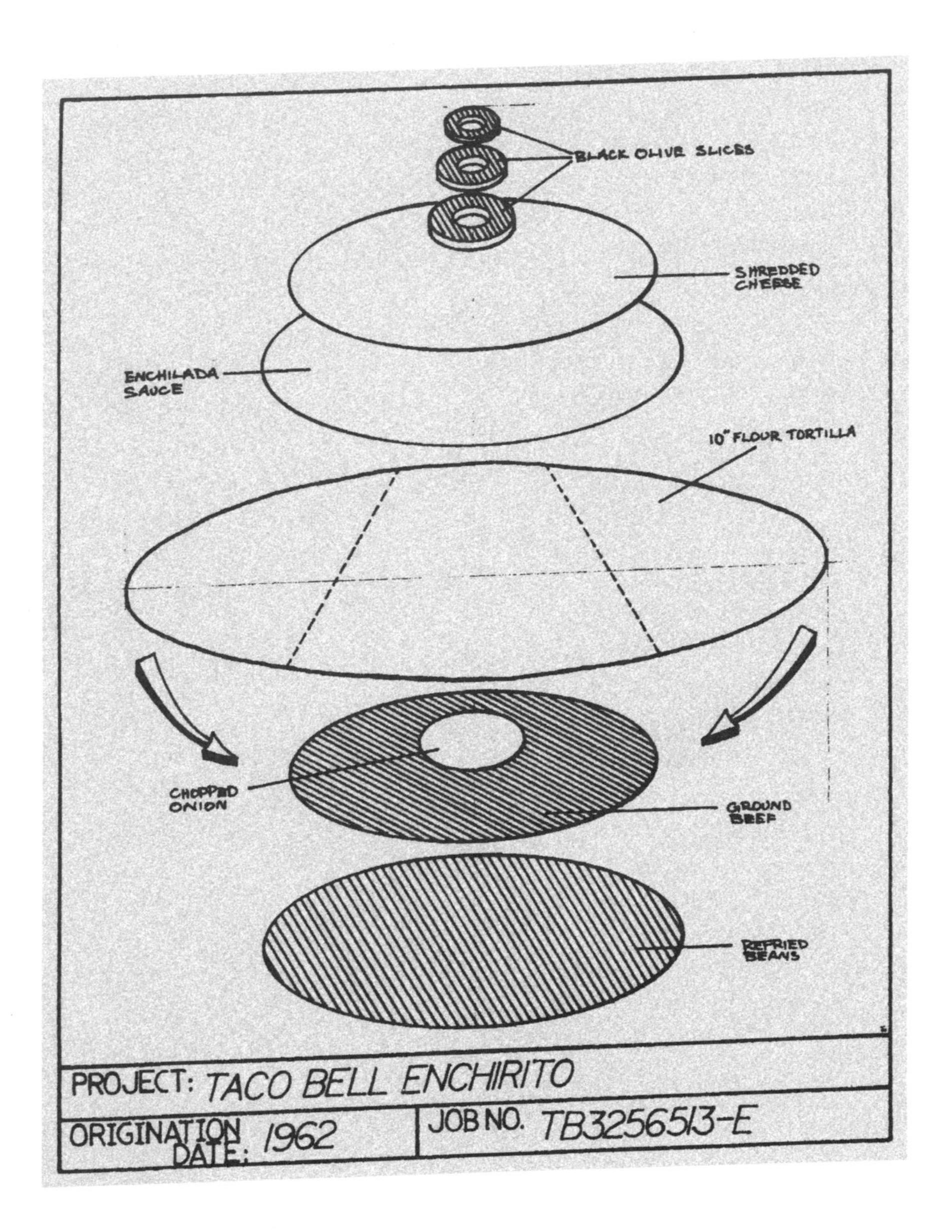
BLACK OLIVE SLICES
SHREDDED CHEESE
ENCHILADA SAUCE
10" FLOUR TORTILLA
CHOPPED ONION
GROUND BEEF
REFRIED BEANS
PROJECT: TACO BELL ENCHIRITO
ORIGINATION DATE: 1962
JOB NO. TB3256513-E

Snacks

TOP SECRET RECIPES VERSION OF

AUNT JEMIMA MAPLE SYRUP

☆ ✌ 💣 ✎ ☯ ✂ ☞

The year 1989 marked the 100th anniversary of the Aunt Jemima trademark. The name was conceived in 1889 by Chris Rutt while he was attending a vaudeville show and watching a New Orleans–style dance number performed to a jazzy tune called "Aunt Jemima." Rutt liked the music so much he stuck the name on his products. The maple syrup came along much later, in 1964, and is now the country's largest-selling syrup.

Today some folks tell the story of how their friends or relatives once met Aunt Jemima many years ago and how she was a kind and cordial woman. Little do they realize these people were fooled by a promotional campaign for the products back in the forties and fifties that used actresses traveling from town to town dressed up and acting like the "famous woman." There never really was an Aunt Jemima.

2 cups water
1 cup granulated sugar
2 cups dark corn syrup
¼ teaspoon salt
1 teaspoon maple flavoring

1. Combine the first four ingredients in a saucepan over medium heat.
2. Stir occasionally, until the mixture comes to a full boil. Let it boil for 7 minutes.
3. Turn the heat off and let the syrup cool for 15 minutes.
4. Add the maple flavoring and stir.

5. When completely cool, transfer the syrup to a covered plastic or glass container.

• MAKES 1 QUART.

TIDBITS

For syrup with a butter flavor, just add 3 tablespoons of butter to the mixture before heating.

For a lighter syrup, use a sugar substitute instead of the granulated sugar.

The absence of natural maple syrup in this recipe is not unusual. In fact, there is no real maple syrup in any Aunt Jemima syrups.

• • • •

TOP SECRET RECIPES VERSION OF

BASKIN-ROBBINS ICE CREAM CAKE

Traditional white birthday cakes are pretty boring by themselves. Scoop a little ice cream onto the plate and I'll perk up a bit. But, hey baby, bring a Baskin-Robbins ice cream cake to the party and I'll be the first one in line with a plastic fork. This 4500-unit ice cream chain stacks several varieties of pre-made ice cream cakes in its freezer, but I've discovered the most popular version, over and over again, is the one made from white cake with pralines and cream ice cream on top. So that's got to be the version we clone here. But don't think you're locked into this formula—you can use any flavor of cake and ice cream you fancy for your homemade masterpiece. Just be sure the ice cream you choose comes in a box. It should be a rectangular shape so that the ice cream layer stacks up right. Then you'll want to find a real sharp serrated knife to cut the ice cream in half while it's still in the box. And check this out: That white stuff that coats the cake is actually softened ice cream spread on in a thin layer like frosting, and then re-frozen. After it sets up, you can decorate the cake any way you like with pre-made frosting in whatever color suits the festive occasion. Voilà! You've just made an ice cream cake at home that looks and tastes exactly like those in the stores that cost around 35 bucks each.

CAKE

1 box white cake mix
1 1/4 cups water
1/3 cup vegetable oil
3 egg whites

1/2-gallon box pralines and cream ice cream
4 cups (2 pints) vanilla ice cream
1 12-ounce container white frosting

OPTIONAL

colored frosting

1. Make your cake following the directions on the box. If you're making the white cake you'll likely blend the cake mix with water, oil, and 3 eggs. Pour the batter into a greased 9 × 13-inch baking pan and bake at 350°F for 30 to 35 minutes. This will make a thin cake for our bottom layer. When the cake is done, let it cool to room temperature.
2. When the cake has cooled, carefully remove it from the pan and place it onto a wax paper–covered cookie sheet, or a platter or tray that will fit into your freezer.
3. Use a sharp serrated knife (a bread knife works great) to slice the ice cream lengthwise through the middle, box and all, so that you have two 2-inch-thick sheets of ice cream. Peel the cardboard off the ice cream and lay the halves next to each other on the cake. Slice the edges of the cake all the way around so that the cake is the same size as the ice cream on top. Work quickly so that the ice cream doesn't melt. When the cake has been trimmed, place it into the freezer for an hour or two.
4. When you are ready to frost the cake, take the 2 pints (4 cups) of vanilla ice cream out of the freezer for 20 to 30 minutes to soften. Stir the ice cream so that it is smooth, like frosting. Use a frosting knife or spatula to coat your cake with about 2 cups of ice cream. Cover the entire surface thoroughly so that you cannot see any of the cake or ice cream underneath. Pop the cake into the freezer for an hour or so to set up.
5. When the cake has set, fill a pastry bag (with a fancy tip) with white frosting to decorate all around the top edge of the cake. Also decorate around the bottom of the cake. Use colored frosting and different tips to add inspired artistic flair and writing on the cake, as needed. Cover the cake with plastic wrap and keep it in your freezer until party time.
6. When you are ready to serve the cake, leave it out for 10 minutes before slicing. Cut the cake with a sharp knife that has been held under hot water.

- Makes 1 large cake (16–20 servings).

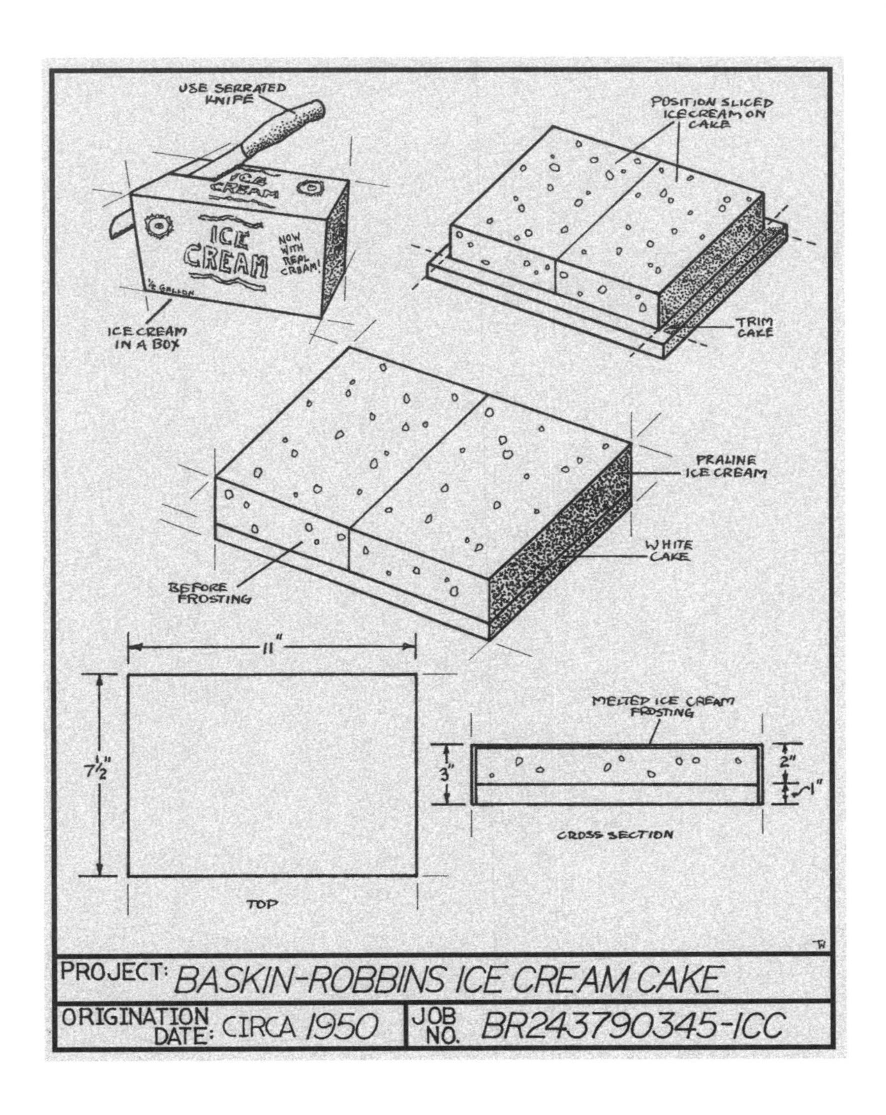
USE SERRATED KNIFE
ICE CREAM
ICE CREAM
½ GALLON
ICE CREAM IN A BOX
POSITION SLICED ICECREAM ON CAKE
TRIM CAKE
PRALINE ICE CREAM
WHITE CAKE
BEFORE FROSTING
11"
7½"
TOP
MELTED ICE CREAM FROSTING
3"
2"
1"
CROSS SECTION
PROJECT: BASKIN-ROBBINS ICE CREAM CAKE
ORIGINATION DATE: CIRCA 1950
JOB NO. BR243790345-ICC

TIDBITS

You may wish to use another flavor cake mix such as chocolate or devil's food for this dessert—even low-fat cake mix works. It's up to you. Just follow the directions on the box for making the cake in a 9×13-inch baking pan.

You can also use any flavor of ice cream. Just be sure to get it in a box.

• • • •

TOP SECRET RECIPES VERSION OF

CRUNCH 'N MUNCH BUTTERY TOFFEE POPCORN WITH PEANUTS

Just look at what F. W. Ruckheim started. He was the guy who, back in the late 1800s made candy-coated popcorn a national treasure with the invention of Cracker Jack. Now we've got Fiddle-Faddle, Screaming Yellow Zonkers, Crunch 'n Munch and several brands of candy-coated microwave popcorn, to name just a few. Sure, these other varieties don't have the traditional prize inside the box, but let's face it, those prizes are pretty weak compared to what used to be found at the bottom of a box of Cracker Jack when I was a kid. And the old-fashioned molasses formula used on Cracker Jack just doesn't have the pizzazz as some of the other tantalizing flavors coating popcorn today. The butter-toffee coating is a good example, so that's what I've reverse-engineered for you here. It's a simple recipe that makes a finished product so addictive you'll have to beg someone to take it away from you before you finish the whole bowl by yourself. All you need is a candy thermometer, some microwave popcorn, a few other basic ingredients, and you're about 15 minutes away from candy-coated heaven.

8 cups popped microwave popcorn (natural flavor)
1/4 cup Spanish peanuts
1/2 cup butter (1 stick)
1/2 cup sugar
1/4 cup light corn syrup

1. Spread popcorn and peanuts on a baking sheet and keep warm in your oven set to 300°F while you prepare the butter toffee. You don't need to preheat the oven.
2. Melt the butter in a medium saucepan over medium-low heat.
3. Add sugar and corn syrup and simmer, stirring occasionally. Pop a candy thermometer into the mixture and watch it closely.
4. When the thermometer reaches 300°F pour the candy over the warm popcorn and peanuts. Stir well so that the candy coats the popcorn. Put the popcorn back into the oven for 5 minutes, then take it out and stir it all around again to coat the popcorn even more. Repeat if necessary to thoroughly coat all of the popcorn.
5. Pour coated popcorn and peanuts onto wax paper. When cool, break up the chunks into bite-size pieces and store it all in a covered container.

- MAKES 8 CUPS.

• • • •

TOP SECRET RECIPES VERSION OF

DOUBLETREE CHOCOLATE CHIP COOKIES

When you check in at one of 240 hotels run by this U.S. chain, you are handed a bag from a warming oven that contains two soft and delicious chocolate chip cookies. This is a tradition that began in the early 90s using a recipe from a small bakery in Atlanta. All of the cookies—which weigh in at an impressive two ounces each—are baked fresh every day on the hotel premises. Raves for the cookies from customers convinced the hotel chain to start selling the chocolatey munchables by the half-dozen. But if you've got an insatiable chocolate chip cookie urge that can't wait for a package to be delivered in the mail, you'll want to try this cloned version fresh out of your home oven.

½ cup rolled oats
2¼ cups all-purpose flour
1½ teaspoons baking soda
1 teaspoon salt
¼ teaspoon cinnamon
1 cup (2 sticks) butter, softened
¾ cup brown sugar, packed
¾ cup granulated sugar
1½ teaspoons vanilla
½ teaspoon lemon juice
2 eggs
3 cups semi-sweet chocolate chips
1½ cups chopped walnuts

1. Preheat oven to 350°F.
2. Grind oats in a food processor or blender until fine. Combine the ground oats with the flour, baking soda, salt, and cinnamon in a medium bowl.
3. Cream together the butter, sugars, vanilla, and lemon juice in another medium bowl with an electric mixer. Add the eggs and mix until smooth.

4. Stir the dry mixture into the wet mixture and blend well. Add the chocolate chips and nuts to the dough and mix by hand until ingredients are well incorporated.
5. Spoon rounded ¼-cup portions onto an ungreased cookie sheet. Place the scoops about 2 inches apart. You don't need to press the dough flat. Bake for 16 to 18 minutes or until cookies are light brown and soft in the middle. Store in a sealed container when cool to keep soft.

- MAKES 20 COOKIES.

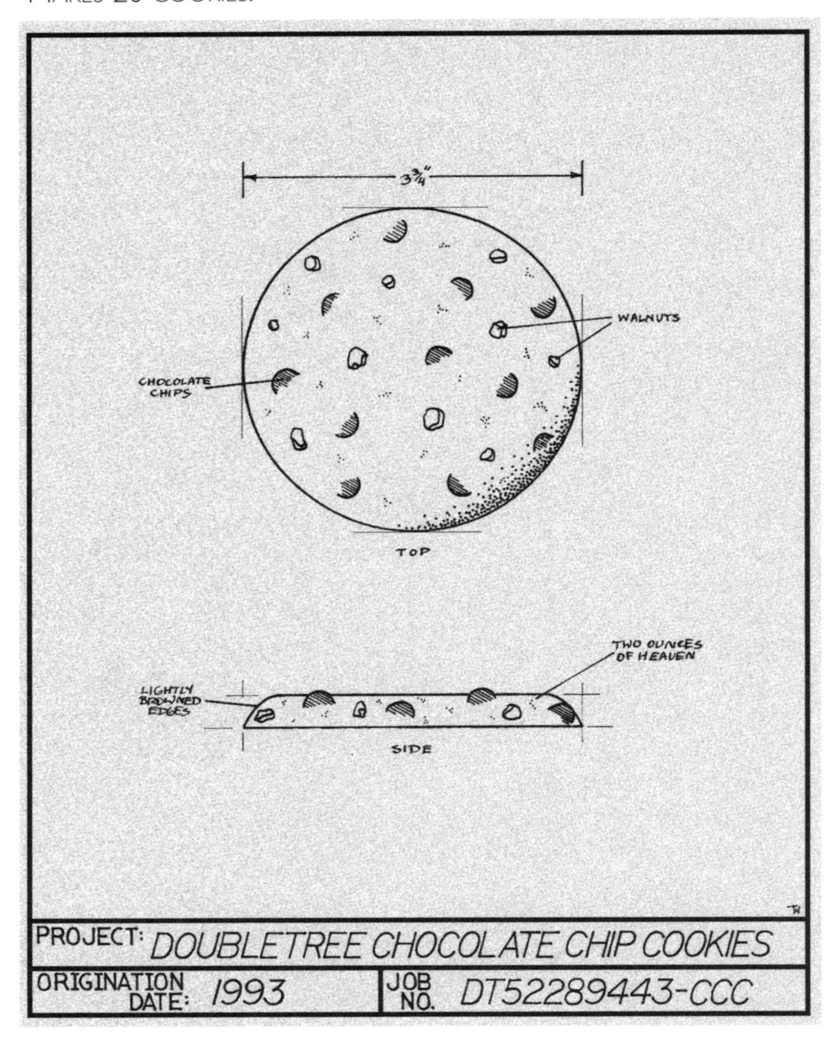

TOP SECRET RECIPES VERSION OF

EMERIL'S ORIGINAL ESSENCE

☆ ✌ 💣 ✏ ☯ ✂ ☞

On his Food Network TV show Emeril Lagasse mentions "Essence" almost as much as "Bam!" and "Kick it up a notch!" He claims to put his special spice blend on "everything but ice cream." He suggests using it on all your meats, veggies, and pasta, and combining it with oil to use as a marinade. If you can't get your hands on the real thing, here's how to whip up a quick clone at home.

4 teaspoons popcorn salt (fine salt)
2 teaspoons paprika
1 teaspoon ground black pepper
½ teaspoon Schilling poultry seasoning
½ teaspoon cayenne pepper
½ teaspoon garlic powder
½ teaspoon onion powder
½ teaspoon dried thyme
½ teaspoon dried oregano

Combine all ingredients in a small bowl. Store in a covered container.

- MAKES ¼ CUP.

• • • •

TOP SECRET RECIPES VERSION OF

FRENCH'S CLASSIC YELLOW MUSTARD

Americans' passion for yellow mustard began in St. Louis at the 1904 World's Fair when the tangy sauce was spread over the top of the classic American hot dog. Today, nearly 100 years later, French's mustard is the top brand found in restaurants, and 80 percent of U.S. households have a bottle of French's somewhere in the pantry or fridge. Another statistic shows that exactly one hundred percent of those bottles will ooze clear, runny mustard goo on the first squirt. And all those bottles will eventually run dry. If that happens just before you throw together some tasty dogs or drippy sandwiches, you may need to whip up some of your own yellow mustard to come to the rescue. If you've got dry ground mustard and turmeric on the spice rack, you can easily clone some yellow mustard sauce in no time at all. This recipe yields just ¼ cup of yellow mustard, but that should hold you over. At least until you can get to the market for more of the real thing.

4 teaspoons dry ground mustard
¼ cup water
3 tablespoons white distilled vinegar
½ teaspoon Wondra flour
¼ teaspoon plus ⅛ teaspoon salt
⅛ teaspoon turmeric
pinch garlic powder
pinch paprika

1. Combine all ingredients in a small saucepan over medium heat. Whisk until smooth.
2. When the mixture comes to a boil, reduce heat and simmer for 5 minutes, stirring often.
3. Remove the pan from the heat and cover until cool. Chill in a covered container.

- MAKES ¼ CUP.

TOP SECRET RECIPES VERSION OF

GOOD SEASONS ITALIAN SALAD DRESSING MIX

☆ ✌ 💣 ✏ ☯ ✂ ☞

Here's a clone for the instant dressing mix you buy in the little .7-ounce packets. When added to vinegar, water, and oil, you get one of the best-tasting instant salad dressings around. But what if you can't find the stuff, or it's no longer sold in your area, as I've heard from so many? Or maybe you want to save some money by making a bunch of your own? Just use the recipe below to make as much dry mix as you want, and save it for when you need instant salad satisfaction. I've used McCormick lemon pepper in the recipe here because it contains lemon juice solids that help duplicate the taste of the sodium citrate and citric acid in the real thing. The dry pectin, which can be found near the canning supplies in your supermarket, is used as a thickener, much like the xanthan gum in the original product.

1 teaspoon carrot, grated and finely chopped
1 teaspoon red bell pepper, finely minced
3/4 teaspoon McCormick lemon pepper
1/8 teaspoon dried parsley flakes
1 teaspoon salt
1/4 teaspoon garlic powder
1/8 teaspoon onion powder
2 teaspoons sugar
1/8 teaspoon black pepper
2 teaspoons dry pectin
pinch ground oregano

1. Place the carrot and bell pepper on a baking pan in an oven set on 250°F for 45 to 60 minutes, or until all of the small pieces are completely dry, but not browned.

2. Combine the dried carrot and bell pepper with the other ingredients in a small bowl. Mix can be stored in a sealed container indefinitely until needed.
3. When ready to use, pour ¼ cup of vinegar into a cruet or jar. Add 3 tablespoons of water, then the dressing mix. Seal and shake vigorously. Add ½ cup of oil and shake until well blended.

• SERVES 8 TO 10.

TIDBITS

If you would like to make the dressing with less oil, follow step 3 above as directed, but substitute ¼ cup of water and ¼ cup of oil in place of the ½ cup of oil.

• • • •

TOP SECRET RECIPES VERSION OF

GREAT AMERICAN COOKIES SNICKERDOODLES

☆ ✌ 💣 ✎ ☯ ✂ ☞

Rather than trying to beat the competitors—especially if they have an exceptional product—Mrs. Fields Famous Brands waves the cash at 'em. With the acquisition of Great American Cookies in 1998 by the company that made chewy mall cookies big business, Mrs. Fields is now peddling her baked wares in more than 90 percent of the premier shopping malls in the United States. That's how you make the dough! One of the all-time favorites you can snag at any of the 364 Great American Cookies outlets is the classic snickerdoodle. Rolled in cinnamon and sugar, it's soft and chewy like the other cookies, and will seem to be undercooked when you take it out of the oven. When it cools it should be gooey, yet firm in the middle. Just a couple bites should make you wonder: "Got milk?!"

½ cup butter (1 stick), softened
½ cup granulated sugar
⅓ cup brown sugar
1 egg
½ teaspoon vanilla
1 ½ cups flour
¼ teaspoon salt
½ teaspoon baking soda
¼ teaspoon cream of tartar

TOPPING
2 tablespoons granulated sugar
1 teaspoon cinnamon

1. In a large bowl, cream together the butter and sugars with an electric mixer on high speed. Add the egg and vanilla and beat until smooth.

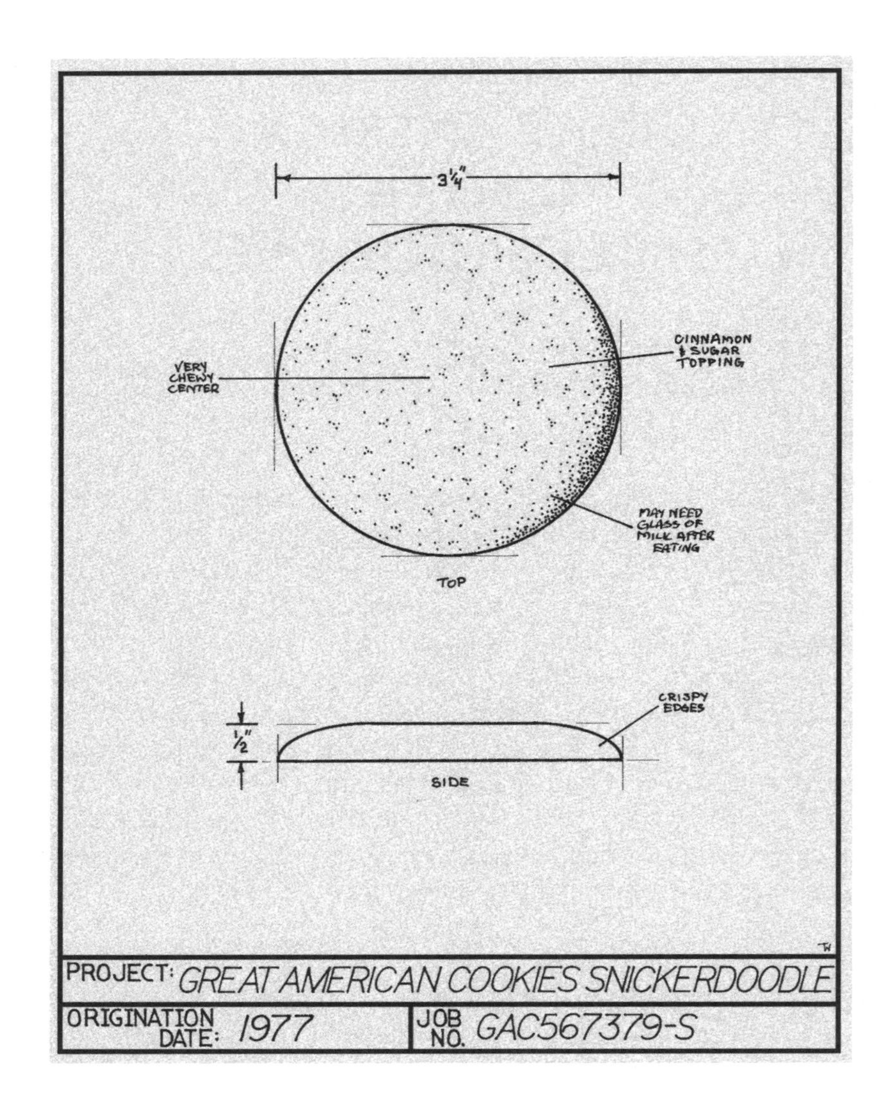
3¼"
VERY CHEWY CENTER
CINNAMON & SUGAR TOPPING
MAY NEED GLASS OF MILK AFTER EATING
TOP
½"
CRISPY EDGES
SIDE
PROJECT: GREAT AMERICAN COOKIES SNICKERDOODLE
ORIGINATION DATE: 1977
JOB NO. GAC567379-S

2. In another bowl, combine the flour, salt, baking soda, and cream of tartar.
3. Pour the dry ingredients into the wet ingredients and mix well.
4. Let the dough rest for 30 to 60 minutes in the refrigerator. Preheat oven to 300°F.
5. In a small bowl, combine the sugar with the cinnamon for the topping.
6. Take about 2½ tablespoons of the dough and roll it into a ball. Roll this dough in the cinnamon/sugar mixture and press it onto an ungreased cookie sheet. Repeat for the remaining cookies.
7. Bake the cookies for 12 to 14 minutes and no more. The cookies may seem undercooked, but will continue to develop after they are removed from the oven. When the cookies have cooled they should be soft and chewy in the middle.

- MAKES 16 TO 18 COOKIES.

• • • •

TOP SECRET RECIPES VERSION OF

GREAT AMERICAN COOKIES WHITE CHUNK MACADAMIA

☆ ✌ 💣 ✎ ☯ ✂ ☞

When Arthur Karp shared his grandmother's favorite chocolate chip cookie recipe with Michael Coles, the business partners knew they had a hit on their hands. They opened their first Great American Cookies store in 1977 in The Perimeter Mall in Atlanta, Georgia. Now with more than 350 stores in the chain, these cookies have quickly become a favorite, just begging to be cloned. The chain bakes the cookies in convection ovens at the low temperature of 280 degrees for around 16 to 17 minutes. But since most of us don't have convection ovens and may have a hard time getting the oven temperature to this odd setting, I've made some adjustments. Just be sure, when you remove the cookies from the oven, that they appear undercooked and light brown around the edges. This will give the cookies the perfect chewy texture when cool.

½ cup butter (1 stick), softened
1 cup brown sugar
½ cup coconut flakes, finely minced
1 egg
1 tablespoon milk
1 teaspoon vanilla
1 ½ cups flour
2 teaspoons baking soda
½ teaspoon baking powder
½ teaspoon salt
8 ounces solid white chocolate, cut into chunks
1 cup macadamia nuts, chopped

1. Cream together the butter and sugar in a large bowl with a mixer on high speed.
2. Add the coconut, egg, milk, and vanilla and mix well.

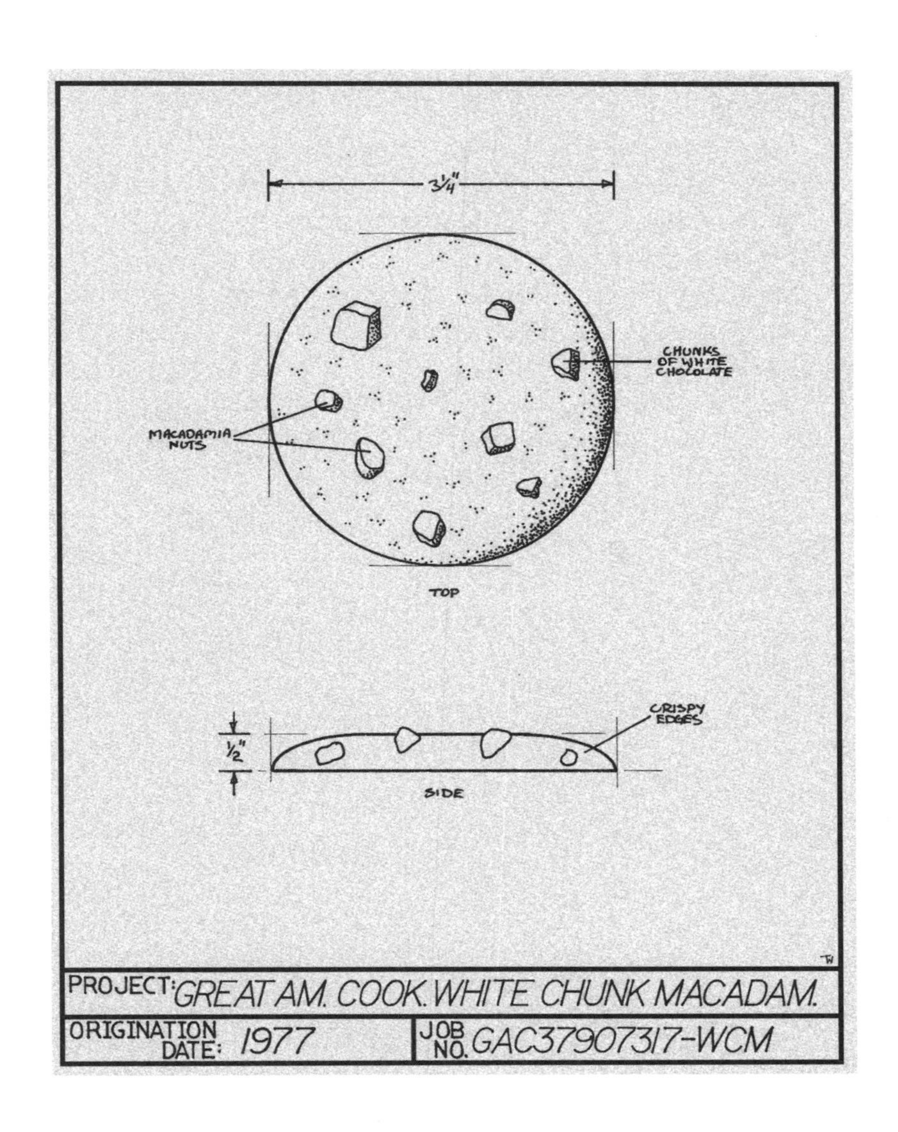
3¼"
CHUNKS OF WHITE CHOCOLATE
MACADAMIA NUTS
TOP
CRISPY EDGES
½"
SIDE
PROJECT: GREAT AM. COOK. WHITE CHUNK MACADAM.
ORIGINATION DATE: 1977
JOB NO. GAC37907317-WCM

3. In another bowl combine the flour, baking soda, baking powder, and salt.
4. Add the dry mixture to the wet mixture and mix until dough forms. Mix in the white chocolate and macadamia nuts.
5. Let the dough rest for 30 to 60 minutes in the refrigerator. Preheat oven to 300°F.
6. Measure out about 2½ tablespoons of the dough and form a ball. Drop each ball of dough onto an ungreased cookie sheet about 3 inches apart and bake for 12 to 14 minutes. Do not overbake! Cookies should come out of the oven appearing slightly browned, yet undercooked. When cooled the cookies will be soft and chewy like the original.

- MAKES 16 TO 18 COOKIES.

• • • •

TOP SECRET RECIPES VERSION OF

HERSHEY'S PAYDAY CANDY BAR

☆ ✌ 💣 ✎ ☯ ✂ ☞

In December of 1996, Hershey Foods snagged the U.S. operations of Leaf Brands for a pretty penny. This added several well-known candies to Hershey's already impressive roster, including Good & Plenty, Jolly Rancher, Milk Duds, Whoppers, Heath, and this delicious peanut roll, which we can now clone at home. The center is sort of a white fudge that we can make by combining a few ingredients on the stove, then getting the mixture up to just the right temperature using a candy thermometer (you've got one, right?). Once cool, this candy center is coated with a thin layer of caramel, then quickly pressed onto roasted peanuts. Looks just like the real thing! This recipe will make eight candy bars. But it's up to you to make the dental appointment.

CENTERS

¼ cup whole milk
5 unwrapped caramels
1 tablespoon light corn syrup
1 teaspoon smooth peanut butter
¼ teaspoon vanilla
¼ teaspoon salt
1 ¼ cups powdered sugar
20 unwrapped caramels
1 ½ teaspoons water
2 cups dry roasted peanuts

1. Combine all ingredients for the centers, except the powdered sugar, in a small saucepan over low heat. Stir often as the caramel slowly melts. When the mixture is smooth, add ¾ cup of powdered sugar. Stir. Save the remaining ½ cup of powdered sugar for later.

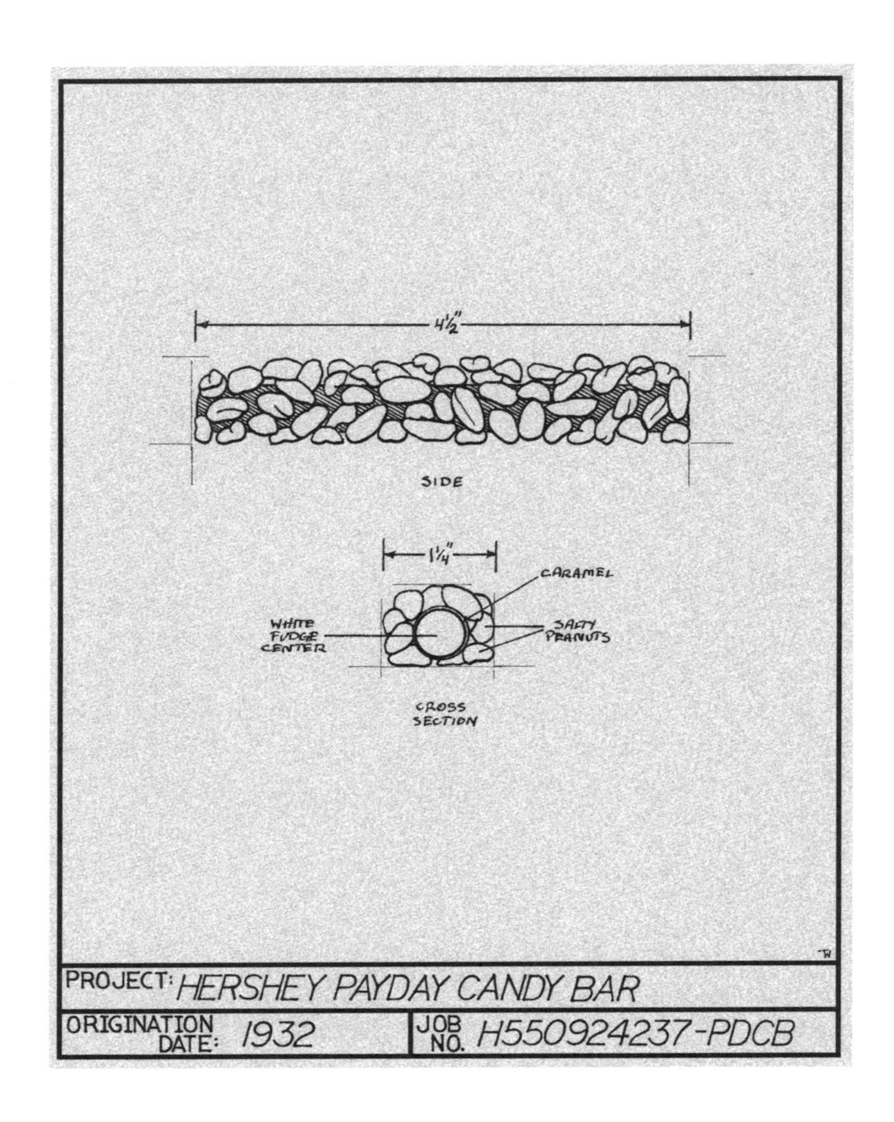
4½"
SIDE
1¼"
CARAMEL
WHITE
FUDGE
CENTER
SALTY
PEANUTS
CROSS
SECTION
PROJECT: HERSHEY PAYDAY CANDY BAR
ORIGINATION DATE: 1932
JOB NO. H550924237-PDCB

2. Use a candy thermometer to bring the mixture to exactly 230°F, stirring often, then turn off the heat.
3. When the temperature of the candy begins to drop, add the remaining ½ cup powdered sugar to the pan, then use a hand mixer on high speed to combine. Keep mixing until the candy cools and thickens and can no longer be mixed. That should take a minute or two.
4. Let the candy cool in the pan for 10 to 15 minutes, or until it can be touched. Don't let it sit too long—you want the candy to still be warm and pliable when you shape it. Take a tablespoon-size portion and roll it between your palms or on a countertop until it forms a roll the width of your index finger and measures about 4½ inches long. Repeat with the remaining center candy mixture and place the rolls on wax paper. You should have 8 rolls. Let the center rolls sit out for an hour or two to firm up.
5. Combine the 20 caramels with the 1½ teaspoons of water in a small saucepan over low heat. Stir often until the caramels melt completely, then turn off the heat. If you work fast this caramel will stay warm while you make the candy bars.
6. Pour the peanuts onto a baking sheet or other flat surface. Using a basting brush and working quickly, "paint" a coating of caramel onto one side of a center roll. Quickly turn the center over, caramel-side-down, onto the peanuts and press gently so that the peanuts stick to the surface of the candy. Paint more caramel onto the other side of the roll and press it down onto the peanuts. The candy should have a solid layer of peanuts covering all sides. If needed, brush additional caramel onto the roll, then turn it onto the peanuts to coat the roll completely. Place the candy bar onto wax paper, and repeat with the remaining ingredients. Eat when completely cool.

- Makes 8 candy bars.

• • • •

TOP SECRET RECIPES VERSION OF

HIDDEN VALLEY ORIGINAL RANCH DRESSING

☆ ✌ 💣 ✎ ☯ ✂ ☞

Ranch dressing was indeed invented at a place called Hidden Valley Ranch near Santa Barbara, California, by a real salad-wranglin' rancher. In the '50s and '60s, Steve Henson and his wife, Gayle, shared their 120-acre dude ranch with University of California at Santa Barbara students and other festive partiers for rousing weekend shindigs. The dozens of guests were served meals of steaks and salads topped with Steve's special blend of herbs, spices, mayonnaise, and buttermilk. As word got out about the fabulous dressing, more guests were showing up at the ranch and walking home with complimentary take-home jars filled with the stuff. Eventually, Steve figured he could make a little cash on the side by packaging the dressing as a dry mix and selling it through the mail. At first he was filling envelopes himself, but within a few months Steve had to hire 12 more people to help with the packaging. Soon, Steve had a multimillion-dollar business on his hands, from a product that for 10 years he had been giving away for free.

½ cup mayonnaise
½ cup buttermilk
½ teaspoon dried parsley flakes
¼ teaspoon ground black pepper
¼ teaspoon MSG (such as Accent)
¼ teaspoon salt
⅛ teaspoon garlic powder
⅛ teaspoon onion powder
pinch dried thyme

1. Combine all ingredients in a medium bowl and whisk until smooth. Cover and chill for several hours before using.

- MAKES 1 CUP.

• • • •

TOP SECRET RECIPES VERSION OF

KEEBLER SOFT BATCH CHOCOLATE CHIP COOKIES

In pre–Civil War Philadelphia, Godfrey Keebler earned a reputation for baking the best cookies and crackers around. Keebler joined in a federation with sixteen local and regional bakeries to help form the United Biscuit Company in 1927. This system lasted for twenty-two years, until 1949, when the conglomerate chose to operate under a single name. *Keebler* was judged to be the most sound and memorable. In 1983 Keebler expanded its distribution to the West Coast, making the conglomerate a national concern.

Today Keebler manufactures more than 200 different products from its 83,000-square-foot facility in Elmhurst, Illinois. Those products, including the chewy Soft Batch cookie, are sold in some 75,000 retail outlets nationwide. Total annual sales for the company are in excess of $1.5 billion, making Keebler the second-largest cookie and cracker manufacturer in the United States, with popular products that have been enjoyed by five generations of Americans.

1 pound (4 sticks) butter, softened
2 eggs
2 tablespoons molasses
2 teaspoons vanilla extract
1/3 cup water
1 1/2 cups granulated sugar
1 1/2 cups packed brown sugar
1 teaspoon baking powder
1 1/2 teaspoons baking soda
1 teaspoon salt
5 cups all-purpose flour
1 1/2 twelve-ounce packages semisweet chocolate chips

1. Preheat the oven to 375°F.
2. Cream the butter, eggs, molasses, vanilla, and water in a medium-size bowl.
3. In a large bowl, sift together the sugars, baking powder, baking soda, salt, and flour.
4. Combine the moist mixture with the dry mixture. Add the chocolate chips.
5. Shape the dough into 1-inch balls, and place them 1 inch apart on an ungreased cookie sheet.
6. Bake for 8 minutes, or until light brown around edges.

• MAKES 4 DOZEN COOKIES.

PEPPERIDGE FARM® CHESAPEAKE® AND SAUSALITO® COOKIES

Pepperidge Farm products bear the name of the farm where Margaret Rudkin lived and created her first product. It was on that farm in Fairfield, Connecticut, in 1937 that Mrs. Rudkin baked her first loaf of homemade bread for her children. Her first few loaves turned out terribly, but she was persistent and eventually came up with a loaf of bread so delicious that friends began requesting it. Soon Mrs. Rudkin was baking as a commercial venture and adding new products. In 1961 Pepperidge Farm was purchased by the Campbell Soup Company. Six years later Margaret Rudkin passed away at the age of sixty-nine.

But Mrs. Rudkin's kitchen enterprise lives on and is bigger than ever. Today Pepperidge Farm has more than 300 products in distribution. One of them is the crispy Chesapeake cookie.

Simply follow the recipe for the Keebler Soft Batch cookie with these exceptions: Omit the water and molasses. Add 3 cups of chopped pecans. (For the Sausalito cookie, substitute macadamia nuts.) Bake at the same temperature, but for 10 to 11 minutes rather than 8 minutes. This will make the cookies crispier.

• • • •

KEEBLER PECAN SANDIES

This company was founded as the United Biscuit Company of America back in 1927. It was made up of sixteen bakeries from Philadelphia to Salt Lake City, marketing cookies and crackers under a variety of brand names. That system lasted for twenty-two years, and eventually the name Keebler was adopted for the entire conglomerate. Keebler was linked with the United Biscuit name once again after it was bought in 1974 by a British company of that name.

Today the company makes 50 billion cookies and crackers each year; among them are the popular Pecan Sandies, first sold in 1955. The Toffee variety came thirty-eight years later.

1 1/2 cups vegetable shortening
4 cups all-purpose flour
3/4 cup granulated sugar
1/4 teaspoon baking soda
1 1/2 teaspoons salt
2 tablespoons water
2 eggs
1 cup shelled pecans

1. Preheat the oven to 325°F.
2. In a large bowl, cream together the shortening, sugar, and salt with an electric mixer on medium speed.
3. Add the eggs and beat well.
4. While mixing, slowly add the flour, baking soda, and water.
5. Chop the pecans into very small bits using a food processor or blender on low speed. Be careful not to overchop; you don't want to make pecan dust. The pieces should be about the size of rice grains.

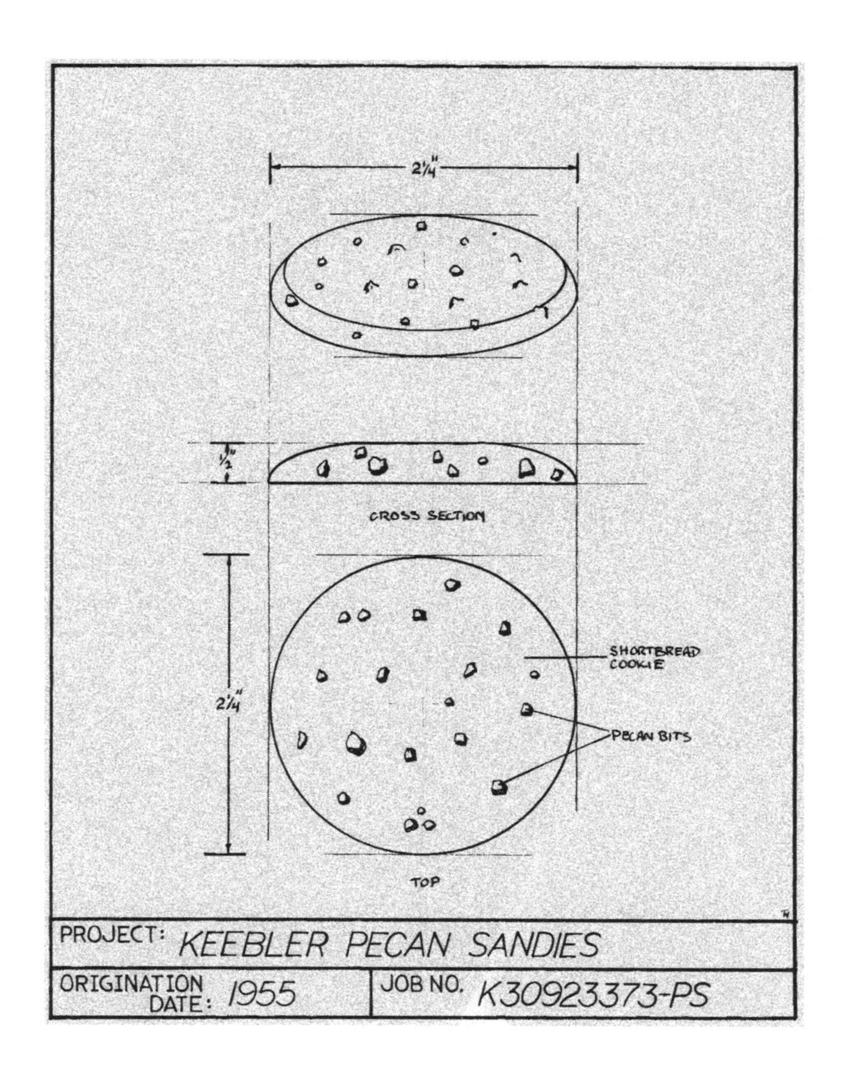
2¼"
CROSS SECTION
SHORTBREAD COOKIE
PECAN BITS
TOP
PROJECT: KEEBLER PECAN SANDIES
ORIGINATION DATE: 1955
JOB NO. K30923373-PS

6. Add the pecans to the dough and knead with your hands until the pecans are well blended into the mixture.
7. Roll the dough into 1-inch balls and press flat with your hands onto ungreased baking sheets. The cookies should be about 2 inches in diameter and 1/2 inch thick.
8. Bake for 25 to 30 minutes, or until the edges of the cookies are golden brown.

- MAKES 4 DOZEN COOKIES.

KEEBLER® TOFFEE SANDIES®

Follow the Pecan Sandies recipe, above, replacing the chopped pecans with one 6-ounce package of Heath® Bits 'o Brickle®.

• • • •

TOP SECRET RECIPES VERSION OF

KELLOGG'S COCOA RICE KRISPIES TREATS

It's the Rice Krispies Treat for all you chocolate lovers. By simply replacing regular Rice Krispies with Kellogg's Cocoa Krispies, then adding a bit of cocoa to the recipe, we can clone the exact flavor of the product you otherwise have to buy in boxes in the grocery store. This recipe makes 16 of the crunchy brown bars, or the equivalent of two boxes of the real thing.

3 tablespoons margarine
¼ teaspoon salt
5 cups miniature marshmallows
½ teaspoon vanilla
4 teaspoons cocoa
6 cups Cocoa Krispies cereal
non-stick cooking spray

1. Combine margarine and salt in a large saucepan over low heat.
2. When margarine has melted, add marshmallows and vanilla and stir until marshmallows have melted. Add cocoa and stir well. Remove from heat.
3. Add Cocoa Krispies and stir until the cereal is well coated with the melted marshmallow mixture.
4. Spray a 9 x 13-inch baking dish with a light coating of non-stick cooking spray. Pour the mixture into the dish and, using wax paper or lightly greased hands, press down until it's flat in the dish. Cool. Slice into 16 bars.

• MAKES 16 BARS.

TOP SECRET RECIPES VERSION OF

KELLOGG'S PEANUT BUTTER CHOCOLATE RICE KRISPIES TREATS

☆ ✌ 💣 ✏ ☯ ✂ ☞

When Kellogg's reacted to spectacular sales of its Rice Krispies Treats with two new varieties of the popular and addictive snack, *TSR* got on the case. It seems we've all tasted the original Rice Krispies Treats. The homemade version is the second homework assignment in Cooking 101, after learning how to boil water. And the Kellogg's store-bought packaged version has been available to the lazier of us for several years now. This variety, however, puts that whole Reese's "You got your peanut butter in my chocolate" thing to work. The crunchy bar has just a touch of nutty essence that builds nicely on the other familiar flavors. But don't be fooled by that dark "chocolatey" coating on top of the real thing. It's not actually chocolate, but rather a melt-resistant custom blend of cocoa and . . . uh, stuff, that tastes a lot like chocolate; and that happens to work better for the product from a manufacturing, shipping, and shelf-life aspect. But here in kitchen cloning land, we don't have to worry about those things. So get ready to walk on the wild side, people, as we step up to the microwave and melt some *real* chocolate chips for topping our cinch of a crunchy clone.

1 tablespoon margarine
3 tablespoons crunchy peanut butter
1/8 teaspoon salt
5 cups miniature marshmallows
1/2 teaspoon vanilla
6 cups Rice Krispies cereal
1 12-ounce bag milk chocolate chips
non-stick cooking spray

1. Combine margarine, peanut butter, and salt in a large saucepan over low heat.
2. When peanut butter and margarine have melted, add marshmallows and vanilla and stir until marshmallows have melted. Remove from heat.
3. Add Rice Krispies and stir until cereal is well coated with the melted marshmallow mixture.
4. Spray a 9 x 13-inch baking dish with a light coating of non-stick cooking spray. Pour the Rice Krispies mixture into the dish and, using wax paper or lightly greased hands, press down until it's flat in the dish. Cool.
5. Prepare the topping by pouring the chocolate chips into a glass dish. Microwave for 2 minutes on 50 percent power. Stir gently. Microwave for an additional minute on 50 percent power. Stir gently once more until smooth. If the mixture hasn't completely melted, zap it again for another 30 seconds.
6. Use a spatula to spread a thin layer of chocolate over the top of the Rice Krispies mixture. Cool at room temperature (at least 72°F), or chill until firm. Slice into 16 bars.

- MAKES 16 BARS.

• • • •

TOP SECRET RECIPES VERSION OF

KRAFT DELUXE MACARONI & CHEESE

☆ ✌ 💣 ✎ ☯ ✂ ☞

It's time to clone America's best-selling brand of instant macaroni & cheese. This recipe is for the "Deluxe" variety of this popular product—that is, the one that comes with an envelope of thick cheese sauce, rather than the dry, powdered cheese. I think the "Deluxe" version, with its two-cheese blend, is the better tasting of the two, although it's gonna hit you a bit harder in the wallet at the supermarket. But now, with this Top Secret Recipe, you can make creamy macaroni & cheese that tastes like Kraft's original at a fraction of the price of the real deal. You gotta love that!

8 cups water
2 cups uncooked elbow macaroni
⅓ cup shredded cheddar cheese
½ cup Cheez Whiz
2 tablespoons whole milk
¼ teaspoon salt

1. Bring 8 cups (2 quarts) of water to a boil over high heat in a large saucepan. Add elbow macaroni to water and cook for 10 to 12 minutes or until tender, stirring occasionally.
2. As macaroni boils, prepare sauce by combining cheddar cheese, Cheez Whiz, and milk in a small saucepan over medium low heat. Stir cheese mixture often as it heats, so that it does not burn. Add salt. When all of the cheddar cheese has melted and the sauce is smooth, cover the pan and set it aside until macaroni is ready.

3. When macaroni is ready, strain the water, but do not rinse the macaroni.
4. Using the same pan you prepared the macaroni in, combine the macaroni with the cheese sauce, and mix well.

- MAKES ABOUT 4 CUPS.

• • • •

KRAFT SHAKE 'N BAKE

Need a recipe that copies Shake 'n Bake in a pinch? Or maybe you don't feel like going to the store for the real thing. Here's the *TSR* solution for a quick clone that will give you the same texture and flavor of Kraft Shake 'n Bake using very common ingredients. You may notice the color is a bit different in this clone when compared to the real thing. That's because this recipe doesn't include beet powder—a hard-to-find ingredient that lends a dark orange tint to the original. But after you sink your teeth into this chicken (baked the same way as described on the Shake 'n Bake box) you'll swear it's the same stuff you buy in a box. When you're ready to get shaking and baking, use this breading on 2½ pounds of chicken pieces or on 2 pounds of skinless chicken breast fillets.

½ cup plus 1 tablespoon corn flake crumbs
2 teaspoons all-purpose flour
1 teaspoon salt
¼ teaspoon paprika
¼ teaspoon sugar
scant ¼ teaspoon garlic powder
scant ¼ teaspoon onion powder

1. Combine all ingredients in a small bowl and stir to combine.
2. Prepare chicken following the same technique as described on the box of the original mix using 2½ pounds of bone-in chicken (6 to 8 pieces, with or without skin) or 2 pounds boneless skinless chicken breast halves. Preheat your oven to 400°F, then moisten the chicken with water. Use a large plastic bag for the coating and use the same steps as described on the original package:

"Shake moistened chicken, 1 to 2 pieces at a time, in shaker bag with coating mixture. Discard any remaining mixture and bag. Bake at 400 degrees in ungreased or foil-lined 15 × 10 × 1-inch baking pan until cooked through—bone-in: 45 minutes/boneless: 20 minutes."

- SERVES 4.

• • • •

TOP SECRET RECIPES VERSION OF

KRAFT STOVE TOP STUFFING

☆ ✌ 💣 ✎ ☯ ✂ ☞

This recipe clones the common 6-ounce box of Stove Top stuffing mix you find in any market. This secret formula duplicates the chicken variety, the brand's most popular version. You know, it's nice to be able to make as much of this as you want prior to the holiday crunch and just keep it sealed up in the pantry until you're ready to use it. Besides, you have enough to worry about deciding which fruits to use in the Jell-O® mold. When it's time to cook, it's just a matter of adding some water and margarine to this mix, and in 10 easy minutes the stuff is all ready to go up a turkey's backside.

DRY MIX

⅓ cup minced fresh celery
4 to 5 slices white bread
3 to 4 slices wheat bread
3 chicken bouillon cubes, crushed
2 teaspoons dried chopped onions
1 ½ teaspoons dried parsley
⅛ teaspoon sugar
⅛ teaspoon onion powder

TO MAKE STUFFING

1 ⅔ cups water
¼ cup margarine

1. Arrange the celery pieces on a plate and set the plate in a warm place—a sunny window is best—for 24 hours or until the celery is thoroughly dry. This is the best way to dry the tiny pieces of celery for the instant stuffing mix. You must be sure to remove all moisture from the celery. You should end up with 2 teaspoons of dried celery from ⅓ cup of freshly minced celery.
2. Prepare bread crumbs by stacking the bread slices on top of each other and squishing them down flat with the palms of

your hands. This will create denser bread crumbs that will not become soggy and pasty when cooking. Use a sharp knife to dice the bread into little pieces. You should have about 2½ cups of white bread and 1½ cups of wheat for a total of around 4 cups of bread.

3. Preheat the oven to 250°F. Spread the bread crumbs on a cookie sheet. Bake for 30 to 40 minutes or until the bread is completely dry. You should now have around 2⅔ cups of dry bread crumbs.
4. To make the vegetable/seasoning mix, combine the dried celery with chicken bouillon powder, onions, parsley, sugar, and onion powder in a small bowl. You now have a stuffing kit that can be sealed up and stored in a dry place until you are ready to use it.
5. To make the stuffing, mix the vegetable/seasoning mix with 1⅔ cups water in a medium saucepan over medium heat. Bring the mixture to a boil, then reduce heat to low, cover, and simmer for 10 minutes. Stir in the bread crumbs, cover, and remove from heat. Let stuffing stand 5 to 7 minutes. Fluff it with a fork before serving.

- MAKES 6 SERVINGS.

• • • •

TOP SECRET RECIPES VERSION OF

KRAFT THOUSAND ISLAND DRESSING

☆ ✌ 💣 ✏ ☯ ✂ ☞

Here's a quick clone for one of the best-selling thousand island dressings around. Use this one on salads or on burgers as a homemade "special sauce." It's easy, it's tasty, it's cheap . . . and it can be made low fat simply by using light mayo. Dig it.

½ cup mayonnaise
2 tablespoons ketchup
1 tablespoon white vinegar
2 teaspoons sugar
2 teaspoons sweet pickle relish
1 teaspoon finely minced white onion
⅛ teaspoon salt
dash black pepper

1. Combine all of the ingredients in a small bowl. Stir well.
2. Place dressing in a covered container and refrigerate for several hours, stirring occasionally, so that the sugar dissolves and the flavors blend.

- MAKES ABOUT ¾ CUP.

• • • •

TOP SECRET RECIPES VERSION OF

LAWRY'S SEASONED SALT

☆ ✌ 💣 ✎ ☯ ✂ ☞

This seven-ingredient clone of Lawry's Seasoned Salt can be made in a small bowl, but it's best stored in an old shaker-top spice bottle that you've cleaned out and saved. You've saved one of those somewhere, right?

2 tablespoons salt
2 teaspoons sugar
½ teaspoon paprika
¼ teaspoon turmeric
¼ teaspoon onion powder
¼ teaspoon garlic powder
¼ teaspoon cornstarch

1. Combine all ingredients in a small bowl and mix well.
2. Pour blend into an empty spice bottle with a shaker top to store.

- MAKES ¼ CUP.

• • • •

TOP SECRET RECIPES VERSION OF

LAWRY'S TACO SPICES & SEASONING

This is a clone for the stuff you buy in 1-ounce packets to create, as the package says, "a fun-filled Mexican fiesta in minutes." Isn't that so true? In fact, thanks to Lawry's, my last Mexican fiesta was filled with so much pure fun that I had to take a siesta the next day. I owe it all to that fabulous little packet of seasoning. And now I promise you just as much super duper fun with this *TSR* clone. Golly, maybe even a tad more fun if you're lucky. Just mix the ingredients together in a small bowl, then add it to 1 pound of browned ground beef along with some water and let it simmer. Before you know it you'll be up to your nostrils in good old-fashioned, taco-making fun.

1 tablespoon flour
1 teaspoon chili powder
1 teaspoon paprika
¾ teaspoon salt
¾ teaspoon minced onion
½ teaspoon cumin
¼ teaspoon cayenne pepper
¼ teaspoon garlic powder
¼ teaspoon sugar
⅛ teaspoon ground oregano

1. Combine all of the ingredients in a small bowl.
2. To prepare the meat filling for the tacos as described on the original package instructions: "In large skillet, brown 1 pound ground beef until crumbly; drain fat. Add spices & seasoning and ⅔ cup water; mix thoroughly. Bring to a boil; reduce heat to low, and cook, uncovered, 7 to 10 minutes, stirring occasionally. Spoon meat filling into warmed taco shells or tortillas. Top with shredded lettuce, grated cheddar cheese, and chopped tomato. Use fresh salsa and guacamole if desired."

• MAKES MEAT FILLING FOR 12 TACOS (ABOUT 3 TABLESPOONS EACH).

TOP SECRET RECIPES VERSION OF

LITTLE DEBBIE OATMEAL CREME PIES

☆ ✌ 💣 ✏ ☯ ✂ ☞

These soft, creme-filled sandwich cookies were the first snacks produced by McKee Foods back in 1960. It was his 4-year-old granddaughter Debbie after whom founder O.D. McKee named his line of snack cakes. O.D. was inspired by a picture of the little girl in play clothes and a straw hat, and that's the image we still find today on every package. The secret to cloning these mouth-watering snacks is re-creating the soft, chewy consistency of the oatmeal cookies. To duplicate the texture, the cookies are slightly underbaked. Then you whip up some of the easy-to-make creme filling with marshmallow creme and spread it between two of the oatmeal cookies to complete the sandwich. Next stop, yum city!

COOKIES

1 cup margarine
3/4 cup dark brown sugar
1/2 cup sugar
1 tablespoon molasses
1 teaspoon vanilla
2 eggs
1 1/2 cups all-purpose flour
1/2 teaspoon salt
1 teaspoon baking soda
1/8 teaspoon cinnamon
1 1/2 cups 1-minute Quaker Oats

CREME FILLING

2 teaspoons very hot water
1/4 teaspoon salt
2 cups marshmallow creme (one 7-ounce jar)
1/2 cup shortening
1/3 cup powdered sugar
1/2 teaspoon vanilla

1. Preheat oven to 350°F.
2. In a large bowl, cream together margarine, sugars, molasses, vanilla, and eggs.

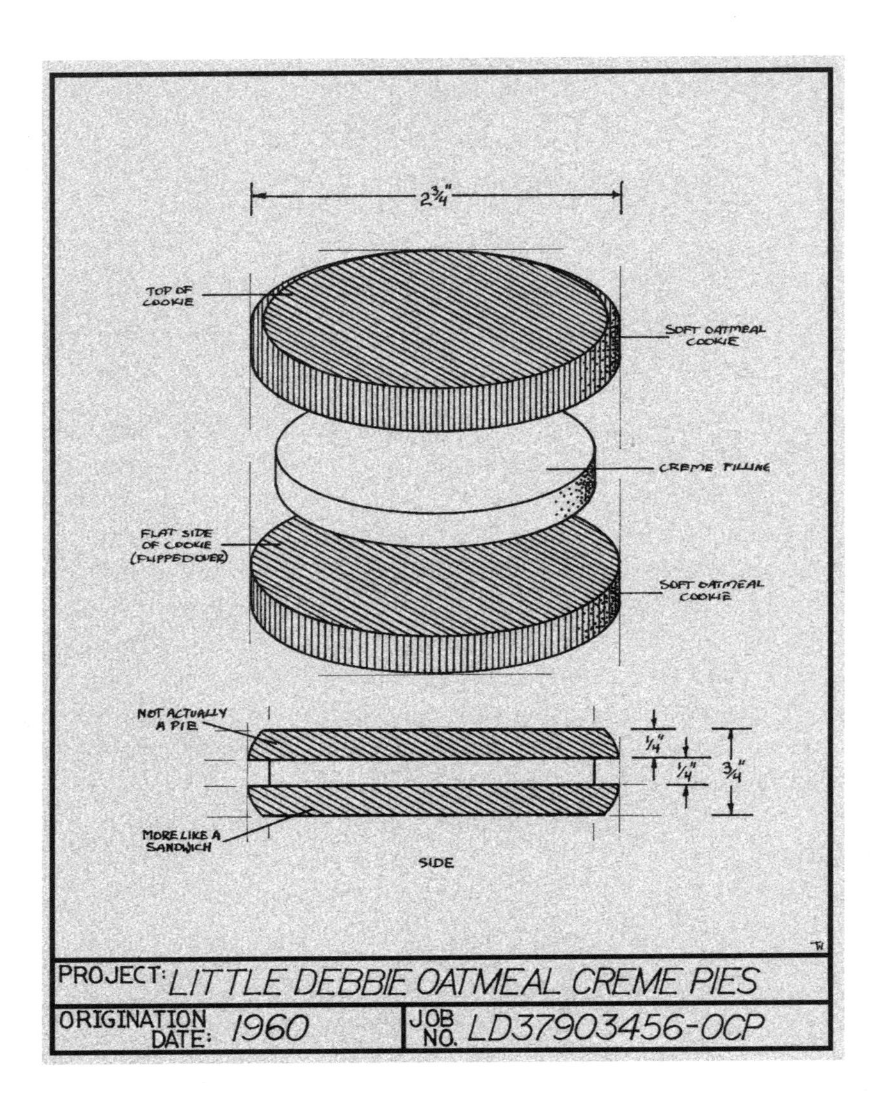
2 3/4"
TOP OF COOKIE
SOFT OATMEAL COOKIE
CREME FILLING
FLAT SIDE OF COOKIE (FLIPPED OVER)
SOFT OATMEAL COOKIE
NOT ACTUALLY A PIE
MORE LIKE A SANDWICH
1/4"
1/4"
3/4"
SIDE
PROJECT: LITTLE DEBBIE OATMEAL CREME PIES
ORIGINATION DATE: 1960
JOB NO. LD37903456-OCP

3. In a separate bowl combine the flour, salt, baking soda, and cinnamon.
4. Combine the dry ingredients with the wet ingredients. Mix in the oats.
5. Drop dough by tablespoonfuls onto an ungreased baking sheet. Bake for 10 to 12 minutes, or until cookies are just starting to darken around the edges. They will still appear moist in the center. Be careful not to overcook—when cooled, the cookies should be soft and chewy.
6. While the cookies bake, prepare the filling. Use a small bowl to dissolve the salt in 2 teaspoons of very hot water. Set this solution aside to cool.
7. Combine the marshmallow creme, shortening, powdered sugar, and vanilla in a medium bowl and mix well with an electric mixer on high speed until fluffy. Add the cooled salt solution to the filling mixture and combine with the mixer.
8. Assemble each creme pie by spreading the filling over one side of a cookie (the flat side) and press another cookie on top, making a sandwich. Repeat for the remaining cookies and filling.

- Makes 2 dozen creme pies.

• • • •

TOP SECRET RECIPES VERSION OF

M&M/MARS CARAMEL TWIX BARS

☆ ✌ 💣 ✎ ☯ ✂ ☞

The process by which M&M/Mars and other candy companies smoothly chocolate-coat their confections is called *enrobing*. Enrobing was created in 1900 to protect the interiors from drying out. The process begins when the uncoated centers pass through a curtain of liquid chocolate on a continuous stainless-steel belt. The top and sides of each bar are coated. The process is repeated a second time, and then the fully coated bar is quickly cooled and wrapped.

Enrobing is the least expensive way for manufacturers to coat their chocolates. At M&M/Mars, the enrobing machines run around the clock to meet the high demand for their products. Unfortunately, traditional kitchen appliances don't include among them an enrobing machine, so in our case, dipping will have to suffice.

The caramel Twix was introduced in 1977, and peanut butter Twix came along in 1982. Other variations of the bar, including cookies & cream and fudge, were introduced in the early nineties.

35 unwrapped Kraft caramels
2 tablespoons water
1 box (40) Nabisco Lorna Doone shortbread cookies
Two 12-ounce bags milk-chocolate chips

1. Combine the caramels with the water in a small pan and melt over low heat.
2. Place the shortbread cookies side by side on an ungreased cookie sheet.

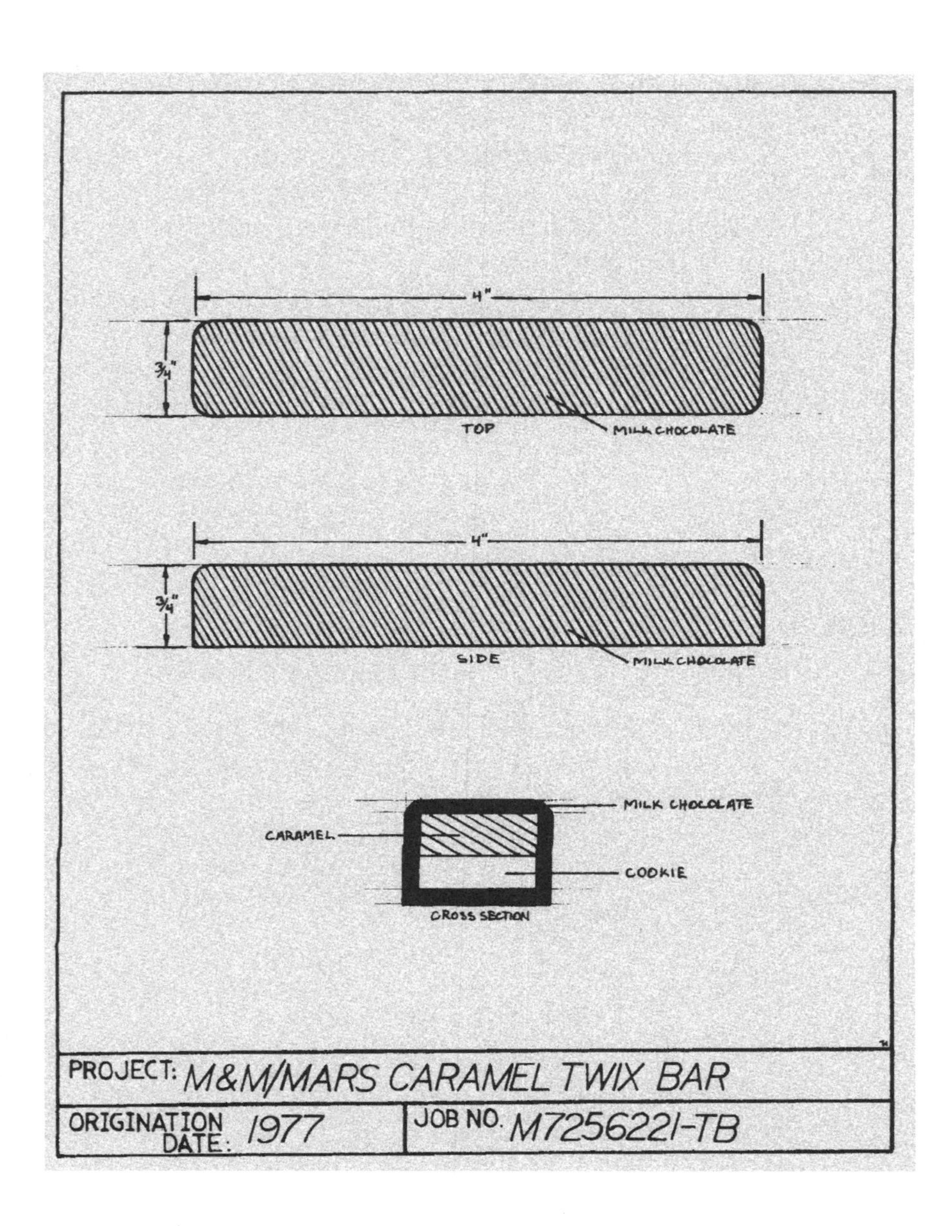
4"
3/4"
TOP
MILK CHOCOLATE
4"
3/4"
SIDE
MILK CHOCOLATE
MILK CHOCOLATE
CARAMEL
COOKIE
CROSS SECTION
PROJECT: M&M/MARS CARAMEL TWIX BAR
ORIGINATION DATE: 1977
JOB NO. M7256221-TB

3. Spoon a dab of caramel onto each cookie. Then place all the cookies in the refrigerator until the caramel firms up.
4. In the meantime, in a double boiler over low heat, melt the chocolate chips. You may also use the microwave for melting the chocolate. Just zap the chips for 1 minute on high, stir, then zap 'em for another minute.
5. Remove the cookies from the refrigerator. Rest each one on a fork and dip it into the chocolate. Tap the fork on the side of the pan or bowl to knock off any excess chocolate. Then place each one on a sheet of waxed paper and let them cool at room temperature (65 to 70°F). This could take several hours, but the bars will set best this way. If you want to speed up the process, put the candy in the refrigerator for 30 minutes.

M&M/MARS PEANUT BUTTER TWIX® BARS

Substitute 1 cup of peanut butter sweetened with ½ cup powdered sugar for the caramels. The peanut-butter mixture will be of a consistency that allows you to spread it on the shortbread cookies with your fingers. Follow the rest of the directions exactly.

- MAKES 40 BARS.

• • • •

TOP SECRET RECIPES VERSION OF

NABISCO CHEESE NIPS

☆ ✌ 💣 ✎ ☯ ✂ ☞

Here's a clone recipe that gets one very important ingredient from another packaged product. The powdered cheese included in the Kraft instant macaroni & cheese kits flavors this homegrown version of the popular bright orange crackers. You'll need a can of Kraft Macaroni & Cheese Cheese Topping or two boxes of the most inexpensive instant variety of macaroni & cheese; you know, the kind with the cheese powder. Two boxes will give you enough cheese to make 300 crackers. As for the macaroni left over in the boxes, just use that for another recipe requiring elbow macaroni.

1 cup sifted all-purpose flour (plus ½ cup divided and reserved for kneading and rolling)
1 teaspoon baking soda
¼ teaspoon baking powder
½ cup Kraft Macaroni & Cheese Cheese Topping powder (or 2 packages dry cheese powder from 2 boxes Kraft Macaroni & Cheese)
3 tablespoons shortening
⅓ cup buttermilk
½ teaspoon salt (for tops, optional)

1. Sift together 1 cup flour, baking soda, baking powder, and cheese powder in a large bowl.
2. Cut in the shortening with a fork and knife with a crosswise motion until dough is broken down into rice-size pieces. Mixture will still be very dry.
3. Stir in buttermilk with a fork until dough becomes very moist and sticky.

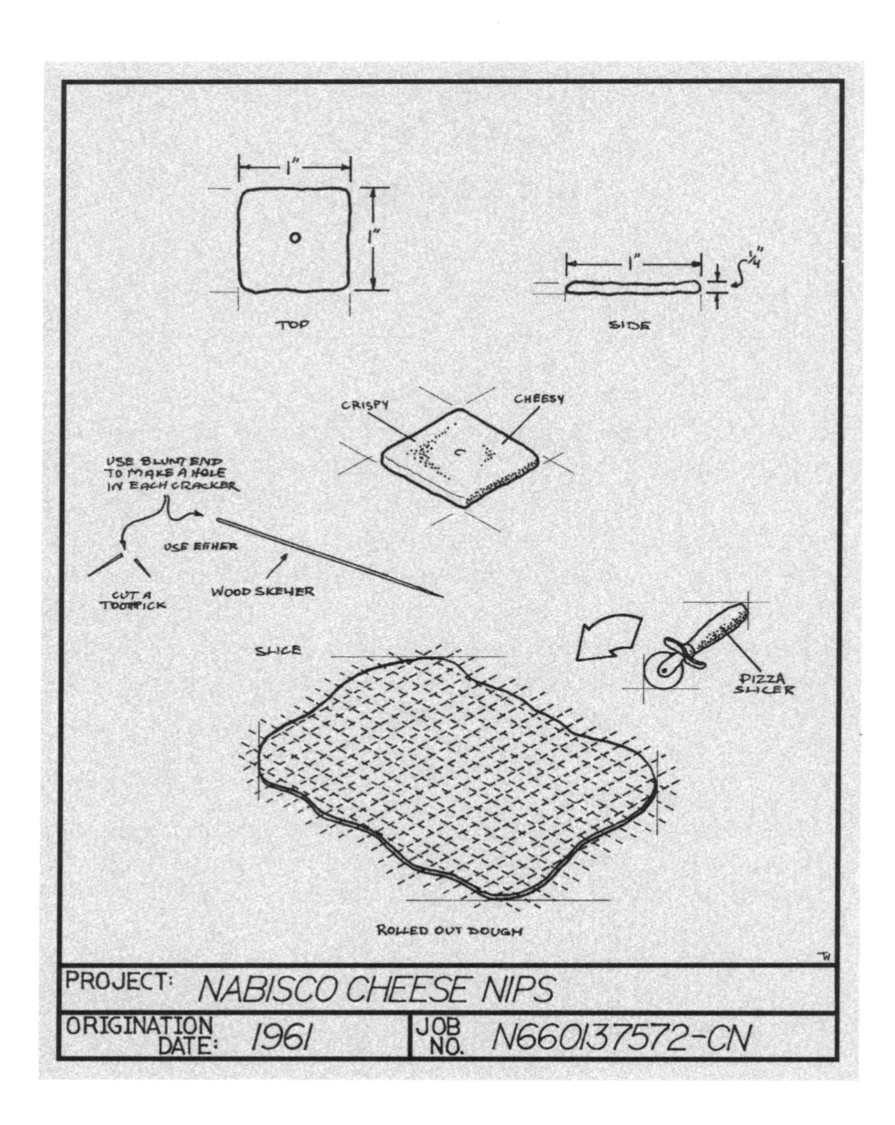
1"
1"
TOP
1"
1/4"
SIDE
CRISPY
CHEESY
USE BLUNT END
TO MAKE A HOLE
IN EACH CRACKER
USE EITHER
CUT A
TOOTHPICK
WOOD SKEWER
SLICE
PIZZA
SLICER
ROLLED OUT DOUGH
PROJECT: NABISCO CHEESE NIPS
ORIGINATION DATE: 1961
JOB NO. N660137572-CN

4. Sprinkle a couple tablespoons of the reserved flour over the dough and work it in until the dough can be handled without sticking, then turn it out onto a floured board, being sure to keep ¼ cup of the reserve flour for later. Knead the dough well for 60 to 90 seconds, until the flour is well incorporated. Wrap the dough in plastic wrap and chill for at least one hour.
5. Preheat oven to 325°F. Spray a light coating of cooking spray on a baking sheet.
6. Remove the dough from the refrigerator and use the remaining reserve flour to dust a rolling surface. Roll about one-third of the dough to just under 1/16 of an inch thick. Trim the edges square (a pizza cutter or wheel works great for this), then transfer the dough to a lightly greased baking sheet. Use the rolling pin to transfer the dough. Simply pick up one end of the dough onto a rolling pin, and roll the dough around the rolling pin. Reverse the process onto the baking sheet to transfer the dough.
7. Use a pizza cutter to cut across and down the dough, creating 1-inch-square pieces. Use the blunt end of a skewer or broken toothpick to poke a hole in the center of each piece.
8. Sprinkle a very light coating of salt over the top of the crackers (crackers will already be quite salty) and bake for 8 to 10 minutes. Mix the crackers around (so those on the edge don't burn) and bake for another 3 to 5 minutes, or until some are just barely turning a light brown. Repeat the rolling and baking process with the remaining dough.

- MAKES APPROXIMATELY 300 CRACKERS.

• • • •

NABISCO NILLA WAFERS

No one knows the exact origin of the vanilla wafer but it's guessed that the recipe was developed in the South. The wafers were being created from scratch at home long before Nabisco introduced the lightweight, poker chip-like packaged cookies in 1945. Back then they were called Vanilla Wafers. But in the 60s Nabisco slapped the trade name Nilla Wafers on the box. Today the real things come about 100 to a box and really fly when whipped into the air with a little flick of the wrist. Here now, you can relive the days of old with a homemade version fresh out of the oven. This clone recipe makes about half a box's worth and they fly just as far.

½ cup powdered sugar
⅓ cup sugar
⅓ cup shortening
1 egg
1 teaspoon vanilla
⅛ teaspoon salt
1 ½ cups cake flour
1 ½ teaspoons baking powder
1 tablespoon water

1. Preheat oven to 325°F.
2. Cream together sugars, shortening, egg, vanilla, and salt in a large bowl.
3. Add the flour and baking powder. Add 1 tablespoon of water and continue mixing until dough forms a ball.
4. Roll dough into ¾-inch balls and flatten slightly onto a lightly

greased cookie sheet. Bake for 15 to 18 minutes or until cookies are light brown.

- MAKES 50 TO 60 COOKIES.

• • • •

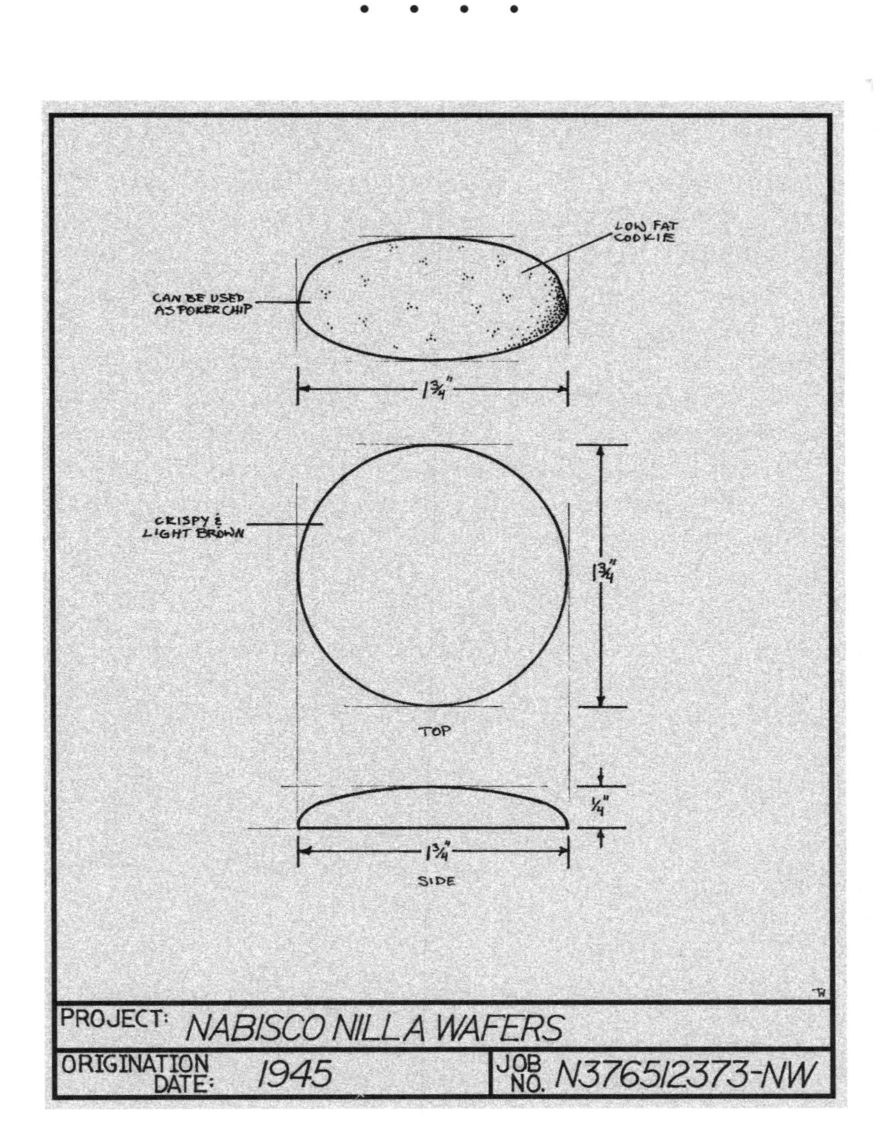

TOP SECRET RECIPES VERSION OF

NABISCO NUTTER BUTTER

Formerly called the National Biscuit Company, Nabisco was formed in the late 1800s by several bakeries that joined together to meet a growing demand. In the 1870s Nabisco's forefathers had introduced the first individually packaged baked goods. Before this, cookies and crackers had been sold from open barrels or biscuit boxes. The company has become the world's largest manufacturer of cookies and crackers, selling some 42 million packages of Nabisco products each day to retail outlets on every continent.

Nutter Butter Cookies were introduced in 1969 and have quickly taken their place alongside Nabisco's most popular products, including Oreos, Chips Ahoy!, and Fig Newtons.

COOKIES

1/2 cup vegetable shortening
2/3 cup granulated sugar
1 egg
1/2 teaspoon salt
3 tablespoons peanut butter
1/2 cup old-fashioned Quaker oats
1 cup all-purpose flour

FILLING

1/2 cup peanut butter
3/4 cup powdered sugar
1 tablespoon fine graham cracker crumbs

1. Preheat the oven to 325°F.
2. In a large bowl, cream together the shortening and sugar with an electric mixer.

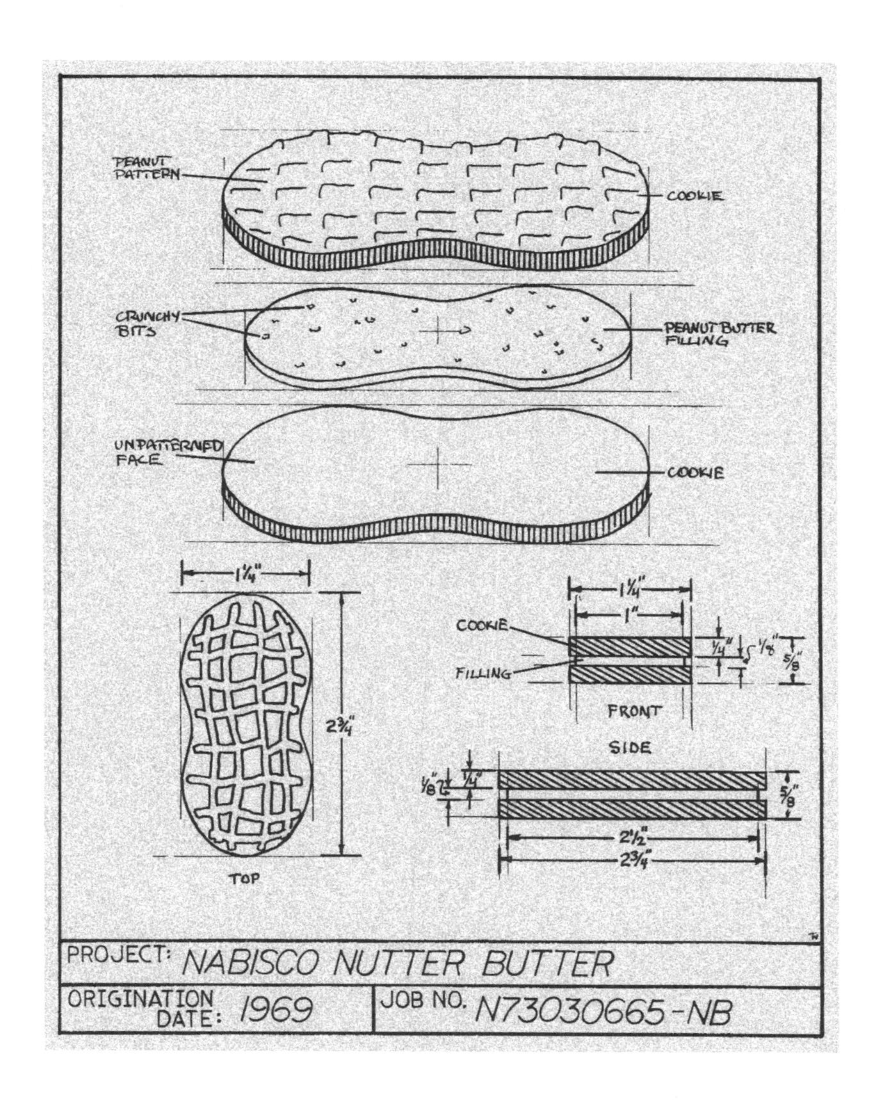
PEANUT PATTERN
COOKIE
CRUNCHY BITS
PEANUT BUTTER FILLING
UNPATTERNED FACE
COOKIE
1¼"
2¾"
TOP
1¼"
1"
COOKIE
FILLING
¼"
⅛"
⅝"
FRONT
SIDE
⅛"
¼"
⅝"
2½"
2¾"
PROJECT: NABISCO NUTTER BUTTER
ORIGINATION DATE: 1969
JOB NO. N73030665-NB

3. Add the egg, salt, and peanut butter and beat until well blended.
4. Put the oats in a blender and blend on medium speed until they are almost as finely ground as flour.
5. Add the oats and flour to the mixture and blend well.
6. Pinch out small portions of dough and roll into 1-inch balls in the palm of your hand. Press these flat on ungreased cookie sheets so that they form 2-inch circles. If you're a stickler for a cookie that looks just like the original, you can form the dough into flat peanut shapes similar to those illustrated.
7. Bake for 8 to 10 minutes, or until light brown around the edges.
8. While the cookies bake, combine the filling ingredients in a small bowl.
9. When the cookies are cool, use a butter knife to spread a thin layer of filling on the flat side of a cookie and press another on top. Repeat.

- MAKES 2 DOZEN COOKIES.

• • • •

TOP SECRET RECIPES VERSION OF

NABISCO OREO COOKIE

☆ ✌ 💣 ✏ ☯ ✂ ☞

At one time Nabisco actually conducted a study that determined that 50 percent of Oreo consumers twist the cookie apart before eating it. I guess this is important information, since it concerns the world's top-selling cookie. Historians at Nabisco aren't sure who came up with the idea for this sandwich cookie back in 1912, but they do know that it was introduced along with two other cookie creations that have long since died. The name may have come from the Greek word for mountain, *oreo,* which would once have made sense because the first test version was hill-shaped. When the Oreo was first sold to the public, it was much larger than today's cookie, but it kept shrinking over the years until Nabisco realized it had become much too small and had to enlarge it again to today's current 1¾-inch diameter.

In 1975, Nabisco figured we couldn't have too much of a good thing, so the company gave us Double Stuf Oreos, with twice the filling. A smart move. Today Double Stuf holds its own rank as the fifth most popular cookie in America.

COOKIE

One 18.25-ounce package Betty Crocker chocolate fudge cake mix
3 tablespoons shortening, melted
½ cup cake flour, measured then sifted
1 egg
3 tablespoons water
*2 tablespoons brown paste food coloring (optional)**

FILLING

3 3/4 cups powdered sugar
1/2 tablespoon granulated sugar
1/2 teaspoon vanilla extract
1/2 cup shortening
2 tablespoons hot water

1. Combine the cookie ingredients in a large bowl. Add the water a little bit at a time until the dough forms. Cover and chill for 2 hours.
2. Preheat oven to 350°F.
3. On a lightly floured surface, roll out a portion of the dough to just under 1/16 inch thick. To cut, use a lid from a spice container with a 1 1/2-inch diameter (Schilling brand is good). Arrange the cut dough rounds on a cookie sheet that is sprayed with a light coating of nonstick spray. Bake for 10 minutes. Remove wafers from the oven and cool completely.
4. As the cookies cool, combine the filling ingredients well with an electric mixer.
5. With your hands form the filling into balls about 1/2 to 3/4 inch in diameter.
6. Place a filling ball in the center of the flat side of a cooled cookie and press with another cookie, flat side down, until the filling spreads to the edge.

- MAKES 60 COOKIES.

TIDBITS

If the cookie dough seems too tacky, you can work in as much as 1/4 cup of flour as you pat out and roll the dough. Use just enough flour to make the dough workable but not tough.

This may be obvious to you, but you can expand your own homemade line of Oreos by creating your own versions of Double Stuf® or the giant Oreos called Oreo Big Stuf®. Just add twice the filling for Double Stuf, or make the cookie twice the size for Big Stuf. Go crazy. Try Triple Stuf or Quadruple Stuf or Quintuple Stuf . . . somebody stop me.

The brown paste food coloring gives the cookies the dark brown, almost black color of the originals. If you do not use the paste food coloring be sure to change the amount of water added to the wafer cookies from 3 tablespoons to 1/4 cup. The coloring can be found with cake decorating supplies at art supply and craft stores.

• • • •

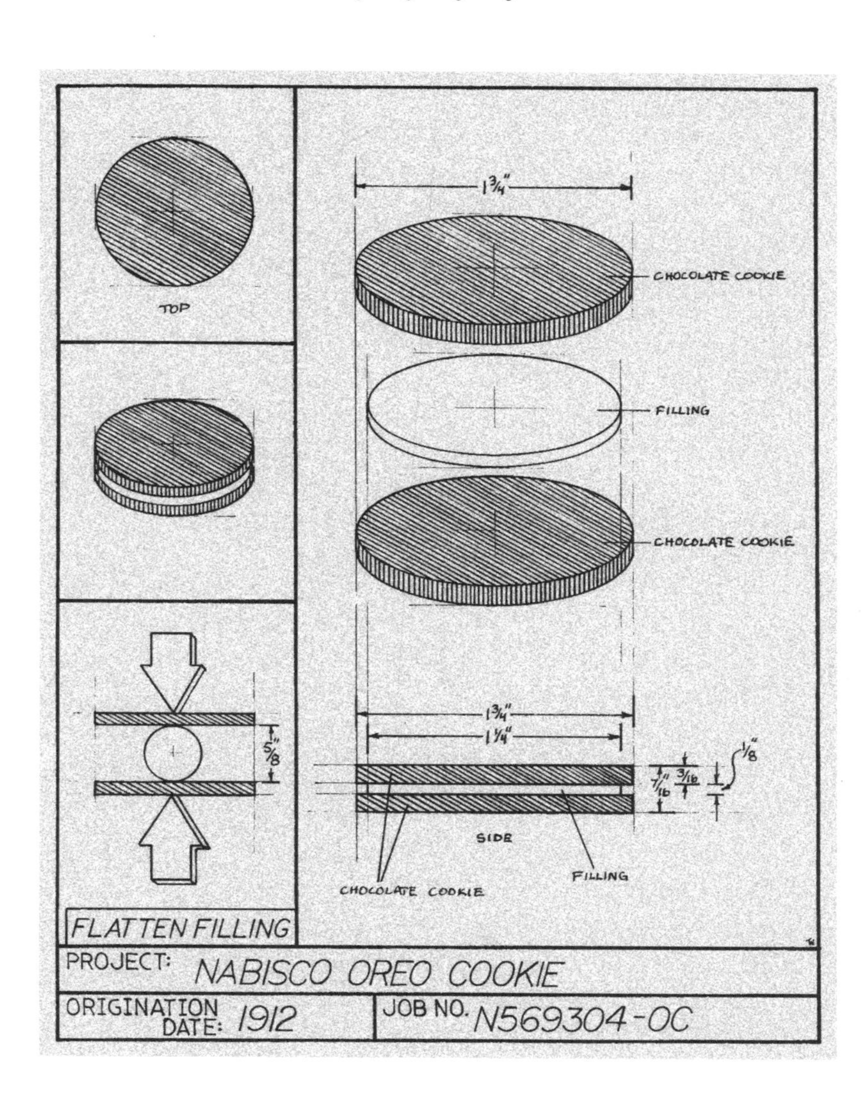

NESTLÉ 100 GRAND BAR

Nestlé is the world's largest packaged food manufacturer, coffee roaster, and chocolate maker. It is the largest single company in Switzerland today, but Nestlé derives only 2 percent of its revenue from its home country.

The company is quite diverse. Nestlé's product lines include beverages and drinks, chocolate and candy, dairy products, and frozen foods. The company also operates more than thirty Stouffer Hotels and owns 25 percent of the French cosmetics giant L'Oréal. In the United States, where the company is called Nestlé USA, it ranks third behind Mars, Inc., and Hershey USA in chocolate sales.

This candy bar was introduced in 1966 as the $100,000 Bar, then its name was changed to 100 Grand Bar in 1985.

30 unwrapped Kraft caramels, at room temperature
3/4 cup Rice Krispies
One 12-ounce bag milk chocolate chips

1. With your fingers, flatten each caramel into a rectangle about 1/4 inch thick.
2. Melt the chocolate chips in a microwave-safe bowl in a microwave set on half power for 2 minutes. Stir halfway through the heating time. Melt thoroughly, but do not overheat.
3. Add the Rice Krispies and stir just until blended.
4. Dip each caramel into the chocolate to coat completely and

then place on waxed paper. Cool until firm at room temperature, 1 to 2 hours.

- MAKES 30 CANDY BARS.

• • • •

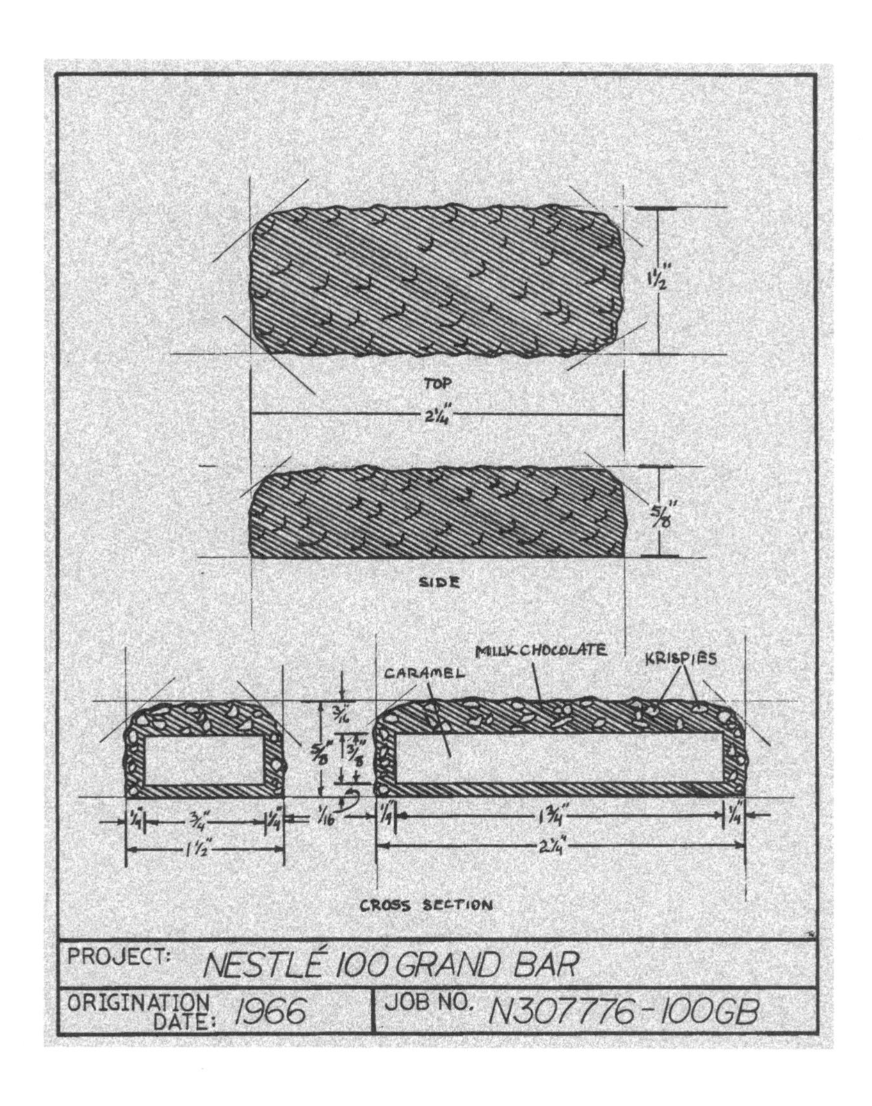

TOP SECRET RECIPES VERSION OF

NEWMAN'S OWN CREAMY CAESAR DRESSING

☆ ✌ 💣 ✎ ☯ ✂ ☞

With over 100 million dollars given to charity since 1982, Newman's Own products have become an American favorite. One variety of the brand's dressings that really stands out is this exceptional Caesar salad dressing, probably the best commercial Caesar dressing on the market. Part of the secret for this special recipe is the inclusion of Worcestershire sauce. The sauce adds a beautiful flavor and color to the dressing, and contains a crucial fishy ingredient: anchovies.

1 cup mayonnaise
3 tablespoons distilled white vinegar
2 tablespoons Kraft grated parmesan cheese
2 teaspoons Worcestershire sauce
½ teaspoon lemon juice
½ teaspoon ground dry mustard
¼ teaspoon salt
¼ teaspoon garlic powder
¼ teaspoon onion powder
¼ teaspoon ground black pepper
pinch dried basil
pinch dried oregano

Combine all ingredients in a medium bowl and mix with an electric mixer for about 30 seconds. Chill the dressing for a couple hours before serving.

- MAKES 1¼ CUPS.

TOP SECRET RECIPES VERSION OF

NUTS 4 NUTS CANDIED NUTS

The streets of New York City are peppered with Nuts 4 Nuts vendors selling freshly candied nuts that you can smell a block away. For a buck or two you get your choice of warm, sugar-coated peanuts, cashews, or almonds wrapped up in a little paper bag with the corners twisted closed. The nuts are candied right there on the carts in a large, metal bowl over a heating element. Sugar and water is added to the nuts, which are stirred often as the water evaporates so they develop a nice, even coating without burning. They're easy to make on the street, which means they're even easier to clone at home. All you need for your own quick version of this addictive street snack is 1¼ cups of your favorite nuts, some sugar, a little water, a hot pan and you're about 5 minutes away from an authentic New York City treat. Give this recipe a try with pecans or walnuts, and then use them on a spinach salad, along with a little goat cheese, and some diced apples or pears for a real gourmet touch.

2 tablespoons water
¼ cup sugar
1¼ cups nuts (almonds, peanuts, or cashews)

1. Bring 2 tablespoons water and ¼ cup sugar to a boil in a medium saucepan over medium heat.
2. Add the nuts and stir often until water evaporates. Continue stirring until the sugar begins to harden on the nuts. When the

sugar on the nuts begins to turn light brown, pour them onto a plate to cool. Be careful not to cook the nuts too long, or the sugar will burn.

- MAKES 1¼ CUPS.

• • • •

TOP SECRET RECIPES VERSION OF

POGEN'S GINGERSNAPS

☆ ✌ 💣 ✎ ☯ ✂ ☞

Back in the 1870s, in the coastal city of Malmö, Sweden, a man named Anders Pahlsson baked the first of his soon-to-be famous gingersnaps in a bakery he named Pogen's. In 1970 Pogen's, Inc., opened in the United States, expanding the line of baked goods that Pahlsson developed in the nineteenth century.

A legend that dates back many years says that if you place a gingersnap in the palm of your hand, press down in the middle, and it breaks into three pieces, good luck will follow. Today, more than 100 years later, good luck and hard work have made Pogen's the third-largest supplier of cookies to the growing vending business.

1/4 cup (1/2 stick) butter
1/2 cup vegetable shortening
1 cup packed brown sugar
1/4 cup molasses
1 egg
2 1/4 cups sifted all-purpose flour
2 teaspoons baking soda
1/2 teaspoon salt
1 teaspoon powdered ginger
2 teaspoons ground cinnamon
1/2 teaspoon ground cloves

1. Preheat the oven to 350°F.
2. Cream the butter, shortening, brown sugar, molasses, and egg until light and fluffy.
3. Sift together the dry ingredients; combine both mixtures.
4. Form the dough into walnut-size balls. With floured fingers, press the balls into flat circles on an ungreased cookie sheet.
5. Bake for 8 minutes, or until golden brown.

6. Remove the gingersnaps from the cookie sheet as soon as they are cool and seal in a covered container to preserve their crunch.

- Makes 4 dozen.

TIDBITS

If you follow the above recipe, you will be making gingersnaps in a simple circular form. However, Pogen's gingersnaps are made in a smattering of animal shapes. If you would like a more accurate clone of the Pogen's variety, simply sprinkle the dough with flour and roll it flat. Then use animal-shaped cookie cutters to form the dough before baking.

• • • •

TOP SECRET RECIPES VERSION OF

RAGU PASTA SAUCE

It's America's most popular pasta sauce and now you can whip up clones of two varieties at home at a fraction of the cost. Just snag yourself a large can of tomato sauce and a few other common ingredients and get simmering. These recipes duplicate the traditional "Meat" variety of the sauce and the newer "Chunky Garden Style" version with tomato, basil, and Italian cheese. Feel free to doctor these sauces up with your own creative additions just as many do to perk up real Ragu.

MEAT

2 ounces ground beef
29-ounce can tomato sauce
5 teaspoons granulated sugar
4 teaspoons olive oil
1 ½ teaspoons minced dried onions
1 ½ teaspoons shredded Romano cheese
⅛ teaspoon ground black pepper
1 bay leaf

1. Brown ground beef in a medium saucepan over medium heat. Add remaining ingredients, bring to a boil, then reduce heat and simmer for 15 to 20 minutes, stirring often.

- MAKES 2½ CUPS.

TOMATO, BASIL, AND ITALIAN CHEESE

29-ounce can tomato sauce
½ cup canned diced tomatoes
5 teaspoons granulated sugar
1 tablespoon olive oil
1 tablespoon shredded Romano cheese
1 teaspoon shredded parmesan cheese
1 teaspoon dried basil
½ teaspoon dried parsley
¼ teaspoon garlic powder
⅛ teaspoon black pepper
1 bay leaf

1. Combine all ingredients in a medium saucepan over medium heat. Bring to a boil then reduce heat and simmer for 15 to 20 minutes, stirring often.

- MAKES 3 CUPS.

• • • •

TOP SECRET RECIPES VERSION OF

SEE'S BUTTERSCOTCH LOLLIPOP

The first See's Candy shop was opened in Los Angeles in 1921 by Charles A. See. He used his mother's candy recipes, and a picture of her at the age of seventy-one embellished every black-and-white box of chocolates. Mary See died in 1939 at the age of eighty-five, but her picture went on to become a symbol of quality and continuity. See's manufacturing plants are still located in California, but because the company will ship anywhere in the United States, it has become a known and respected old-fashioned-style chocolatier across the country.

In an age of automation, many companies that manufacture chocolate have resorted to automated enrobing machines to coat their chocolates. But See's workers still hand-dip much of their candy.

One of the company's most popular sweets isn't dipped at all. It's a hard, rectangular lollipop that comes in chocolate, peanut butter, and butterscotch flavors. The latter, which tastes like caramel, is the most popular flavor of the three, and this recipe will enable you to clone the original, invented more than fifty years ago.

You will need twelve shot glasses, espresso cups, or sake cups for molds, and twelve lollipop sticks or popsicle sticks.

1 cup granulated sugar
1 cup heavy cream
3 tablespoons light corn syrup
2 tablespoons butter or margarine
1 teaspoon vanilla extract
nonstick spray

1. Combine the first four ingredients in a saucepan over medium heat. Stir until the sugar has dissolved.
2. Let the mixture boil until it reaches 310°F on a cooking thermometer (this is called the *hard-crack stage*), or until a small amount dropped in cold water separates into hard, brittle threads.
3. Stir in the vanilla, then remove from the heat.
4. Coat the molds with nonstick spray and pour the mixture in. (If you are using shot glasses, be sure to cool the mixture first so that the glass won't crack.)
5. Place a small piece of aluminum foil over each mold and press a lollipop stick or popsicle stick in the center.
6. When cool, remove from molds.

- MAKES 1 DOZEN LOLLIPOPS.

• • • •

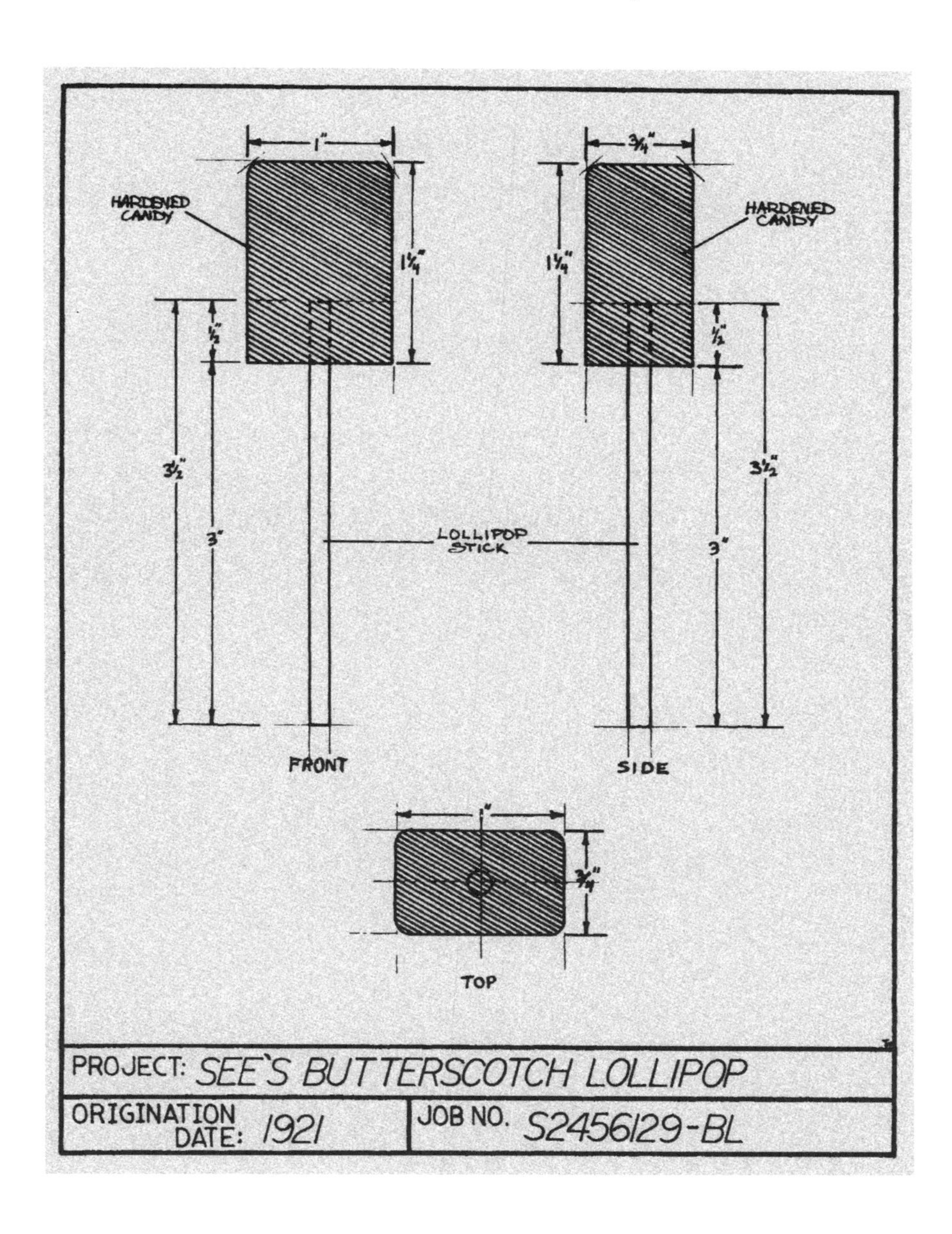
1"
3/4"
HARDENED CANDY
HARDENED CANDY
1¼"
1¼"
½"
½"
3½"
3½"
3"
3"
LOLLIPOP STICK
FRONT
SIDE
1"
3/4"
TOP
PROJECT: SEE'S BUTTERSCOTCH LOLLIPOP
ORIGINATION DATE: 1921
JOB NO. S2456129-BL

TWIN DRAGON ALMOND COOKIES

According to Main On Foods, the manufacturer and distributor of Twin Dragon Almond Cookies, the original recipe was brought to this country in 1951 by a Chinese baker who owned a small corner shop in downtown Los Angeles. That retail bakery is gone now, but its most popular product, the world's best-tasting almond cookie, is still selling big.

3 cups all-purpose flour
1 teaspoon baking soda
½ teaspoon salt
1 cup blanched almonds
1 cup granulated sugar
1½ cups lard (see Tidbits, next page)
1 teaspoon almond extract
1 egg, beaten
⅛ cup water

1. Preheat the oven to 350°F.
2. Mix the flour, baking soda, and salt.
3. In a blender, grind ½ cup blanched almonds to a fine powder. Add to the flour mixture.
4. Cream the sugar, lard, almond extract, egg, and water, and add to the dry mixture. Mix thoroughly.
5. Form into 1-inch balls and place on an ungreased cookie sheet 2 inches apart.
6. Press one of the remaining almonds into the center of each ball, while flattening it slightly with fingers.
7. Brush each cookie lightly with beaten egg.
8. Bake for 20 minutes, or until cookies are light brown around edges.

- Makes 2 dozen cookies.

TIDBITS

If your daily allowance of lard will be exceeded by this recipe, feel free to substitute vegetable shortening.

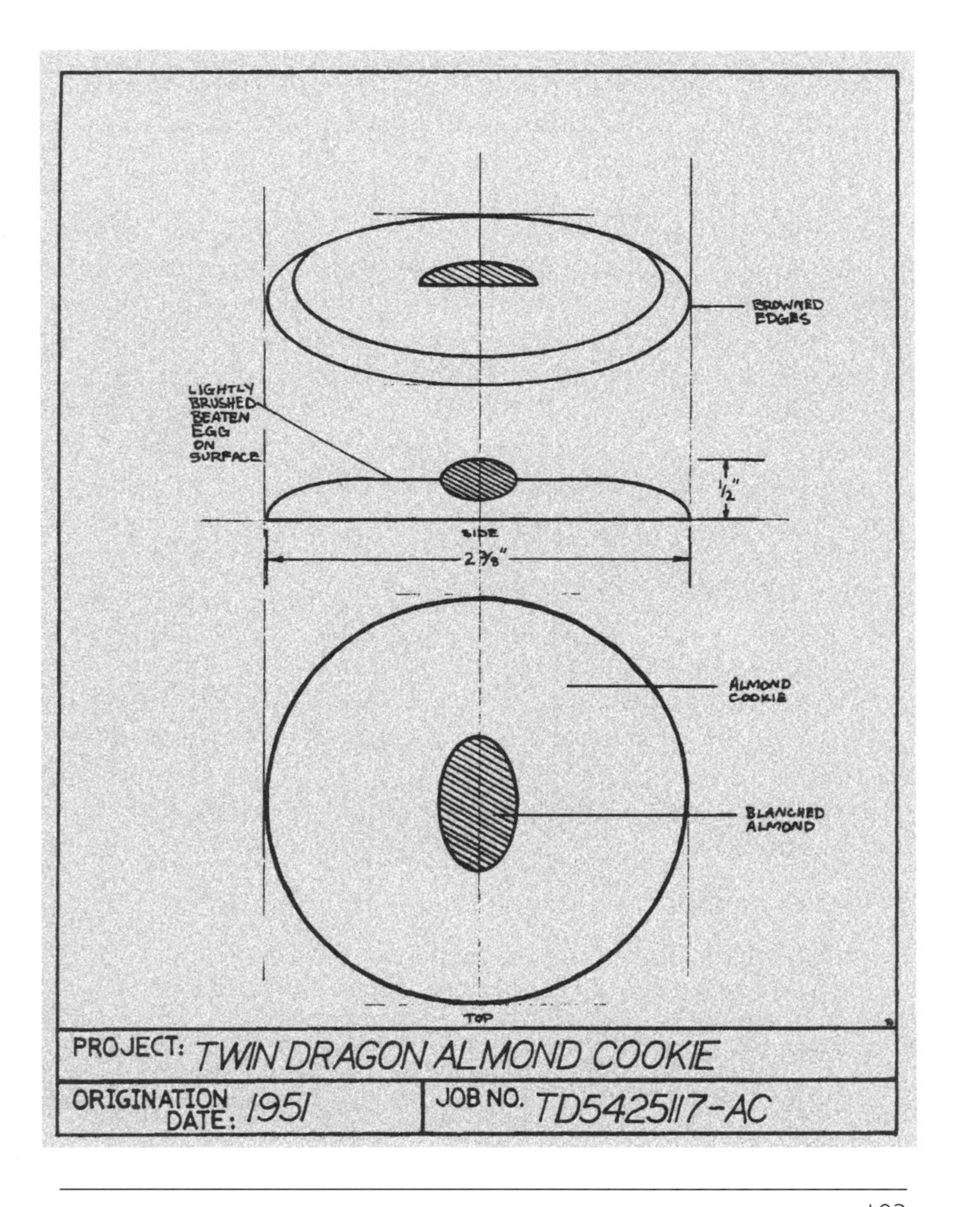

TOP SECRET RECIPES VERSION OF

YORK PEPPERMINT PATTIE

In York, Pennsylvania, Henry C. Kessler first concocted this confection in the late 1930s at his candy factory, the York Cone Company. The company was originally established to make ice cream cones, but by the end of World War II, the peppermint patty had become so popular that the company discontinued all other products. In 1972, the company was sold to Peter Paul, manufacturers of Almond Joy and Mounds. Cadbury USA purchased the firm in 1978, and in 1988 the York Peppermint Pattie became the property of Hershey USA.

Many chocolate-covered peppermints had been made before the York Peppermint Pattie came on the market, but Kessler's version was firm and crisp, while the competition was soft and gummy. One former employee and York resident remembered the final test the patty went through before it left the factory. "It was a snap test. If the candy didn't break clean in the middle, it was a second."

For years, seconds were sold to visitors at the plant for fifty cents a pound.

1 egg white
4 cups powdered sugar
1/3 cup light corn syrup
1/2 teaspoon peppermint oil or extract
Cornstarch for dusting
One 12-ounce bag semisweet chocolate chips

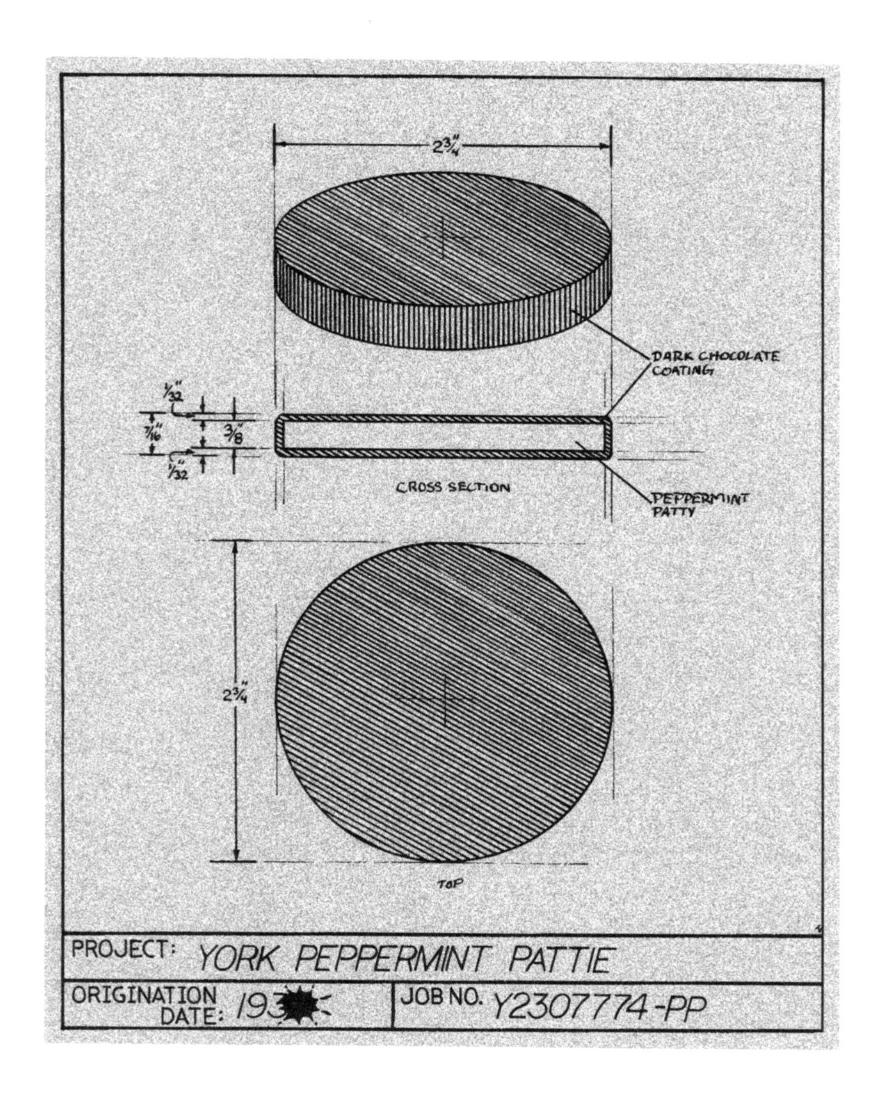
2¾"
DARK CHOCOLATE COATING
1/32"
7/16"
3/8"
1/32"
CROSS SECTION
PEPPERMINT PATTY
2¾"
TOP
PROJECT: YORK PEPPERMINT PATTIE
ORIGINATION DATE: 193
JOB NO. Y2307774-PP

1. In a medium bowl, beat the egg white until frothy but not stiff. Don't use a plastic bowl for this.
2. Slowly add the powdered sugar while blending with an electric mixer set on medium speed.
3. Add the corn syrup and peppermint oil or extract and knead the mixture with your hands until it has the smooth consistency of dough. Add more powdered sugar if necessary, until mixture is no longer sticky.
4. Using a surface and rolling pin heavily dusted with cornstarch, roll out the peppermint dough until it is about 1/4 inch thick.
5. Punch out circles of peppermint dough with a biscuit cutter or a clean can with a diameter of about 2 1/2 inches. Make approximately 20, place them on plates or cookie sheets, and let them firm up in the refrigerator, about 45 minutes.
6. Melt the chocolate chips in a microwave set on high for 2 minutes. Stir halfway through the heating time. Melt thoroughly, but do not overheat.
7. Drop each patty into the chocolate and coat completely. Using a large serving fork, or 2 dinner forks, one in each hand, lift the coated patty from the chocolate. Gently tap the forks against the bowl to knock off the excess chocolate, and place each patty on wax paper.
8. Chill the peppermint patties until firm, about 30 minutes.

- MAKES 20 PEPPERMINT PATTIES.

• • • •

TOP SECRET RECIPES VERSION OF

APPLEBEE'S PIZZA STICKS

☆ ✌ 💣 ✎ ☯ ✂ ☞

MENU DESCRIPTION: "PARMESAN: *Thin crusty strips of pizza dough topped with herbs & melted Italian cheese, served with marinara sauce.* **LOADED:** *Add Italian sausage & pepperoni."*

Each Applebee's makes an effort to decorate the inside of the restaurant with pictures and memorabilia from the neighborhood in which it is located. You'll see photographs of local heroes and students, license plates, banners, old souvenirs, trinkets, and antiques—all representing area history. Take a look around the walls of the next Applebee's you visit. Maybe you can find something you lost several years ago.

Meanwhile, here's a find: pizza sticks that are made from dough that is proofed, fried, and then broiled. The frying adds a unique flavor and texture to the dough that you won't get with traditional pizza. I've designed this recipe to use the premade dough that comes in tubes (you know, like the stuff from that dough boy). But you can make this with any dough recipe you might like. Just roll the dough into a 10 × 15-inch rectangle before slicing.

These appetizers can be made either in the Parmesan version without meat, or "loaded" with sausage and pepperoni. This recipe yields a lot, so it makes good party food.

MARINARA DIPPING SAUCE

1 8-ounce can tomato sauce
1 tomato, chopped
1 tablespoon diced onion
1 teaspoon sugar
½ teaspoon dried oregano
⅛ teaspoon salt
⅛ teaspoon dried basil

PARMESAN PIZZA STICKS

1 10-ounce tube instant pizza dough (Pillsbury is good)
2 to 4 cups vegetable oil for frying
1¾ cups grated mozzarella cheese
¼ cup grated fresh Parmesan cheese
½ teaspoon dried oregano
¼ teaspoon dried basil
¼ teaspoon caraway seeds

¼ teaspoon garlic salt

OPTIONAL (FOR THE "LOADED")
3 ounces pepperoni, diced
3 ounces Italian sausage, cooked and crumbled

1. Preheat the oven to 425°F.
2. Prepare the dipping sauce by combining all of the marinara ingredients in a small, uncovered saucepan and bringing the mixture to a boil. Reduce the heat, cover, and simmer the sauce for ½ hour. (The sauce can be made ahead and kept, refrigerated, for several days.)
3. Prepare the pizza sticks by first proofing the dough. Unroll the dough onto a cutting board and straighten the edges. It should form a rectangle that is longer from left to right than top to bottom. With a sharp knife or pizza cutter, slice through the middle of the dough lengthwise. This will divide the rectangle into two thinner rectangles that will measure 4 to 5 inches from top to bottom.
4. Slice the dough from top to bottom into 1 1/2-inch-wide pieces. You should have somewhere between 20 and 24 dough slices.
5. Place the slices onto a greased cookie sheet about ½ inch apart and bake for 3 minutes. You may have to use more than one cookie sheet. This will proof the dough so that it becomes stiff.
6. Heat vegetable oil in a frying pan or deep fryer to 350°F. Oil should be at least ½ inch deep if using a stovetop pan. You will want to use more oil with a deep fryer.
7. Fry pizza sticks 5 to 6 at a time for about 1 minute per side or until they are a dark golden brown. Remove them from the oil onto a cloth or paper towel to drain.
8. When all the pizza dough sticks are fried, arrange them once again on the cookie sheet(s). You may want to line the cookie sheets with foil to make cleanup easier. Preheat the broiler.
9. Sprinkle the mozzarella cheese evenly over the dough.
10. Sprinkle the Parmesan cheese evenly over the mozzarella.
11. Combine the oregano, basil, caraway seeds, and garlic salt in a small bowl. If your oregano and basil are fairly coarse you can use your thumb and first finger to crunch the spice up a little, making it a finer blend.

12. Sprinkle the spice mixture over the cheese.
13. If you want to make the "loaded" variety, sprinkle the pepperoni and sausage over the top of the pizza sticks.
14. Broil the pizza sticks for 2 minutes or until the cheese is melted. Serve hot with dipping sauce on the side.

- SERVES 6 TO 8 AS AN APPETIZER.

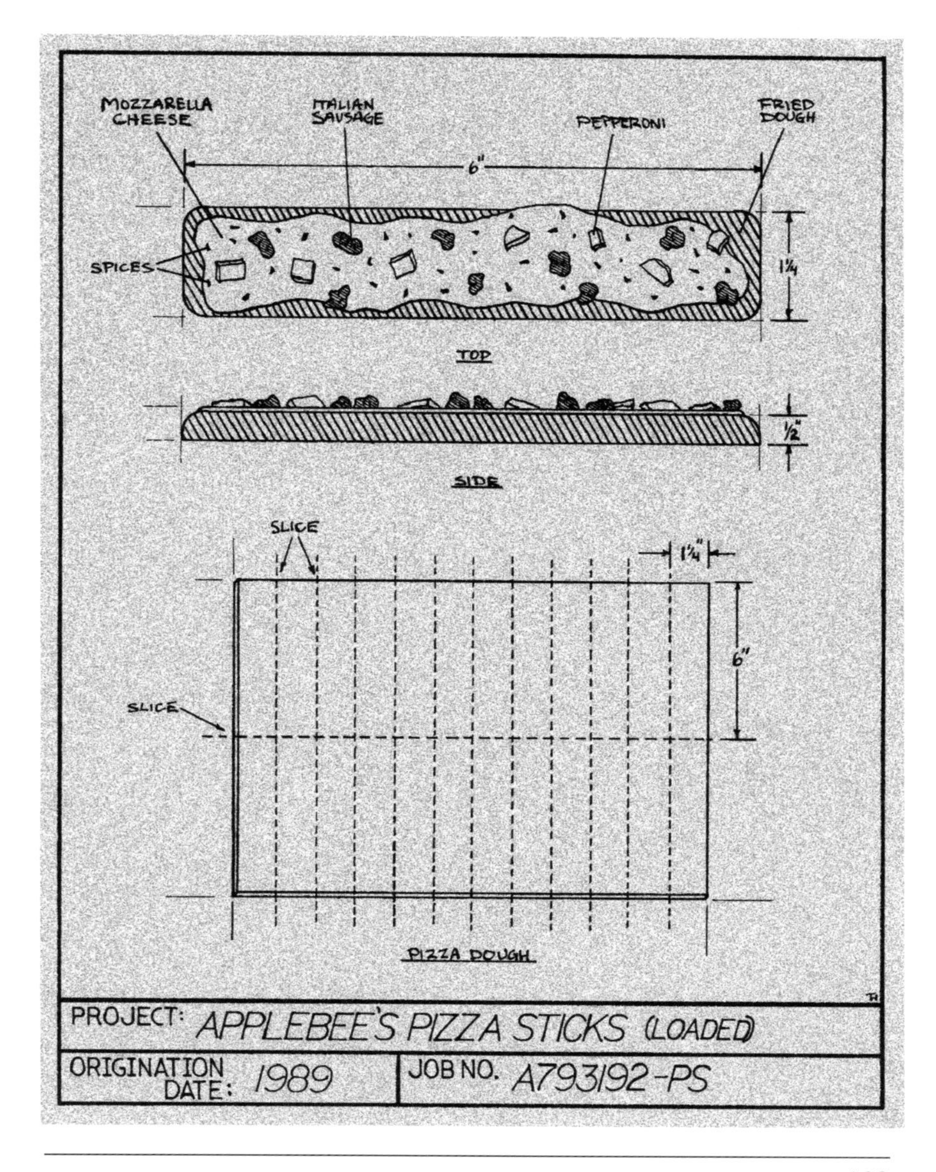

TOP SECRET RECIPES VERSION OF

APPLEBEE'S ORIENTAL CHICKEN SALAD

☆ ✌ 💣 ✏ ☯ ✂ ☞

MENU DESCRIPTION: *"Crisp Oriental greens topped with chunks of crunchy Chicken Fingers, toasted almonds & crispy rice noodles tossed in a light Oriental vinaigrette."*

Applebee's 60-item menu is revised at least twice a year. That means about 40 percent of the entire menu changes on a regular basis, with those selections varying from location to location. The other 60 percent are items found on menus in all of the Applebee's restaurants, and they seldom change. This practice of constant menu retooling is becoming more frequent in all of the large restaurant chains these days. As competition grows, the chains find they must alter their menus regularly to keep discriminating customers interested.

Even though the Oriental Chicken Salad, which is considered one of the restaurant's signature items, has been on the menu for some time now, it's possible that by the time you are reading this book it has been replaced by another salad selection. If that happens, here's the only way you can still enjoy this salad creation—by making your own. You'll love the Oriental dressing with the unique, nutty flavor of roasted sesame oil. This type of oil is becoming quite popular today and can be found in the supermarket near the other oils or where the Asian food is displayed.

ORIENTAL DRESSING

3 tablespoons honey
1 1/2 tablespoons white vinegar
4 teaspoons mayonnaise
1 tablespoon Grey Poupon Dijon mustard
1/8 teaspoon sesame oil

SALAD

2 to 4 cups vegetable oil for frying
1 egg
½ cup milk
½ cup all-purpose flour
½ cup cornflake crumbs
1 teaspoon salt
¼ teaspoon pepper
1 boneless, skinless chicken breast half
3 cups chopped romaine lettuce
1 cup chopped red cabbage
1 cup chopped napa cabbage
½ carrot, julienned or shredded
1 green onion, sliced
1 tablespoon sliced almonds
⅓ cup chow mein noodles

1. Using an electric mixer, blend together all the ingredients for the dressing in a small bowl. Put the dressing in the refrigerator to chill while you prepare the salad.
2. Preheat the oil in a deep fryer or frying pan over medium heat. You want the temperature of the oil to be around 350 degrees F. If using a frying pan, the oil should be around ½ inch deep. More oil can be used in a deep fryer so that the chicken is immersed.
3. In a small, shallow bowl beat the egg, add the milk, and mix well.
4. In another bowl, combine the flour with the cornflake crumbs, salt, and pepper.
5. Cut the chicken breast into 4 or 5 long strips. Dip each strip of chicken first into the egg mixture then into the flour mixture, coating each piece completely.
6. Fry each chicken finger for 5 minutes or until the coating has darkened to brown.
7. Prepare the salad by tossing the romaine with the red cabbage, napa cabbage, and carrot.
8. Sprinkle the green onion on top of the lettuce mixture.
9. Sprinkle the almonds over the salad, then the chow mein noodles.
10. Cut the chicken into bite-size chunks. Place the chicken on the salad, forming a pile in the middle. Serve with the salad dressing on the side.

- SERVES 1 AS AN ENTREE (CAN BE DOUBLED).

TOP SECRET RECIPES VERSION OF

APPLEBEE'S CLUB HOUSE GRILL

☆ ✌ 💣 ✏ ☯ ✂ ☞

MENU DESCRIPTION: *"Applebee's signature hot club sandwich with warm sliced ham & turkey, Cheddar, tomatoes, mayonnaise & Bar-B-Que sauce on thick-sliced grilled French bread. Served with a side of coleslaw."*

Here's a sandwich which Applebee's claims is a signature item for the chain. I can see why—it's creative, yet simple. And pretty tasty. It's a cross between a club sandwich and a grilled cheese. So, if you like both of those, you'll love this. And it helps that the sandwich is easy to make when you're as lazy as I am.

For the sliced turkey and ham, go to your deli service counter in the supermarket and get the stuff they machine-slice real thin for sandwiches. This usually tastes the best. If you don't have a service counter, you can find the thin-sliced meats prepackaged near the hot dogs and bologna.

2 thick slices French bread
1 tablespoon butter, softened
2 teaspoons mayonnaise
1/3 cup shredded Cheddar cheese
2 slices deli-sliced turkey breast
2 slices deli-sliced ham
2 slices tomato
2 teaspoons barbecue sauce (Bull's Eye is best)

1. Spread the butter evenly over one side of each slice of bread.
2. Put one slice of bread, butter side down, into a preheated frying pan over medium heat.
3. Spread the mayonnaise over the unbuttered side of the grilling bread.
4. Sprinkle half of the Cheddar cheese over the mayonnaise.
5. Lay the turkey and ham in the pan next to the bread for about 30 seconds to heat it up.
6. When it's warm, lay the turkey on the cheese.

7. Place the tomato slices on the turkey.
8. Spread the barbecue sauce over the tomato slices.
9. Lay the ham on the tomatoes.
10. Sprinkle the remainder of the cheese over the ham.
11. Top off the sandwich with the other slice of bread, being sure that the buttered side is facing up.
12. By now the first side of bread should be golden brown. Flip the sandwich over and grill the other side for 2 to 3 minutes or until golden brown as well.
13. Remove the sandwich from the pan and cut in half diagonally. Serve with additional barbecue sauce on the side.

- SERVES 1 AS AN ENTREE (CAN BE DOUBLED).

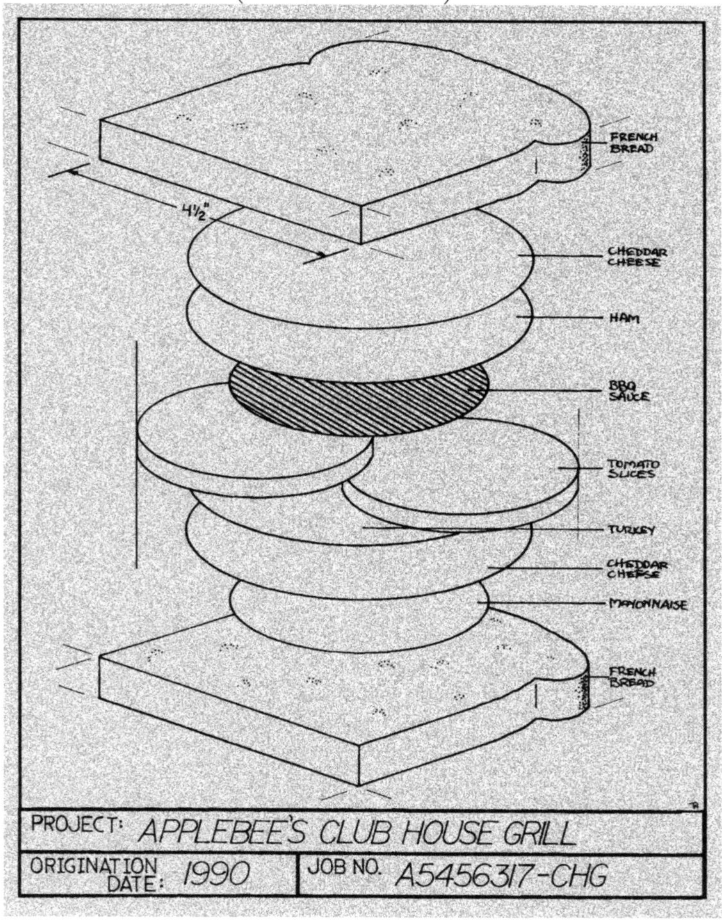

TOP SECRET RECIPES VERSION OF

CARNEGIE DELI CLASSIC NEW YORK CITY CHEESECAKE

☆ ✌ 💣 ✏ ☯ ✂ ☞

Carnegie Deli's huge pastrami sandwiches were selected as the best in New York by *New York Magazine* in 1975, but it's the cheesecakes, which can be shipped anywhere in the country, that really put this famous deli on the map. The secret to accurately cloning a traditional New York cheesecake is in creating the perfect, not-too-sweet, sugar-cookie crust, and varying the baking temperature so that we get a nicely browned top before cooking the cheesecake through. Get ready for the best deli-style cheesecake to ever come out of your oven.

COOKIECRUST

½ cup butter, softened
¼ cup granulated sugar
½ teaspoon vanilla
dash salt
1 egg
1½ cups flour

5 8-ounce packages cream cheese, softened
1⅓ cups sugar
2 teaspoons vanilla extract
4 teaspoons lemon juice
⅓ cup sour cream
2 tablespoons flour
3 eggs

1. Leave the butter and cream cheese out of the refrigerator for 30 to 60 minutes to soften. Make the crust by creaming together butter, ¼ cup sugar, ½ teaspoon vanilla, and salt. Add 1 egg and mix well. Add 1½ cups flour and stir well to combine.
2. Preheat oven to 375°F, then press half of the dough onto the bottom of a 9-inch springform pan. Bake for 5 to 7 minutes or until edge of dough begins to turn light brown. Cool.

3. When the pan has cooled, take the remaining dough and press it around the inside edge of the pan. Don't go all the way up to the top though. Leave about a ½-inch margin from the top of the pan.
4. Crank oven up to 500ºF. Combine cream cheese, 1⅓ cups sugar, 2 teaspoons vanilla extract and lemon juice with an electric mixer in a large bowl until smooth. Mix in sour cream and 2 tablespoons flour. Add the eggs and mix on slow speed until combined.
5. Pour cream cheese filling into the pan and bake at 500ºF for 10 minutes. Reduce heat to 350ºF and bake for 30 to 35 minutes more, or until the center is firm. Cover and cool in refrigerator for several hours or overnight before serving.

- SERVES 8.

• • • •

TOP SECRET RECIPES VERSION OF

CRACKER BARREL HASH BROWN CASSEROLE

☆ ✌ 💣 ✏ ☯ ✂ ☞

MENU DESCRIPTION: *"Made from scratch in our kitchens using fresh Grade A Fancy Russet potatoes, fresh chopped onion, natural Colby cheese and spices. Baked fresh all day long."*

In the late sixties Dan Evins was a Shell Oil "jobber" looking for a new way to market gasoline. He wanted to create a special place that would arouse curiosity, and would pull travelers off the highways. In 1969 he opened the first Cracker Barrel just off Interstate 40 in Lebanon, Tennessee, offering gas, country-style food, and a selection of antiques for sale. Today there are over 260 stores in 22 states, with each restaurant still designed as a country reststop and gift store. In fact, those stores (which carry an average of 4,500 different items apiece) have made Cracker Barrel the largest retailer of American-made finished crafts in the United States.

Those who know Cracker Barrel well love the restaurant for its delicious home-style breakfasts. This casserole, made with hash browns, Colby cheese, milk, beef stock, and spices is served with many of the classic breakfast dishes at the restaurant. The recipe here is designed for a skillet that is also safe to put in the oven. If you don't have one of those, you can easily transfer the casserole to a baking dish after it is done cooking on the stove.

1 26-ounce bag frozen country-style hash browns
2 cups shredded Colby cheese
1/4 cup minced onion
1 cup milk
1/2 cup beef stock or canned broth
2 tablespoons butter, melted
dash garlic powder
1 teaspoon salt
1/4 teaspoon ground black pepper

1. Preheat the oven to 425°F.
2. Combine the frozen hash browns, cheese, and onion in a large bowl.
3. Combine the milk, beef stock, half the melted butter, the garlic powder, salt, and black pepper in another bowl. Mix until well blended, then pour the mixture over the hash browns and mix well.
4. Heat the remaining butter in a large, ovenproof skillet over high heat.
5. When the skillet is hot, spoon in the hash brown mixture. Cook the hash browns, stirring occasionally, until hot and all of the cheese has melted (about 7 minutes).
6. Put the skillet into the oven and bake for 45 to 60 minutes or until the surface of the hash browns is dark brown.

TIDBITS

If your skillet isn't ovenproof (because it has a plastic handle, for example), you can also spoon the potatoes into a glass 9 × 9-inch baking dish and microwave the potatoes until they are hot and the cheese has melted. Then put that baking dish into the 425°F oven until the surface of the hash browns has browned.

If you can't find Colby cheese, you can also use Cheddar cheese for this recipe. Colby, however, is preferred.

- SERVES 4 TO 6 AS A SIDE DISH.

• • • •

TOP SECRET RECIPES VERSION OF

CRACKER BARREL EGGS-IN-THE-BASKET

☆ ✌ 💣 ✎ ☯ ✂ ☞

MENU DESCRIPTION: *"Two slices of sourdough bread grilled with an egg in the middle, served with thick sliced bacon or smoked sausage patties and fried apples or hash brown casserole."*

Breakfast is a popular meal at Cracker Barrel restaurants. Just to prove it, the restaurant has some amazing statistics printed on the back of their breakfast menus:

"Each Spring 607,142 Sugar Maple Trees must be tapped to produce enough pure maple syrup for our guests.

"It takes 5,615,00,000 (THAT'S BILLION!) coffee beans each year to satisfy our guests' needs for coffee. Each tree produces only 1 pound of coffee per year . . . that's 1,560,000 trees."

And if you've ever wondered who the man is on the restaurant's logo:

"Uncle Herschel, the country gentleman on our logo, really is the uncle of Cracker Barrel president, Dan Evins."

This recipe is from an old-fashioned egg-in-the-hole meal that I used to make all the time as a kid. Heck, I thought my family had invented it! I was surprised to see this offered on the Cracker Barrel menu, and then I was thrilled to find it tasted just like the homemade version we used to make years ago. This version of the Cracker Barrel classic goes great with the Hash Brown Casserole recipe (page 196). If you're making this for more than just one person, the recipe is easily doubled or quadrupled.

2 thick slices sourdough bread
2 tablespoons butter, softened
2 eggs
Salt to taste

ON THE SIDE
Sausage
Thick-sliced bacon

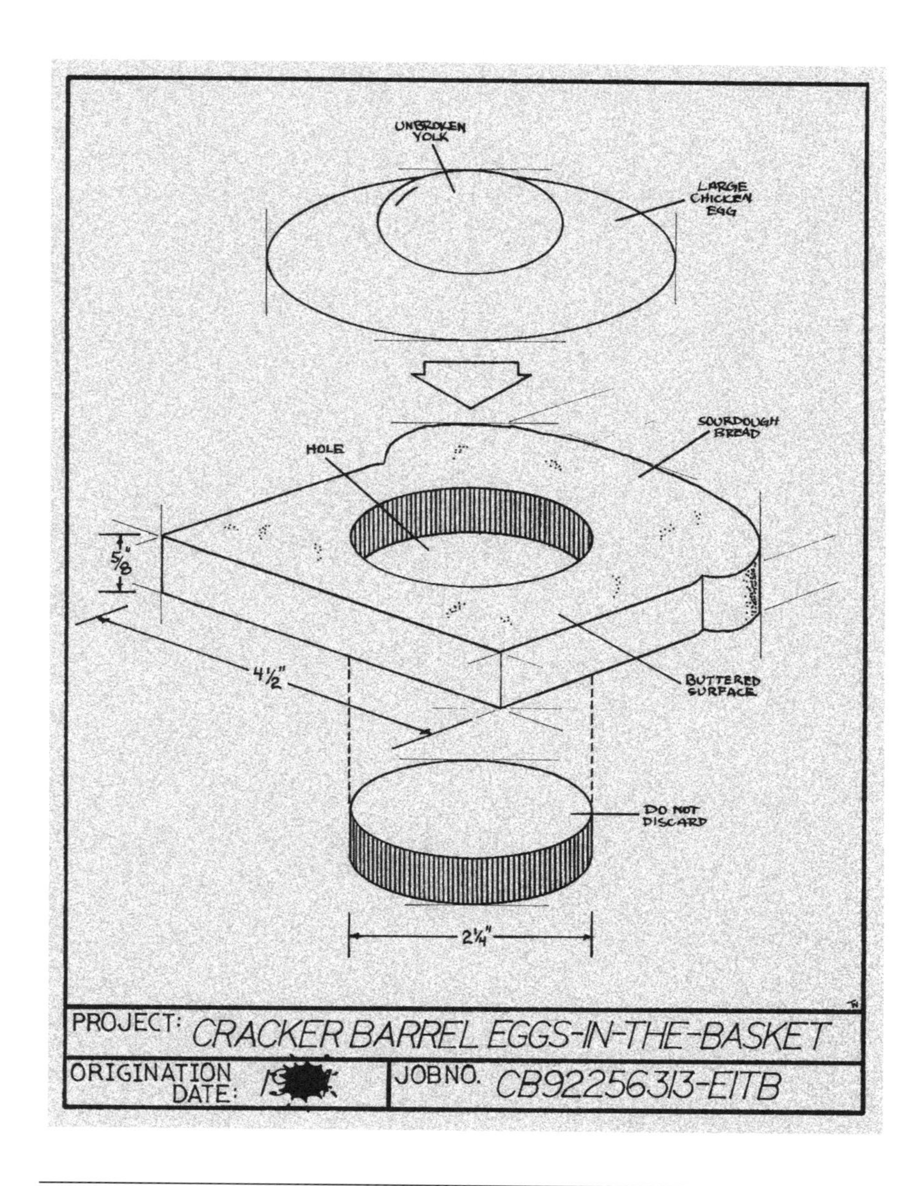

1. Heat a large frying pan or griddle over medium heat.
2. Spread the butter evenly over one face of each slice of bread.
3. Use a biscuit cutter or any jar or container you can find with a diameter of about 2¼ inches to cut a circle out of the center of each slice of bread.
4. Grill the bread and the hole you cut out, butter side down, in the hot pan for 2 minutes or until it just starts to turn brown.
5. Drop a little butter in the hole of each slice of bread, then carefully crack an egg into each hole. Be sure not to break the yolks. Salt lightly.
6. When the eggs have cooked for 1 to 2 minutes, carefully flip each one over without breaking the yolks or flinging raw egg goo all over the stovetop. Also, flip the cut-out "holes."
7. Cook for another minute or so until the eggs are cooked the way you like them. Serve the eggs, grilled bread, and "holes" with hash browns or Hash Brown Casserole, and bacon or sausage.

• SERVES 1 (CAN BE DOUBLED).

• • • •

TOP SECRET RECIPES VERSION OF

CRACKER BARREL CHICKEN & DUMPLINS

☆ ✌ 💣 ✏ ☯ ✂ ☞

MENU DESCRIPTION: *"We use only the 'best of the breast' chicken tenderloin in our recipe. Our dumplins are made from scratch, then hand rolled and cut into strips before simmering to perfection in chicken stock."*

By 1977 there were 13 Cracker Barrel stores located in Georgia and Tennessee, with all of them based on founder Dan Evins' original concept of a restaurant and store built around gasoline pumps. But with the oil embargo and energy crisis of the mid-seventies, Cracker Barrel started building stores that did not offer gas. Soon all of the original 13 stores were converted so that today not one Cracker Barrel lets you "filler-up" while you fill yourself up.

Another old-time favorite at Cracker Barrel is the Chicken & Dumplins on the lunch and dinner menu. The nice thing about this version of the popular classic dish is that it creates its own tasty gravy. As the "dumplins" dissolve some, the flour thickens the stock into a creamy sauce. Just remember to let your dough rest a bit before rolling it to cut out the dumplins. This will allow the gluten in the flour to work much better. Use extra flour on your cutting board and rolling pin if the dough is too tacky, and try not to roll the dough too thin.

CHICKEN AND BROTH

3 quarts water
1 3- to 4-pound chicken, cut up
1 1/2 teaspoons salt
1 small onion, sliced
2 stalks celery, chopped
1 clove garlic, peeled and quartered
1 bay leaf
4 to 6 whole parsley leaves
1 teaspoon coarsely ground black pepper
1 tablespoon lemon juice

"DUMPLINS"

2 cups all-purpose flour
1 tablespoon baking powder
1 ¼ teaspoons salt
1 cup plus 2 tablespoons milk

1. Bring the water to a boil in a large pot. Add the chicken, 1 teaspoon of salt, onion, celery, garlic, bay leaf, and parsley to the pot. Reduce the heat to simmer and cook the chicken, uncovered, for 2 hours. The liquid will reduce by about one third.
2. When the chicken has cooked, remove it from the pot and set it aside. Strain the stock to remove all the vegetables and floating scum. You only want the stock and the chicken, so toss everything else out.
3. Pour 1 ½ quarts (6 cups) of the stock back into the pot (keep the leftover stock, if any, for another recipe—it can be frozen). You may also want to use a smaller pot or a large saucepan for this. Add coarsely ground pepper, the remaining ½ teaspoon salt, and the lemon juice, then reheat the stock over medium heat while preparing the dumplins.
4. For dumplins, combine the flour, baking powder, 1 ¼ teaspoons salt, and milk in a medium bowl. Stir well until smooth, then let the dough rest for to 5 to 10 minutes. Roll the dough out onto a floured surface to about a ½-inch thickness.
5. Cut the dough into ½-inch squares and drop each square into the simmering stock. Use all of the dough. The dumplins will first swell and then slowly shrink as they partially dissolve to thicken the stock into a white gravy. Simmer for 20 to 30 minutes until thick. Stir often.
6. While the stock is thickening, the chicken will have become cool enough to handle. Tear all the meat from the bones and remove the skin. Cut the chicken meat into bite-size or a little bigger than bite-size pieces and drop them into the pot. Discard the skin and bones. Continue to simmer the chicken and dumplins for another 5 to 10 minutes, but don't stir too vigorously or the chicken will shred and fall apart. You want big chunks of chicken in the end.
7. When the gravy has reached the desired consistency, ladle four portions onto plates and serve hot. Serve with your choice of steamed vegetables, if desired.

- SERVES 4 AS AN ENTREE.

TOP SECRET RECIPES VERSION OF

HARD ROCK CAFE FILET STEAK SANDWICH

☆ ✌ 💣 ✏ ☯ ✂ ☞

MENU DESCRIPTION: *"Filet mignon grilled to perfection, sliced thin, with shredded lettuce, tomato and spicy mustard. Served on a sourdough French roll with fries and a salad."*

When the first Hard Rock Cafe opened in 1971 on Old Park Lane in London, England, not one guitar or gold record decorated the walls. The burger joint was the inspiration of two Americans, Peter Morton and Isaac Tigrett, who couldn't find a decent American-style hamburger anywhere in London and decided to do something about it. The restaurant soon became famous only for its food, until along came Eric Clapton, who donated his guitar as a joke. Up on the wall it went. Not wanting to be outdone, Pete Townsend of The Who soon offered up a guitar of his own to be hung on the wall next to Clapton's with a note: "Mine's as good as his." That started a wave of donations from rock and rollers through the decades; and thus was born the world's first theme restaurant. Soon more Hard Rock Cafes were opening around the world, with the first one in America opening in Los Angeles in 1982. After that came New York City, San Francisco, Chicago, Houston, New Orleans, Maui, Las Vegas, Aspen, Newport Beach, and many more—a total of 58 so far. The success of the Hard Rock Cafe spawned a trend which now includes other restaurants built around themes ranging from movies to fashion to motorcycles to blues.

Here is an easy-to-make sandwich that features a tender, sliced filet mignon. It's a clone of one of the Hard Rock's more popular recent additions to the menu. This recipe suggests another way you can serve those filet mignons you've been saving in the freezer.

2 6- to 8-ounce filet mignon steaks
Salt and pepper
2 sourdough French rolls
3 tablespoons mayonnaise
3 tablespoons spicy mustard
6 slices tomato
1 cup shredded iceberg lettuce

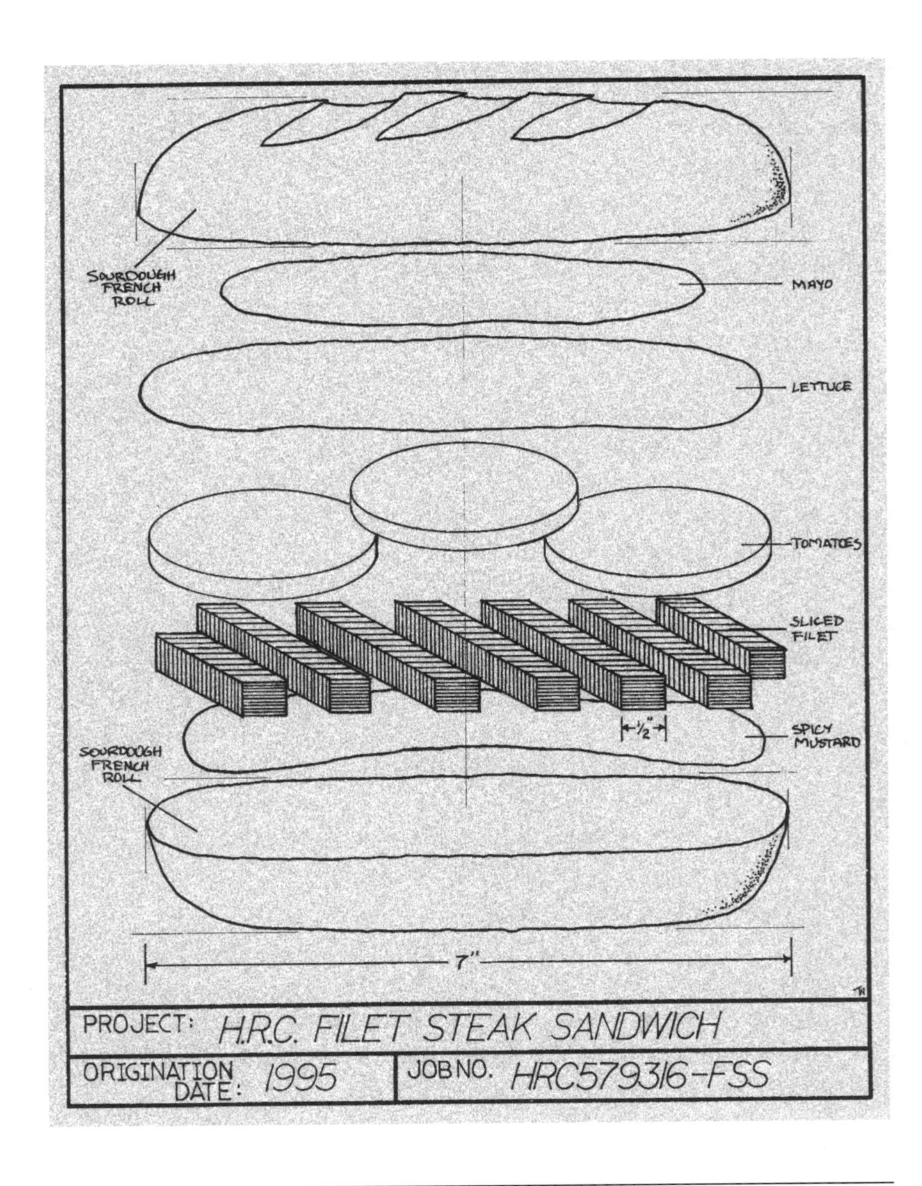

1. Preheat the barbecue or stovetop grill.
2. Since most filets are usually cut pretty thick (1 inch or more) you will want to slice your filets through the middle before grilling, making four thinner filets that are around ½ inch each.
3. Cook your filets over a hot grill for 2 to 4 minutes per side or until cooked to your preference. Be sure to salt and pepper both sides of each filet.
4. As the meat cooks, prepare your rolls by slicing them into top and bottom halves.
5. Spread the mayonnaise on the face of each top half.
6. Spread the mustard onto the face of each bottom half.
7. When the filets are done, slice them into ½-inch-thick strips.
8. Arrange the sliced filets evenly over the mustard on each bottom roll.
9. Place the tomato slices over the filets.
10. Put the shredded lettuce on top of the tomatoes.
11. Place the top buns on the lettuce and slice the sandwiches diagonally into two even halves. Hold each sandwich half together with toothpicks to serve.

- SERVES 2 AS AN ENTREE.

• • • •

HARD ROCK CAFE GRILLED VEGETABLE SANDWICH

MENU DESCRIPTION: *"Grilled eggplant, zucchini, summer squash, and roasted red peppers. Served on a sourdough French roll with your choice of fries or watermelon."*

Pop artist Andy Warhol called Hard Rock Cafe the "Smithsonian of Rock and Roll." In fact, the Hard Rock Cafe chain owns more artifacts of rock history than anyone in the world—somewhere around 30,000 in all. The chain has been collecting the artifacts, which decorate each of the 58 Hard Rock Cafes, for more than two decades. Because of this, some of the memorabilia you see in the restaurants, especially the older ones, were donated from artists even before they were famous.

As the chain grew larger over the years, cofounders Peter Morton and Isaac Tigrett grew tired of their business relationship. The company was eventually divided, with Isaac operating foreign Hard Rocks, and Peter taking over the stateside cafes. In 1988, Isaac sold his shares to Britain's Rank Organization and then partnered with actor Dan Aykroyd to open the House of Blues chain. In 1996, just a week before the Hard Rock celebrated its 25th anniversary, Peter sold his shares to Rank as well (for $410 million in cash!), consolidating the chain once again.

If you don't eat meat, or even if you do, you'll find this grilled vegetable sandwich makes a great meal in itself for lunch or dinner. I'm not usually one to go for strictly vegetarian sandwiches, but when I first tried this one I was surprised at how good it was. Now I veg out with this sandwich regularly. Hopefully you will too.

6 tablespoons mayonnaise
1/2 teaspoon chopped fresh parsley
Pinch dried oregano
Salt
1 red bell pepper
1 small zucchini
1 yellow summer squash
1/4 eggplant
1/4 cup olive oil
2 sourdough French rolls
1 tablespoon freshly grated Parmesan cheese
6 to 8 separated onion ring slices (2 whole slices)
3 to 4 slices tomato (1 medium tomato)
2 leaves red leaf lettuce

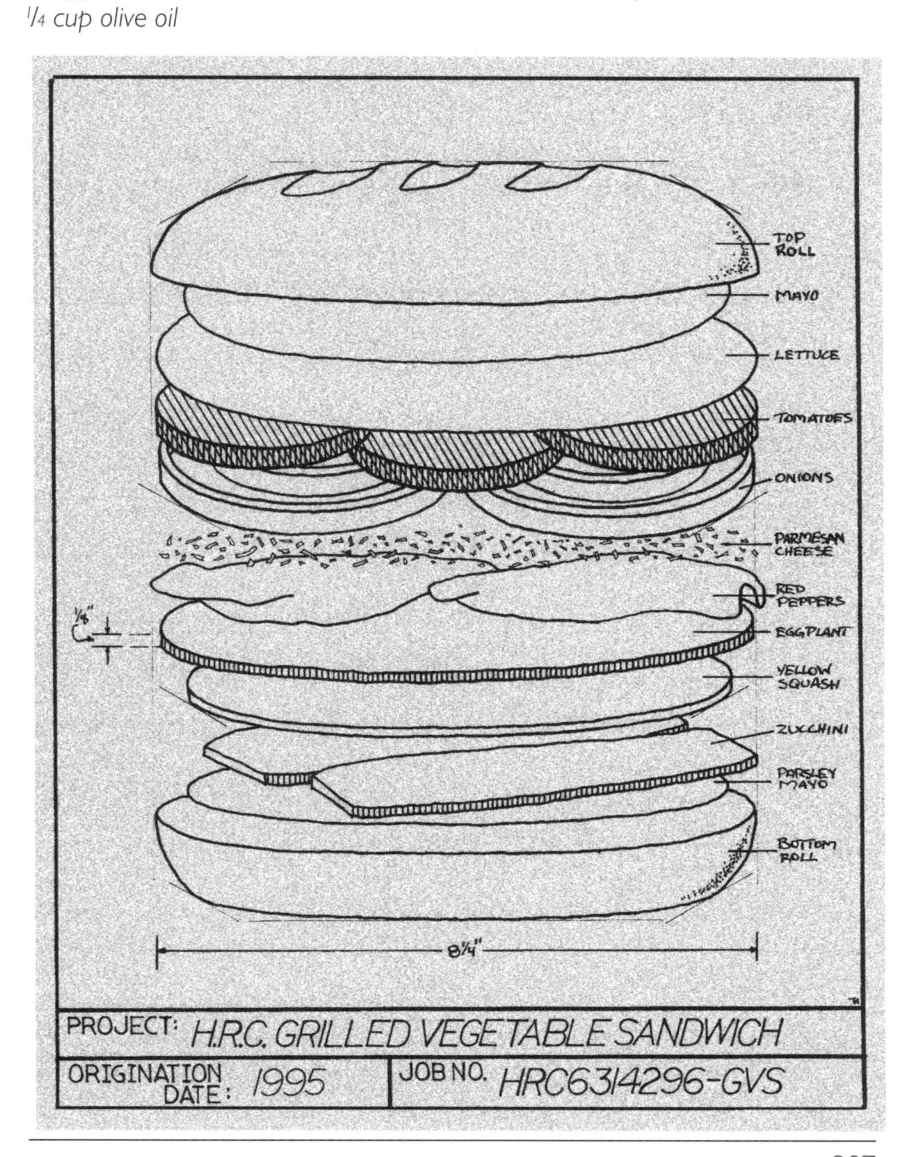

1. Preheat the barbecue or stovetop grill.
2. To prepare a spread, put 3 tablespoons of the mayo into a small bowl and add the parsley, oregano and a pinch of salt. Set this and the remaining mayonnaise aside until you're ready to make the sandwich.
3. Prepare the bell pepper by cutting it into quarters and seeding it. Brush the entire surface of the pepper with olive oil.
4. Slice the zucchini, squash, and eggplant into lengthwise slices no more than 1/8 to 1/4 inch thick. Brush these slices with oil as well.
5. Cook the red pepper on a hot grill for 2 or 3 minutes. At that point add the remaining vegetables to the grill and cook everything for 4 to 5 more minutes or until all the vegetables are tender. Be sure to salt the vegetables and, of course, turn them halfway through the cooking time.
6. When the veggies are tender and begin to char, remove them from the grill and prepare each sandwich by first cutting the French rolls in half lengthwise through the middle.
7. Spread the parsley-mayonnaise over the face of the bottom halves.
8. Arrange the zucchini onto the rolls.
9. Stack the yellow squash next.
10. Eggplant goes on top of that.
11. Peel the skin off the red peppers, then stack the peppers on the eggplant.
12. Divide the Parmesan cheese and sprinkle it over the peppers.
13. Arrange the onions on the peppers.
14. Tomato slices go on the onions.
15. Tear the red lettuce leaves so that they fit on the tomatoes.
16. Divide the remaining 3 tablespoons of mayonnaise and spread it on the face of the top rolls and stack the rolls on the lettuce to finish off your sandwiches.
17. Cut the sandwiches diagonally through the middle and pierce each half with a toothpick before serving.

- SERVES 2 AS AN ENTREE.

• • • •

TOP SECRET RECIPES VERSION OF

HARD ROCK CAFE FAMOUS BABY ROCK WATERMELON RIBS

☆ ✌ 💣 ✏ ☯ ✂ ☞

MENU DESCRIPTION: *"Texas style ribs basted in our special watermelon B.B.Q. sauce, grilled and served with fries and a green salad."*

The collection of rock and roll memorabilia is different in each Hard Rock Cafe. You may find artifacts that come from recording stars of the fifties, like Elvis Presley and Fats Domino, to more contemporary artists such as Prince, Pearl Jam, and Nirvana. Usually there are several gold and platinum records donated from artists, sequined stage costumes, and famous guitars, some even left in a smashed condition as they were donated straight from a performance. The Hard Rock also collects movie memorabilia, such as Tom Cruise's pilot helmet from the movie *Top Gun* and the Indiana Jones jacket from *Raiders of the Lost Ark.*

In 1995, Hard rock cofounder Peter Morton opened the world's first rock-and-roll hotel, The Hard Rock Hotel and Casino, in Las Vegas. Peter now operates the hotel and his swank restaurant Morton's in Hollywood, California—the famous location of many a celebrity power meal over the years.

I thought these ribs with a barbecue sauce made from watermelon rind had a unique and memorable flavor begging to be duplicated at your next power meal. The sauce is sweet and slightly tangy, and the ribs are so tender they melt in your mouth. It's the slow-cooking process that makes them that way. Throwing them on the grill at the last minute is not meant to cook them so much as it is to add the smoky flavor and slight charring that good ribs require. If possible, make the watermelon barbecue sauce a day ahead so the ribs can marinate in it overnight. If you don't have time for that, at least marinate the ribs for a couple of hours.

Watermelon rind from about ½ of a small watermelon
1 cup dark corn syrup
½ cup water
¼ cup tomato ketchup
¼ cup distilled vinegar
¾ teaspoon crushed red pepper flakes
½ teaspoon liquid smoke
¼ teaspoon black pepper
4 pounds baby back ribs

1. For the puréed watermelon rind, you want to cut off the green skin and about half an inch of the hard white part, keeping the part of the watermelon that is lighter red to white. This is the tender part of the rind. Try to stay away from the harder, white rind just inside the green skin. Put the rind into a food processor and purée for only about 10 seconds. Strain the liquid from the pulp and use 1 cup of pulp, measured after straining.
2. Combine the watermelon pulp with the remaining ingredients for the sauce in a medium saucepan over high heat. Bring the mixture to a boil, then reduce the heat and simmer, covered, for about 1 hour or until it's as thick as you like it.
3. Cut racks of ribs into plate-size portions of about 6 or 7 rib bones each. Brush the ribs with the barbecue sauce and wrap each rack individually in aluminum foil. Be sure to save some sauce for later. Let the ribs marinate in the refrigerator for a couple of hours at least. (Overnight is best.)
4. Preheat the oven to 300°F. To cook the ribs, set them with the seam of the foil facing up, into the oven. Bake for 2 to 2½ hours or until the rib meat has pulled back from the cut end of the bones by about ½ inch. They should be very tender.
5. Remove the ribs from the foil and brush on some additional sauce. Grill the ribs on a hot barbecue for 2 to 4 minutes per side or until you see several spots of charred sauce. Be sure to watch the ribs so that they do not burn. Serve with leftover sauce on the side.

- SERVES 2 TO 4 AS AN ENTREE.

HARD ROCK CAFE ORANGE FREEZE

MENU DESCRIPTION: *"Fresh squeezed O.J. and orange sherbet."*

The Hard Rock Cafe chain has been committed to a "Save the Planet" campaign for some time now. The chain recycles all of the glass bottles, paper, and cardboard boxes, and uses no polystyrene. Water in the restaurant is only served on request. At the restaurants in Los Angeles and Newport Beach electronic tote boards have been erected to "tick away by the second the acres of remaining rainforest on the planet while also displaying the world's population count as it continues to explode, reminding us all to be conscious of our decreasing natural resources." In addition, any leftover food is donated to local charities that feed the homeless. That's cool, eh?

You'll find the Orange Freeze is pretty cool also, especially on a hot summer day. This refreshing dessert item at the Hard Rock is easy to duplicate at home with just a few ingredients and a couple minutes in front of a blender.

2 cups orange sherbet or sorbet
1 cup fresh squeezed orange juice
1/4 cup milk
1 sprig of fresh spearmint

1. Put the sherbet, juice, and milk in a blender and blend for 15 seconds or just until all the sherbet is smooth. You may have to stop the blender and stir the sherbet up a bit to help it combine.
2. Pour the orange freeze into a tall, chilled glass. Place a sprig of fresh spearmint in the top and serve immediately.

TIDBITS

This is also good with a little whipped cream on top.

- SERVES 1 AS DESSERT OR BEVERAGE.

OLIVE GARDEN TOSCANA SOUP

MENU DESCRIPTION: *"Spicy sausage, russet potatoes, and cavolo greens in a light creamy broth."*

For two years after the first Olive Garden restaurant opened in 1982, operators were still tweaking the restaurant's physical appearance and the food that was served. Even the tomato sauce was changed as many as 25 times.

This soup blends the flavors of potatoes, kale, and Italian sausage in a slightly spicy chicken and cream broth. When I first tried the soup at the restaurant I was surprised at how good it was. I'd never had any soup with the leafy, healthy, spinach-like kale in it (found in most produce sections), and the combination of flavors was addicting. When you try this version for yourself I think you'll agree.

2¾ cups chicken stock or broth
¼ cup heavy cream
1 medium russet potato
2 cups chopped kale
½ pound spicy Italian sausage
¼ teaspoon salt
¼ teaspoon crushed red pepper flakes

1. Combine the stock and cream in a saucepan over medium heat.
2. Slice the unpeeled potato into ¼-inch slices, then quarter the slices and add them to the soup.
3. Add the kale.
4. Grill or sauté the sausage. When cooked and cooled, cut the sausage at an angle into slices about ½ inch thick. Add the sausage to the soup.
5. Add the spices and let the soup simmer for about 1 hour. Stir occasionally.

- SERVES 4 AS AN APPETIZER, 2 AS AN ENTREE.

OLIVE GARDEN ALFREDO PASTA

MENU DESCRIPTION: *"Our classically rich blend of cream, butter and parmesan cheese with a hint of garlic."*

The Alfredo Pasta served at the Olive Garden is a tasty, classic recipe. Although rich and creamy, the simplicity of this recipe made it hard for me to resist. This is one of those fail-safe recipes that can be made quickly and easily with just a few ingredients.

Serve this dish with a Toscana soup appetizer and some garlic bread and you've got a tasty meal just like one you might get at the restaurant chain—except this version will cost less, you can enjoy it in the comfort of home, and you won't have to tip.

1/2 cup (1 stick) butter
2 cups heavy cream
1/8 teaspoon garlic powder
1/8 teaspoon ground black pepper
1 12-ounce box fettuccine pasta (or your choice of pasta)
1/4 cup grated Parmesan cheese

1. Melt the butter in a medium saucepan over medium heat.
2. Add the cream, garlic powder, and pepper and simmer for 10 to 12 minutes or until thick.
3. At the same time, bring 4 to 6 quarts of water to a boil and add the pasta.
4. When the Alfredo sauce has reached your desired consistency, stir in the Parmesan cheese.
5. When the pasta is cooked, drain it. Serve the pasta on plates with Alfredo sauce poured over the top.

- SERVES 2 TO 3 AS AN ENTREE.

RED LOBSTER BROILED LOBSTER

The namesake of the Red Lobster chain is the delicious broiled lobster, lightly seasoned, served with lemon and melted butter. Two varieties are most often available at the restaurant: Maine lobster and rock lobster. The Maine lobsters are purchased live, while rock lobster tails come frozen; and both are available in stores across the country. Rock lobsters, also known as spiny lobsters, are found in warmer waters. They have no claws, which is why you only get rock lobster tails. Each Red Lobster restaurant has a special device that bakes and broils the lobsters without burning them. Since these special broilers don't come with most homes, I've created a cooking method using a conventional oven that produces broiled lobster just like that which you can enjoy at the restaurant.

2 6-ounce rock lobster or Maine lobster tails
Melted butter
1/4 teaspoon salt
1/4 teaspoon paprika
dash ground black pepper
dash cayenne pepper
dash allspice
Lemon wedges

1. Thaw lobster tails if frozen, then preheat the oven to 425°F.
2. Each tail is prepared differently for cooking. The meat from the rock lobster is fully exposed on top of the shell for broiling, while the meat of the Maine lobster is left in the shell.

   To prepare the rock lobster, use a kitchen scissors to cut along the top of the shell down to the tail. Crack the ribs of the shell underneath so that you can spread the shell open on top and pull the meat out down to the tail. You may have to use a spoon to pull the meat away from inside of the shell so that it will come free. Leave the end of the meat attached to the shell when you pull it out, then close the shell underneath it. Now you should be able to rest the meat back down on top of the shell. Cut about 1/4 inch deep down the center of the meat so that you can pull the colored part of the meat over, exposing the white center. This may have already happened when you cut the shell open.

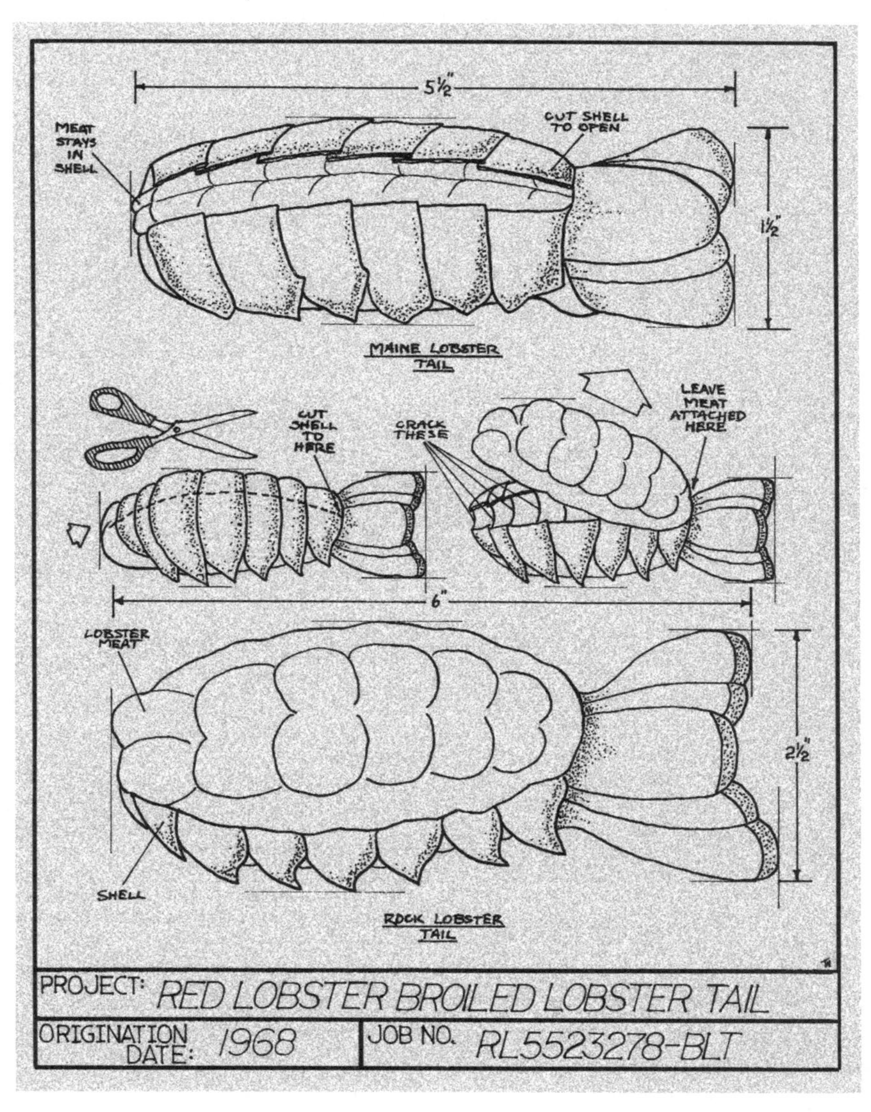

For the Maine lobster, slice down the top of the shell to the tail Crack the ribs in the center along the bottom of the tail so that you can hinge the shell open from the top. Use a spoon to pull the meat away from the inside of the shell so that it is easy to eat when cooked, but leave the meat inside the shell. Slice down the middle of the meat so that you can spread open the colored part. This may have already happened when you cut the top of the shell open.

3. Brush the lobster meat with melted butter.
4. Combine the salt, paprika, peppers, and allspice in a small bowl. Sprinkle a dash of this spice combination on the top of each lobster.
5. Bake in the oven on a broiling pan for 15 minutes.
6. Turn the oven to broil and broil for an additional 6 to 8 minutes or until the meat or shell just begins to turn a light brown on top. Be careful not to burn the lobster meat. Remove from the broiler and serve with melted butter and a lemon wedge.

TIDBITS

If you like, you can take the Maine lobster meat out of the shell as explained in the method for the rock lobster. That's not the way Red Lobster does it, but, hey, you're not eating at Red Lobster.

- SERVES 2 AS AN ENTREE.

• • • •

TOP SECRET RECIPES VERSION OF

RED LOBSTER SCALLOPS AND BACON

☆ ✌ 💣 ✎ ☯ ✂ ☞

At the time I was researching this book there were two ways you could have your bacon and scallops at Red Lobster: wrapped and broiled, or grilled on a skewer. The former is a smaller portion to be served as an appetizer, while the skewers may be served as a main entree or part of one. I've included recipes to clone both versions.

BROILED BACON-WRAPPED SCALLOPS

4 medium sea scallops
2 slices bacon
Melted butter
Salt
Paprika
Ground pepper
1 tablespoon warm bottled clam juice
4 toothpicks

1. Preheat the broiler to high.
2. Boil 2 to 3 cups of water in a small pan over high heat. Salt the water.
3. Boil the scallops in the water for 3 to 4 minutes, or until they firm up. Drain the scallops when they're done.
4. Cook the bacon slices for a couple minutes per side. Don't cook until crispy or you won't be able to fold the bacon around the scallops.
5. When the scallops are cool enough to touch, cut or tear a piece of partially cooked bacon in half and wrap one half over the top of the scallop so that it meets itself underneath. Put a

toothpick through the bacon to stick it in place. If you have a problem wrapping your bacon (story of my life) because it is too crispy, dip the bacon into hot or boiling water to make it more flexible. Repeat this with the remaining scallops.

6. Put the scallops on their side in an oven-safe dish and brush with melted butter.
7. Lightly season the scallops with salt, paprika, and a dash of ground pepper.
8. Broil the scallops for 5 to 6 minutes, or just until the edges begin to brown.
9. Remove the scallops from the oven and add warm clam juice to the bottom of the baking dish. Serve in the same dish.

- SERVES 2 AS AN APPETIZER.

• • • •

TOP SECRET RECIPES VERSION OF

RED LOBSTER GRILLED SCALLOP AND BACON SKEWERS

☆ ✌ 💣 ✎ ☯ ✂ ☞

1 teaspoon salt
16 sea scallops
4 round zucchini slices, 1/2 inch thick
2 slices bacon, cooked soft
1 tablespoon melted butter
4 8-inch skewers

ON THE SIDE
Brown rice

1. Preheat the barbecue grill to medium/high heat.
2. In a large saucepan, heat 3 to 4 cups of water until boiling. Add a teaspoon or so of salt to the water.
3. Boil the scallops for 4 minutes or until they firm up.
4. Remove the scallops from the water and drain.
5. When the scallops have cooled enough to handle, begin building your 4 skewers.
6. Cut a zucchini slice in half and pierce it, round edge first, onto the skewer.
7. Slide the zucchini to the end until there's about 1 inch left on the end of the skewer.
8. Slide one scallop on next, piercing through the rounded edges.
9. Break the bacon into quarters and slide one piece of bacon on next.
10. Add two more scallops, one more piece of bacon, another scallop, and the other half of the zucchini slice (this one goes cut side first).

11. Make three more skewers exactly the same way.
12. Generously brush the skewers with melted butter.
13. Lightly season with salt, paprika, and a dash of black pepper.
14. Grill the skewers for 4 to 5 minutes per side or until the zucchini has softened. Serve the skewers over a bed of brown rice.

TIDBITS

For a healthier alternative, try turkey bacon with either of these recipes as a substitute for the pork bacon.

- SERVES 2 AS AN ENTREE.

• • • •

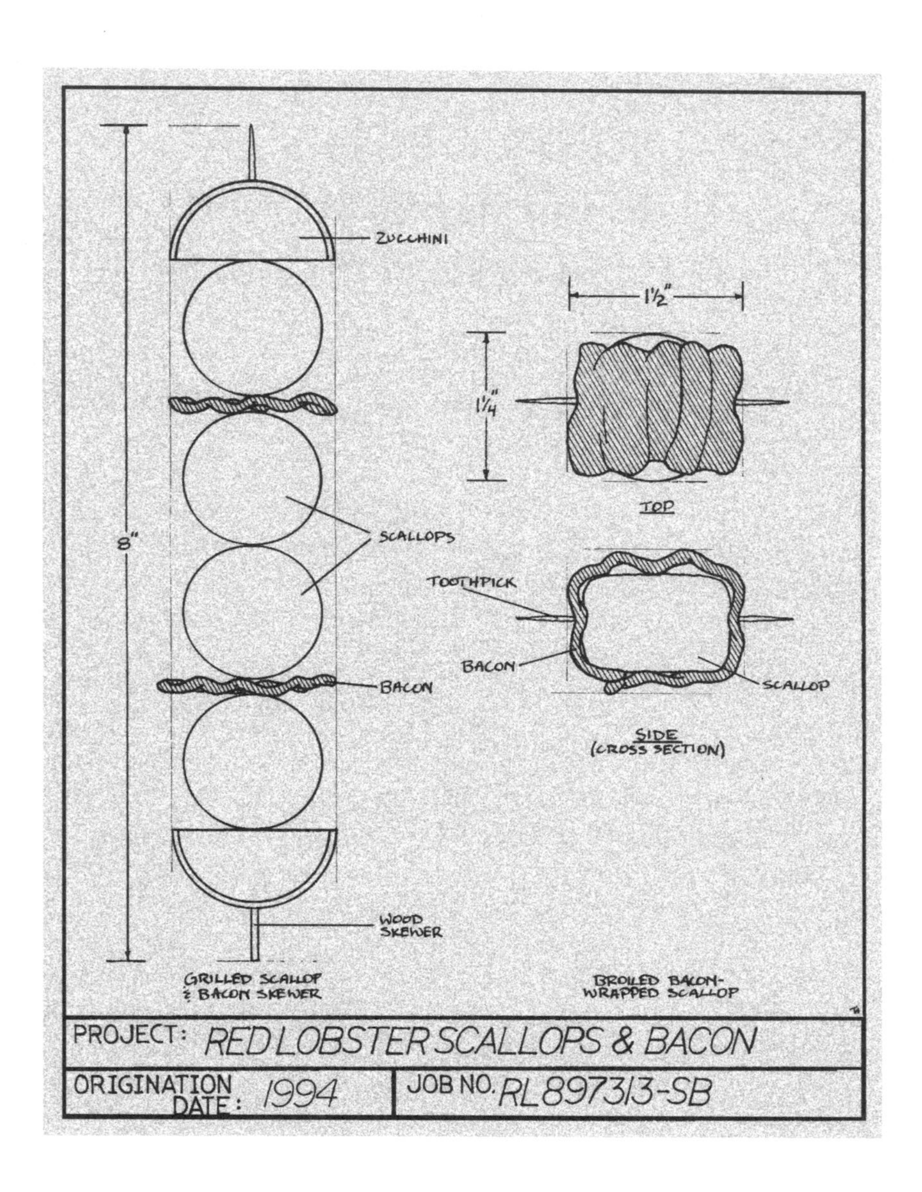
ZUCCHINI
1½"
1¼"
8"
TOP
SCALLOPS
TOOTHPICK
BACON
BACON
SCALLOP
SIDE
(CROSS SECTION)
WOOD
SKEWER
GRILLED SCALLOP
& BACON SKEWER
BROILED BACON-
WRAPPED SCALLOP
PROJECT: RED LOBSTER SCALLOPS & BACON
ORIGINATION DATE: 1994
JOB NO. RL 897313-SB

TOP SECRET RECIPES VERSION OF

RED LOBSTER STUFFED SHRIMP AND STUFFED MUSHROOMS

Bill Darden was only 19 when he started his restaurant career in 1939 by opening a 25-seat lunch counter called The Green Frog in Waycross, Georgia. From the start Bill's business was a hopping success. That success helped Bill to springboard into other restaurant acquisitions throughout the years including 20 Howard Johnson's restaurants. Then, in 1968, as he reached his mid-fifties, Bill took another gamble and opened a seafood restaurant in Lakeland, Florida. When deciding on a name for the new restaurant, someone suggested that since he had great luck with the name "Green Frog" in the past, why not name this one "Red Lobster." And so it was.

Here are a couple of great dishes to serve as appetizers or on the side with an entree such as broiled lobster or fish. These recipes include a stuffing that varies in the restaurants only in the type of seafood used—the stuffed shrimp contains crabmeat and the stuffed mushrooms contain lobster meat. If you like, you can use the stuffings interchangeably in the mushrooms caps and shrimp.

- SERVES 4 TO 6 AS AN APPETIZER.

STUFFED SHRIMP

1/2 cup water
3 tablespoons butter
1 tablespoon minced celery
1 tablespoon minced onion
1 tablespoon finely chopped red chili pepper
1 tablespoon finely chopped green chili pepper
1/4 teaspoon dried parsley
1/2 teaspoon salt
dash pepper
1/2 tablespoon sugar
3/4 cup cornbread crumbs (Pepperidge Farm cornbread stuffing mix is good)
1 cup lump crab meat (fresh, frozen, or one 6-ounce can)
1 egg, beaten
20 large shrimp
1/4 to 1/2 pound Cheddar cheese, thinly sliced
Paprika

1. Preheat the oven to 375°F.
2. Boil the water and 2 tablespoons butter in a medium saucepan.
3. Add the celery, onion, peppers, parsley, salt, pepper, and sugar.
4. Reduce the heat to low and let it simmer for 5 minutes.
5. Add the bread crumbs and remove from the heat.
6. Mix the crab meat with the beaten egg. Add to the bread-crumb mixture, cover, and let it sit for 5 minutes.
7. In the meantime, prepare each shrimp by cutting along the back to remove the vein and removing all of the shell except the last joint and the tip of the tail. Cut deep into the shrimp where the vein was, but not all of the way through, and spread the meat open (butterfly slice) so that each shrimp will sit in a roasting pan, cut side up, with its tail sticking up. Repeat for all of the shrimp and arrange in a baking dish.
8. Scoop about 1 tablespoon of stuffing onto the top of the spread-out portion of each shrimp.
9. Melt the remaining tablespoon of butter and brush it over the surface of each stuffed shrimp. Scoot all the shrimp close together after you do this.

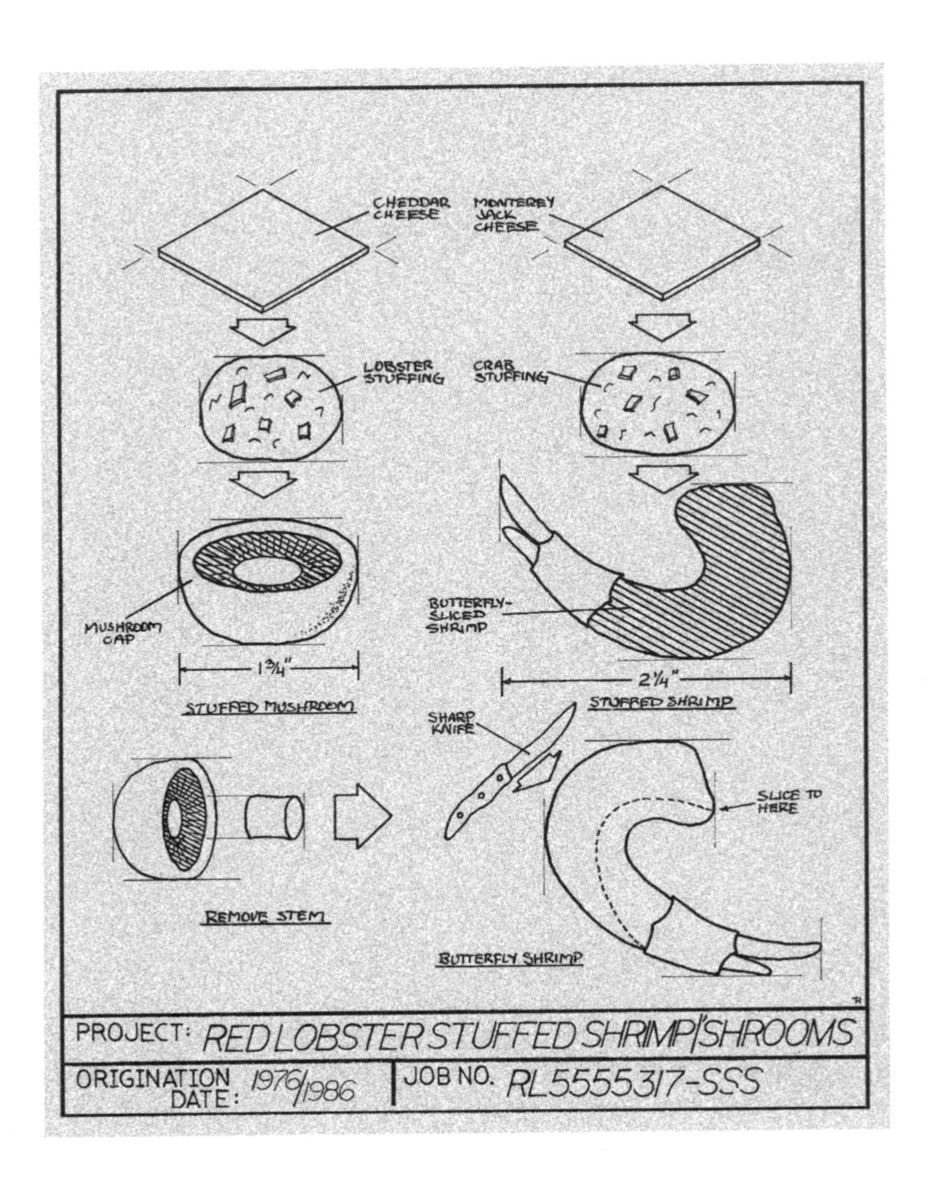
CHEDDAR CHEESE
MONTEREY JACK CHEESE
LOBSTER STUFFING
CRAB STUFFING
MUSHROOM CAP
1¾"
STUFFED MUSHROOM
BUTTERFLY-SLICED SHRIMP
2¼"
STUFFED SHRIMP
SHARP KNIFE
SLICE TO HERE
REMOVE STEM
BUTTERFLY SHRIMP
PROJECT: RED LOBSTER STUFFED SHRIMP/SHROOMS
ORIGINATION DATE: 1976/1986
JOB NO. RL5555317-SSS

10. Spread thin slices of cheddar cheese evenly over the entire surface of all of the shrimp. Sprinkle on a dash of paprika.
11. Bake the shrimp for 15 to 20 minutes or until the shrimp are completely cooked. Broil for an additional 1 to 2 minutes to brown the cheese just slightly.

STUFFED MUSHROOMS

1. Follow the above directions for the stuffing, but substitute 1 cup cooked lobster meat for the crab meat. If you broil the tail from a live lobster for another recipe, such as the one on page 229, you can use the meat from the legs and claws for this recipe. Simply cook the remaining lobster in the shell for 15 to 20 minutes in rapidly boiling salted water. Use a nut cracker to remove the meat. You may also use canned lobster meat for this recipe, although fresh lobster meat tastes much better.
2. Instead of shrimp, use 20 to 24 (about 1 pound) mushrooms with stems removed.
3. Fill the mushroom caps with 2 to 3 teaspoons of stuffing, brush with melted butter, and top with slices of Monterey Jack cheese rather than Cheddar.
4. Season lightly with paprika, then bake the mushrooms in a roasting pan or baking dish in a preheated oven set on 375 degrees F for about 12 minutes, or until the cheese is melted. Broil for 1 to 2 minutes to slightly brown the cheese.

• • • •

RED ROBIN NO-FIRE PEPPERS

MENU DESCRIPTION: *"Full-flavored jalapeños stuffed with cool cream cheese and deep-fried in a cracker-crumb coating. Served with sweet jalapeño jelly & sour cream."*

Red Robin was one of the first restaurant chains to serve No-Fire Peppers, an item which can be found on many restaurant menus today under a variety of different names. The cream cheese–filled, battered and fried jalapeño peppers are actually called Poppers by their creators, Anchor Foods, a restaurant food supply company which manufactures Poppers and a variety of other appetizers for sale to restaurant chains everywhere. According to *a* magazine, Poppers were the #1 food item added to restaurant menus in 1995, with restaurants purchasing over 700 million of the little suckers.

It's important when you make these that you allow time for them to freeze. The freezing stage ensures that the coating stays on when the peppers are fried and prevents the cream cheese from squirting out as it heats up.

4 large, fresh jalapeño peppers
1/4 pound cream cheese
2 eggs
3/4 teaspoon salt
1 teaspoon vegetable oil
2/3 cup self-rising flour
1/8 teaspoon garlic powder
dash paprika
dash onion powder
1/2 cup cornflake crumbs
Vegetable oil for frying

ON THE SIDE
Hot pepper jelly
Sour cream

1. Remove the stems from the jalapeños, then slice each one down the middle lengthwise and remove the seeds and inner membranes. Be careful to wash your hands afterward.
2. Poach the jalapeño halves in a saucepan half-filled with boiling water for 10 to 15 minutes or until tender. Drain and cool.
3. Blot with a cloth or paper towel to dry the inside of each jalapeño slice, then use a teaspoon to spread about ½ ounce of cream cheese into each jalapeño half.

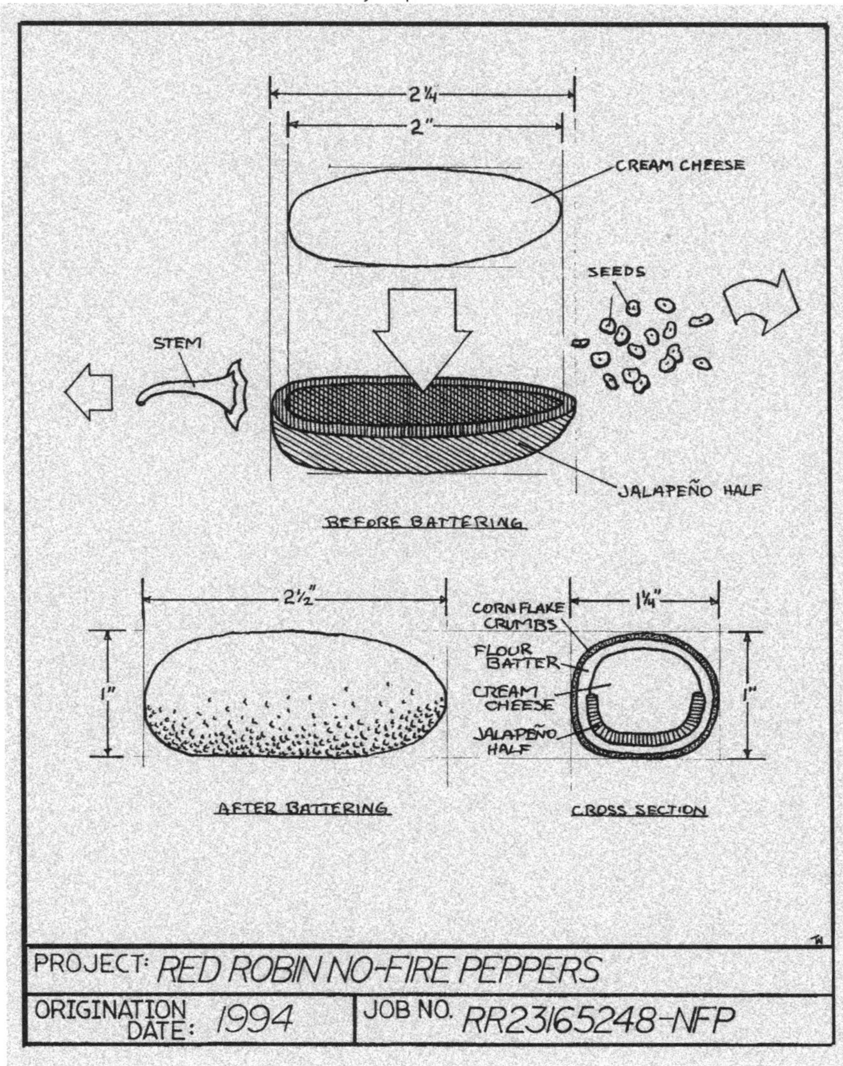

4. Beat the eggs in a small, shallow bowl, then add ¼ teaspoon salt and the oil and combine with a whisk.
5. In another shallow bowl, combine the flour, ½ teaspoon salt, garlic powder, paprika, and onion powder.
6. Add the cornflake crumbs to a third shallow bowl.
7. Working one at a time, dip each stuffed jalapeño into the egg mixture, then into the flour mixture. Repeat, by again dipping the jalapeño into the egg and then back into the flour. Finally, dip the jalapeño back into the egg, then into the cornflake crumbs.
8. Put the coated peppers side by side on a plate and into the freezer for at least 2 hours. This way when the peppers are fried, the breading won't fall off and the cheese in the center won't ooze out.
9. When the peppers are frozen, heat vegetable oil in a deep fryer or deep saucepan to about 350°F. Use enough oil to cover the jalapeños when frying. Fry the peppers for 3½ to 4 minutes or until the outside is a dark golden brown. Drain on a rack or paper towels. Serve hot with pepper jelly and sour cream on the side.

TIDBITS

You can also make these ahead of time by frying them for only 1½ minutes and then refreezing them until you are ready to serve them. Then cook the frozen jalapeños in hot oil for 3½ minutes or until they are hot all the way through. You may also bake the frozen jalapeños in a 450 degrees F oven on a greased baking pan for 10 to 15 minutes, turning them over halfway through the heating time.

- SERVES 2 TO 4 AS AN APPETIZER.

• • • •

TOP SECRET RECIPES VERSION OF

RED ROBIN BBQ CHICKEN SALAD

☆ ✌ 💣 ✎ ☯ ✂ ☞

MENU DESCRIPTION: *"Breast of chicken basted with BBQ sauce & topped with cheddar cheese, tomato, fresh avocado, and black beans. Served with Ranch dressing & garlic cheese bread."*

In 1969, Gerald Kingen bought a beat-up 30-year-old bar called Red Robin in Seattle across the road from the University of Washington. The pub did a booming business with the college and local crowd, but in 1973 building officials gave their opinion of the bar: Either fix it up or shut it down. Jerry not only fixed up the 1200-square-foot building, but also expanded it to three times its old size, to 3600 square feet, and added a kitchen to start making food. Red Robin soon became popular for its wide selection of gourmet burgers in addition to the designer cocktails served in kooky glasses. Jerry says he set out to create a chain of restaurants that would be recognized as "the adult McDonald's and poor man's Trader Vic's."

2 cups chopped romaine lettuce
2 cups chopped green leaf or iceberg lettuce
1/2 cup chopped red cabbage
1 small tomato, chopped (1/4 cup)
1 boneless, skinless chicken breast half
1/3 cup barbecue sauce (Bullseye or K.C. Masterpiece work well)
1/2 cup canned refried black beans
1/2 cup shredded Cheddar cheese
1/4 cup French's French Fried Onions (onion straws)
3 avocado slices (1/4 avocado)
1/4 cup ranch dressing

1. Toss the lettuces and cabbage together and arrange on a large plate.
2. Arrange the tomato on the lettuce mixture at the bottom of the plate.
3. Grill the chicken breast on a hot barbecue grill for 4 to 5 minutes per side or until done. Brush a generous coating of barbecue sauce over the chicken as it grills.

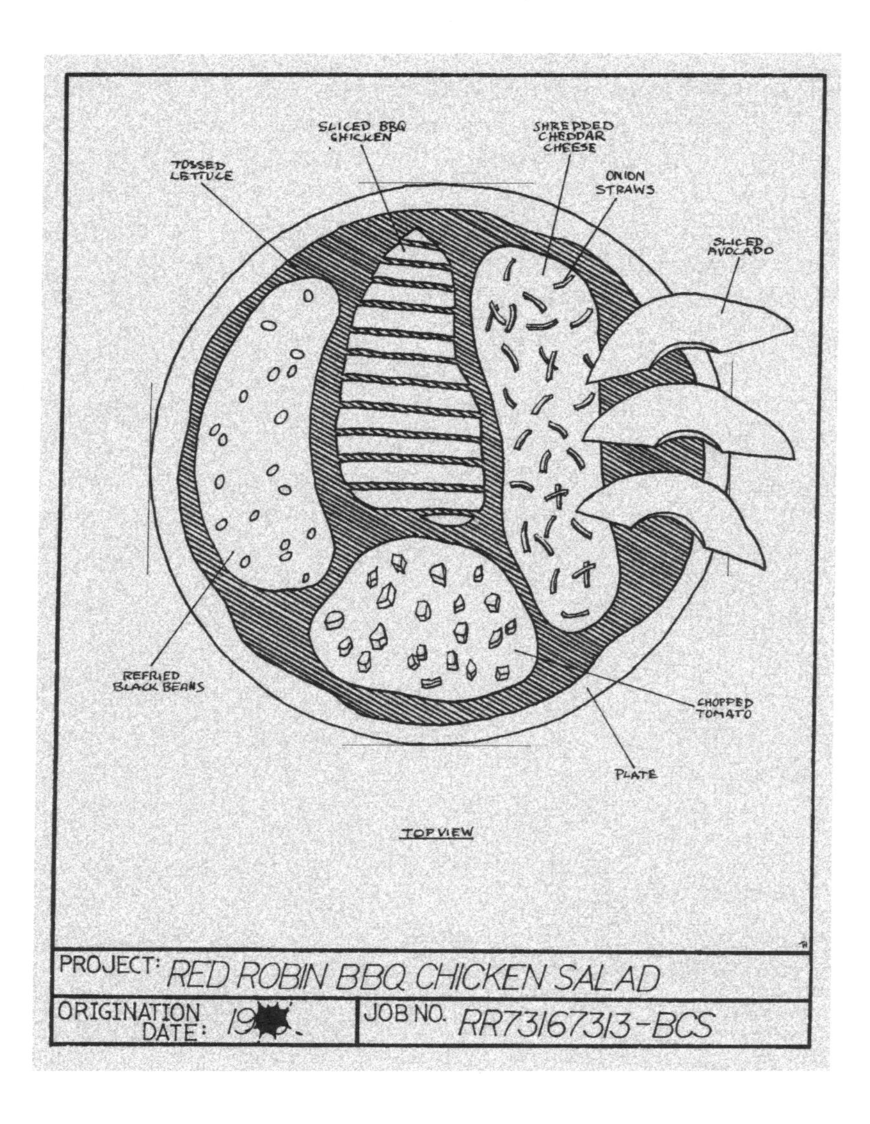

4. Heat the black beans in the microwave or in a saucepan over medium heat.
5. Spread the black beans over the lettuce on the left side of the plate.
6. Slice the warm chicken into bite-size pieces and arrange them neatly over the lettuce in the center of the plate.
7. Sprinkle the cheese over the lettuce on the right side of the plate.
8. Sprinkle the onion straws over the cheese.
9. Garnish the salad with 3 slices of avocado arranged side by side on the right rim of the plate. Serve with the ranch dressing and the remaining barbecue sauce on the side.

- SERVES 1 AS AN ENTREE (CAN BE DOUBLED).

TIDBITS

You can also make the onion straws yourself by following this simple recipe:

ONION STRAWS

2 cups vegetable oil
1/4 cup very thinly sliced white onion
1/2 cup all-purpose flour
1/2 teaspoon baking soda
1/4 teaspoon salt
2/3 cup cold water

1. Heat the oil in a wide saucepan to about 350°F.
2. Slice the onion into very thin onion rings and then cut the rings in half, making long strips or straws. Try to slice the onion as thin as possible.
3. Combine the flour, baking soda, and salt in a large bowl. Add the cold water and whisk until the batter is smooth.
4. When the oil is hot, drop the onions into the batter. Remove the onions one at a time, let them drip off a bit, and then place them into the hot oil. You will want to cook these for about 2 minutes apiece, or until you see them turn a golden brown. Drain the onion straws on a paper towel.

TOP SECRET RECIPES VERSION OF

RED ROBIN MOUNTAIN HIGH MUDD PIE

☆ ✌ 💣 ✎ ☯ ✂ ☞

Gerald Kingen is a man with a mission. In 1985 he sold his successful Red Robin chain of restaurants to Tokyo-based Skylark Co. Ltd. Unhappy with the changes the new owners were implementing, Jerry and a partner purchased a "substantial equity position" of the Irvine, California–based Red Robin in March of 1996. Now Jerry is once again at the helm of the company, with a goal of reviving old menu items and living up to the old slogan as "the world's greatest gourmet burger maker & most masterful mixologists."

A unique signature dessert item is the Mountain High Mudd Pie, which servers claim is one of the most ordered desserts on the menu. Save some room for this giant-size sundae made from chocolate and vanilla ice cream with peanut butter, caramel, and fudge sauce. There are several stages of freezing, so give yourself at least seven hours to allow for these steps. This dessert is big and serves at least a dozen, so it's good for a small party or gathering, or makes a unique birthday cake. If there's only a few of you, leftovers can be frozen in a sealed container for several weeks and enjoyed later.

6 cups chocolate ice cream
1 cup peanut butter cookie pieces
6 cups vanilla ice cream
1⅔ cups creamy peanut butter
4 chocolate-flavored graham crackers
1 cup fudge topping
1 20-ounce squirt bottle chocolate topping
1 20-ounce squirt bottle caramel topping
1 can whipped cream
¾ cup chopped peanuts
12 maraschino cherries, with stems

1. Soften the chocolate ice cream and load it into the bottom of a 2½- to 3-quart mixing bowl. Make sure the surface of the ice cream is smooth and leveled.
2. Spread the peanut butter cookie pieces evenly over the top of the ice cream, then cover the bowl and put it back into the freezer for at least 1 hour. (If you can't find packaged peanut butter cookies, use the recipe in "Tidbits.")
3. Soften the vanilla ice cream and spread it over the chocolate ice cream and cookie pieces. Again, be sure to smooth and level the surface of the ice cream. Cover the bowl with plastic wrap and put it back into the freezer for at least 1 hour.
4. Use a spatula to spread ⅔ cup of peanut butter over the surface of the ice cream. Be sure the ice cream has hardened before you do this or it could get sloppy.
5. Crush the chocolate graham crackers into crumbs and spread them evenly over the peanut butter. Put the bowl back into the freezer for at least 1 hour.
6. Remove the bowl from the freezer and hold it in a sink filled with warm water for about 1 minute. You want the ice cream around the edges to soften just enough that you can invert the ice cream onto a plate.
7. Turn a large plate upside down and place it on top of the bowl. Flip the bowl and plate over together, and tap gently on the bowl until the ice cream falls out onto the plate. You may have to put the bowl back into the water if it's stubborn. Once the ice cream is out, cover it with plastic wrap and place it back in the freezer for another 1 or 2 hours.
8. Without heating it up, spread the fudge evenly over the entire surface of the ice cream mountain. Put the fudge-coated ice cream back into the freezer for 1 hour.
9. When the fudge has hardened, spread the remaining 1 cup of peanut butter over the entire surface as well. Once again, back into the freezer for at least 1 hour. We're almost there.
10. Slice the ice cream with a warm knife into 12 pieces. Put wax paper between the cuts so that when you serve it later, it is easy to divide. Then slip it back into the freezer, covered.
11. When serving, first coat a plate with a criss-cross pattern of chocolate and caramel sauce. Make three parallel lines down the

plate with the squirt bottle of chocolate sauce. Then three parallel horizontal lines made with the bottle of caramel sauce.

12. Place the slice of ice cream upright onto the plate toward the back of the design.

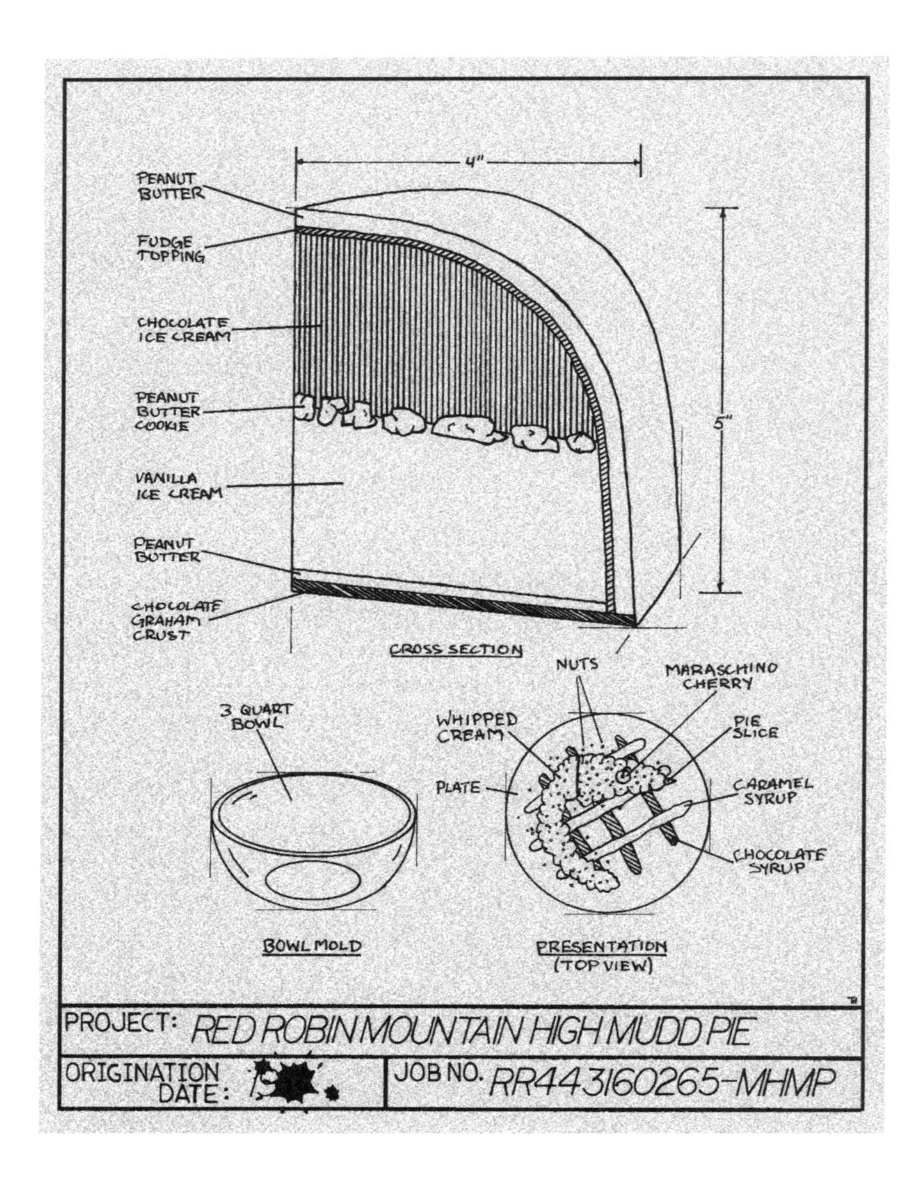

13. Spray whipped cream on top and down the curved edge of the ice cream slice, onto the plate over the sauces. Be generous.
14. Sprinkle about a tablespoon of chopped nuts over your creation.
15. Add a cherry to the top. Marvel at the beauty, then dig in or serve it before it melts. Repeat for the remaining slices.

• SERVES 12.

TIDBITS

If you would like to make your own peanut butter cookies, rather than buying them pre-made, here is a recipe that makes about 2 dozen tasty cookies—more than enough for the ice cream dessert.

PEANUT BUTTER COOKIES

1/2 cup butter, softened
1/2 cup granulated sugar
1/2 cup firmly packed brown sugar
1/2 cup creamy peanut butter
1 egg
1 1/4 teaspoons vanilla extract
1 1/2 cups all-purpose flour
1 teaspoon baking soda
1/2 teaspoon salt

1. Preheat the oven to 325°F.
2. Use an electric mixer to combine the butter with the sugars in a large bowl until creamy.
3. Add the peanut butter, egg, and vanilla and mix until smooth.
4. Sift together the flour, baking soda, and salt, and combine with the moist ingredients in the large bowl. Mix the dough until all of the ingredients are smooth and well blended.
5. Drop rounded tablespoons of the dough onto an ungreased cookie sheet. Press the dough flat with a fork and bake for 15 to 18 minutes, until the edges of the cookies begin to turn light brown.

• • • •

TOP SECRET RECIPES VERSION OF

RUBY TUESDAY POTATO CHEESE SOUP

Sandy Beall started managing Pizza Huts while a freshman at the University of Tennessee, to get out of fraternity house duties. It was just three years later that Sandy's boss at Pizza Hut would favor him with quite a nice gift: $10,000 to invest in a dream. With that, Sandy and four of his fraternity buddies pitched in to open the first Ruby Tuesday on the university campus in Knoxville, Tennessee, in 1972. Sandy was only 21 at the time.

Here's a great soup that can be served by the cup or in large bowls as a meal in itself. Along with the potatoes is a little bit of minced celery, some minced onion, and a small amount of grated carrot for color. An additional pinch of cheese, crumbled bacon, and chopped green onion make a tasty garnish just like on the Ruby Tuesday original.

2 large russet potatoes
2 tablespoons finely minced celery (1/2 stalk)
1 tablespoon finely minced onion
1 tablespoon grated carrot (1/4 carrot)
2 cups chicken stock or broth
1 teaspoon salt
2 teaspoons white vinegar
2 tablespoons flour
1 1/2 cups milk
1 cup plus 1 tablespoon shredded Cheddar cheese
1 tablespoon shredded Monterey Jack cheese
2 slices bacon, cooked
1 tablespoon chopped green onion

1. Peel the potatoes and chop them into bite-size pieces—you should have about 4 cups. Make sure the celery and onion are minced into very small pieces about the size of a grain of rice. The carrot should be grated into very small pieces, not shredded.
2. Combine the vegetables with the chicken stock, salt, and vinegar in a large saucepan over medium heat. Bring the stock to a boil, then turn down the heat, cover the pan, and simmer for 20 minutes.
3. Whisk together the flour and milk in a medium bowl.
4. Remove the saucepan of vegetables from the heat and add the flour and milk mixture. Put the pan back on the heat and simmer, uncovered, for 5 to 8 minutes or until the soup has thickened.
5. Add 1 cup Cheddar cheese to the soup and simmer until melted. By this time the potatoes should be tender and falling apart. If not, continue to cook until the soup is as thick as you like it.
6. To serve, spoon the soup into bowls. Divide the remaining 1 tablespoon of Cheddar and the Monterey Jack and sprinkle on the soup. Crumble the bacon and sprinkle it evenly on top of the cheese. Top off each bowl of soup with chopped green onion.

- SERVES 4 AS AN APPETIZER, 2 AS AN ENTREE.

• • • •

TOP SECRET RECIPES VERSION OF

RUBY TUESDAY SMOKEY MOUNTAIN CHICKEN

MENU DESCRIPTION: *"Chicken breast topped with ham, barbecue sauce, tomatoes, scallions and cheese. Served with fries."*

When the founder of Ruby Tuesday, Sandy Beall, was reviewing some early designs of printed materials for his planned restaurant, he saw that some of the art featured the faces of University of Tennessee students printed in red. At that moment Sandy knew he wanted to call the eatery "ruby something." Meanwhile, he and the four fraternity friends who joined him in the investment had been listening to lots of Rolling Stones music. One day when Sandy heard "Ruby Tuesday" come on the jukebox, he convinced his partners that they had finally found a name.

You may find a little something unusual in the name for this dish. Ruby Tuesday's menu became a victim of a common spelling error in the word "smoky." Apparently the dish is named after the Great Smoky Mountains that lie between North Carolina and Tennessee, but there's no "e" in that name or in the general spelling of the word "smoky." But, hey, what do you want: good spelling or good taste? And this dish, which combines chicken breast, ham and barbecue sauce, topped with tomatoes, scallions and cheese, tastes great no matter how you spell it. Thanks, Rubey Tuesday.

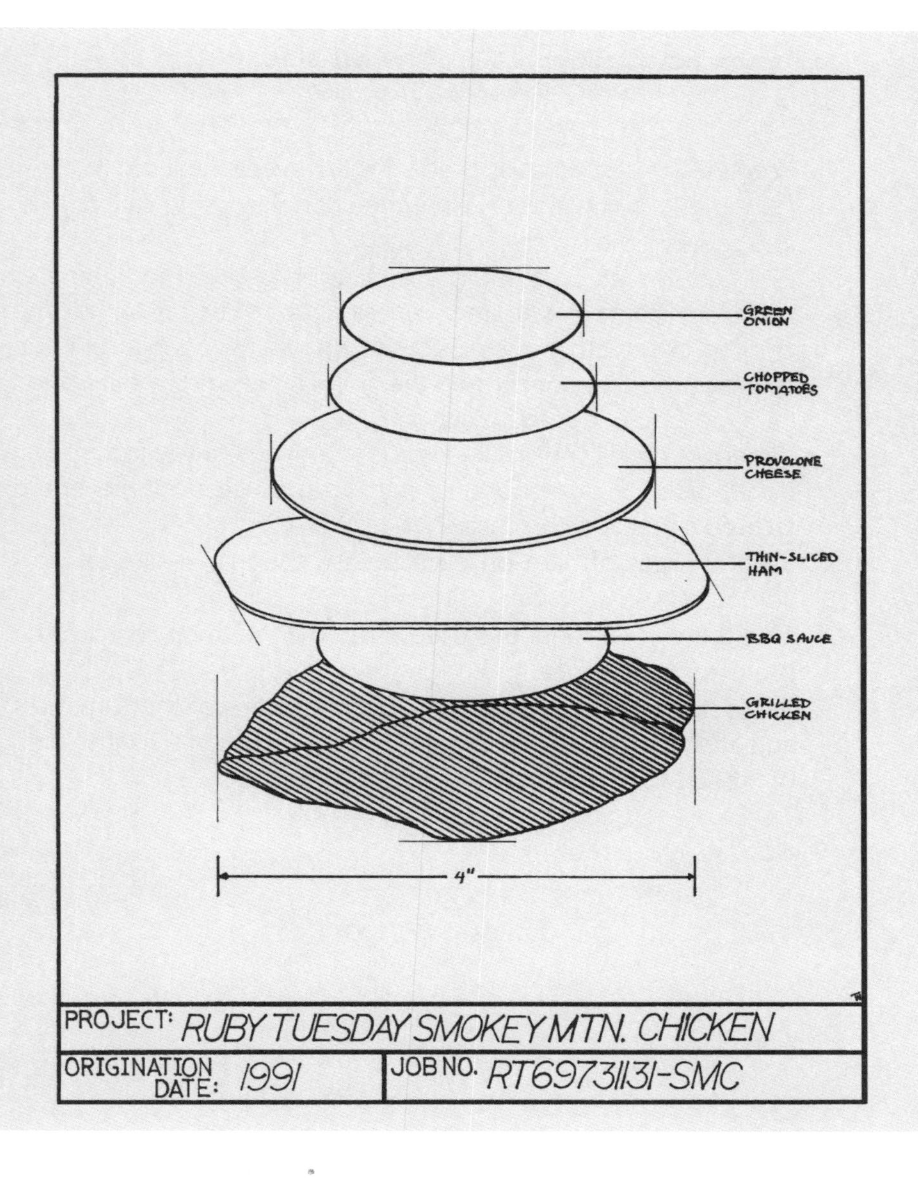
GREEN ONION
CHOPPED TOMATOES
PROVOLONE CHEESE
THIN-SLICED HAM
BBQ SAUCE
GRILLED CHICKEN
4"
PROJECT: RUBY TUESDAY SMOKEY MTN. CHICKEN
ORIGINATION DATE: 1991
JOB NO. RT6973II3I-SMC

2 whole boneless chicken breasts (with skin)
Vegetable or olive oil
Salt
Pinch dried thyme
Pinch dried summer savory
4 slices deli-sliced smoked ham
2 tablespoons hickory smoke barbecue sauce (Bullseye is good)
2 slices provolone cheese
½ medium tomato, chopped (¼ cup)
1 green onion, chopped (2 tablespoons)

ON THE SIDE

French fries
Rice

1. Prepare the barbecue or preheat the stovetop grill.
2. Rub a little oil on the chicken, then sprinkle some salt, thyme, and savory on each chicken breast.
3. Grill the chicken on a hot, covered barbecue for 4 to 5 minutes per side, starting with the skin side up. When you flip the chicken over with the skin side down, wait a couple minutes, then put the slices of ham on the grill. This is just to heat up the ham; be careful not to scorch it.
4. When you think the chicken is about a minute away from being done, brush 1 tablespoon of barbecue sauce over the entire face-up surface of the chicken.
5. Stack 2 slices of ham on each breast, then lay a slice of provolone on top.
6. Grill the chicken until the cheese has melted, then remove the breasts from the heat.
7. Serve each breast topped with 2 tablespoons of the tomatoes and a tablespoon of green onion. Serve immediately with a side of French-fried potatoes or rice if desired.

- SERVES 2 AS AN ENTREE.

• • • •

TOP SECRET RECIPES VERSION OF

SIZZLER CHEESE TOAST

In Los Angeles in 1957, Del Johnson noticed an article in the *Wall Street Journal* about a successful $1.09 per steak steakhouse chain with locations in New York, Chicago, and San Francisco. Inspired by the article, Del decided to open his own steakhouse in L.A., but with a twist that would save him money. His idea was to develop a steakhouse where customers would order their food at a food counter and pick it up when it was ready. Doesn't sound that exciting, but the concept was a hit. After the first Sizzler was open for a year, Del decided to run a two-day, one-cent anniversary sale: buy one steak at the regular price and get a second for just a penny. Del said, "We opened at 11:00. People were lined up from 11:00 until 9:00 at night, and we sold 1050 steaks in one day and about 1200 the second day."

With every meal, Sizzler serves a slice of tasty cheese toast. It's a simple recipe that goes well with just about any entree.

4 tablespoons butter
4 slices thick-sliced French bread
4 teaspoons Kraft grated Parmesan cheese

1. Melt the butter in a small saucepan or in the microwave.
2. Use a brush to spread the butter evenly over one face of each slice of bread.
3. Sprinkle the Parmesan cheese over the butter.
4. Grill the bread, buttered side down, on a frying pan or griddle over medium/low heat for 5 minutes or until golden brown. Grill only the buttered side.

- SERVES 2 TO 4.

TOP SECRET RECIPES VERSION OF

SIZZLER CHICKEN CLUB SANDWICH

When Del Johnson and his wife were trying to think of a name for their new restaurant concept they were looking for the perfect single-word name. "Something that would merchandise well," said Del. "In the old days, they served steaks on those sizzling platters. In a first class restaurant when you ordered a steak, they'd bring it out, put the butter on that steak and that plate was hot, it was aluminum and it would sizzle when they put it down in front of you. That's how we came up with the name. I knew we wanted to use those sizzling platters."

Eventually the restaurant would diversify the menu to include items other than the sizzling steak. One of those on the menu today is the chicken club sandwich, which you can now easily duplicate at home.

1 boneless, skinless chicken breast half
Vegetable oil
Salt
1 hamburger bun
1/4 cup chopped lettuce
1 slice Swiss cheese
2 slices bacon, cooked
1 small slice onion, separated
2 slices tomato
1/2 tablespoon Thousand Island dressing

1. Prepare the barbecue or preheat the stovetop grill or broiler.
2. Lightly brush the chicken breast with oil, and grill it over medium heat for 5 minutes per side or until done. Salt the chicken.
3. Brown the faces of the bun top and bottom on the grill or in a skillet over medium heat.
4. Stack the sandwich in the following order from the bottom up:

a. bottom bun   b. lettuce   c. chicken breast
d. Swiss cheese   e. bacon slices, crisscrossed   f. onion
g. tomato slices

5. Spread the Thousand Island dressing on the face of the top bun, and top off your sandwich with it.

- SERVES 1 AS AN ENTREE (CAN BE DOUBLED).

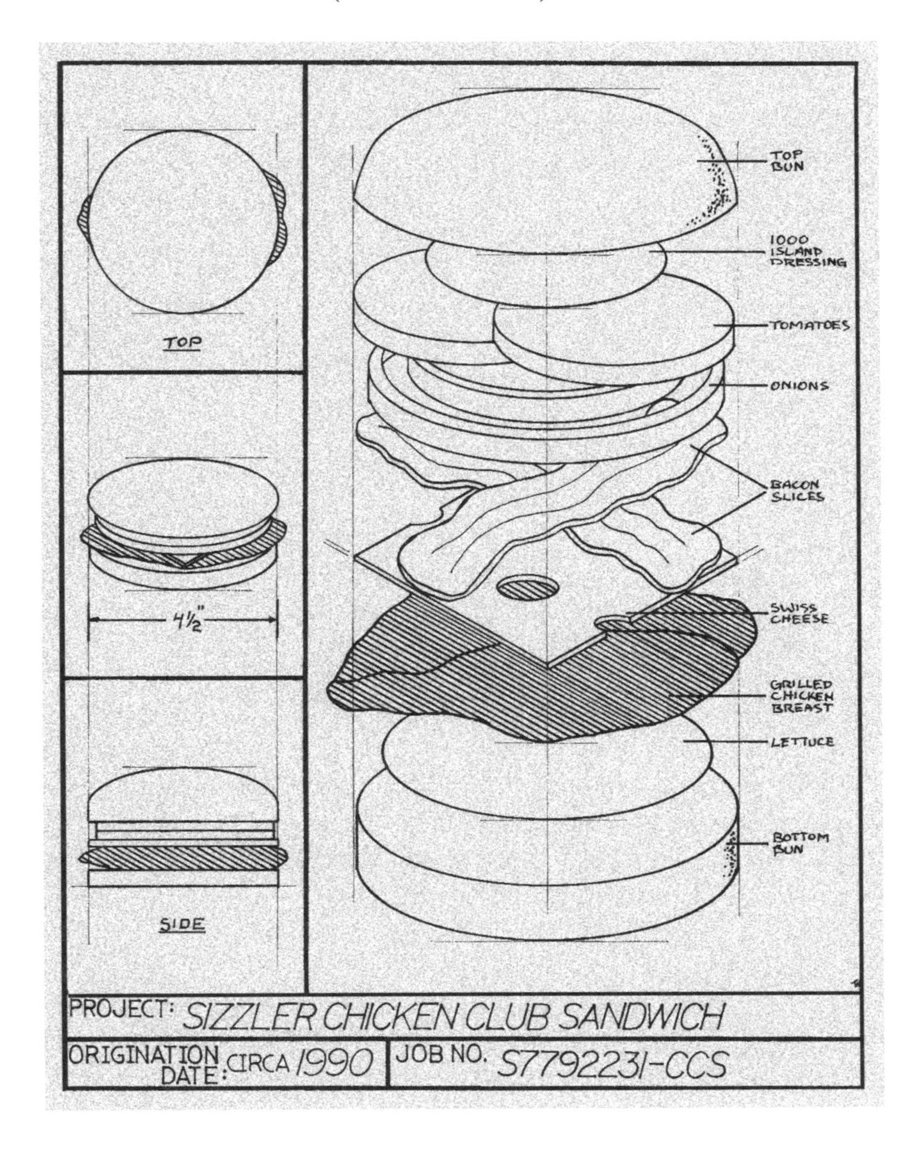

TOP SECRET RECIPES VERSION OF

SIZZLER SOUTHERN FRIED SHRIMP

☆ ✌ 💣 ✏ ☯ ✂ ☞

One of the most popular items on the Sizzler menu is the fried shrimp, which is often offered as a belly-stuffing, all-you-can-eat deal.

12 medium shrimp (1/3 pound)
1 cup plain bread crumbs
1 1/2 teaspoons salt
1/2 teaspoon dried basil, crushed fine
1/2 teaspoon dried parsley, crushed fine
1/8 teaspoon garlic powder
1/8 teaspoon onion powder
1 egg, beaten
1/2 cup milk
1 cup all-purpose flour
Vegetable oil for frying

ON THE SIDE *Lemon wedge* *Cocktail sauce*

1. Prepare the shrimp by removing all of the shell except the last section and the tailfins. Butterfly the shrimp by cutting most of the way through along the back of the shrimp on the side with the dark vein. Remove the vein and rinse each shrimp.
2. Combine the bread crumbs, salt, basil, parsley, garlic powder, and onion powder in a small bowl.
3. Combine the beaten egg and milk in another small bowl.
4. Sift the flour into a third small bowl.
5. Heat oil in a deep fryer or large saucepan over medium heat. You want the oil to be around 350°F and it should be deep enough to cover the shrimp.

6. Coat the shrimp one at a time, using one hand for the wet mixture and one hand for the dry stuff. First dip the shrimp into the egg and milk mixture, then drop it into the flour. Coat the shrimp with the flour with the dry hand and then drop it back into the milk mixture. When it's completely moistened drop it into the bread crumbs and coat it again. Set each shrimp on a plate until all of them are coated.
7. Drop the shrimp into the hot oil and cook for 3 to 4 minutes or until the outside is golden. Serve with a wedge of lemon and cocktail sauce for dipping.

TIDBITS

This is also great with cornflake crumbs rather than bread crumbs.

- SERVES 1 AS AN ENTREE, OR 2 AS AN APPETIZER.

• • • •

TOP SECRET RECIPES VERSION OF

RUTH'S CHRIS STEAK HOUSE BARBECUED SHRIMP

In 1965, Ruth Fertel, divorced with two kids in their teens, was looking for a better way to support herself in her native New Orleans. Her job as a lab technician wasn't paying enough for her to send the kids to college, so she went to the classifieds to find something better. There she found a steakhouse for sale, and determined that this might be her ticket. She mortgaged her house to raise $18,000 (against the advice of her attorney) and purchased the restaurant, then called Chris Steak House. Ruth sold 35 steaks on opening day—not much for a restaurant that now sells 10,000 a day. But the restaurant would eventually become a big hit, and within the first year Ruth was making more than twice her salary at the lab.

In keeping with the New Orleans flavor of many of the Ruth's Chris dishes, this barbecued shrimp is actually Cajun-style broiled shrimp with a little kick to it.

5 to 6 large uncooked shrimp
1/4 cup (1/2 stick) butter, melted
1 tablespoon Louisiana hot sauce (Frank's Red Hot or Crystal are good)
2 cloves garlic, pressed
1/4 teaspoon salt
1/2 teaspoon coarsely ground or cracked black pepper
1/2 teaspoon finely chopped fresh parsley
Pinch dried rosemary
Lemon wedges

1. Preheat the oven to 400°F.
2. Shell and devein the shrimp.
3. In a small baking dish, combine the melted butter with the hot sauce, garlic, salt, cracked pepper, parsley, and rosemary. Stir.
4. Arrange the shrimp side by side in the baking dish and bake for 6 to 8 minutes. Immediately broil the shrimp for 2 to 4 minutes or until the shrimp are done, but not chewy. Squeeze some lemon juice over the shrimp. Serve the shrimp sizzling hot in the baking dish.

• SERVES 2 AS AN APPETIZER.

RUTH'S CHRIS STEAK HOUSE PETITE FILET

MENU DESCRIPTION: *"A smaller, but equally tender filet . . . the tenderest corn-fed Mid-western beef. So tender it practically melts in your mouth."*

This is the signature item for the Ruth's Chris chain. It's a delicious filet mignon that comes to your table sizzling hot and does seem to melt in your mouth as the menu claims. If you want to prepare filets the Ruth's Chris way you first need some corn-fed filets, which can be found in specialty meat markets or through mail-order outlets such as Omaha Steaks. If you can't find corn-fed beef, you can still use this cooking method with filet purchased at your supermarket, but the meat will likely not be as tasty and tender.

I've designed this recipe to duplicate the petite filet on the Ruth's Chris menu, since the larger filet is around 14 ounces. That size can be difficult to obtain unless you cut your own. Ruth's Chris uses a special broiler which reaches temperatures as high as 1800 degrees F. It's likely you don't have such an oven, so you will have to use a conventional oven set on high broil, with the rack placed up near the top. You want to be sure the filet is about 5 to 6 inches away from the heat source, and if you have gas, be very careful to watch for flame-ups from spattering. If you begin to get flames, move the rack to a lower level so that you don't start a fire. Also, you need to have ceramic oven-safe plates to serve this meat properly sizzling. This recipe assumes that your broiler is located at the top of the oven. If not, you won't be able to use this technique until you get a new oven. Sorry.

4 8-ounce filet mignon steaks
6 tablespoons butter, softened
Salt
Pepper
2 teaspoons chopped fresh parsley

1. Preheat the broiler.
2. Prepare the filets by drying them with a cloth or paper towel and rubbing ½ tablespoon of butter per steak over the top and bottom. Salt and pepper the filet.
3. Make sure your broiler is on high and that it is good and hot. It should have preheated for *at least* 30 minutes. Put four oven-safe ceramic serving plates on the bottom rack in the oven when you start to preheat the broiler and through the entire cooking time. Move another rack up to the top so that when you put the filets in they will be about 5 to 6 inches from the heat. You will have to check the filets periodically to be sure they haven't flamed up. Cook the meat in a broiler pan, turning halfway through cooking time for the following length of time based on your preference:

COOKING CHART

4 to 6 minutes per side——Rare
5 to 7 minutes per side——Medium Rare
6 to 8 minutes per side——Medium
7 to 9 minutes per side——Medium Well
8 to 11 minutes per side——Well

4. When the meat is done, carefully remove the ceramic plates from the oven. On each of them, place 1 tablespoon of butter. It should sizzle.
5. When the butter has melted, place a steak in the center of the plate.
6. Sprinkle a pinch of the parsley on top of the meat, and another pinch around it onto the butter.
7. Serve the dishes sizzling hot.

TIDBITS

Try cooking other cuts of meat using this same method—delicious! Of course, the broiling time will vary depending on the thickness of your meat.

- Serves 4 as an entree.

TOP SECRET RECIPES VERSION OF

RUTH'S CHRIS STEAK HOUSE POTATOES AU GRATIN

☆ ✌ 💣 ✏ ☯ ✂ ☞

MENU DESCRIPTION: *"In cream sauce, topped with melted sharp cheddar."*

There are many ways to order potatoes from the Ruth's Chris menu including steak fries, julienne fries, shoestring fries, cottage fries, Lyonnaise, baked, and au gratin.

Here is a traditional, classic recipe for the delicious side dish inspired by the Ruth's Chris creation. You may use less of the cream and milk mixture in your version depending on the size baking dish you use and the size of your potatoes. Stop adding the creamy mixture when it is level with the sliced potatoes in the baking dish. Be sure to use a casserole dish that has a lid for the first stage of the baking.

3 to 4 medium russet potatoes, peeled
1 cup heavy cream
1/2 cup milk
1 1/2 tablespoons flour
1 large clove garlic, pressed
1/4 teaspoon salt
1/8 teaspoon pepper
1 tablespoon butter, softened
1 1/2 cups grated Cheddar cheese
1 teaspoon finely chopped fresh parsley

1. Preheat the oven to 400°F.
2. Cut the potatoes into 1/4-inch slices, then quarter each of those slices.
3. Beat together the cream, milk, flour, garlic, salt, and pepper by hand just until well combined.

4. Coat the inside of a large baking dish with the softened butter.
5. Arrange one-fourth of the potatoes on the bottom of the dish. Pour some of the cream mixture over the potatoes. Repeat this layering step three more times.
6. Cover the potatoes and bake for 20 minutes. Uncover, and bake another 40 minutes or until the potatoes are starting to brown on top.
7. Sprinkle grated cheese over the top of the potatoes and continue to bake for 5 to 10 minutes or until the cheese is melted and slightly browned and the potatoes are tender.
8. Sprinkle the parsley on top and serve.

- SERVES 4 TO 6 AS A SIDE DISH.

• • • •

TOP SECRET RECIPES VERSION OF

SHONEY'S COUNTRY FRIED STEAK

☆ ✌ 💣 ✎ ☯ ✂ ☞

MENU DESCRIPTION: *"Tender steak, lightly breaded and golden fried. Smothered with country milk gravy."*

Alex Schoenbaum opened the doors to his first restaurant, Parkette, a drive-in in Charleston, West Virginia, in 1947, at the start of a boom in popularity of the classic American drive-in restaurants many of us now know only from reruns of *Happy Days*. Schoenbaum's restaurant did very well and he decided, in 1951, to purchase a Big Boy franchise, the fastest growing chain at the time. In 1953, Parkette changed its name to Shoney's Big Boy.

Today Shoney's is no longer affiliated with Big Boy, but maintains a menu that features the Southern homestyle favorites that have made it so successful for so long. One of the old-time favorites is the Country Fried Steak smothered in peppered milk gravy. The technique here is to freeze the steaks after they have been breaded with flour. This way the coating won't wash off when the steaks are fried—the same technique the restaurants use.

2 cups all-purpose flour
1 tablespoon salt
1/4 teaspoon ground black pepper
2 cups whole milk
2 cups water
4 4-ounce cube steaks
Vegetable oil for frying

COUNTRY GRAVY

1 1/2 tablespoons ground beef
1/4 cup all-purpose flour
2 cups chicken stock
1/4 teaspoon coarsely ground black pepper
1/4 teaspoon salt

1. Prepare the steaks at least several hours before you plan to serve this meal. First, sift the flour, salt, and pepper together into a large, shallow bowl. Pour the water into another shallow bowl.
2. Trim the steaks of any fat, then use your hand to press down firmly on each cube steak on a hard surface to flatten it out a bit. You don't want the steaks too thick.
3. Dredge each steak, one at a time, first in the water and then in the flour. Repeat this one more time so that each steak has been coated twice.
4. When all four steaks have been coated, place them on waxed paper and put them into the freezer for several hours until they are solid. This is the same technique used at the restaurant chain to ensure that the flour coating won't fall off when frying the steaks.
5. About 10 minutes before you are ready to cook the steaks, prepare the gravy by browning the ground beef in a small frying pan. Crumble the meat into tiny pieces as you cook it.
6. Transfer the meat to a medium saucepan over medium heat. Add ¼ cup flour and stir it in with the ground beef. Add the remaining ingredients for the gravy and bring to a boil, stirring often. Cook for 10 to 15 minutes until thick. Reduce the heat to low to keep the gravy warm while the steaks are prepared.
7. As the gravy is cooking, heat oil in a deep fryer or a deep frying pan over medium/high heat to 350 degrees F. You want enough oil to cover the steaks when frying.
8. When the oil is hot, drop the steaks, one at a time, into the oil. Fry for 8 to 10 minutes or until golden brown, then drain on paper towels.
9. Serve the steaks with gravy poured over the top, with a side of mashed potatoes, grits, or steamed vegetables, if desired.

- SERVES 4 AS AN ENTREE.

• • • •

TOP SECRET RECIPES VERSION OF

SHONEY'S SLOW-COOKED POT ROAST

☆ ✌ 💣 ✏ ☯ ✂ ☞

MENU DESCRIPTION: *"Tender roast beef and carrots slow-simmered and served in a rich brown gravy."*

Remember Mom's delicious pot roast? Shoney's tender slow-cooked entree is just as good, if not better than, many home recipes. The secret to making tender, flaky pot roast is the long slow-cooking process with frequent basting—and then cooking in the pan juices after flaking the meat. This recipe, based on Shoney's popular dish, requires 3 to 4 hours of cooking to make the meat tender. The meat is then flaked apart, put back into the pot with the pan juices and carrots, and cooked more to infuse the meat with flavor. The original recipe requires a rump roast, a tough cut of meat before cooking, which is reasonably low in fat. If you like, you can also use the more tender and less costly chuck roast. This cut of meat requires about an hour less time in the oven to tenderize it because of its higher fat content.

POT ROAST

2 tablespoons butter
1 4-pound rump roast
1 onion, chopped
2 stalks celery, chopped
1 bay leaf
1 large clove garlic, chopped
20 whole peppercorns
1 1/2 teaspoons fresh thyme (or 1/2 teaspoon dried)
1 1/2 teaspoons fresh parsley (or 1/2 teaspoon dried)
2 cups beef stock or canned beef broth
1 teaspoon salt
2 large carrots, sliced

GRAVY

2 cups beef stock or canned beef broth
1/3 cup all-purpose flour
Salt and pepper to taste

ON THE SIDE

Mashed potatoes

1. Preheat the oven to 325°F.
2. Melt the butter in a large oven-safe pot or Dutch oven and sear all sides of the roast in the melted butter for 2 to 3 minutes per side, or until all sides are browned.
3. Remove the meat from the pot to a plate. Add the onion, celery, bay leaf, garlic, peppercorns, thyme, and parsley to the pot that the meat was in and sauté over high heat for 5 minutes until the onion starts to brown.
4. Put the roast back in the pot with the vegetables. Add the beef stock and ½ teaspoon salt.
5. Cook the meat in the oven, covered, for 4 hours or until the meat is tender enough to tear apart. Every half hour or so baste the meat with the broth so that it doesn't dry out.
6. When the roast is tender, remove it from the pot and strain the stock into a medium bowl. Discard the vegetables and spices, but keep the stock.
7. Using two forks, shred the roast apart into slightly bigger than bite-size chunks. Put the meat back into the pot and pour the stock over it. Add the remaining ½ teaspoon salt and the carrots.
8. Put the pot back into the oven and cook for 40 to 50 minutes. This will make the meat even more tender and fill it with flavor. By this time the carrots should be tender.
9. Just before serving the pot roast make a gravy by straining the stock from the pot roast and combining it with an additional 2 cups of beef stock. Sprinkle the flour into a medium saucepan and stir in the liquid. (You should have about 3 cups of stock altogether. If not, add water until you have 3 cups of liquid.) Bring the mixture to a boil, stirring often until thick. Remove from the heat.
10. Serve the pot roast and carrots on a bed of mashed potatoes with the gravy poured over the top. Salt and pepper to taste.

- SERVES 6 TO 8 AS AN ENTREE.

• • • •

TOP SECRET RECIPES VERSION OF

APPLEBEE'S BANANABERRY FREEZE

☆ ✌ 💣 ✎ ☯ ✂ ☞

Ah, if only kitchen cloning were an exact science. While researching this one I saw the same bartender make the drink two different ways on two different days. Only after a firm grilling did I get her to admit to her personal "improvement" to the chain's secret recipe. The official clone includes the ingredients found below. But if you want to add a little pineapple juice—as some independent-thinking bartenders are apt to do—you might discover you have indeed created a tastier version of this refreshing smoothie. On that day the cloning gods shall be looking the other way.

But, for heaven's sake, be sure your banana is soft and ripe. This is a detail the gods won't ignore.

1 10-ounce box frozen sweetened sliced strawberries, thawed
⅓ cup pina colada mix (from recipe on page 230)
2 cups ice
2 ripe bananas

GARNISH
whipped cream
2 fresh strawberries

1. Use a blender to puree the entire contents of the thawed box of frozen strawberries.
2. Add ⅓ cup pina colada mix and 2 cups of ice to the blender.
3. Cut the end off each banana—set these pieces aside to use later as a garnish—then put the bananas into the blender.
4. Blend on high speed until the ice is crushed and the drink is smooth. Pour into two tall stemmed glasses, such as daiquiri glasses.

5. Slice each strawberry halfway up through the middle and add one to the rim of each glass.
6. Cut each banana slice halfway through the middle and add one to the rim of each glass next to the strawberry. Top with whipped cream and serve with a straw.

- Makes 2 drinks.

• • • •

TOP SECRET RECIPES VERSION OF

BASKIN-ROBBINS STRAWBERRY SMOOTHIE

When Irv Robbins was discharged from the army in 1945, he hooked up with his brother-in-law Burt Baskin and the two opened an ice cream parlor in Glendale, California. A simple coin flip determined whose name would go first on the sign. By 1948 six Baskin-Robbins stores had opened their doors and the concept of franchising in the ice cream industry was born.

As in the previous recipe, you may want to let the fruit thaw out a bit here so that you can chop up the strawberries and get a more accurate measure. The word on the street is that some of those frozen whole strawberries can be quite big. Chopping them up first also helps you get a smoother blend going.

1 cup Kern's strawberry nectar
¾ cup frozen whole strawberries, chopped
1 scoop fat-free vanilla frozen yogurt
3 or 4 ice cubes

Combine all ingredients in a blender and blend on high speed until all the ice is crushed and the drink is smooth.

- MAKES 1 16-OUNCE DRINK.

• • • •

BASKIN-ROBBINS B.R. BLAST

Burt Baskin and Irv Robbins' idea to franchise their ice cream stores for rapid growth was so inspired that the company's former milk shake machine salesman, Ray Kroc, adopted the technique to successfully expand his new chain of McDonald's hamburger outlets.

Ice cream is this chain's staple. So this coffee drink, unlike the Frappuccino made famous by Starbucks, requires adding ice cream for a creamy texture and rich taste. If you've got a blender you can clone either of the two varieties of this refreshing coffee beverage. For chocoholics bent on everything mocha, just add some chocolate syrup to the mix.

CAPPUCCINO

1 cup cold espresso or double-strength coffee (see Tidbits)
1 cup milk
1/3 cup granulated sugar
1 heaping cup vanilla ice cream
2 cups crushed ice or ice cubes

GARNISH
whipped cream
cinnamon

1. Combine the espresso, milk, and sugar in a blender and mix on medium speed for 15 seconds to dissolve sugar.
2. Add ice cream and ice, then blend on high speed until smooth and creamy.
3. Pour drink into two 16-ounce glasses. If desired, add whipped cream to the top of each drink followed by a sprinkle of cinnamon.

• Makes 2 large drinks.

MOCHA

For this version, add 2 tablespoons of chocolate syrup to the recipe above and prepare as described.

TIDBITS

Make double-strength coffee in your coffee maker by adding half the water suggested by the manufacturer. Allow coffee to chill in the refrigerator before using it in this recipe.

• • • •

CINNABON ICESCAPE

In a blender, Cinnabon adds concentrated flavoring, some ice and a curious secret ingredient referred to only as a "dairy product." When blended smooth, out come these thick, refreshing drinks that look and taste like they were made with ice cream. For this clone we just need a little half-and-half to give our version the exact same creamy consistency as the original with that custom "dairy" ingredient.

STRAWBERRY

1 cup water
¼ cup granulated sugar
3 cups crushed ice
½ cup frozen whole strawberries (4 large strawberries)
½ cup half-and-half
¼ cup lemon juice
¼ cup Hershey's strawberry syrup

1. Combine the water and sugar in a cup and stir until the sugar is dissolved.
2. Combine this sugar syrup with remaining ingredients in a blender. Blend on high speed until the drink is smooth. Serve in two 16-ounce glasses.

- MAKES 2 LARGE DRINKS.

ORANGE

3 cups crushed ice
1 cup water
⅔ cup orange juice
½ cup half-and-half
3 tablespoons Tang orange drink mix

Mix all ingredients in a blender set on high speed until smooth and creamy. Serve in two 16-ounce glasses.

- MAKES 2 LARGE DRINKS.

• • • •

CINNABON STRAWBERRY LEMONADE

Cinnabon, the 470-unit chain famous for its gooey cinnamon rolls, gives lemonade a twist by adding strawberry syrup. It's a simple clone when you snag some Hershey's strawberry syrup (near the chocolate syrup in your supermarket), and a few juicy lemons. While you're at it, toss in a straw.

½ cup lemon juice (from 3 or 4 fresh lemons)
¼ cup sugar
2 cups water
2 tablespoons Hershey's strawberry syrup

Mix ingredients together in a pitcher. Serve over ice with a straw, if you've got one.

- MAKES 2 DRINKS.

• • • •

TOP SECRET RECIPES VERSION OF

HOT DOG ON A STICK MUSCLE BEACH LEMONADE

☆ ✌ 💣 ✏ ☯ ✂ ☞

Entrepreneur Dave Barham opened the first Hot Dog on a Stick location in Santa Monica, California, near famed Muscle Beach. That was in 1946, and today the chain has blossomed into a total of more than 100 outlets located in shopping malls across America. You've probably seen the bright red, white, blue, and yellow go-go outfits and those cylindrical fez-style bucket hats on the girls behind the counter.

In giant clear plastic vats at the front of each store floats ice, fresh lemon rinds, and what is probably the world's most thirst-quenching substance—Muscle Beach Lemonade. Our clone is a simple concoction really, with only three ingredients. And with this *TSR* formula, you'll have your own version of the lemonade in the comfort of your own home at a fraction of the price.

1 cup fresh-squeezed lemon juice (about 5 lemons)
7 cups water
1 cup granulated sugar

1. Combine the lemon juice with the water and sugar in a 2-quart pitcher. Stir or shake vigorously until all the sugar is dissolved.
2. Slice the remaining lemon rind halves into fourths, then add the rinds to the pitcher. Add ice to the top of the pitcher and chill.
3. Serve the lemonade over ice in a 12-ounce glass and add a couple of lemon rind slices to each glass.

• MAKES 2 QUARTS, OR 8 SERVINGS.

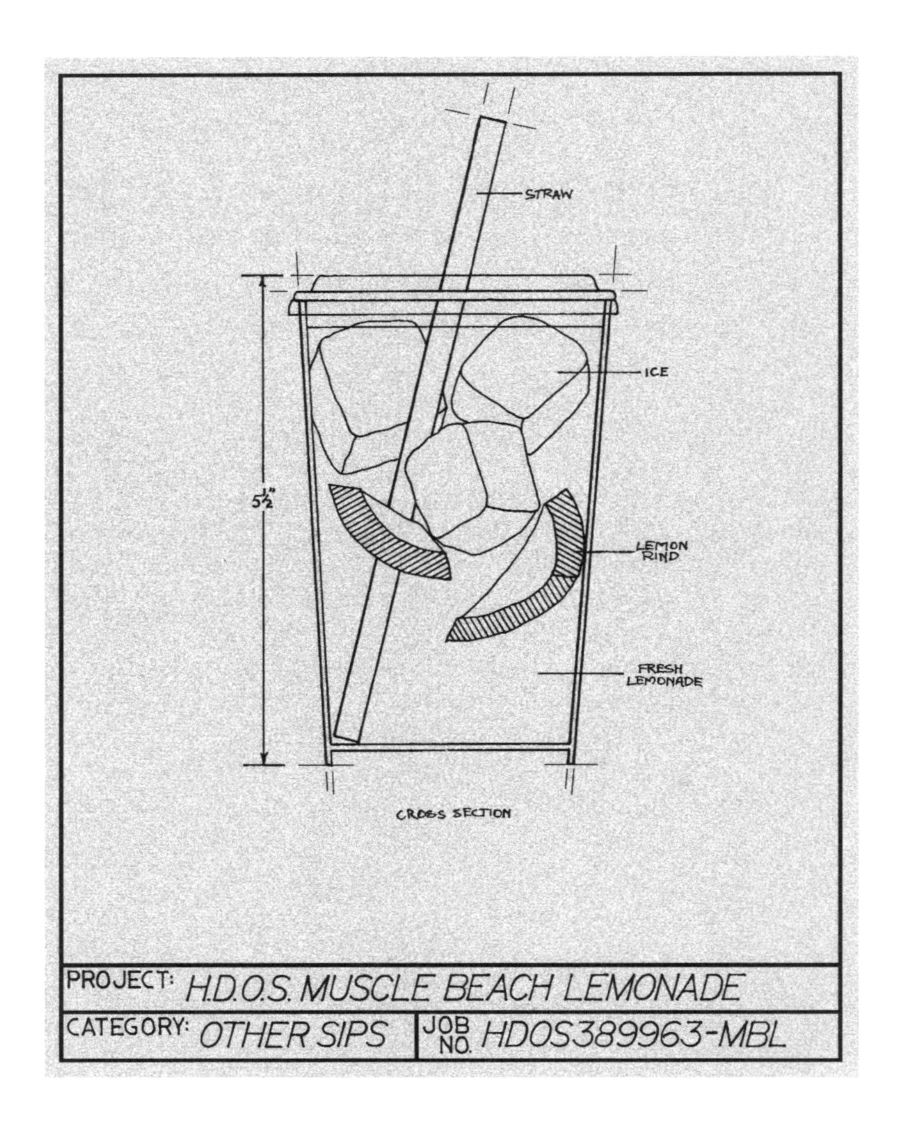
STRAW
ICE
5½"
LEMON RIND
FRESH LEMONADE
CROSS SECTION
PROJECT: H.D.O.S. MUSCLE BEACH LEMONADE
CATEGORY: OTHER SIPS
JOB NO. HDOS389963-MBL

TOP SECRET RECIPES VERSION OF

JACK IN THE BOX OREO COOKIE SHAKE

If you live in one of the 15 Western states served by Jack in the Box, you have no doubt cracked a gut from the hilarious TV ads produced by this popular hamburger chain. In the spots a suit-wearing "Jack" runs the company, even though he's got a bulbous antenna ball for a head with a smiley-face painted on it. He has a private jet, he plays golf, and he even has kids with mini antenna-ball heads.

Jack also has a featured shake flavor that, as it turns out, is very easy to make at home with a blender, ice cream, milk, and a handful of Oreo cookies. Sure, the drive-thru is convenient and easy. But if you don't feel like getting out, now you can enjoy this clone at home from the first fast food chain in the country to use a drive-thru window way back when.

3 cups vanilla ice cream
1 ½ cups milk
8 Oreo cookies

1. Combine the ice cream and milk in a blender and mix on low speed until smooth. Stir the shake with a spoon to mix, if necessary.
2. Break Oreo cookies while adding them to the blender. Mix on low speed for 5 to 10 seconds or until cookies are mostly pureed into the shake, but a few larger pieces remain. Stir with a spoon to help combine the cookies, if necessary.
3. Pour shake into two 12-ounce glasses.

• SERVES 2.

TOP SECRET RECIPES VERSION OF

NESTEA NATURAL LEMON FLAVORED ICED TEA

☆ ✌ 💣 ✏ ☯ ✂ ☞

For five thousand years tea was served hot. But when a heat wave hit the World's Fair in St. Louis in 1904, tea plantation owner Richard Blechynden couldn't give the steamy stuff away. So he poured it over ice, creating the first iced tea, and the drink became the hit of the fair. Today Nestle's drink division, which markets Nestea, produces somewhere in the area of 50 percent of the world's processed tea. That's huge business when you consider that tea is second only to water in worldwide consumption.

2 quarts (8 cups) water
2 Lipton tea bags
¾ cup plus 2 tablespoons granulated sugar
¼ cup bottled lemon juice

1. Bring 2 quarts of water to a boil. Add tea bags and let the tea steep for 1 to 2 hours.
2. Remove the tea bags and pour the tea into a 2-quart pitcher. Add sugar and lemon juice. Cover and chill.

• MAKES 2 QUARTS.

• • • •

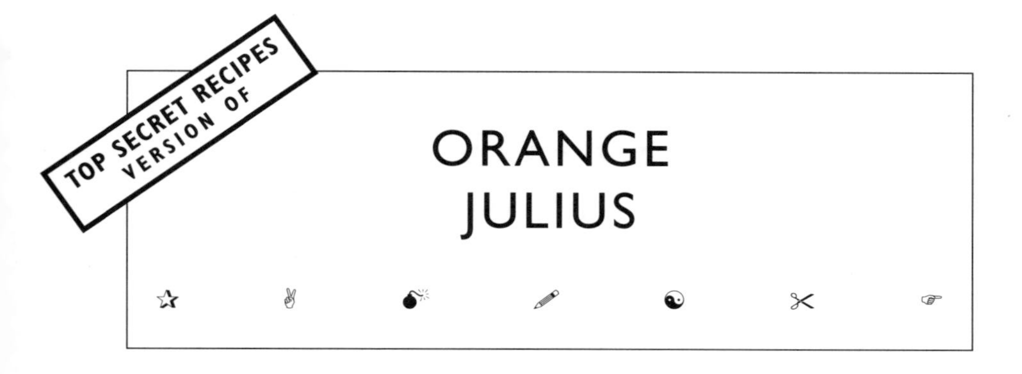

ORANGE JULIUS

In 1926 a man named Julius Freed opened a fresh-orange-juice shop in downtown Los Angeles, initially ringing up sales of $20 a day. The real estate agent who helped locate his first store just so happened to be an ex-chemist named Bill Hamlin. The two became good friends. One day Hamlin, drawing on his chemistry background, presented Freed with an idea for a compound, using all natural ingredients, that would give his orange juice a creamy, frothy texture. When the two began selling the new drink, response was so tremendous that sales skyrocketed to $100 a day. An increasing number of customers would come by the store saying, "Give me an orange, Julius," and so the name was born. By 1929 the chain had opened 100 stores across the United States.

In 1987 International Dairy Queen bought the Orange Julius chain, and today you'll find more than 500 Orange Julius outlets nationwide serving the drink in a variety of natural flavors, including strawberry and pineapple.

1 cup orange juice
1 cup water
2 egg whites
¾ teaspoon vanilla extract
¼ cup granulated sugar
1 heaping cup ice

Combine all of the ingredients in a blender set on high speed for 15 to 30 seconds.

• • • •

RED ROBIN CHILLIN' MANGO SMOOTHIE

Masterful mixologists make this drink as a special limited-time-only summer refresher at the popular eatery. The chain uses a special pureed mango fruit mix made by Torani, the same company that makes the flavoring syrups used in coffeehouses. But since this special ingredient can be hard to come by, we'll substitute with canned mango chunks that you'll find in jars in the produce section.

¾ cup canned mango, with juice
¾ ounce grenadine
¼ cup orange juice
1 cup ice

GARNISH
orange wedge
maraschino cherry

1. Combine all ingredients in a blender on high speed and mix until smooth.
2. Pour into a 12-ounce glass, then add an orange wedge and maraschino cherry speared on a toothpick. Serve with a straw.

• MAKES 1 DRINK.

• • • •

TOP SECRET RECIPES VERSION OF

RED ROBIN GROOVY SMOOTHIE

The strawberries used for this drink come in 10-ounce boxes in the freezer section of your local supermarket. These berries work great because when thawed they wind up swimming in a juicy sweet syrup that's perfect for this clone recipe. The restaurant adds a special blend of apple, raspberry, and blackberry juices called "Groovy Mix" to the drink, but we can still create an excellent carbon copy using a blend of apple and berry juices made by Langer's. If you can't find that brand, use any berry juice blend you can get your hands on and you'll still have an extremely groovy drink.

1/3 cup frozen sweetened sliced strawberries, thawed
1/2 ripe banana
1/3 cup Langer's berry juice (a blend of berry and apple juices)
1/4 cup Kern's peach nectar
1/2 cup ice
1/2 cup vanilla ice cream

GARNISH
orange wedge
maraschino cherry

1. Combine all ingredients in a blender and blend on high speed until smooth. Pour into a 16-ounce glass.
2. Add an orange wedge and a maraschino cherry speared on a toothpick. Serve with a straw.

• MAKES 1 DRINK.

• • • •

TOP SECRET RECIPES VERSION OF

RED ROBIN FRECKLED LEMONADE

☆ ✌ 💣 ✎ ☯ ✂ ☞

This is Red Robin's signature non-alcoholic drink, and is simple to make with pre-made lemonade (unless you want to use one of the fresh lemonade recipes from page 88 or 90) and the strawberries that come frozen in sweet syrup. When added to the top of the ice-filled lemonade glass the strawberries and syrup speckle the drink. Serve this one without stirring it up, or the freckles will be gone.

⅓ cup frozen sweetened sliced strawberries, thawed
1 cup lemonade

GARNISH
lemon wedge

1. Fill a 16-ounce glass with ice.
2. Ladle strawberries with syrup over the top of the ice.
3. Fill the glass with lemonade. Add a lemon wedge and serve with a straw.

• MAKES 1 DRINK.

• • • •

TOP SECRET RECIPES VERSION OF

RED ROBIN STRAWBERRY ECSTACY

After adding the juices to the blender the restaurant does a "flash blend." That means you use just a couple of pulses on high speed so that the ice is broken up into small pieces, without being completely crushed to a slushy consistency.

½ cup orange juice
⅓ cup pineapple juice
½ ounce grenadine
1 cup ice
⅓ cup frozen sweetened sliced strawberries, thawed

1. Add orange juice, pineapple juice, grenadine, and ice to a blender. Blend the drink with just a couple pulses on high speed so that the ice is still a bit chunky.
2. Pour into a 16-ounce glass and ladle strawberries with the syrup into the drink.
3. Add a wedge of orange and a maraschino cherry speared on a toothpick. Serve with a straw.

- Makes 1 drink.

• • • •

TOP SECRET RECIPES VERSION OF

SONIC DRIVE-IN STRAWBERRY CHEESECAKE SHAKE

☆ ✌ 💣 ✎ ☯ ✂ ☞

The cool thing about this Top Secret Recipe is that many of the ingredients come in a kit designed for making strawberry cheesecake. Find Jell-O® No Bake Strawberry Cheesecake mix near the puddings in your supermarket, and you have half of the ingredients locked up. Inside the box are three separate packets: strawberries, the cheesecake mix for flavoring, and graham cracker crumbs to sprinkle over the top of your shake as they do at the restaurant. To complete your clone, you'll just need some vanilla ice cream, a cup of milk, and a little whipped cream. The recipe below makes two regular-size shakes, but you can make another two drinks with the remaining strawberries that come in the mix. If you thaw out some frozen, sweetened strawberries (those syrupy strawberries that come in a box), you can make as many as 8 more shake clones with the remaining cheesecake mix powder and graham cracker crumbs.

1 cup milk
3 cups vanilla ice cream
½ cup strawberries and syrup (from Jell-O® No Bake Strawberry Cheesecake kit)
3 tablespoons cheesecake mix powder (from cheesecake kit)

ON TOP

canned whipped cream
2 teaspoons graham cracker crumbs (from cheesecake kit)

1. Combine milk, ice cream, strawberries, and cheesecake mix in a blender and mix on high speed until smooth. Pour into two 12-ounce glasses.
2. Garnish the top with a squirt of whipped cream from a can and about a teaspoon of graham cracker crumbs from the cheesecake kit. Serve each shake with a straw.

- MAKES 2 REGULAR-SIZE DRINKS.

• • • •

TOP SECRET RECIPES VERSION OF

SONIC DRIVE-IN CHERRY LIMEADE

☆ ✌ 💣 ✎ ☯ ✂ ☞

Here's the signature drink from the chain that's reviving the drive-in burger joint, just like a scene out of *American Graffiti* or *Happy Days*.

It was in 1953 that Troy Smith obtained the parcel of land in Shawnee, Oklahoma, that was big enough to fit the new steakhouse and root beer stand that was his dream. Troy thought he'd make the steakhouse his primary operation, but as it turned out folks preferred the hot dogs and cold drinks over at the root beer stand. So Troy did the smart thing and ditched the steakhouse to focus all his efforts on the other joint. At first he called the root beer stand "Top Hat," but when Troy found out later that name was already being used, he came up with "Sonic" to signify "service at the speed of sound." Today the chain is the sixth-largest hamburger outlet in the country.

This recipe makes a simple, old-fashioned drink by combining Sprite with cherry juice and some lime wedges. Use cherry juice made by Libby under the brand name Juicy Juice for the best clone.

12 ounces cold Sprite (1 can)
3 lime wedges (1/8 of a lime each)
1/4 cup cherry juice (Libby's Juicy Juice is best)

1. Fill a 16-ounce glass 2/3 full with ice.
2. Pour Sprite over the ice.
3. Add the juice of three lime wedges and drop them into the drink.
4. Add the cherry juice and serve with a straw.

• MAKES 1 16-OUNCE DRINK (MEDIUM SIZE).

TOP SECRET RECIPES VERSION OF

SONIC DRIVE-IN STRAWBERRY LIMEADE

☆ ✌ ● ✎ ☯ ✂ ☞

Troy Smith isn't the one who came up with the idea to use an intercom system in the parking lot so that customers could pull up to order, and then eat while still in their cars. He was inspired by another hamburger stand he saw while driving through Louisiana, and had the same system designed for his place. Troy's borrowed concept survived the generations thanks to a menu of food with wide appeal. Today Sonic is the only major fast food chain still incorporating the nearly 50-year-old service concept. And just as in the 50s, roller-skating carhops still bring the food right to the car window so diners can stay comfortably seated behind the wheel.

This is a flavor variation of Sonic's signature Cherry Limeade. This version is just as good, even with the minor inconvenience of little chunks of strawberry clogging up the straw.

12 ounces cold Sprite (1 can)
3 lime wedges (1/8 of a lime each)
2 tablespoons frozen sweetened sliced strawberries, thawed

1. Fill a 16-ounce glass 2/3 full with ice.
2. Pour Sprite over the ice.
3. Add the juice of three lime wedges.
4. Add two tablespoons of strawberries with the syrup. Serve with a straw.

- MAKES 1 16-OUNCE DRINK (MEDIUM SIZE).

TOP SECRET RECIPES VERSION OF

SONIC DRIVE-IN OCEAN WATER

☆ ✌ 💣 ✏ ☯ ✂ ☞

Any Sonic Drive-In regular knows the four or five unique fountain drink favorites on the menu. There's the Limeade, the Diet Limeade, Strawberry Limeade, and, of course, the Cherry Limeade. But that bright blue stuff called Ocean Water has become a recent favorite for anyone who digs the taste of coconut—it's like a pina colada soda. The server simply squirts a bit of blue coconut-flavored syrup into a cup of cold Sprite. The big secret to duplicating this one at home is re-creating that syrup, so that's the first step. After that's done, you make the drink as they do at the restaurant in less time than it takes to say, "Does my blue tongue clash with what I'm wearing?"

3 tablespoons water
2 tablespoons sugar
1 teaspoon imitation coconut extract
2 drops blue food coloring
2 12-ounce cans cold Sprite
ice

1. Combine the water and the sugar in a small bowl. Microwave for 30 to 45 seconds, and then stir to dissolve all of the sugar. Allow this syrup to cool.
2. Add coconut extract and food coloring to the cooled syrup. Stir well.
3. Combine the syrup with two 12-ounce cans of cold Sprite. Divide and pour over ice. Add straws and serve.

• MAKES 2 12-OUNCE SERVINGS.

TOP SECRET RECIPES VERSION OF

SONIC DRIVE-IN CREAM PIE SHAKES

☆ ✌ 💣 ✏ ☯ ✂ ☞

If you placed all the cups end to end that Sonic uses in a year, they would circle the earth twice. That's including the detour the cups would make to avoid passing through downtown Detroit.

These awesome shakes are unique for the graham cracker crumbs in the mix that make them taste as if you're slurping up a creamy chilled pie. You can either crumble up your own graham crackers or use the already ground stuff in a box that's used most often to make graham cracker pie crusts.

BANANA

If you love banana cream pies, you'll love this shake. Just be sure your banana is ripe.

2½ cups vanilla ice cream
½ cup milk
1 ripe banana
2 tablespoons graham cracker crumbs

GARNISH
whipped cream
graham cracker crumbs

1. Put all ingredients in a blender and mix until smooth. You may have to stop the blender and stir the shake with a spoon so that it blends evenly.
2. Pour the shake into two 12-ounce glasses. Garnish each serving with a dollop of whipped cream, and shake some graham cracker crumbs over the top. Serve with a straw.

• MAKES 2 12-OUNCE SHAKES.

CHOCOLATE

Simply add a little chocolate syrup to the shake if chocolate is your thing. This recipe makes two medium shakes or one big one for real chocoholics.

2½ cups vanilla ice cream
½ cup milk
2 tablespoons Hershey's chocolate syrup
2 tablespoons graham cracker crumbs

GARNISH
whipped cream
graham cracker crumbs

1. Put all ingredients in a blender and mix until smooth. You may have to stop the blender and stir the shake with a spoon so that it blends evenly.
2. Pour the shake into two 12-ounce glasses. Garnish each serving with a dollop of whipped cream, and shake some graham cracker crumbs over the top. Serve with a straw.

- MAKES 2 12-OUNCE SHAKES.

COCONUT

This shake uses cream of coconut for flavoring. This is the canned ingredient used most often to make pina coladas, and can be found near the bar mixers in your supermarket.

2½ cups vanilla ice cream
½ cup milk
¼ cup cream of coconut
2 tablespoons graham cracker crumbs

GARNISH
whipped cream
graham cracker crumbs

1. Put all ingredients in a blender and mix until smooth. You may have to stop the blender and stir the shake with a spoon so that it blends evenly.
2. Pour the shake into two 12-ounce glasses. Garnish each serving

with a dollop of whipped cream, and shake some graham cracker crumbs over the top. Serve with a straw.

• MAKES 2 12-OUNCE SHAKES.

STRAWBERRY

This flavor uses the frozen sliced strawberries that are found in boxes in the freezer section with the other frozen fruit. Thaw out a box and measure the berries along with the syrup into the blender.

2½ cups vanilla ice cream
½ cup milk
¼ cup frozen sweetened sliced strawberries, thawed
2 tablespoons graham cracker crumbs

GARNISH
whipped cream
graham cracker crumbs

1. Put all ingredients in a blender and mix until smooth. You may have to stop the blender and stir the shake with a spoon so that it blends evenly.
2. Pour the shake into two 12-ounce glasses. Garnish each serving with a dollop of whipped cream, and shake some graham cracker crumbs over the top. Serve with a straw.

• MAKES 2 12-OUNCE SHAKES.

• • • •

HIRAM WALKER CRÈME DE STRAWBERRY LIQUEUR

1 cup very hot water
⅔ cup granulated sugar
1 cup 80-proof vodka
¾ teaspoon imitation strawberry extract

1. Dissolve the sugar in the hot water.
2. Add the vodka and strawberry extract. Stir well and store in a sealed container.

- MAKES 2½ CUPS.

• • • •

TOP SECRET RECIPES VERSION OF

HIRAM WALKER RAZZ ATTACK RASPBERRY SCHNAPPS

To make this delicious raspberry schnapps you'll need to track down the raspberry flavoring syrup used in coffeehouses with the brand name Torani. A few of the more popular flavors, raspberry included, are now available in most supermarkets.

1 cup very hot water
⅓ cup sugar
1 cup 80-proof vodka
½ cup Torani raspberry flavoring syrup

1. Dissolve the sugar in the hot water.
2. Add vodka and flavoring syrup and stir well. Store in a covered container.

- Makes 2⅔ cups.

• • • •

TOP SECRET RECIPES VERSION OF

HIRAM WALKER ROOT BEER SCHNAPPS

☆ ✌ 💣 ✏ ☯ ✂ ☞

You could use this liqueur to make a teddy bear shooter: Layer ½ ounce of vodka over ½ ounce of root beer schnapps in a shot glass. Or you could make a root beer float as described on the bottle of the real Hiram Walker Root Beer Schnapps by adding 1 part Root Beer Schnapps to 2 parts milk or cream, and 4 parts 7UP or Sprite, then combining it all in a blender with ice until smooth. Or you could just pour it over some ice cream and dive in.

1 cup very hot water
¾ cup granulated sugar
1 cup 80-proof vodka
¼ teaspoon root beer concentrate

1. Dissolve the sugar in the hot water.
2. Add the vodka and root beer concentrate. Store in a sealed container.

• MAKES 2½ CUPS.

• • • •

TOP SECRET RECIPES VERSION OF

KAHLÚA COFFEE LIQUEUR

No one knows for sure the true origin of Kahlúa, the largest-selling imported liqueur in America, but we do have a few clues. The oldest proof of Kahlúa's date of origin is a bottle found by Maidstone Co., a former distributor of the liqueur. The bottle came from Mexico, where the drink is now made, and is dated 1937. The world *Kahlúa* was discovered to have ties to ancient Arabic languages, and the old label, which bears a similarity to the current label, shows a turbaned man smoking a pipe beneath a Moorish archway. The only obvious change in the current label is that the man has become a sombrero-wearing Mexican napping beneath the same Moorish archway.

In 1959 Jules Berman discovered Kahlúa in Mexico and started importing it to the United States. In 1991 Kahlúa had annual worldwide sales of more than 2½ million cases, or the equivalent of 750 million drinks a year.

You will need an empty 750-ml. liquor bottle with a top for storing the liqueur.

2 cups water
1½ cups granulated sugar
1½ tablespoons instant coffee
2 cups 80-proof vodka
1½ tablespoons vanilla extract

1. Combine water, sugar, and coffee in a covered saucepan over high heat. Bring mixture to a boil, and continue to boil for 10 minutes. Be sure mixture does not boil over.
2. Remove the mixture from the heat and let it cool for 5 minutes.

3. Add vodka and vanilla. Stir.
4. Store in an empty 750-ml. liquor bottle with a screw top or another bottle with a resealable lid.

• Makes 750 ml.

TIDBITS

It is very important that you use a covered saucepan when making this drink. The alcohol will boil away if the solution is not covered when it gets hot.

Also, the longer this drink is bottled and stored in a dark, cool place, the better it will taste. For the best flavor, store it for at least thirty days before drinking. Probably the hardest part of making this simple recipe is not drinking the stuff before it matures!

• • • •

TOP SECRET RECIPES VERSION OF

MARIE BRIZARD WATERMELON LIQUEUR

☆ ✌ 💣 ✏ ☯ ✂ ☞

This delicious brand of watermelon liqueur is easy to duplicate by pureeing fresh watermelon. You'll need a cup of pureed melon that comes from about ⅛ of a medium watermelon. I suggest you get the seedless kind.

1 cup pureed watermelon (no seeds)
1 cup 80-proof vodka
½ cup plus 1 tablespoon granulated sugar

1. Make pureed watermelon by removing the seeds and rind from about ⅛ of a medium watermelon (seedless watermelon is the easiest to use). Use a large fork or potato masher to mash the watermelon in a large bowl. You don't need to puree it in the bowl, just mash it up enough to create some liquid so that the fruit will puree well in the blender. Pour the melon and sugar into your blender and blend for 15 seconds or so, or until the sugar has dissolved.
2. Pour the watermelon puree into a container with a lid, add the vodka, and cover. Store at room temperature for a week.
3. Strain the melon pulp from the liquid by pouring it through a paper towel–lined strainer. Store in a sealed container.

• MAKES 2½ CUPS.

• • • •

TOP SECRET RECIPES VERSION OF

MIDORI MELON LIQUEUR

☆ ✌ 💣 ✎ ☯ ✂ ☞

The world's most famous melon liqueur can be imitated at home by pureeing fresh honeydew melon. After the liqueur sits for a week or so, strain out the melon, put on your drinking cap, and enjoy thoroughly.

1 cup pureed honeydew melon
¾ cup granulated sugar
1 cup 80-proof vodka
4 drops green food coloring
3 drops yellow food coloring

1. Puree the honeydew melon by first slicing ¼ of the melon away from the rind. Remove the seeds and then slice the melon into big chunks. Put the chunks into a medium bowl and mash with a potato masher to create some juice. Pour the mashed melon and juice into a blender and blend on medium speed for 10 to 15 seconds or until pureed. Measure 1 cup of melon into a jar with a lid.
2. Add sugar, vodka, and food coloring to the jar. Cover and shake until sugar is dissolved.
3. Store liqueur at room temperature for a week, then strain the melon pulp from the liquid by pouring it through a paper towel–lined strainer.

• MAKES 2 CUPS.

• • • •

RESTAURANT-STYLE MAI TAI MIX

Use this in restaurant drink clones that require fresh mai tai mix. To make it you'll need passion fruit nectar, which can be hard to find in some stores. In that case use passion fruit juice that's blended with another juice, such as Mauna Lai Paradise Passion guava/passion fruit blend.

¼ cup orange juice
¼ cup pineapple juice
¼ cup passion fruit juice
2 tablespoons maraschino cherry juice
1 ½ tablespoons simple syrup (from page 226)

Combine ingredients in a pitcher. Cover and refrigerate until needed.

- MAKES APPROX. 1 CUP.

• • • •

TOP SECRET RECIPES VERSION OF

RESTAURANT-STYLE PINA COLADA MIX

Use this in restaurant drink clones that require fresh pina colada mix. This tastes exactly five-and-a-half times better than any pina colada mix you get out of a bottle.

1⅓ cups cream of coconut (one 15-ounce can)

3½ cups pineapple juice

Combine ingredients in a pitcher. Cover and refrigerate until needed.

- MAKES APPROX. 4¾ CUPS.

• • • •

TOP SECRET RECIPES VERSION OF

APPLEBEE'S LOW-FAT VEGGIE QUESADILLA

☆ ✌ 💣 ✏ ☯ ✂ ☞

The menu description's got the scoop: "Fresh mushrooms, red pepper, onion, broccoli, & carrots smothered in nonfat shredded Cheddar/Mozzarella blend & sandwiched between two wheat tortillas. Served with fat-free sour cream & shredded lettuce. Less than 10 grams of fat."

The TSR version of this tasty favorite appetizer comes in with a fat gram count that's even slightly lower than that, at only 6 grams. The fat-free cheese is where you're spared the major fat gram dosage. And the fat-free sour cream on the side, which nicely completes this guilt-free veggie-filled finger food, certainly helps to keep the waistline in check.

½ tablespoon canola oil
½ cup sliced mushrooms
⅓ cup shredded carrot
⅓ cup chopped broccoli
2 tablespoons diced onion
1 tablespoon diced red bell pepper
1 teaspoon soy sauce
dash cayenne pepper
dash black pepper
dash salt
2 10-inch whole wheat flour tortillas
¼ cup shredded fat-free cheddar cheese
¼ cup shredded fat-free mozzarella cheese
nonstick cooking spray

ON THE SIDE

fat-free sour cream
Pace picante salsa
shredded lettuce

1. In a frying pan that has a bigger diameter than the tortillas, sauté the vegetables in the oil over medium/high heat for 5 to 7 minutes. Season with soy sauce, peppers, and salt.
2. Pour the vegetables into a bowl, and place the frying pan back on the heat, but reduce the heat to medium/low.
3. Place one of the tortillas in the pan, and sprinkle half of the cheeses on the tortilla. Spread the vegetables over the cheese, then sprinkle the rest of the cheeses over the vegetables. Put the second tortilla on top, and cook for 1 to 2 minutes, or until heated through and the cheese is melted. Flip the quesadilla over and cook for 1 to 2 more minutes.
4. Slide the quesadilla onto a cutting board and slice it like a pizza into 6 equal pieces. Serve hot with fat-free sour cream, salsa, and shredded lettuce on the side.

- SERVES 2 AS AN APPETIZER.

Nutrition Facts

SERVING SIZE— ½ QUESADILLA
TOTAL SERVINGS—2
FAT (PER SERVING)—6G
CALORIES (PER SERVING)—274

• • • •

TOP SECRET RECIPES VERSION OF

ARBY'S LIGHT MENU ROAST TURKEY DELUXE

It was in 1991 that Arby's saw a market for a selection of sandwiches that weighed in with very little fat. The chain was able to create three sandwiches that had 10 grams of fat or less, with whole wheat hamburger buns, light mayonnaise, lettuce, and tomato. Of the three selections, it is the Roast Turkey Deluxe that has the least fat, with only 6 grams per sandwich.

Now you can make a clone of that light creation, with deli-sliced roast turkey breast that you can pick up at any deli counter at your local supermarket. You can also find the turkey in prepackaged portions near the luncheon meats.

butter-flavored spray or spread
1 whole wheat hamburger bun
2 ounces deli-sliced roast turkey breast
salt
½ tablespoon light mayonnaise
1 to 2 tomato slices
¼ cup shredded lettuce

1. Preheat a frying pan or griddle to medium heat. Apply butter-flavored spread or spray to the faces of the top and bottom wheat buns. Grill the faces of the buns lightly on the hot pan.
2. Build the sandwich by first placing the sliced turkey on the bottom bun. Salt the turkey.
3. Spread the mayonnaise on the face of the top bun.
4. Invert the top bun. On the bun, stack the tomatoes, then the lettuce on top of that.
5. Turn the top of the sandwich over onto the bottom and serve.

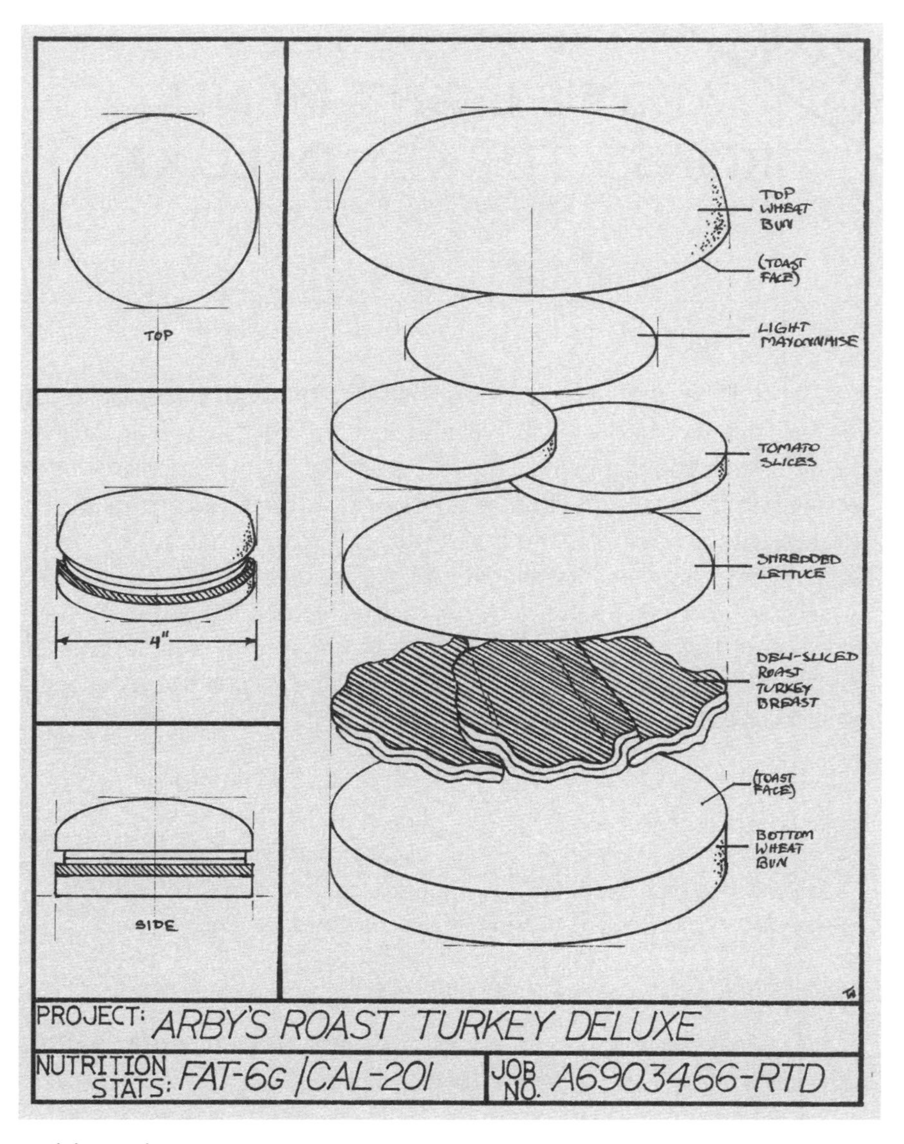

- Makes 1 sandwich.

Nutrition Facts

Serving size—1 sandwich
Total servings—1
Fat (per serving)—6g
Calories (per serving)—201

• • • •

TOP SECRET RECIPES VERSION OF

CHILI'S GUILTLESS GRILL GUILTLESS CHICKEN SALAD

This salad was one of the first six selections offered when Chili's Guiltless Grill premiered on the chain's menu in 1993. You'll love the Southwestern flavors in this delicious and healthy salad clone. The marinated grilled chicken has a sweet, smoky taste, and the pico de gallo lends a nice zing to the dish. Top it all off with irresistible Southwest dressing and you'll have a meal-size salad that comes in at only 5 grams of fat.

Fat-free sour cream and low-fat milk help to keep the slightly spicy dressing remarkably low in fat grams. It's a dressing that's so tasty you'll want to use it for other low-fat salad creations.

CHICKEN MARINADE

1 cup water
1/4 cup pineapple juice
1 tablespoon soy sauce
1/2 teaspoon salt
1/4 teaspoon liquid smoke
1/4 teaspoon onion powder
dash garlic powder

2 chicken breast fillets

LOW-FAT SOUTHWEST DRESSING

1/4 cup low-fat milk
1 tablespoon vinegar
2 tablespoons minced tomato
1 tablespoon minced white onion
2 teaspoons minced canned Ortega chili
1 teaspoon sugar
1/4 teaspoon salt
1/8 teaspoon chili powder
1/8 teaspoon cumin
dash thyme
dash oregano
1/2 cup fat-free sour cream

PICO DE GALLO

1 large tomato
1/4 cup diced Spanish onion
1 teaspoon chopped fresh jalapeño pepper, seeded
1 teaspoon finely minced fresh cilantro
pinch of salt

4 cups chopped iceberg lettuce
4 cups chopped green leaf lettuce
1 cup shredded red cabbage
1/4 cup shredded carrot
2 cups alfalfa sprouts
2/3 cup canned dark red kidney beans
2 green onions, diced (green part only)

1. Make the chicken marinade by combining the ingredients in a medium bowl. Add the chicken fillets and marinate for at least 24 hours.
2. Prepare the dressing by combining all ingredients, except the sour cream, in a blender. Blend on low speed for about 15 seconds or until the onion is pulverized.
3. Pour the mixture into a medium bowl and add the sour cream. Whisk until smooth. Cover and chill.
4. Prepare the pico de gallo by combining all of the ingredients in a small bowl. Cover and chill.
5. When you are ready to build the salads, cook the chicken fillets on a preheated barbecue or indoor grill set to high for 4 to 7 minutes per side, or until done.
6. To build the salad, first toss the lettuces, cabbage, and shredded carrot together. Divide this lettuce mixture and arrange it on two plates.
7. Divide the sprouts and sprinkle them over the lettuce around the edge of each plate.
8. Divide the kidney beans and sprinkle them over the lettuce on each plate.
9. Divide the pico de gallo and sprinkle it over the top of the salads.
10. Divide the green onion and sprinkle it over the top of each salad.
11. Slice the chicken fillets into bite-size pieces and arrange

over the top of each salad. Serve with the low-fat dressing on the side.

- MAKES 2 LARGE ENTRÉE SALADS.

Nutrition Facts

SERVING SIZE—1 SALAD
TOTAL SERVINGS—2
FAT (PER SERVING)—5G
CALORIES (PER SERVING)—558

• • • •

TOP SECRET RECIPES VERSION OF

CHILI'S GUILTLESS GRILL GUILTLESS CHICKEN SANDWICH

☆ ✌ 💣 ✎ ☯ ✂ ☞

Here's another item that has been on Chili's Guiltless Grill menu from the start. It's a chicken sandwich that gets its sweet smoky flavor from the marinated chicken that is grilled over an open flame. The chicken is stacked on whole wheat buns with lettuce and tomato; and a tasty, yet simple-to-make honey mustard sauce is drizzled over the top. If your chicken fillets are too plump, just give 'em a few whacks with a tenderizing mallet and rejoice in the extra calories you work off.

MARINADE

1 cup water
¼ cup pineapple juice
1 tablespoon soy sauce
½ teaspoon salt
¼ teaspoon liquid smoke
¼ teaspoon onion powder
dash garlic powder

4 chicken breast fillets

FAT-FREE HONEY MUSTARD DRESSING

2 tablespoons Grey Poupon Dijon mustard
2 tablespoons honey
1 tablespoon fat-free mayonnaise
1 teaspoon vinegar

4 whole wheat hamburger buns
1 cup shredded lettuce
4 large tomato slices

1. Prepare the chicken marinade by combining the marinade ingredients in a medium bowl. Add the chicken fillets, cover, and refrigerate for several hours. Overnight is even better.
2. When the chicken has marinated, cook the fillets on a preheated barbecue or indoor grill set to a high temperature for 4 to 7 minutes per side or until done.
3. While the chicken is grilling, make the fat-free dressing by mixing together the dressing ingredients in a small bowl.
4. Build each sandwich by first stacking one-quarter of the lettuce on the bottom hamburger bun.
5. Stack the tomato slice on the lettuce.
6. Stack the chicken fillet on the tomato.
7. Cover each sandwich with the top bun and serve with the fat-free honey mustard dressing on the side.

- Serves 4.

Nutrition Facts

Serving size—1 sandwich
Total servings—4
Fat (per serving)—8g
Calories (per serving)—378

• • • •

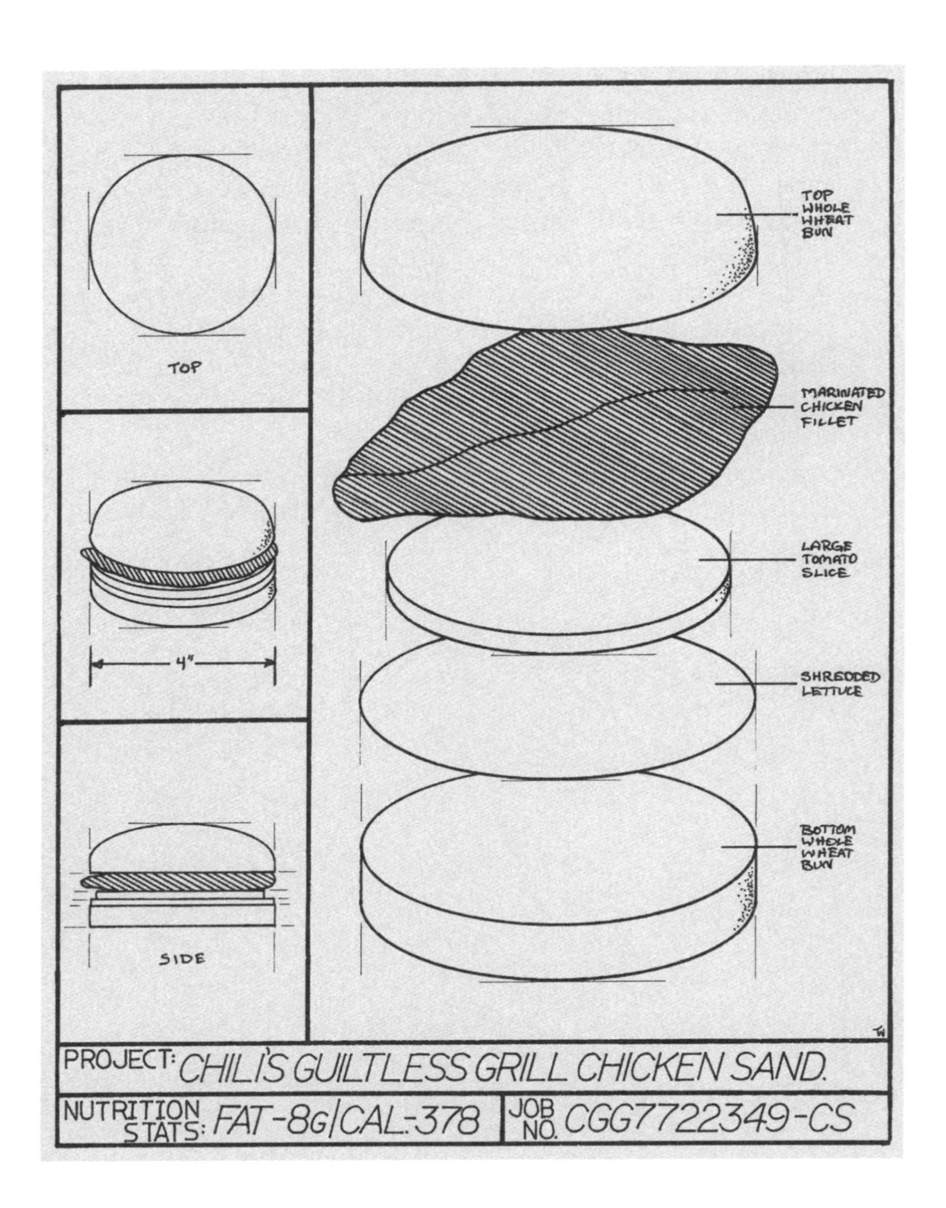
TOP
4"
SIDE
TOP WHOLE WHEAT BUN
MARINATED CHICKEN FILLET
LARGE TOMATO SLICE
SHREDDED LETTUCE
BOTTOM WHOLE WHEAT BUN
TW
PROJECT: CHILI'S GUILTLESS GRILL CHICKEN SAND.
NUTRITION STATS: FAT-8G/CAL-378
JOB NO. CGG7722349-CS

TOP SECRET RECIPES VERSION OF

EINSTEIN BROS. BAGELS

According to legend, in 1683 a Jewish baker shaped dough into the form of a riding stirrup to honor King John Sobieski of Poland, a skilled horseman who had saved the Austrian people from Turkish invaders. Three hundred years later, this Boulder, Colorado, chain is the biggest seller of what has become America's favorite low-fat munchies. Since the first Einstein Bros. Bagel store opened in 1995, the chain has quickly expanded into 38 states. Today there are around 450 Einstein Bros. Bagel stores serving 16 varieties of the chewy bread snack. The company also owns Noah's bagels, giving them another 140 stores. Each company has its own style of bagel, but both brands often win awards in local bagel contests. The company strives to open a new Einstein Bros. or Noah's somewhere in the country each business day.

Here are clones for six of the chain's most popular bagels. You'll notice that the special ingredient that sets these bagels apart from others is molasses. It's an ingredient that adds a unique sweetness and slightly dark color to these tasty, soft bagels.

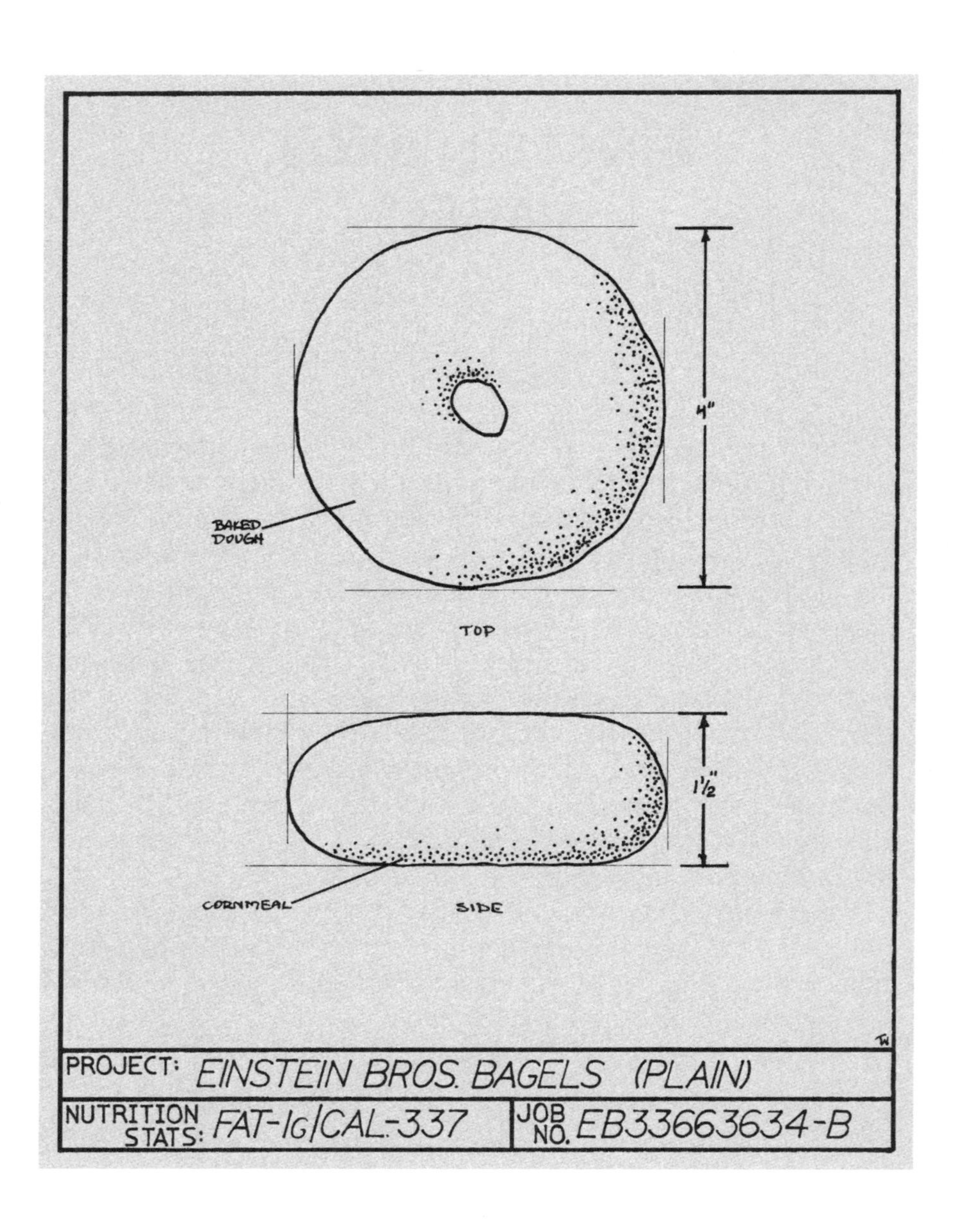
4"
BAKED DOUGH
TOP
1½"
CORNMEAL
SIDE
TW
PROJECT: EINSTEIN BROS. BAGELS (PLAIN)
NUTRITION STATS: FAT-1G/CAL-337
JOB NO. EB33663634-B

PLAIN

1 cup very warm water (110 to 115 degrees, not steaming)
½ tablespoon yeast
1 tablespoon plus 1 teaspoon light corn syrup
1 tablespoon plus 1 teaspoon molasses
½ teaspoon vegetable oil
1 teaspoon salt
2 cups bread flour (plus about ⅔ cup to incorporate while kneading)
1½ tablespoons sugar (for water bath)
cornmeal (for dusting)

1. Combine the warm water and yeast in a medium bowl and stir until the yeast is dissolved. Be sure the water is not too hot, or it may kill the yeast.
2. Add the corn syrup, molasses, and oil to the bowl and stir thoroughly. Add the salt.
3. Pour the 2 cups of bread flour into the bowl and incorporate it with the other ingredients.
4. Sprinkle a little of the reserved flour over the dough in the bowl and turn it out onto a surface that has been dusted with more of the reserved flour. Knead the dough, while working in the remaining reserve flour (depending on your climate you may not have to use all of the reserve flour, but you will surely use most of it). The dough should become very smooth and elastic, dry to the touch, and not tacky. You will have to knead for 6 or 7 minutes to get the right consistency.
5. Put the dough back into the bowl or another container, cover, and let it rise in a warm place for 30 to 40 minutes. The dough should double in size.
6. Punch down the dough and cut it into 4 even portions. Working with one portion of the dough at a time, form the dough into a ball. Turn the edge of the dough inward with your fingers while punching a hole in the center with your thumbs. Work the dough in a circle while stretching it out and enlarging the center hole, so that it looks like a doughnut. The hole should be between 1 to 1½ inches in diameter. Place the 4 portions of shaped dough onto a greased board or baking sheet,

cover (a clean towel works well), and allow the dough to rise for 20 to 30 minutes. The dough should nearly double in size.

7. Preheat the oven to 400°F.
8. Fill a medium saucepan ⅔ full of water and bring it to a boil. Add 1½ tablespoons of sugar to the water.
9. Working with one bagel at a time, first enlarge the hole if it has closed up to less than ¾ of an inch. Be careful not to overwork the dough at this point or it won't have the proper consistency. Drop the bagel into the water, cover the saucepan, and boil for 20 seconds. Flip the bagel over, and boil for another 20 seconds. Immediately take the bagel out of the water with a slotted spoon, let the water drip off for about 10 seconds, then place the bagel onto a baking sheet that has been dusted with cornmeal. Repeat for the remaining bagels. Be sure the bagels do not touch each other.
10. Bake the bagels for 26 to 30 minutes, or until they are light brown.

- MAKES 4 BAGELS.

Nutrition Facts

SERVING SIZE—1 BAGEL
TOTAL SERVINGS—4
FAT (PER SERVING)—1 G
CALORIES (PER SERVING)—337

CINNAMON SUGAR

1 cup very warm water (110 to 115 degrees, not steaming)
½ tablespoon yeast
1 tablespoon plus 1 teaspoon light corn syrup
1 tablespoon plus 1 teaspoon molasses
½ teaspoon vegetable oil
1 teaspoon salt
2 cups bread flour (plus about ⅔ cup to incorporate while kneading)
1½ tablespoons sugar (for water bath)
2 tablespoons superfine sugar
1½ teaspoons cinnamon
nonstick spray

1. Follow steps 1 to 8 for the plain bagels.
2. Combine superfine sugar and cinnamon in a small bowl (or use a premixed cinnamon/sugar, such as the one made by Schilling). If you have an empty shaker bottle—an empty spice bottle works well—you can put the cinnamon and sugar in it and use it to sprinkle an even coating on the bagel when the time comes.
3. Working with one bagel at a time, first enlarge the hole if it has closed up to less than ¾ of an inch. Be careful not to overwork the dough at this point or it won't have the proper consistency. Drop the bagel into the water, cover the saucepan, and boil for 20 seconds. Flip the bagel over, and boil for another 20 seconds. Immediately take the bagel out of the water with a slotted spoon, let the water drip off for about 10 seconds, sprinkle a light coating of the cinnamon/sugar over the entire surface of the bagel, then place the bagel onto a lightly greased baking sheet. Repeat for the remaining bagels. Be sure the bagels do not touch each other.
4. Bake the bagels for 26 to 30 minutes, or until they are light brown.

- Makes 4 bagels.

Nutrition Facts

Serving size—1 bagel
Total servings—4
Fat (per serving)—1 g
Calories (per serving)—360

JALAPEÑO

⅓ cup canned jalapeño slices (nacho slices)
⅛ teaspoon red pepper flakes
1 cup very warm water (110 to 115 degrees, not steaming)
½ tablespoon yeast
1 tablespoon plus 1 teaspoon light corn syrup
1 tablespoon plus 1 teaspoon molasses
½ teaspoon vegetable oil
1 teaspoon salt
2 cups bread flour (plus about ⅔ cup to incorporate while kneading)
1 ½ tablespoons sugar (for water bath)
cornmeal (for dusting)

1. Finely mince the jalapeño slices, then combine with the red pepper flakes in a small bowl and set aside.
2. Follow all of the steps for the plain bagels, adding the jalapeño mixture to the dough in step 2.
3. Rise and bake using the same steps as for the plain bagels.

- MAKES 4 BAGELS.

Nutrition Facts

SERVING SIZE—1 BAGEL
TOTAL SERVINGS—4
FAT (PER SERVING)—1G
CALORIES (PER SERVING)—340

CHOPPED GARLIC

1 cup very warm water (110 to 115 degrees, not steaming)
½ tablespoon yeast
1 tablespoon plus 1 teaspoon light corn syrup
1 tablespoon plus 1 teaspoon molasses
2 teaspoons vegetable oil
1 teaspoon salt
2 cups bread flour (plus about ⅔ cup to incorporate while kneading)
1 ½ tablespoons sugar (for water bath)
cornmeal (for dusting)
1 tablespoon dry minced garlic
1 teaspoon sesame seeds

1. Follow the same steps as for the plain bagels through step 9. After the bagels have been arranged on the cornmeal-dusted baking sheet, and while they are still moist, sprinkle a scant teaspoon of dry minced garlic over the top of each one. Sprinkle about ¼ teaspoon of sesame seeds over the top of each bagel as well.
2. Bake the bagels for 26 to 30 minutes, or until they are light brown.

- MAKES 4 BAGELS.

Nutrition Facts

SERVING SIZE—1 BAGEL
TOTAL SERVINGS—4
FAT (PER SERVING)—3G
CALORIES (PER SERVING)—366

CHOPPED ONION

1 cup very warm water (110 to 115 degrees, not steaming)
½ tablespoon yeast
1 tablespoon plus 1 teaspoon light corn syrup
1 tablespoon plus 1 teaspoon molasses
½ teaspoon vegetable oil
1 teaspoon salt
1 teaspoon poppy seeds
2 cups bread flour (plus about ⅔ cup to incorporate while kneading)
1½ tablespoons sugar (for water bath)
cornmeal (for dusting)
1 tablespoon dry minced onion

1. Follow the directions for the plain bagels through step 9, but add the poppy seeds to the mixture in step 2.
2. After the bagels have been arranged on the cornmeal-dusted baking sheet, and while they are still moist, sprinkle a scant teaspoon of dry minced onion over the top of each one.
3. Bake the bagels for 26 to 30 minutes, or until they are light brown.

• MAKES 4 BAGELS.

Nutrition Facts

SERVING SIZE—1 BAGEL
TOTAL SERVINGS—4
FAT (PER SERVING)—1 G
CALORIES (PER SERVING)—340

EVERYTHING

1 cup very warm water (110 to 115°F, not steaming)
½ tablespoon yeast
1 tablespoon plus 1 teaspoon light corn syrup
1 tablespoon plus 1 teaspoon molasses
1 teaspoon vegetable oil
1 teaspoon salt
2 cups bread flour (plus about ⅔ cup to incorporate while kneading)
1½ tablespoons sugar (for water bath)
cornmeal (for dusting)
1 tablespoon dry minced onion
1 tablespoon dry minced garlic
½ teaspoon poppy seeds
½ teaspoon caraway seeds
½ teaspoon sesame seeds
½ teaspoon kosher salt

1. Follow the directions for the plain bagels through step 9.
2. After the bagels have been arranged on the cornmeal-dusted baking sheet, and while they are still moist, sprinkle a scant teaspoon each of dry minced onion and dry minced garlic over the top of each bagel. Combine the poppy seeds, caraway seeds, sesame seeds, and kosher salt in a small bowl. Sprinkle ¼ of the mixture over the top of each bagel.
3. Bake the bagels for 26 to 30 minutes, or until they are golden brown.

• Makes 4 bagels.

Nutrition Facts

Serving size—1 bagel
Total servings—4
Fat (per serving)—2g
Calories (per serving)—356

• • • •

TOP SECRET RECIPES VERSION OF

ENTENMANN'S LIGHT FAT-FREE CHEESE-FILLED CRUMB COFFEE CAKE

Take a close look at the Entenmann's logo sometime. You'll see a drawing of the same type of horse-drawn delivery wagon that William Entenmann drove back in 1898 in Brooklyn, New York, when he started his home-delivery baking service. The successful family business was passed on through the generations with little change in philosophy or goals. Then in 1951, the family realized the best way to reach the growing numbers of customers was by selling the products in New York-area supermarkets. The delivery business went retail, but the company was still a local New York-area business.

All that changed in 1982, when General Foods purchased the company. Not only did distribution go national, but at the same time food scientists at General Foods were working hard to develop the first line of fresh-baked fat-free cakes and pastries. When those products hit store shelves in 1989, the fat-shunning fad was in its infancy, and Entenmann's was able to grab a big chunk of the market.

Now you can sink your teeth into a big chunk of this homemade version of the popular cheese-filled crumb cake. This clone recipe of the popular treat makes two cakes the same size as the original, by dividing a standard 9 x 13-inch pan in half with a large piece of aluminum foil.

CAKE

½ cup Duncan Hines yellow cake mix
2½ cups cake flour (unsifted)
3 tablespoons Butter Buds Sprinkles
1 package rapid-rise yeast (2¼ teaspoons)
¾ teaspoon baking soda
½ teaspoon salt
1¼ cups fat-free milk
¾ teaspoon vanilla
1 tablespoon white vinegar

FILLING

2 8-ounce packages fat-free cream cheese
⅓ cup powdered sugar
1 tablespoon cornstarch
1 teaspoon Butter Buds Sprinkles
½ teaspoon white vinegar
½ teaspoon vanilla
¼ teaspoon salt

TOPPING

1 tablespoon yellow cake mix
¼ cup plus 1 tablespoon sugar
¼ cup all-purpose flour
2 teaspoons Butter Buds Sprinkles
½ teaspoon baking powder
dash salt
2 to 3 tablespoons fat-free ricotta cheese

GLAZE

1 cup powdered sugar
½ teaspoon vanilla (clear is best)
1 tablespoon plus 1 teaspoon fat-free milk
¼ teaspoon Butter Buds Sprinkles
pinch of salt

1. Preheat the oven to 350°F.
2. To make the cake, in a large bowl, combine the cake mix, cake flour, Butter Buds, yeast, baking soda, and salt.
3. In a separate, smaller bowl, combine the milk, vanilla, and vinegar, then microwave on high heat for 1½ to 2 minutes until very warm. Add the wet ingredients to the dry and beat until the mixture is well combined. Cover the bowl and set it in a warm place to rise for 10 minutes.
4. While the cake batter rises, make a custom cake pan using a 16- to 18-inch piece of foil and a 9 × 13-inch baking pan. Fold the foil in half lengthwise, then bend it up again about 1 inch to the left and right of the middle fold. Place this foil down into the

pan. This will make a liner for the baking pan with a foil divider down the middle. Spray the foil with nonstick cooking spray.

5. Pour 1 cup of the batter into each side of the pan. Bake for 5 minutes, then remove it from the oven and cool for 15 minutes.
6. As the cake cools, prepare the filling by first warming the cream cheese in the microwave on 50 percent power for 3 minutes. Add the remaining filling ingredients and beat with an electric mixer until smooth.
7. Prepare the crumb topping by combining all of the topping ingredients, except the cheese, in a small bowl. Cut the fat-free ricotta into the mixture with a knife or pastry blender until it makes crumbs about one-half to one-quarter the size of a pea.
8. Divide the cheese filling and spread half onto the top of each cake. Cover the filling with the remaining batter. Sprinkle the crumb topping over the top of the batter. Bake for 25 to 30 minutes, or until the cake begins to brown. Remove the pan from the oven and allow the cake to cool completely.
9. Make the glaze by combining the glaze ingredients in a small bowl. When the cake is cool, drizzle the glaze over the top. Store uncovered for the first day.

- MAKES 2 CRUMB CAKES.

TIDBITS

It is important to eat these cakes shortly after adding the glaze. Once the cakes are stored in a sealed container, moisture will begin to liquefy the glaze. If you plan to keep the cakes longer than a day or two, hold off on frosting the cakes until just before you eat them.

Nutrition Facts

SERVING SIZE—2.6-OUNCE SLICE FAT (PER SERVING)—0G
TOTAL SERVINGS—18 CALORIES (PER SERVING)—140

• • • •

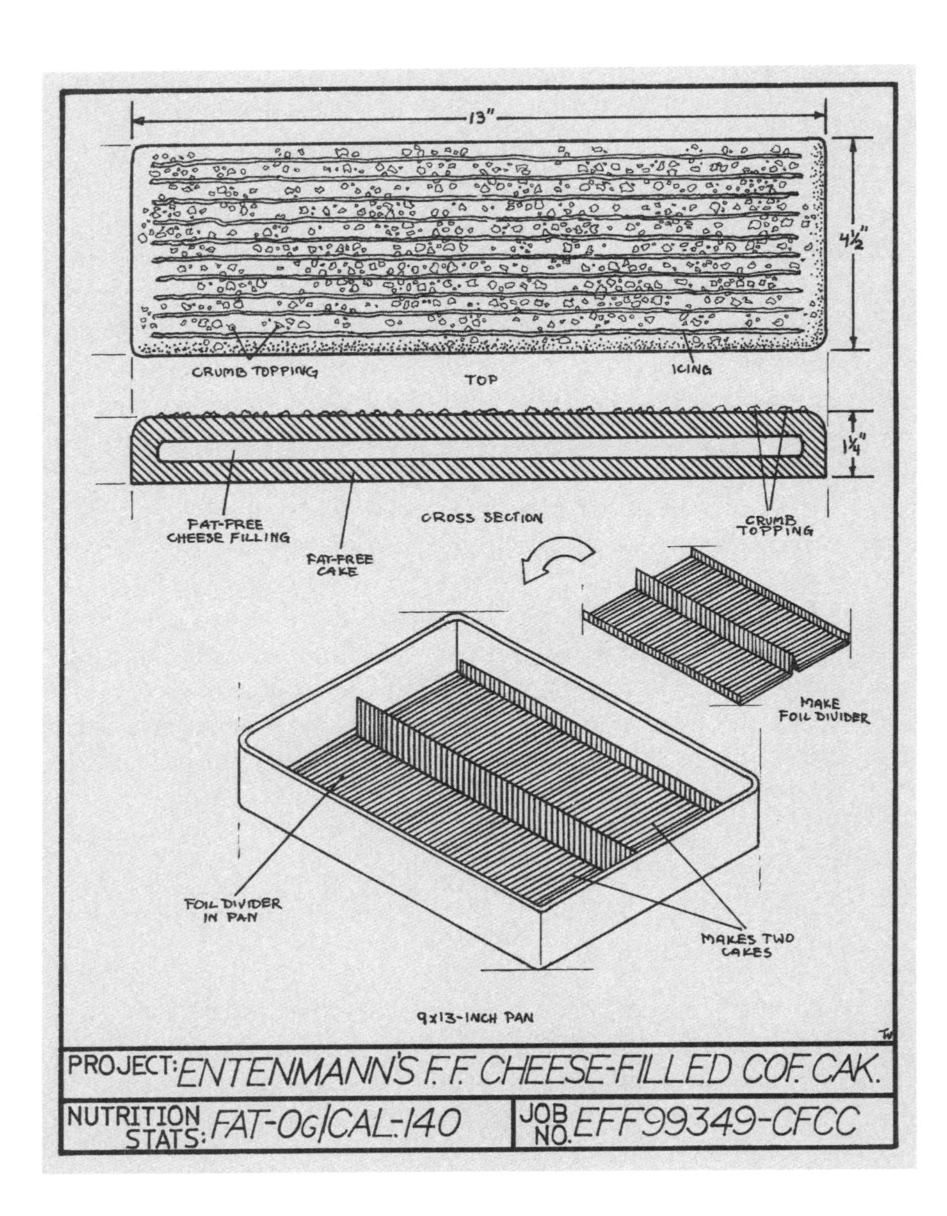
13"
4½"
CRUMB TOPPING
TOP
ICING
1¼"
FAT-FREE CHEESE FILLING
FAT-FREE CAKE
CROSS SECTION
CRUMB TOPPING
MAKE FOIL DIVIDER
FOIL DIVIDER IN PAN
MAKES TWO CAKES
9x13-INCH PAN
PROJECT: ENTENMANN'S F.F. CHEESE-FILLED COF. CAK.
NUTRITION STATS: FAT-0G/CAL-140
JOB NO. EFF99349-CFCC

TOP SECRET RECIPES VERSION OF

ENTENMANN'S LIGHT FAT-FREE GOLDEN LOAF

☆ ✌ 💣 ✎ ☯ ✂ ☞

How would you like this job? Three times a day, each day, the chief bakers at Entenmann's gather in "scoring sessions," wherein they taste and rate products that come off the factory line. If a product doesn't earn at least an 8 out of 10 rating, it never makes it onto a delivery truck.

In the last ten years, Entenmann's has become known as a company that makes delicious baked fat-free products that do not taste fat-free. Today the company boasts around 50 products that carry the low-fat and fat-free labels. One of those products is a delicious pound cake, called Golden Loaf, cloned with this recipe. It makes an excellent dessert or snack when sliced and served with strawberries and low-fat whipped topping, or beneath a big scoop of light ice cream.

However you decide to serve this versatile dessert, you will amaze your guests when you tell 'em it's fat-free fare. And, yes, I realize that the reduced-fat yellow cake mix contains fat, but we have stretched out the product with cake flour so that each slice of these cakes (the recipe makes two) contains less than ½ gram. Check it out.

1 18.25-ounce package reduced-fat yellow cake mix (Betty Crocker Sweet Rewards)
¾ cup cake flour (unsifted)
1 teaspoon vanilla
2 tablespoons Butter Buds Sprinkles
½ cup sugar
1 cup egg substitute
1⅔ cups water

1. Preheat the oven to 325°F.
2. Mix together all the ingredients in a large bowl with an electric mixer on medium speed.
3. Spray two 9 x 5-inch loaf pans with nonstick spray. Pour half of the batter into each pan and bake for 25 minutes. Using a knife, slice down the middle of each cake (about ½-inch into the cake). This will give the cakes the same look on top as the original. Bake for an additional 20 to 25 minutes, or until the cakes are golden brown on top. Cut each cake into 13 slices.

• MAKES 2 POUND CAKES, 13 SLICES EACH.

Nutrition Facts

SERVING SIZE—1.7-OUNCE SLICE
TOTAL SERVINGS—26
FAT (PER SERVING)—0G
CALORIES (PER SERVING)—106

• • • •

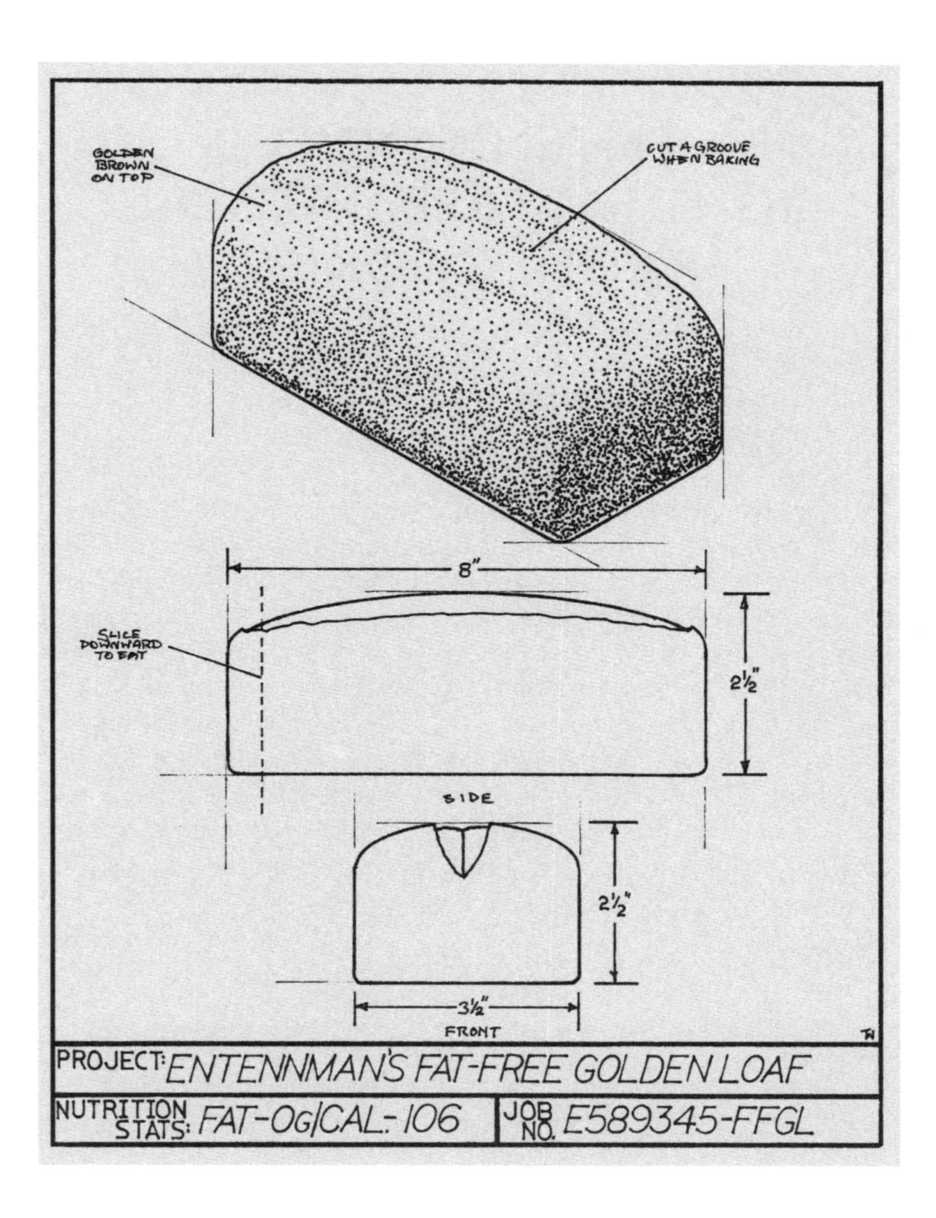
GOLDEN BROWN ON TOP
CUT A GROOVE WHEN BAKING
8"
SLICE DOWNWARD TO EAT
2½"
SIDE
2½"
3½"
FRONT
PROJECT: ENTENNMAN'S FAT-FREE GOLDEN LOAF
NUTRITION STATS: FAT-0G/CAL.-106
JOB NO. E589345-FFGL

TOP SECRET RECIPES VERSION OF

ENTENMANN'S LIGHT FAT-FREE OATMEAL RAISIN COOKIES

☆ ✌ 💣 ✎ ☯ ✂ ☞

These chewy little fat-free cookies have become quite popular in recent years. And they're pretty tasty considering there's a big goose egg in the fat column. A typical oatmeal cookie would have somewhere in the neighborhood of 3 grams of fat . . . each. Since we're removing all the fat, we'll have to resort to some of our *Top Secret* tricks to keep these clones nice and chewy like the original.

The sweetened condensed milk, molasses, and raisin puree will certainly help by not only giving the cookies a delicious flavor, but will also create the perfect chewy texture. Sweetened condensed milk can be found in a fat-free variety that is made with skim milk, and raisin puree is easy to make in a blender. Plus, that raisin flavor is just what we want for this recipe.

2 egg whites
½ cup sugar
3 tablespoons sweetened condensed skim milk
1 teaspoon vanilla extract
2 tablespoons molasses
2 tablespoons raisin puree (see Tidbit)
½ cup quick-cooking oats
¾ cup unbleached flour
¾ cup whole wheat flour
¼ cup dry nonfat milk
½ teaspoon salt
½ teaspoon baking powder
½ teaspoon baking soda
¼ teaspoon cinnamon
½ cup dark raisins

1. Preheat the oven to 325°F.
2. Whip the egg whites with an electric mixer until they form soft peaks. Add the sugar, a little bit at a time, while beating.
3. Add the condensed milk, vanilla, molasses, and raisin puree and beat until well combined.
4. Use a blender or food processor to grind the oats into coarse flour. Pulse the machine a few times to pulverize the oats, but don't grind too long. You still want to see some of the oats in the cookie.
5. Combine the ground oatmeal with the remaining ingredients, except for the raisins, in another bowl and mix by hand.
6. Pour the dry mixture into the wet. Mix by hand until well combined.
7. Add the raisins to the cookie dough, and mix once again by hand.
8. Drop the dough by the tablespoonful onto a greased cookie sheet. Form the cookies into circles, and press down on them to flatten a bit.
9. Bake the cookies for 10 to 15 minutes or until they begin to turn slightly brown around the edges.

- MAKES 2 DOZEN COOKIES.

TIDBIT

Make raisin puree by combining ¼ cup raisins with ½ cup water in a blender. Blend on high speed until smooth.

Nutrition Facts

SERVING SIZE—2 COOKIES
TOTAL SERVINGS—12
FAT (PER SERVING)—0G
CALORIES (PER SERVING)—120

• • • •

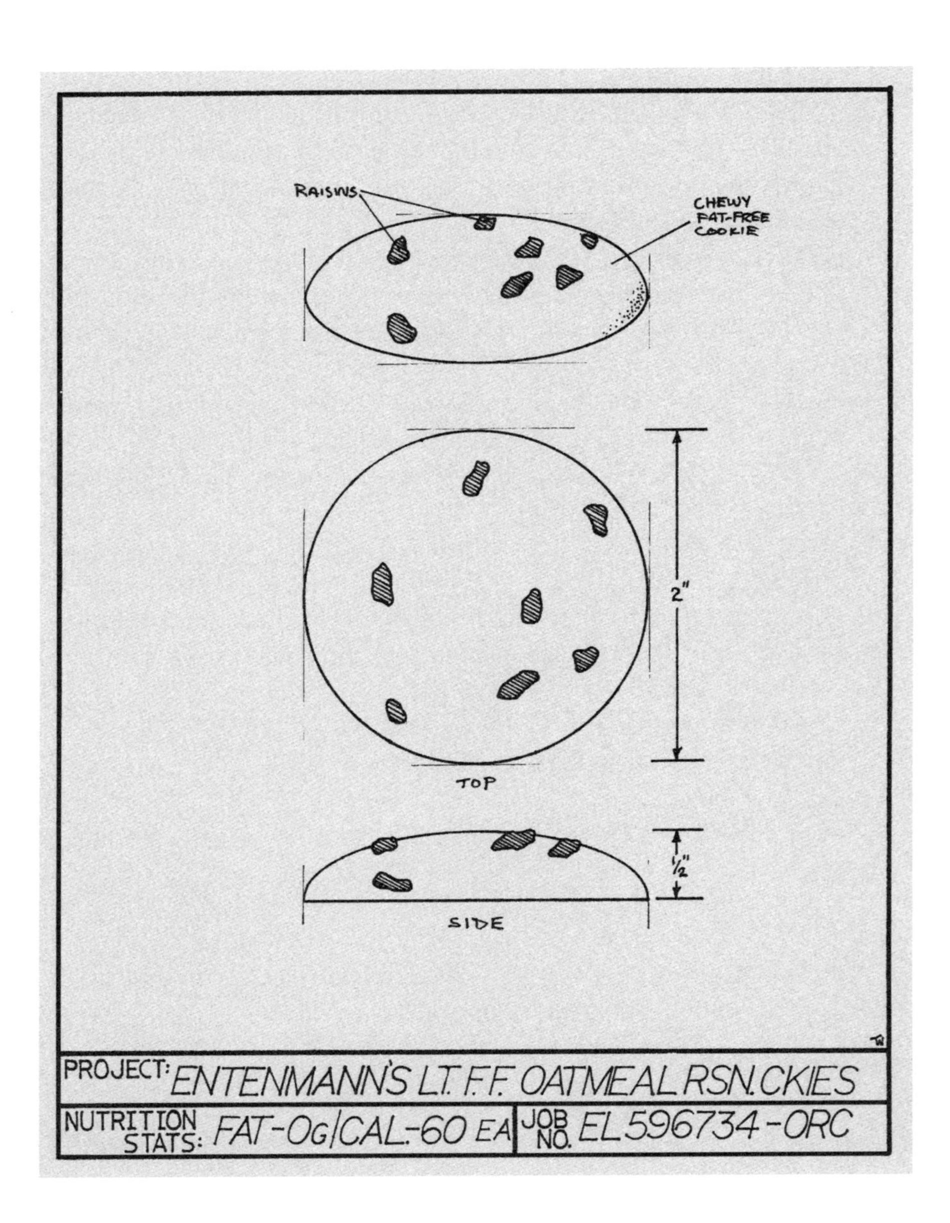
RAISINS
CHEWY FAT-FREE COOKIE
2"
TOP
1/2"
SIDE
PROJECT: ENTENMANN'S LT. F.F. OATMEAL RSN. CKIES
NUTRITION STATS: FAT-0G/CAL.-60 EA
JOB NO. EL596734-ORC

TOP SECRET RECIPES VERSION OF

KOO KOO ROO ORIGINAL SKINLESS FLAME-BROILED CHICKEN

This fast-growing West Coast chain is another popular contender in the home meal replacement biz, which includes Boston Market and Kenny Rogers' Roasters. In 1990, shortly after Kenneth Berg sold his mortgage banking business for $125 million, he came across a little two-unit chicken chain in Los Angeles that seemed to attract clientele from an income bracket above that of typical burger chain customers. Kenneth discovered that the chicken served in these stores was not only delicious but also prepared with a secret marinade and baste that allowed the chicken to be cooked in a more health-conscious way—without skin. The owners of the restaurants, brothers Michael and Raymond Badalian, had created a marinade of juices and spices that kept the chicken moist and juicy inside. The company claims the chicken is marinated for up to seventy-two hours in this secret concoction and then brushed with a tangy orange baste when grilling. Just three months later, Kenneth purchased the chain for $2.5 million—ten times what it was earning each year—and expanded into other Western states, growing the restaurant to around forty units strong. That's about the time the company merged with Family Restaurants, the corporation behind the El Torito and Chi-Chi's Mexican food chains.

MARINADE

1 cup water
1 cup apple juice
1 cup V-8 juice
1 tablespoon lemon juice
½ cup pineapple juice
1 cup chopped onion
2 teaspoons salt
2 teaspoons ground black pepper

1 whole chicken, skinned and cut into 8 pieces (legs, thighs, breasts, and wings)

BASTE

2 tablespoons plus 1 teaspoon vegetable oil
½ cup thinly sliced onions
1 10¾-ounce can tomato puree
¼ cup water
1 tablespoon white vinegar
1 tablespoon lemon juice
¼ teaspoon salt
dash ground black pepper
dash garlic powder

1. Combine all of the ingredients for the marinade in a medium bowl. Mix well.
2. Add chicken to the marinade and leave it for at least 24 hours. It is even better if you let the chicken marinate longer, for as much as 48 to 72 hours.
3. Sometime before the chicken is done marinating, prepare the basting sauce by heating 1 teaspoon of the oil in a medium skillet. Sauté the sliced onions until they begin to blacken a bit. Pour the onions into a medium saucepan with the other baste ingredients. Bring mixture to a full boil, then reduce heat and simmer for 5 to 7 minutes. Remove from heat. When cool, cover the baste and chill it until it's needed.
4. When you are ready to cook the chicken, fire up your grill to medium heat. Grill the chicken for 5 to 6 minutes, then turn it over and grill for another 5 to 6 minutes. Turn chicken over once more and brush the top with the baste. Grill for another 5 to 6 minutes, then turn the chicken over again, baste the other side, and cook it until it's done—around 25 to 35 minutes total cooking time. You should see a few charred black spots on the surface of the chicken, but don't let it burn.

- Serves 4.

Nutrition Facts

Serving size—2 pieces
Total servings—4
Fat (per serving)—8 g
Calories (per serving)—195

• • • •

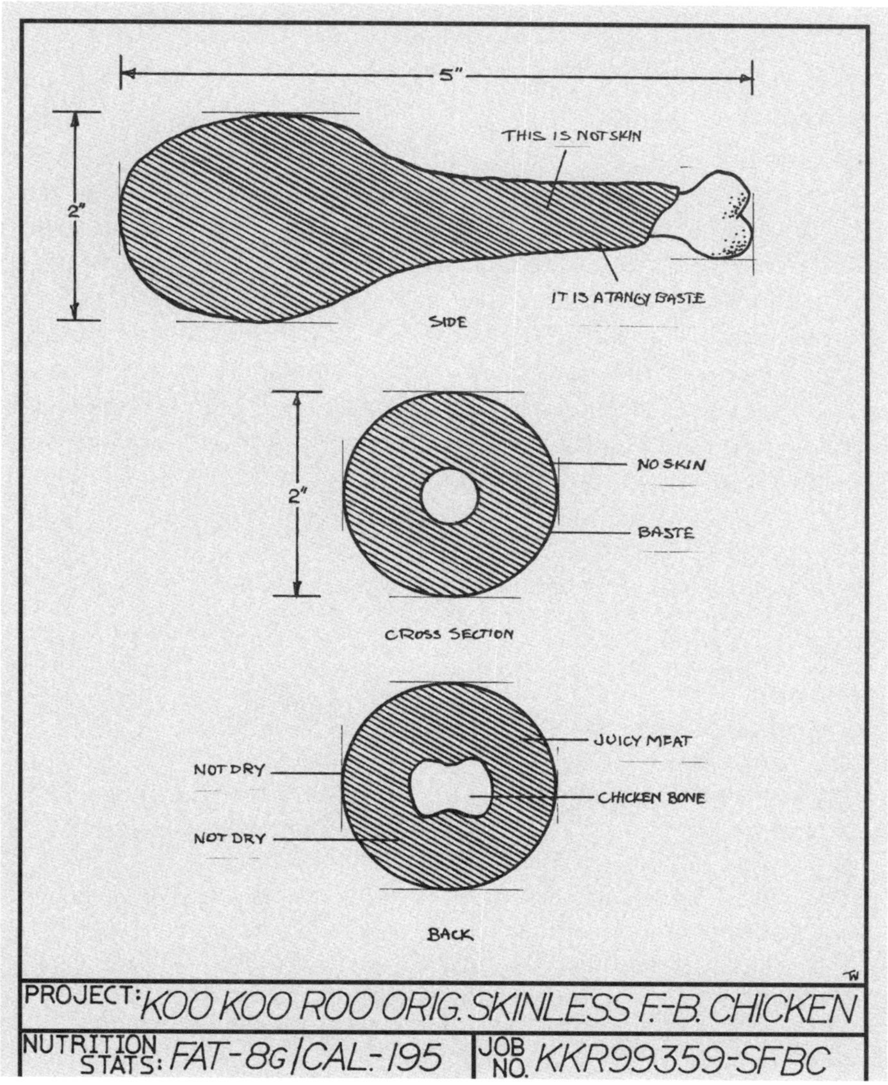

TOP SECRET RECIPES VERSION OF

KOO KOO ROO SANTA FE PASTA

☆ ✌ 💣 ✏ ☯ ✂ ☞

In 1998, ex–Chrysler chairman Lee Iacocca took the reins at the struggling chicken chain. Lee had been an investor in the company since 1995, so when increasing competition from chains like Boston Market and Kenny Rogers' Roasters caused the Koo Koo Roo bottom line to sag, he was called in to rescue it. Can Lee perform the same comeback magic as he did with Chrysler's historic turnaround in the early '80s? While we wait to find out, let's make some pasta. This one goes great with the chicken from the previous recipe or with just about any other meal. The Southwestern-style dressing includes a small amount of oil, but the total fat grams per six-ounce serving stays quite modest.

1 16-ounce package rotini pasta
4 to 5 quarts water

DRESSING
1 cup V-8 juice
2 tablespoons olive oil
4 teaspoons red wine vinegar
1 teaspoon chili powder
½ teaspoon paprika
¾ teaspoon salt
¼ teaspoon ground black pepper
⅛ teaspoon garlic powder

⅔ cup grated Parmesan cheese
½ cup cooked yellow corn kernels
¼ cup chopped fresh cilantro
¼ cup chopped green onion
2 tablespoons diced red bell pepper
2 tablespoons diced green bell pepper
1 boneless chicken breast fillet, cooked and diced

1. Prepare the pasta by bringing 4 to 5 quarts of water to a rolling boil in a large saucepan. Add pasta to the pan, and when water begins to boil again, cook for 8 to 11 minutes. Pasta should be *al dente*, or mostly tender but with a slight toughness in the middle.
2. Whisk all of the dressing ingredients together in a small bowl. Cover and chill the dressing until you're ready to use it.
3. When pasta is done, drain it and pour it into a large bowl to cool. Add the dressing, then toss.
4. Add the remaining ingredients to the pasta and toss until pasta is well coated. Cover and chill for several hours before serving.

- SERVES 10 AS A SIDE DISH.

Nutrition Facts

SERVING SIZE—6 OUNCES
TOTAL SERVINGS—10
FAT (PER SERVING)—5 G
CALORIES (PER SERVING)—230

• • • •

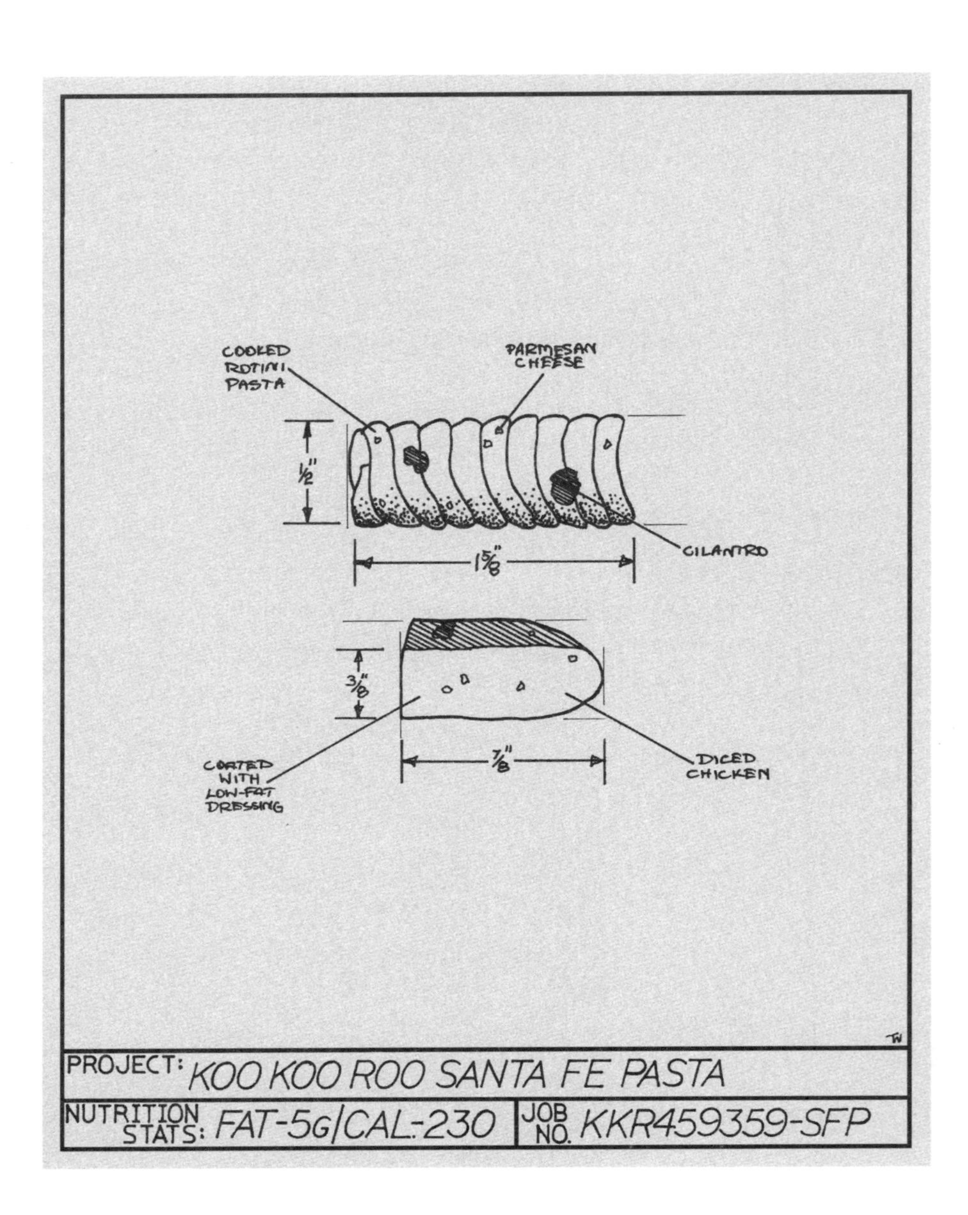
COOKED ROTINI PASTA
PARMESAN CHEESE
1/2"
CILANTRO
1 5/8"
3/8"
COATED WITH LOW-FAT DRESSING
7/8"
DICED CHICKEN
TW
PROJECT: KOO KOO ROO SANTA FE PASTA
NUTRITION STATS: FAT-5G/CAL-230
JOB NO. KKR459359-SFP

TOP SECRET RECIPES VERSION OF

RAINFOREST CAFE REGGAE BEAT SEASONING

☆ ✌ 💣 ✎ ☯ ✂ ☞

Walk inside Steve Schussler's house in Minneapolis, Minnesota, and you'd think you had stepped into a jungle. That's because seventeen years of research and seven years of construction went into re-creating a working rain forest inside the doors of his not-exactly-humble abode. This is how Steve presented the idea for his theme restaurant chain to the numerous potential investors. One of them, Lyle Berman, liked the idea and helped to provide the financing to open the first Rainforest Cafe in Minneapolis's Mall of America in 1994.

The popular chain has always used the Reggae Beat Seasoning in several of its recipes. In 1998, Rainforest Cafe decided to bottle the spice and sell it in the gift shops attached to each of its thirty-three units around the world.

2 teaspoons minced dried onion
1 teaspoon minced dried garlic
1 teaspoon granulated sugar
¾ teaspoon salt
½ teaspoon crushed red pepper
½ teaspoon cayenne pepper
½ teaspoon ground black pepper
½ teaspoon allspice
¼ teaspoon cinnamon
¼ teaspoon ground clove
dash cornstarch
dash dried savory
dash dried thyme

1. Combine all ingredients in a small cup or bowl.
2. Crush with the back of a spoon until finer in texture. Store in a covered container.

• MAKES ABOUT 3 TABLESPOONS.

• • • •

TOP SECRET RECIPES VERSION OF

RAINFOREST CAFE THE PLANT SANDWICH

☆ ✌ 💣 ✎ ☯ ✂ ☞

Inside each Rainforest Cafe, customers are immersed in a thunder and lightning storm every twenty minutes. But don't worry, you don't have to bring your umbrella, since the rain only falls over specially designed troughs that recycle the water and ready it for the next downpour.

This sandwich was introduced in 1998 and uses Rainforest Cafe's delicious balsamic vinaigrette to marinate the mushrooms, making it one of the most delicious portobellos you've ever munched on. For this clone, prepare the vinaigrette and marinate the mushrooms a couple hours before you plan to assemble the sandwich.

BALSAMIC VINAIGRETTE

½ cup mayonnaise
5 teaspoons balsamic vinegar
1 tablespoon water
½ teaspoon cracked black pepper
¼ teaspoon garlic powder
⅛ teaspoon onion powder
⅛ teaspoon lemon juice
dash ground black pepper
dash salt

SANDWICH

4 portobello mushroom caps
1 medium zucchini, sliced thinly lengthwise
1 red bell pepper, seeded and quartered
4 large romaine lettuce leaves, chopped
2 tablespoons Caesar salad dressing
fat-free butter-flavored spray
a handful fresh spinach leaves
8 slices 7- or 9-grain bread

1. Prepare the balsamic vinaigrette by mixing the ingredients in a small bowl until smooth.
2. Place the mushroom caps into a large resealable plastic bag. Pour the balsamic vinaigrette into the bag, seal it up, and chill for an hour or two.
3. When the mushrooms have marinated, preheat your barbecue or indoor grill to high temperature.
4. Place the mushroom caps on the grill along with the zucchini and quartered bell pepper with the skin side down. Cook the zucchini for 3 to 4 minutes per side, and the mushrooms for 5 to 7 minutes per side. Leave the bell pepper with the skin side facing the heat for the entire time, until the skin is well charred.
5. In a medium bowl, toss the chopped lettuce with the Caesar dressing until well coated.
6. Preheat a large skillet over medium heat.
7. When you are ready to build the sandwiches, spray a light coating of butter spray over the face of each slice of bread. Grill the faces of the bread in the hot skillet until light brown.
8. Build each sandwich by first arranging a few spinach leaves on the face of one slice of bread, followed by about ¼ of the tossed romaine lettuce.
9. Place a grilled portobello mushroom cap on the lettuce.
10. Remove the charred skin from one of the bell pepper quarters and then slice the pepper in half, lengthwise. Place the two slices on the sandwich.
11. Cut one grilled zucchini slice in half, across the middle, and arrange the slices on the sandwich.
12. Top the sandwich with a grilled slice of bread. Cut the sandwich diagonally and stick a toothpick in each half. Repeat for the remaining sandwiches.

- MAKES 4 SANDWICHES.

Nutrition Facts

SERVING SIZE—1 SANDWICH	FAT (PER SERVING)—11 G
TOTAL SERVINGS—4	CALORIES (PER SERVING)—335

• • • •

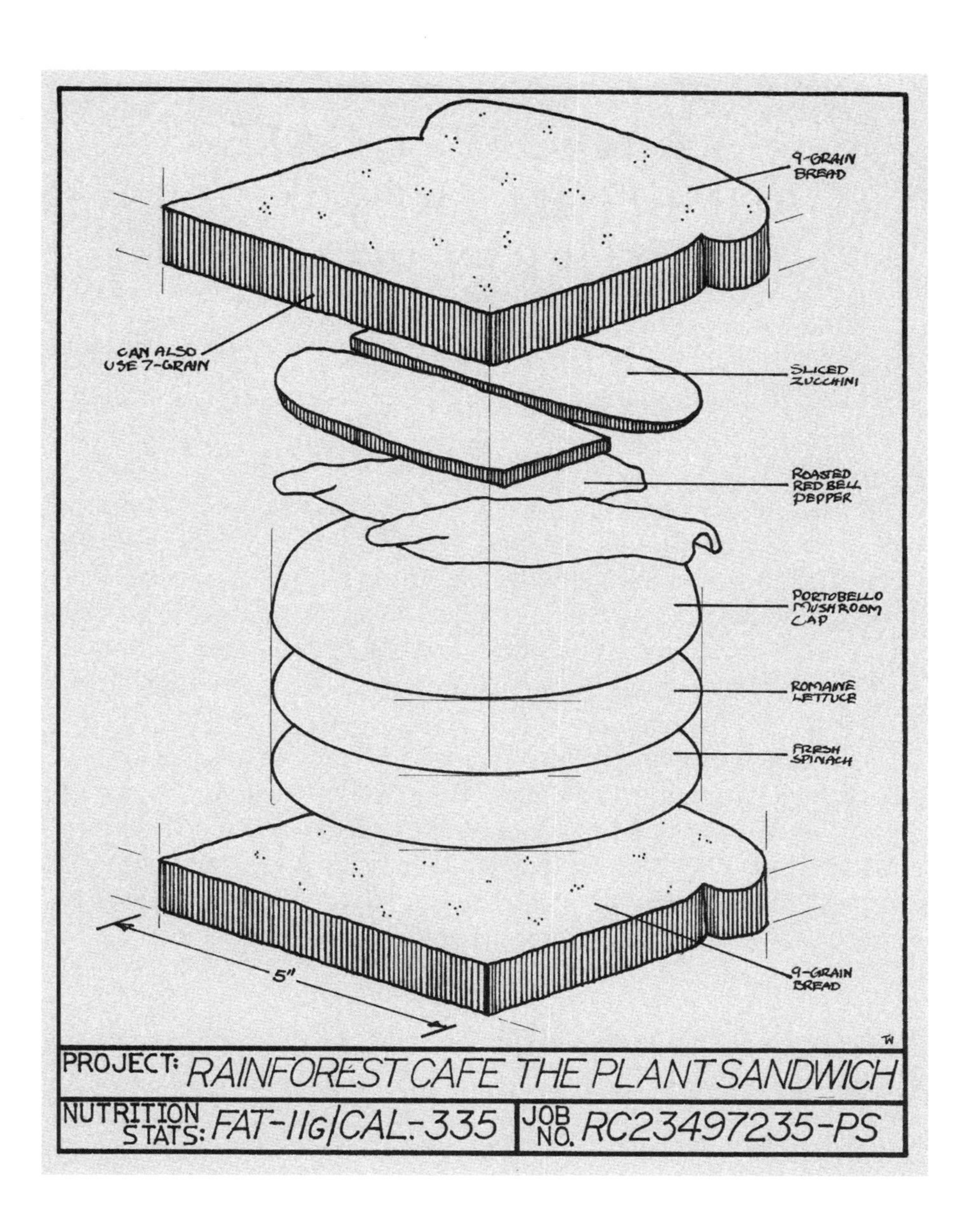
9-GRAIN BREAD
CAN ALSO USE 7-GRAIN
SLICED ZUCCHINI
ROASTED RED BELL PEPPER
PORTOBELLO MUSHROOM CAP
ROMAINE LETTUCE
FRESH SPINACH
5"
9-GRAIN BREAD
TW
PROJECT: RAINFOREST CAFE THE PLANT SANDWICH
NUTRITION STATS: FAT-11G/CAL.-335
JOB NO. RC23497235-PS

TOP SECRET RECIPES VERSION OF

RAINFOREST CAFE RUMBLE IN THE JUNGLE TURKEY PITA

☆ ✌ 💣 ✎ ☯ ✂ ☞

No two Rainforest Cafes are the same. While they all include plant-covered walls and ceilings, waterfalls, starry skies, and live birds, you will find many unique features in each of the restaurants. The Las Vegas store includes an aquarium archway under which you must walk to enter the restaurant, and the original store in the Mall of America features a talking banyan tree spouting ecological messages twice a minute.

The turkey pita sandwich has been on the menu since the first restaurant opened in 1994, and our clone is a great way to use up your leftover Thanksgiving turkey and cranberry sauce. We can use full-fat Caesar dressing for our clone, just like the restaurant uses, and still keep the fat reasonably low. But if you find a tasty lower-fat substitute, you can knock those fat grams down even further.

CRANBERRY RELISH (OPTIONAL)

1 16-ounce can whole berry cranberry relish
½ cup orange juice
¼ cup raisins
¼ cup gold raisins

PITA

10 large leaves romaine lettuce, chopped (5 to 6 cups)
¼ cup Caesar dressing
4 large pita breads
2 Roma tomatoes, sliced (16 slices)
1 cooked turkey breast, chilled (about 12 ounces)
½ cup French's french fried onions

1. Prepare the cranberry relish, if you plan to use it, by combining all of the ingredients in a medium saucepan over medium/high heat. Bring mixture to a boil, then reduce heat and simmer for 5 to 7 minutes. Remove mixture from heat, and cool. Pour mixture into a covered container and chill until cold.
2. Toss the lettuce with the Caesar dressing in a large bowl.
3. Wrap the pitas in a moist towel and heat in the microwave on high for about 1 minute or until all of the pitas are hot.
4. To make a sandwich, fold a pita like a taco and fill it with about ¼ the romaine lettuce.
5. Arrange four of the Roma tomato slices along one side of the pita.
6. Spoon 3 ounces (about ¾ cup) of the turkey over the lettuce and tomato slices, then sprinkle 2 tablespoons of fried onions on top. Serve with cranberry relish on the side, if desired. Repeat for the remaining sandwiches.

• MAKES 4 SANDWICHES.

Nutrition Facts

SERVING SIZE—1 SANDWICH
TOTAL SERVINGS—4
FAT (PER SERVING)—13 G
CALORIES (PER SERVING)—350

• • • •

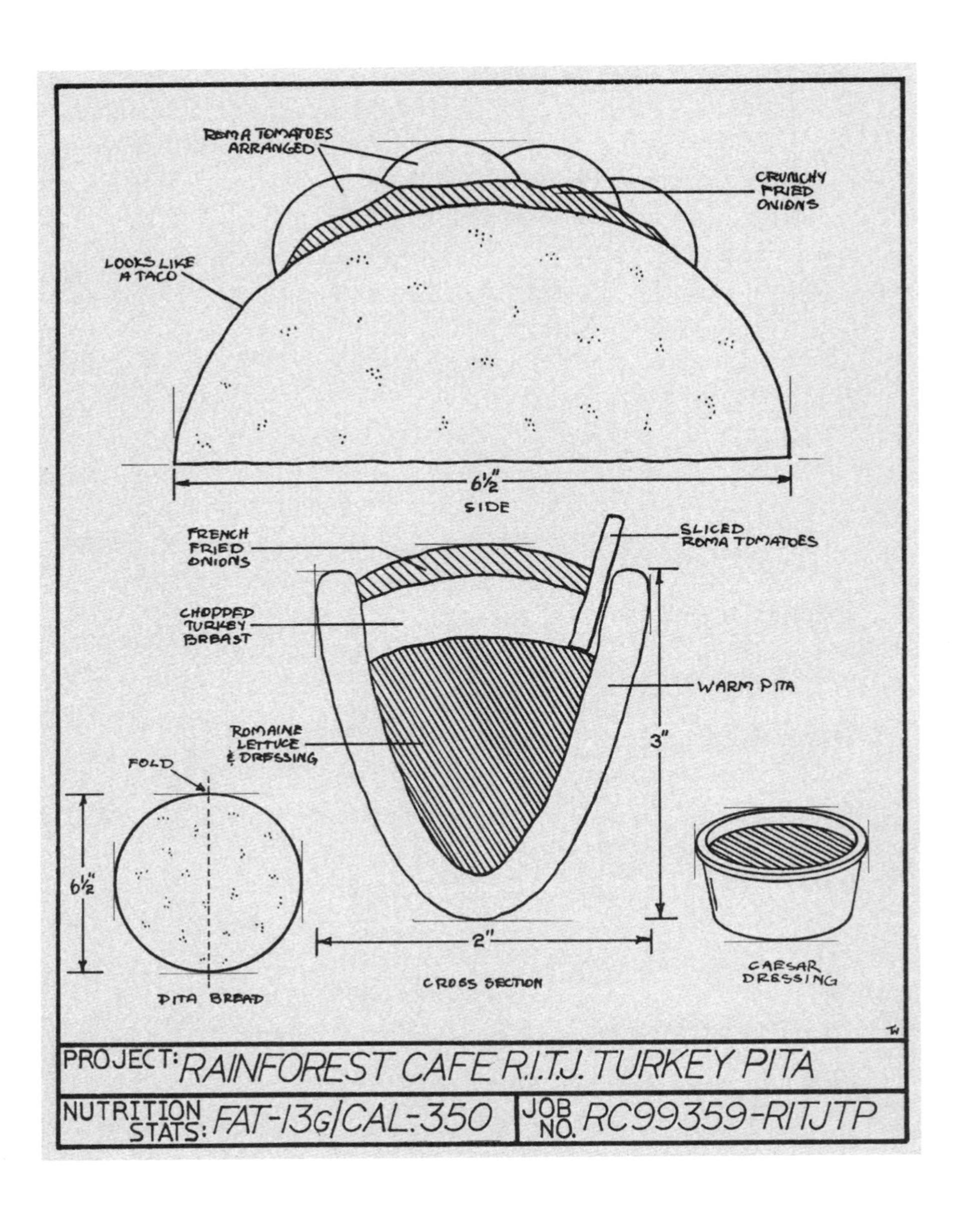
ROMA TOMATOES ARRANGED
CRUNCHY FRIED ONIONS
LOOKS LIKE A TACO
6½"
SIDE
FRENCH FRIED ONIONS
SLICED ROMA TOMATOES
CHOPPED TURKEY BREAST
WARM PITA
ROMAINE LETTUCE & DRESSING
3"
FOLD
6½"
2"
CROSS SECTION
PITA BREAD
CAESAR DRESSING
PROJECT: RAINFOREST CAFE R.I.T.J. TURKEY PITA
NUTRITION STATS: FAT-13G/CAL-350
JOB NO. RC99359-RITJTP

TOP SECRET RECIPES VERSION OF

SEVEN SEAS FREE RED WINE VINEGAR FAT-FREE DRESSING

☆ ✌ 💣 ✎ ☯ ✂ ☞

The original version of this bright red dressing is made with a generous amount of oil and is filled with gobs of greasy fat grams. The trend toward fat-free foods was in its infancy when Seven Seas went to work on a nonfat variety of the Red Wine Vinegar Dressing that would taste as good as the original. They did a pretty darn good job, too. Just by tasting the Seven Seas version of this clone, it's hard to believe there's not a speck of fat in the bottle.

We can replace the oil by thickening the dressing with a top secret combination of water, cornstarch, and a little gelatin. A couple drops of food coloring will give your clone the bright, beet-red hue of the original. Of course, you can leave the coloring out of the recipe if you like, but when you see the color without the red, you'll understand why it's in there.

1 1/3 cups water
1/4 cup granulated sugar
2 teaspoons cornstarch
1/8 teaspoon Knox unflavored gelatin
1 1/2 teaspoons dried minced onion
1 teaspoon salt
1/2 cup red wine vinegar
7 drops red food coloring

1. Combine water, sugar, cornstarch, gelatin, onion, and salt in a small saucepan. Whisk to dissolve cornstarch, then set pan over medium/low heat.
2. Heat mixture until boiling, stirring often. When mixture begins

to boil, cook for 2 additional minutes, stirring constantly, then remove from heat. Let mixture cool for 5 minutes.

3. Add vinegar and food coloring to saucepan and stir. Transfer dressing to a covered container and refrigerate—preferably overnight—before serving.

• MAKES 1½ CUPS.

Nutrition Facts

SERVING SIZE—2 TABLESPOONS
TOTAL SERVINGS—12
FAT (PER SERVING)—0 G
CALORIES (PER SERVING)—15

• • • •

TOP SECRET RECIPES VERSION OF

TOOTSIE ROLL MIDGEES

How would you react if your dentist suddenly whipped out a giant Tootsie Roll for you to bite down on so that he could make a mold of your teeth? Ask patients of a dentist in Philadelphia who does just that. This is just one of many facts that you learn researching the history of the Tootsie Roll, which, by the way, was named after the inventor's five-year-old daughter. Leo Hirschfield created the chewy brown candy in his small store in New York in 1896. In those days, the candy was hand rolled and delivered to customers by horse-drawn carriage. Over one hundred years later, more than forty-nine million Tootsie Rolls are produced each day from operations all over the world. And that's not counting the sixty bite-size clones—Tootsie Roll calls them "Midgees"—you'll make with this secret recipe.

1 cup granulated sugar
½ cup light corn syrup
2½ tablespoons shortening
4 teaspoons cocoa
2 tablespoons condensed skim milk
½ teaspoon vanilla

1. Combine sugar, corn syrup, shortening, and cocoa in a medium saucepan over medium/high heat.
2. Bring mixture to a boil, then reduce heat to medium, and simmer candy until temperature comes to 275°F on a candy thermometer.
3. Remove pan from heat. When bubbling stops, add condensed milk and beat in pan with electric mixer for about 30 seconds.

4. Add vanilla, then continue to beat candy until it begins to firm up and you can no longer beat it.
5. Pour candy out onto wax paper. When it is cool, divide candy into several portions and roll into long ropes that are approximately ½ inch thick.
6. Use a sharp knife to slice candy into 1⅛-inch-long portions.
7. Arrange the candy on a plate and let it sit out overnight so that it firms up.

- MAKES 60 PIECES.

Nutrition Facts

SERVING SIZE—6 PIECES
TOTAL SERVINGS—10
FAT (PER SERVING)—3 G
CALORIES (PER SERVING)—180

• • • •

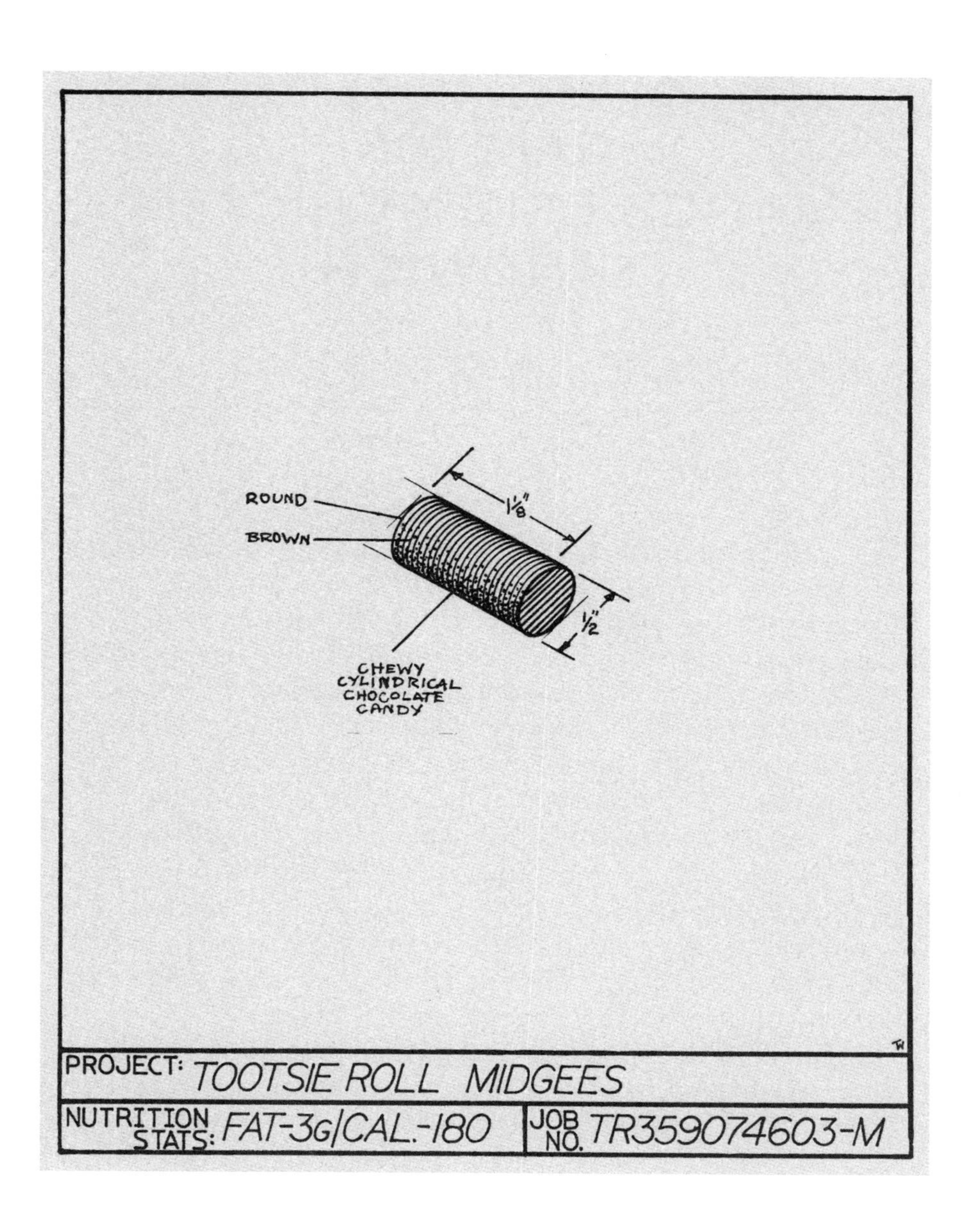
ROUND
BROWN
1⅛"
½"
CHEWY CYLINDRICAL CHOCOLATE CANDY
PROJECT: TOOTSIE ROLL MIDGEES
NUTRITION STATS: FAT-3G/CAL.-180
JOB NO. TR359074603-M

TOP SECRET RECIPES VERSION OF

CARL'S JR. RANCH CRISPY CHICKEN SANDWICH

The 1980s were the beginning of tough times for one of the world's largest burger chains. Carl Karcher had built the little hot-dog cart he purchased for $311 in 1941 into a successful West Coast hamburger chain 600 units strong; but his luck was about to change. Carl took his company public, then opened several Carl's Jr. restaurants in Texas. The bottom line for the Texas stores fell way below expectations, and the stock began to skid. In 1988, Carl was charged with insider trading for selling stock just before its price fell, and he paid almost $1 million in fines. When poor Southern California real estate investments left him millions of dollars in debt, Carl was desperate to find a way out of the hole. He proposed to the board of directors that Carl's Jr. should sell Mexican food. The board rejected the plan, so Carl tried to fire its members. In 1993, the board voted to fire Carl instead, and the man with the vision was ousted from the very company he had founded.

For this reduced-fat clone of an excellent chicken sandwich, we'll make the ranch dressing from scratch with fat-free ingredients. Then we'll use a special Top Secret Recipes baking technique cooked up in the underground test kitchen that eliminates much of the fat we can't avoid when frying.

FAT-FREE RANCH DRESSING

⅓ cup fat-free mayonnaise
2 tablespoons fat-free sour cream
1 tablespoon reduced-fat buttermilk
1 ½ teaspoons white vinegar
1 teaspoon granulated sugar
¼ teaspoon lemon
⅛ teaspoon salt
⅛ teaspoon dried parsley
⅛ teaspoon onion powder
1/16 teaspoon dried dillweed
dash garlic
dash ground black pepper
½ teaspoon unflavored gelatin
2 teaspoons hot water

SANDWICH

¼ cup egg substitute
1 cup water
1 cup flour
2½ teaspoons salt
1 teaspoon paprika
1 teaspoon onion powder
⅛ teaspoon garlic powder
2 skinless chicken breast fillets
vegetable oil cooking spray
4 sesame seed hamburger buns
4 lettuce leaves
4 tomato slices

1. Prepare the ranch dressing by combining all ingredients except the gelatin and hot water in a medium bowl. Combine the gelatin with the hot water in a small bowl and stir to dissolve all of the gelatin. Add this to the other ingredients and stir well. Cover and chill (best to chill for at least a couple hours).
2. Preheat oven to 475°F.
3. Combine the egg substitute and water in a large, shallow bowl.
4. Combine the flour, salt, paprika, onion powder, and garlic powder in another shallow bowl.
5. Cut each chicken breast in half across the middle. Wrap each half in plastic wrap and pound it to about ¼ inch thick. Trim each piece so that it is round.
6. Working with one fillet at a time, coat each with the flour, then dredge it in the egg and water mixture. Coat the chicken once again with the flour and set it aside until all of the fillets have been breaded.
7. Line a large baking sheet with aluminum foil. Spray the foil with a generous coating of cooking oil. Place the chicken fillets on

the baking sheet, then coat each one with a light layer of cooking spray.

8. Bake the fillets for 12 minutes, then crank the oven up to broil for 4 to 5 minutes, then flip the chicken over and broil for another 2 to 4 minutes or until the chicken is browned and crispy on both sides.
9. As chicken is cooking, prepare each sandwich by grilling the faces of the hamburger buns on a hot skillet over medium heat. Spread about 1½ teaspoons of the ranch dressing on the face of the top and bottom buns.
10. On the bottom bun, stack a leaf of lettuce and a tomato slice.
11. When the chicken is done cooking, stack a fillet over the tomato onto the bottom of the sandwich, then top off the sandwich with the top bun. Repeat for the remaining sandwiches.

- MAKES 4 SANDWICHES.

Nutrition Facts *(per serving)*

SERVING SIZE—1 SANDWICH   TOTAL SERVINGS—4

	LOW-FAT	ORIGINAL
CALORIES	580	620
FAT	11G	29G

• • • •

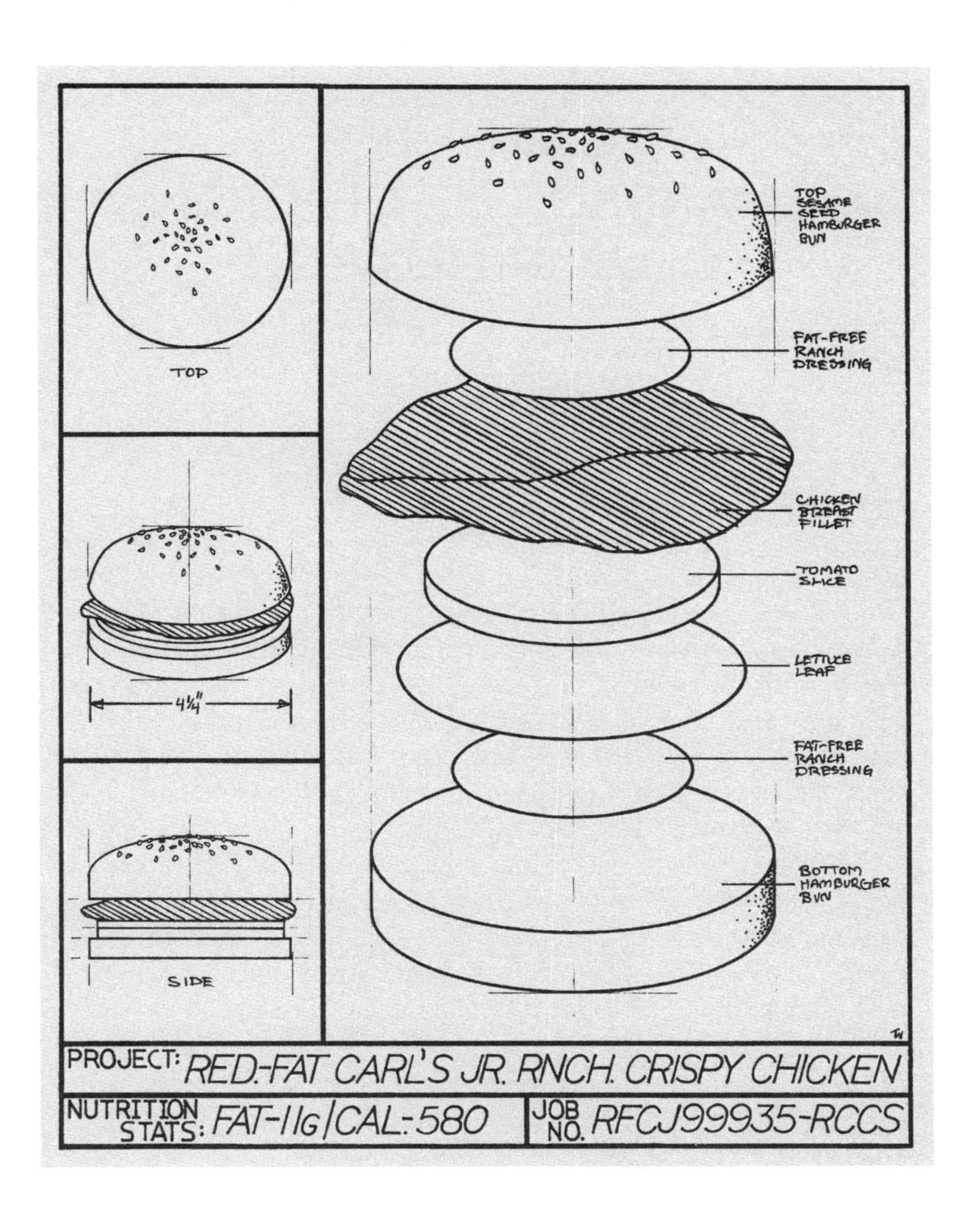
TOP
4¼"
SIDE
TOP SESAME SEED HAMBURGER BUN
FAT-FREE RANCH DRESSING
CHICKEN BREAST FILLET
TOMATO SLICE
LETTUCE LEAF
FAT-FREE RANCH DRESSING
BOTTOM HAMBURGER BUN
PROJECT: RED-FAT CARL'S JR. RNCH. CRISPY CHICKEN
NUTRITION STATS: FAT-11G | CAL-580
JOB NO. RFCJ99935-RCCS

TOP SECRET RECIPES VERSION OF

CARL'S JR. CHARBROILED CHICKEN CLUB SANDWICH

Eight weeks after the board of directors locked seventy-six-year-old Carl Karcher out of his office in 1993, he was engineering a takeover of the "Happy Star" company that he had built over five decades. Crafty Carl found financier William P. Foley to assume his debts in exchange for stock and take control of the company as the new chairman of the board. Carl was named chairman emeritus and finally got his desk back. His plan to sell Mexican food at Carl's Jr. restaurants was later adopted and became a huge success for the chain, and almost all of the executives who had fired him have since left the company.

Here's one of Carl's delicious sandwiches that we can clone with much fewer fat grams by using turkey bacon, fat-free mayonnaise, and fat-free Swiss cheese. These substitutions for full-fat ingredients can bring the fat down from twenty-nine grams to just over ten without compromising that distinctive Carl's Jr. taste.

2 skinless chicken breast fillets
½ cup teriyaki marinade (thick style)
4 whole wheat hamburger buns
8 slices turkey bacon
¼ cup fat-free mayonnaise
1 cup alfalfa sprouts
4 lettuce leaves
4 large tomato slices
4 slices fat-free Swiss cheese slices

1. Cut each chicken breast in half across the middle, then wrap the halves, one at a time, in plastic wrap. Pound each one with a mallet until it is about ¼ inch thick.

2. Pour the teriyaki marinade over the meat. Cover and chill the meat and let it marinate for at least two hours. Marinating them overnight is even better.
3. When the chicken is well marinated, heat up a skillet and toast the face of each of the buns. Keep the pan hot. Preheat your barbecue or indoor grill to medium heat.
4. Fry the turkey bacon in the skillet for 5 to 6 minutes or until it's crispy, turning each slice over halfway through the cooking time.
5. As the bacon is frying, cook the chicken on the grill for 3 to 4 minutes per side or until done.
6. Build the sandwiches by first spreading ½ tablespoon of fat-free mayo on each toasted face of the buns.
7. Divide the sprouts into four even portions and stack a mound on each of the bottom buns.
8. On the sprouts, stack a lettuce leaf, and then a slice of tomato.
9. Place a piece of chicken on the tomato slice on each of the sandwiches.
10. Next, place a slice of Swiss cheese on the chicken, and then two pieces of bacon, crossed over each other.
11. Finish building the sandwiches by adding the top bun.
12. Microwave each sandwich for 15 seconds on high, and serve.

- MAKES 4 SANDWICHES.

Nutrition Facts *(per serving)*

SERVING SIZE—1 SANDWICH   TOTAL SERVINGS—4

	LOW-FAT	ORIGINAL
CALORIES	366	570
FAT	10.5G	29G

• • • •

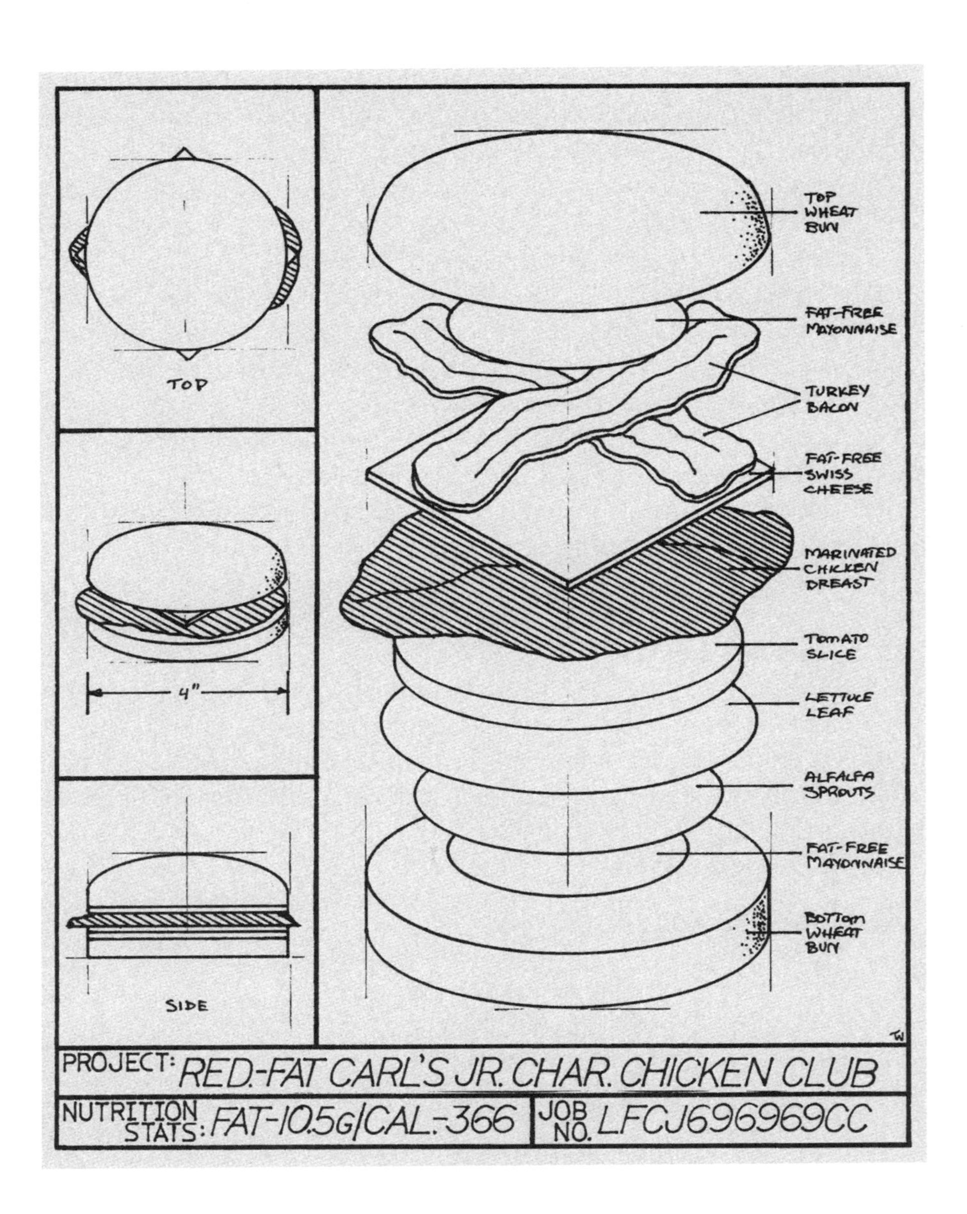
TOP
SIDE
4"
TOP WHEAT BUN
FAT-FREE MAYONNAISE
TURKEY BACON
FAT-FREE SWISS CHEESE
MARINATED CHICKEN BREAST
TOMATO SLICE
LETTUCE LEAF
ALFALFA SPROUTS
FAT-FREE MAYONNAISE
BOTTOM WHEAT BUN
TW
PROJECT: RED.-FAT CARL'S JR. CHAR. CHICKEN CLUB
NUTRITION STATS: FAT-10.5G/CAL.-366
JOB NO. LFCJ696969CC

TOP SECRET RECIPES VERSION OF

CARL'S JR. CHARBROILED SANTA FE CHICKEN SANDWICH

☆ ✌ 💣 ✎ ☯ ✂ ☞

In the last few years, Carl's Jr. has become one of the fastest-growing fast-food chains in the country. In 1997, the burger joint grew from 930 restaurants in nine states to nearly 3,900 in forty-four states with its purchase of Hardee's hamburger outlets. This makes Carl's Jr. the fourth-largest burger chain in the country, behind McDonald's, Burger King, and Wendy's.

One of the unique sandwiches that makes Carl's a popular stop for the lunch crowd is this Charbroiled Santa Fe Chicken Sandwich with the delicious spicy sauce. It's that tasty sauce that gives the real thing much of its fat, so by cloning it with nonfat ingredients, we can cut the grease on this sandwich to one-fifth of that of the original, while keeping all of the zing.

SANTA FE SAUCE

1/3 cup fat-free mayonnaise
1/4 teaspoon paprika
1/4 teaspoon curry powder
1/8 teaspoon cayenne pepper
1/8 teaspoon salt

SANDWICH

2 skinless chicken breast fillets
1/2 cup teriyaki marinade (thick style)
4 whole wheat hamburger buns
4 lettuce leaves
2 large canned mild green chili peppers, halved
4 slices fat-free American cheese

1. Make the sauce by combining all of the ingredients in a small bowl, and stir well. Cover and chill until needed.
2. Cut each chicken breast in half across the middle, and then wrap the halves, one at a time, in plastic wrap. Pound each one with a mallet until it is about ¼ inch thick.
3. Pour the teriyaki marinade over the chicken. Cover and chill the chicken and let it marinate for at least two hours. Marinating it overnight is even better.
4. When the chicken is well marinated, heat up a skillet and toast the face of each of the buns. You may also toast the buns in a toaster oven.
5. Cook the chicken on the grill for 3 to 4 minutes per side or until done.
6. Build the sandwiches by first spreading ½ tablespoon of the Santa Fe sauce on each toasted face of the buns.
7. Stack the lettuce on next.
8. Spread out a pepper half and place it on top of the lettuce on each sandwich. Depending on the size of the pepper, you may have to trim the pepper or add more. You want to have just enough to fit on the sandwich without too much excess falling over the side.
9. Place a piece of chicken on the pepper on each of the sandwiches.
10. Next, place a slice of American cheese on the chicken.
11. Finish building the sandwiches by adding the top bun.
12. Microwave each sandwich for 15 seconds on high.

- MAKES 4 SANDWICHES.

Nutrition Facts *(per serving)*

SERVING SIZE—1 SANDWICH TOTAL SERVINGS—4

	LOW-FAT	ORIGINAL
CALORIES	305	530
FAT	5.5G	29G

• • • •

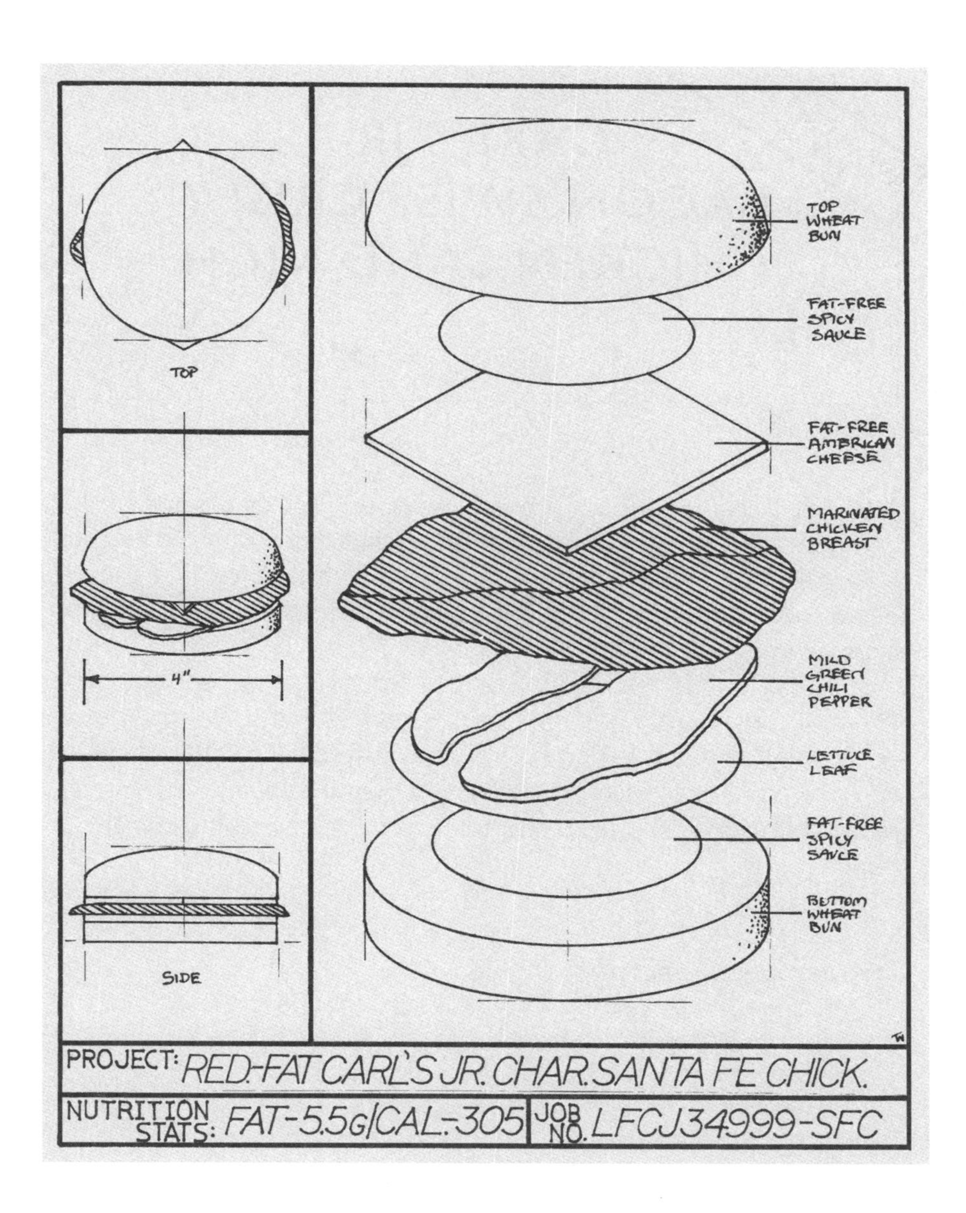
TOP
SIDE
4"
TOP WHEAT BUN
FAT-FREE SPICY SAUCE
FAT-FREE AMERICAN CHEESE
MARINATED CHICKEN BREAST
MILD GREEN CHILI PEPPER
LETTUCE LEAF
FAT-FREE SPICY SAUCE
BOTTOM WHEAT BUN
PROJECT: RED-FAT CARL'S JR. CHAR. SANTA FE CHICK.
NUTRITION STATS: FAT-5.5G/CAL.-305
JOB NO. LFCJ34999-SFC

TOP SECRET RECIPES VERSION OF

CARL'S JR. BACON SWISS CRISPY CHICKEN SANDWICH

☆ ✌ 💣 ✎ ☯ ✂ ☞

Helping Carl's Jr. rebound from its sales slump was a series of TV commercials featuring oversauced sandwiches that splattered ketchup and mayo onto floors, clothes, and shoes. The tag line, "If it doesn't get all over the place, it doesn't belong in your face," made sloppy synonymous with tasty.

If you look forward to messing up your clean clothes but don't need all the saturated fat that usually comes with this drippy fare, you'll want to give this clone a try. The fat-free ranch dressing saves you from oodles of nasty fat grams, and then the special baking technique that clones the taste and texture of deep frying eliminates a bunch more.

FAT-FREE RANCH DRESSING

1/3 cup fat-free mayonnaise
2 tablespoons fat-free sour cream
1 tablespoon reduced-fat buttermilk
1 1/2 teaspoons white vinegar
1 teaspoon granulated sugar
1/4 teaspoon lemon juice
1/8 teaspoon salt
1/8 teaspoon dried parsley
1/8 teaspoon onion powder
1/16 teaspoon dried dillweed
dash garlic
dash ground black pepper
2 teaspoons hot water
1/2 teaspoon unflavored gelatin

SANDWICH

8 slices lean turkey bacon, cooked
1/4 cup egg substitute
1 cup water
1 cup flour

2½ teaspoons salt
1 teaspoon paprika
1 teaspoon onion powder
⅛ teaspoon garlic powder
2 skinless chicken breast fillets
vegetable oil cooking spray
4 sesame seed hamburger buns
4 lettuce leaves
4 tomato slices
4 Kraft fat-free Swiss cheese singles

1. Prepare the ranch dressing by combining the ingredients in a small bowl. Cover and chill.
2. Preheat oven to 475°F.
3. Cook bacon following directions on package. Drain on paper towels and set aside.
4. Combine the egg substitute and water in a large, shallow bowl.
5. Combine the flour, salt, paprika, onion powder, and garlic powder in another shallow bowl.
6. Cut each chicken breast in half across the middle, and then wrap the halves, one at a time, in plastic wrap. Pound each one with a mallet until it is about ¼ inch thick. Trim each fillet until it is round.
7. Working with one fillet at a time, first coat each fillet with the flour, then dredge it in the egg and water mixture. Coat the chicken once again in the flour, and set it aside until all of the fillets have been breaded.
8. Line a large baking sheet with aluminum foil. Spray the foil with a generous coating of cooking oil. Place the chicken fillets on the baking sheet, then coat each one with a coating of cooking spray.
9. Bake the fillets for 12 minutes, then crank the oven up to broil for 4 to 5 minutes, then flip the chicken over and broil for another 2 to 4 minutes or until the chicken is browned and crispy on both sides.
10. As chicken is cooking, prepare each sandwich by grilling the face of the hamburger buns on a hot skillet over medium heat. Spread about 1½ teaspoons of the ranch dressing on the face of the top and bottom buns.
11. On the bottom bun, stack a leaf of lettuce and a tomato slice.
12. When the chicken is done cooking, place a fillet over the

tomato onto the bottom of the sandwich, then stack a slice of the fat-free Swiss cheese onto the chicken.

13. Arrange the bacon, crosswise, on top of the Swiss cheese, then top off the sandwich with the top bun. Repeat the stacking process for each of the remaining sandwiches.

- MAKES 4 SANDWICHES.

Nutrition Facts *(per serving)*

SERVING SIZE—1 SANDWICH TOTAL SERVINGS—4

	LOW-FAT	ORIGINAL
CALORIES	660	720
FAT	19G	36G

• • • •

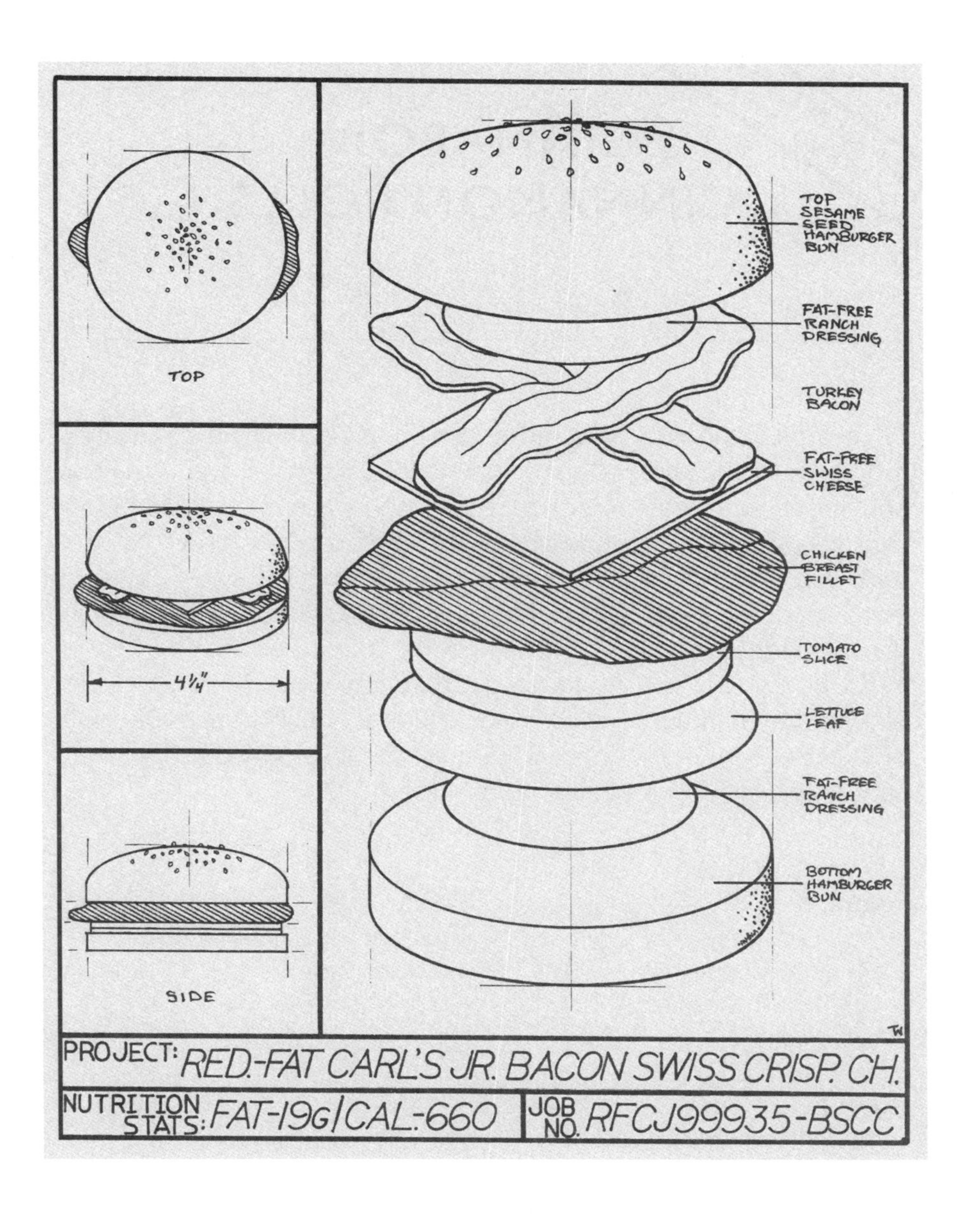
TOP
4 1/4"
SIDE
TOP SESAME SEED HAMBURGER BUN
FAT-FREE RANCH DRESSING
TURKEY BACON
FAT-FREE SWISS CHEESE
CHICKEN BREAST FILLET
TOMATO SLICE
LETTUCE LEAF
FAT-FREE RANCH DRESSING
BOTTOM HAMBURGER BUN
TW
PROJECT: RED.-FAT CARL'S JR. BACON SWISS CRISP. CH.
NUTRITION STATS: FAT-19G/CAL.-660
JOB NO. RFCJ99935-BSCC

TOP SECRET RECIPES VERSION OF

CINNABON CINNAMON ROLLS

☆ ✌ 💣 ✏ ☯ ✂ ☞

How sinfully delicious are these cinnamon rolls? Their intoxicating aroma wafts through shopping malls and airports all over America, and at one time or another you've probably been a victim of that irresistible, gooey swirl of delight. Sometimes, though, for a treat this delicious, you just have to say "What the heck!" Right? There's a good chance that same thought has gone through the minds of millions since the first Cinnabon was served at Seattle's Sea-Tac Mall in 1985. But what if you could still get that marvelous Cinnabon taste with better than an 80 percent reduction in fat? Not possible, you say? Get out the rolling pin and prepare for an amazing reduced-fat conversion of America's favorite mall food.

ROLLS

1 ¼-ounce package active dry yeast
1 cup warm fat-free milk (105 to 110 degrees)
½ cup sugar
¼ cup butter
6 tablespoons egg substitute
1 teaspoon salt
4 cups all-purpose flour

FILLING

1 cup dark brown sugar, packed
⅓ cup Wondra flour
2½ tablespoons cinnamon
½ cup fat-free butter spread

ICING

1 8-ounce package fat-free cream cheese
1 ½ cups powdered sugar
1 tablespoon Butter Buds
½ teaspoon vanilla
⅛ teaspoon salt

1. Make the rolls by dissolving the yeast in the warm milk in a large bowl. Add the sugar and let the mixture sit for 5 minutes.
2. Melt the butter in the microwave or in a saucepan over low heat and add it to the mixture in the large bowl.
3. Add the egg substitute, salt, and flour to the large bowl, mix to incorporate the ingredients, then use flour-dusted hands to knead the dough into a large ball. Put the dough back into the bowl, cover it, and let it rise in a warm place for about 1 hour, or until it has doubled in size.
4. Make the filling by combining the brown sugar, Wondra flour, and cinnamon in a small bowl. Preheat the oven to 400°F.
5. Roll the dough out onto a lightly floured surface. Roll the dough into a flat rectangle until it is approximately 21 inches long and 16 inches wide. It should be about ¼-inch thick.
6. Spread ½ cup of the butter-flavored spread over the surface of the dough. Sprinkle the brown sugar and cinnamon mixture over the spread.
7. Working from the top (a 21-inch side), roll the dough down to the bottom edge.
8. Cut the rolled dough into 1¾-inch slices and place 6, evenly spaced, into each of two 9 x 13-inch lightly greased baking pans. Cover the baking pans and let the rolls rise for another 45 to 60 minutes, then bake for 15 to 22 minutes or until the rolls are light brown on top.
9. While the rolls bake, combine the icing ingredients in a medium bowl and beat well with an electric mixer at high speed until smooth and creamy.
10. Cool the rolls for 3 to 5 minutes after removing them from the oven, then spread icing over the top of each one.

- MAKES 1 DOZEN ROLLS.

Nutritional Facts *(per serving)*

SERVING SIZE—1 ROLL TOTAL SERVINGS—12

	LITE	ORIGINAL
CALORIES	370	730
FAT	4G	24G

• • • •

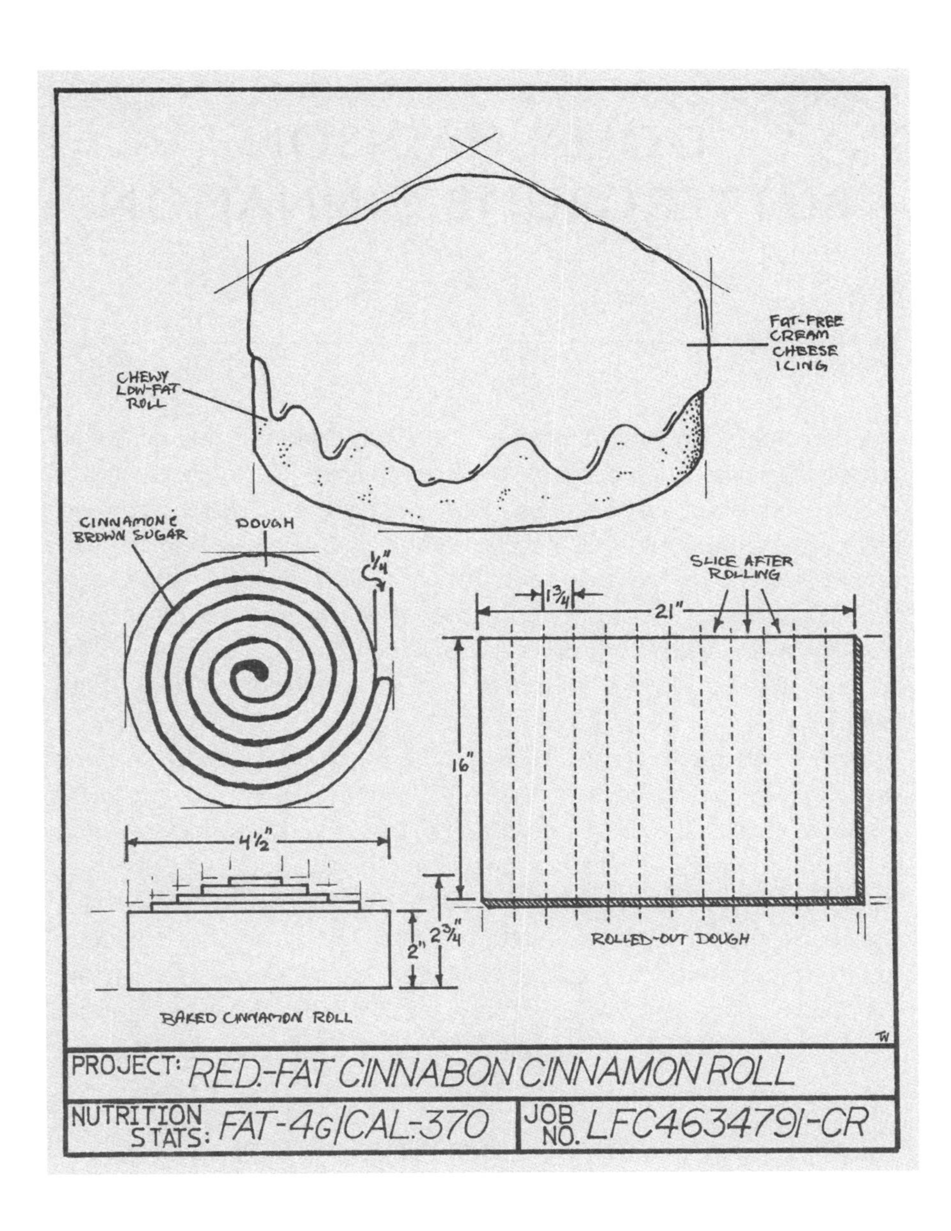
FAT-FREE CREAM CHEESE ICING
CHEWY LOW-FAT ROLL
CINNAMON & BROWN SUGAR
DOUGH
1/4"
SLICE AFTER ROLLING
1 3/4
21"
16"
4 1/2"
2 3/4"
2"
ROLLED-OUT DOUGH
BAKED CINNAMON ROLL
TW
PROJECT: RED.-FAT CINNABON CINNAMON ROLL
NUTRITION STATS: FAT-4G/CAL.-370
JOB NO. LFC4634791-CR

TOP SECRET RECIPES VERSION OF

DOLLY MADISON BUTTERCRUMB CINNAMON

☆ ✌ 💣 ✎ ☯ ✂ ☞

When Interstate Brands started the Dolly Madison line of baked goods that has today become the convenience store leader, it was known as Interstate Bakeries. Roy Nafziger started the bakery in 1927, and he could only have dreamed that one day his company would ring up more than one billion dollars in sales. One item that contributes to those impressive sales figures are these little brown sugar/cinnamon–topped cakes, which have become a popular addition to the Dolly Madison line of baked goods since the late eighties.

We can easily create a low-fat home clone of the real thing with only seven ingredients, thanks to white cake mix that can be found in practically all stores. Notice that the cake mix is not a reduced-fat variety. That's not necessary for the recipe to produce little cakes that taste just like the real thing, but still have less than one-third the fat. And even though the original is sort of square-shaped, we'll use a couple of 12-cup muffin pans to simplify the process. The shape will be different, but the flavor will be right on.

1 18.25-ounce box white cake mix
1 ¼ cups water
½ cup egg substitute
1 tablespoon Butter Buds Sprinkles

TOPPING
⅔ cup dark brown sugar
2 tablespoons sugar
1 tablespoon cinnamon

1. Preheat the oven to 350°F.
2. Combine the cake mix, water, egg substitute, and Butter Buds in a large bowl and mix with an electric mixer for 2 minutes.
3. Grease the cups of two 12-cup muffin tins (if you only have one, just be sure to clean it well after the first batch). Fill each cup about half full with batter.
4. Combine the ingredients for the topping in a small bowl and mix well.
5. Sprinkle about 2 teaspoons of the topping over the batter in each cup. Use a knife to slightly swirl the topping into the batter.
6. Bake the cakes for 20 to 25 minutes or until light brown on top. Store the cakes in a sealed container after they have cooled to keep them fresh.

- MAKES 24 CAKES.

Nutritional Facts *(per serving)*

SERVING SIZE—1 CAKE TOTAL SERVINGS—24

	LITE	ORIGINAL
CALORIES	111	170
FAT	1.7G	6G

• • • •

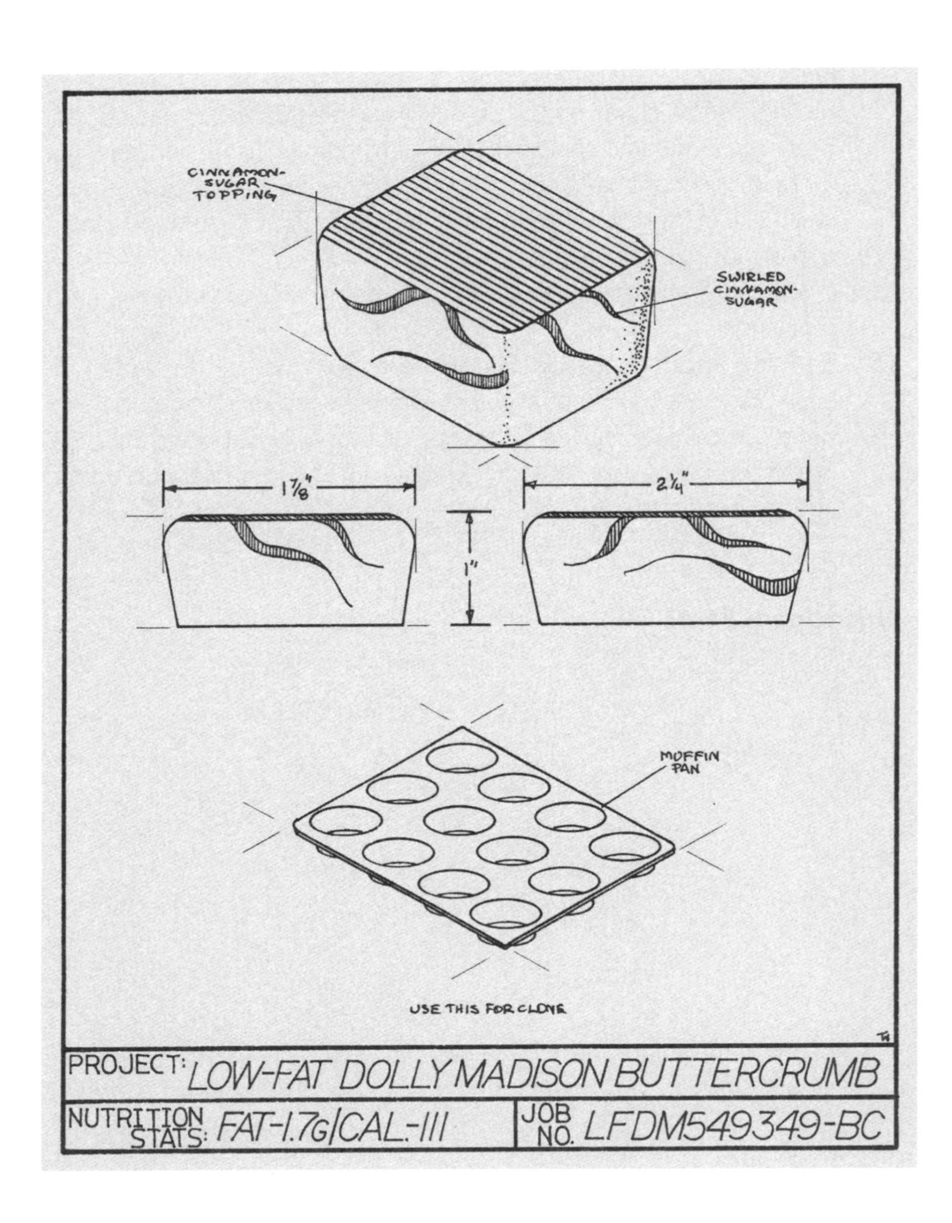
CINNAMON-SUGAR TOPPING
SWIRLED CINNAMON-SUGAR
1 7/8"
2 1/4"
1"
MUFFIN PAN
USE THIS FOR CLONE
PROJECT: LOW-FAT DOLLY MADISON BUTTERCRUMB
NUTRITION STATS: FAT-1.7G/CAL.-111
JOB NO. LFDM549349-BC

TOP SECRET RECIPES VERSION OF

KELLOGG'S RICE KRISPIES TREATS

☆ ✌ 💣 ✎ ☯ ✂ ☞

It wasn't long after the cereal's 1928 introduction that Kellogg Kitchens invented a way to mix Rice Krispies with melted marshmallows and butter to produce with an alternative, nonbreakfast use for the product. In the early forties the Rice Krispies Treats recipe was printed on boxes of Rice Krispies cereal and became a great recipe for kids since it was very easy to make, required no baking, and could be eaten almost immediately. The popularity of these treats inspired two additional cereals in the early nineties: Fruity Marshmallow Krispies, and Rice Krispies Treats Cereal. And at the same time, Kellogg came out with individually packaged Rice Krispies Treats, for those who wanted instant satisfaction without having to spend time in the kitchen. But that product, just like the popular recipe printed on the cereal box, contained 2 grams of fat. And since the packaged Treats are small, it's tough to eat just one (tell me about it).

By using Butter Buds Sprinkles and making some other important changes to the recipe, I have come up with a treat recipe for bars that taste like the packaged product, at considerably less cost (the recipe makes the equivalent of three boxes of the real thing), and with not one gram of fat.

nonstick cooking spray
7 cups miniature marshmallows
3 tablespoons Butter Buds Sprinkles
2 tablespoons water
¼ teaspoon vanilla
¼ teaspoon salt
6 cups Rice Krispies cereal

1. Lightly coat a large nonstick saucepan or pot with cooking spray.
2. Add the marshmallows, Butter Buds, water, vanilla, and salt to the pan and set over medium/low heat. Stir the mixture constantly while cooking until the marshmallows are completely melted. Turn off the heat.
3. Add the Rice Krispies and stir until the cereal is completely coated.
4. Spray a 9 x 13-inch baking pan with a light coating of the cooking spray. Pour the Rice Krispies mixture into the pan. Moisten your hands and press the mixture into the pan until flat.
5. When the mixture cools completely, cut four times down and four across, making 25 bars.

- MAKES 25 BARS.

Nutritional Facts *(per serving)*

SERVING SIZE—1 BAR TOTAL SERVINGS—25

	LITE	ORIGINAL
CALORIES	90	90
FAT	0G	2G

• • • •

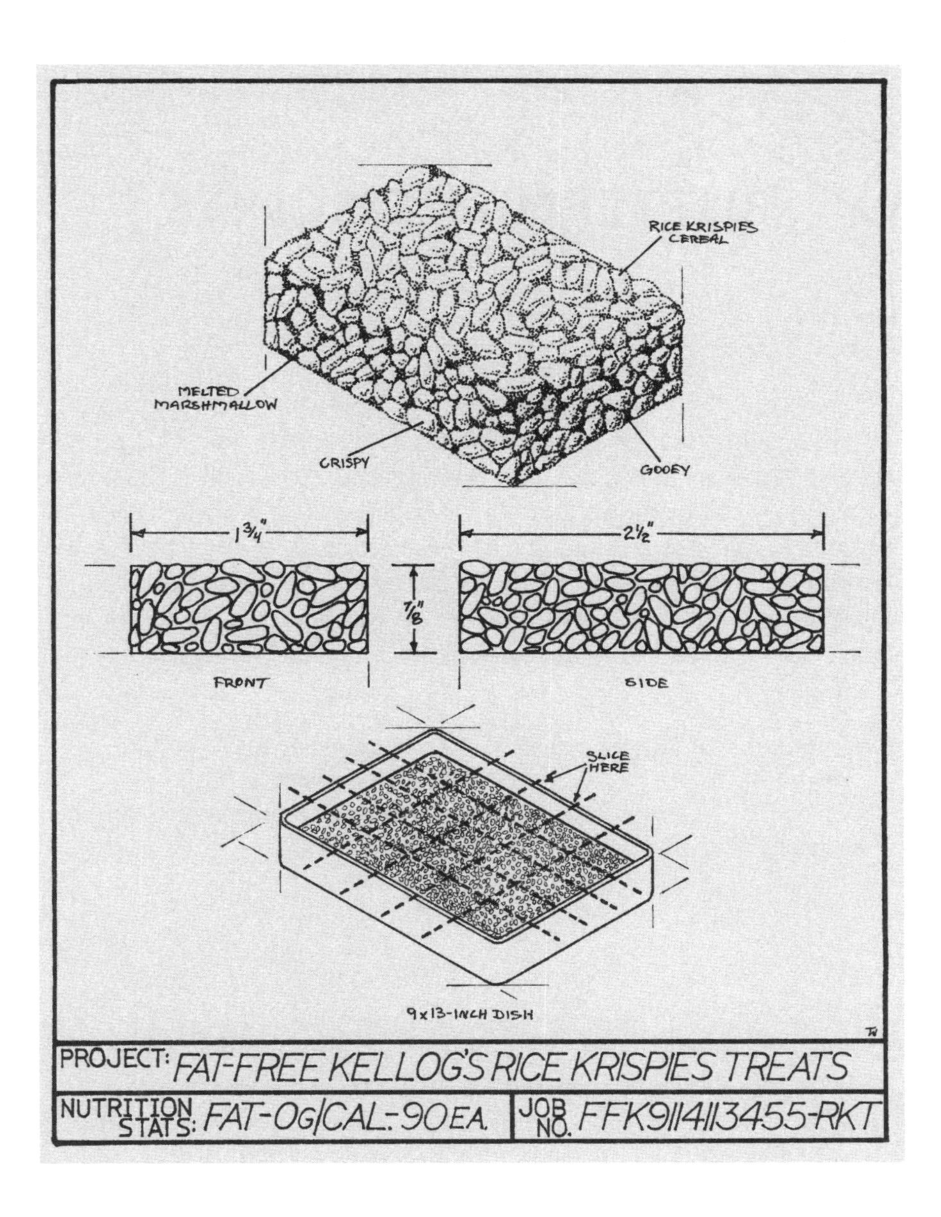
RICE KRISPIES CEREAL
MELTED MARSHMALLOW
CRISPY
GOOEY
1 3/4"
2 1/2"
7/8"
FRONT
SIDE
SLICE HERE
9x13-INCH DISH
PROJECT: FAT-FREE KELLOG'S RICE KRISPIES TREATS
NUTRITION STATS: FAT-0G/CAL.-90 EA.
JOB NO. FFK9114113455-RKT

TOP SECRET RECIPES VERSION OF

KFC BUTTERMILK BISCUITS

How would you like a killer biscuit recipe that has 75 percent less fat than typical biscuits, and tastes great? And what if I told you they would still taste like those introduced to the world in 1982 by the world's largest chicken chain? Here you go—a clone recipe for making a low-fat version of KFC's Buttermilk Biscuits. Reduced-fat Bisquick and Butter Buds Sprinkles are the secret ingredients that help make this TSR low-fat conversion of a fast food favorite.

2 cups reduced-fat Bisquick baking mix
¾ cup low-fat (1 percent) buttermilk
2 teaspoons Butter Buds Sprinkles
2 teaspoons sugar
¼ teaspoon salt
1 tablespoon margarine, melted

1. Preheat the oven to 450°F.
2. Combine the baking mix, buttermilk, Butter Buds, sugar, and salt in a medium bowl. Mix by hand until well blended.
3. Turn the dough out onto a floured surface and knead for about 30 seconds, or until the dough becomes elastic.
4. Roll the dough to about ¾-inch thick and punch out biscuits using a 3-inch cutter. Arrange the punched-out dough on an ungreased baking sheet, and bake for 10 to 12 minutes or until the biscuits are golden on top and have about doubled in height.
5. Remove the biscuits from the oven and immediately brush the

top of each one with a light coating of the melted margarine. Serve warm.

- Makes 8 biscuits.

Nutritional Facts *(per serving)*

Serving size—1 biscuit   Total servings—8

	Lite	Original
Calories	115	180
Fat	2.5g	10g

• • • •

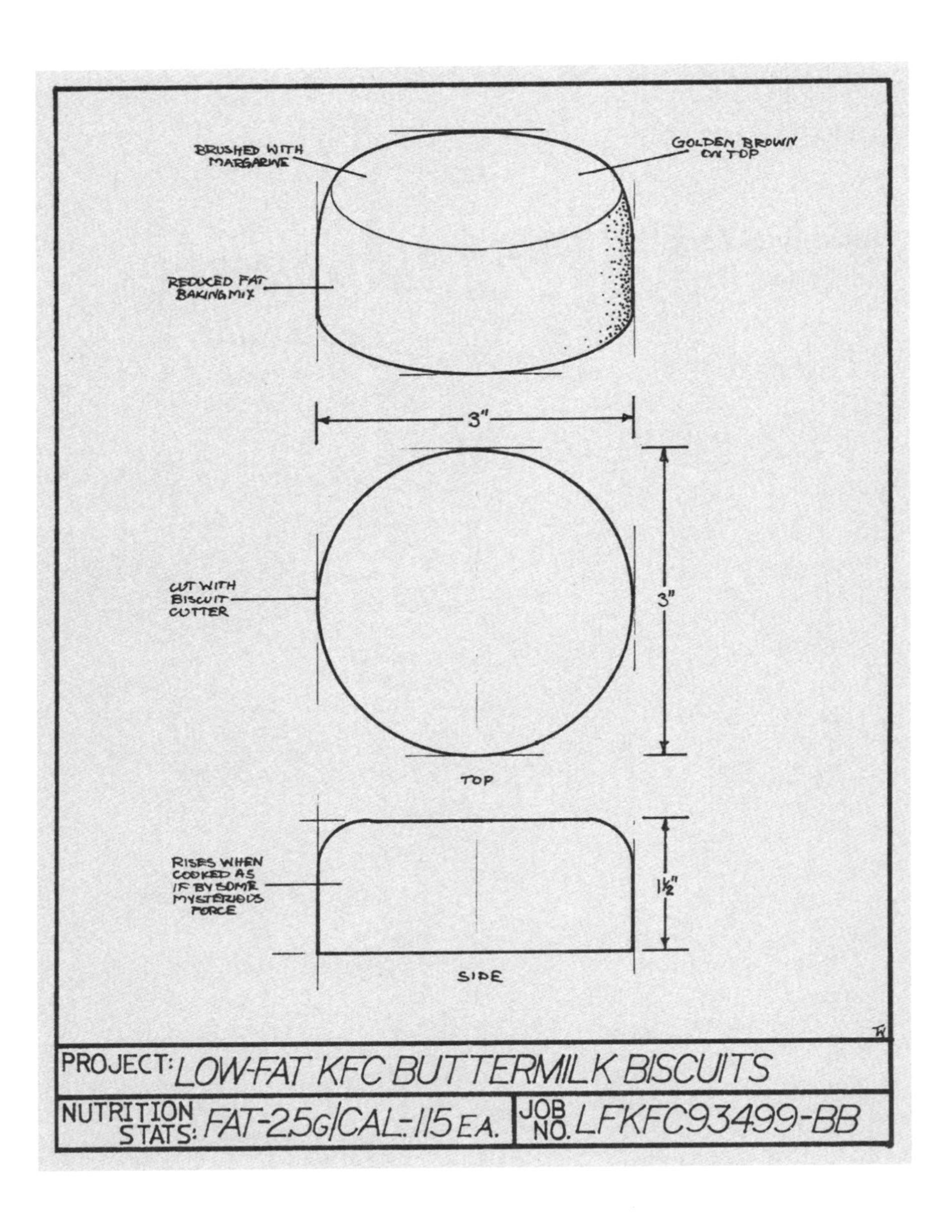
BRUSHED WITH MARGARINE
GOLDEN BROWN ON TOP
REDUCED FAT BAKING MIX
3"
CUT WITH BISCUIT CUTTER
3"
TOP
RISES WHEN COOKED AS IF BY SOME MYSTERIOUS FORCE
1½"
SIDE
PROJECT: LOW-FAT KFC BUTTERMILK BISCUITS
NUTRITION STATS: FAT-2.5G/CAL-115 EA.
JOB NO. LFKFC93499-BB

TOP SECRET RECIPES VERSION OF

KFC MASHED POTATOES & GRAVY

The secret to cloning the Colonel's famous gravy at home is to first darken the chicken broth with a roux. Roux is a mixture of flour and oil that is cooked in a saucepan over low heat until it's browned, but not burned. This magical mixture not only colors the gravy for us, but also thickens it. The small amount of oil used here and no addition of drippings will give you gravy that tastes as good as the stuff from the world-famous chicken chain, but with significantly less fat.

And when you're done with the gravy, you can easily make mashed potatoes that taste just like KFC's with those popular Potato Buds. The taste of the real thing is imitated with fat-free butter-flavored spread that adds no fat. You're going to love this one.

GRAVY

1 tablespoon vegetable oil
5 tablespoons all-purpose flour
1 can Campbell's chicken broth (plus 1 can of water)
¼ teaspoon salt
⅛ teaspoon pepper

MASHED POTATOES

1 ½ cups water
⅓ cup reduced-fat (2 percent) milk
2½ tablespoons Fleischmann's Fat-Free Buttery Spread
½ teaspoon salt
1 ⅓ cups instant mashed potato flakes (Potato Buds)

1. Make the gravy by first preparing a roux: Combine the oil with 1½ tablespoons of flour in a medium saucepan. Cook over low heat for 20 to 30 minutes or until the mixture becomes a chocolate color.
2. Remove the pan from the heat and add the chicken broth, 1 can of water, the remaining flour, ¼ teaspoon of salt, and pepper. Put the pan back on the heat and bring the heat up to medium. When the mixture begins to boil, reduce the heat and simmer the gravy for 15 minutes or until thick.
3. As the gravy is reducing, prepare the potatoes by combining 1½ cups of water, ⅓ cup of milk, the fat-free buttery spread, and ½ teaspoon of salt in a medium saucepan over medium heat. Bring to a boil, add the potato flakes, and whip with a fork until smooth.
4. Serve the mashed potatoes with gravy poured over the top.

- Makes 4 servings.

Nutritional Facts *(per serving)*

Serving size—½ cup potatoes and 3 tablespoons gravy   Total servings—4

	Lite	Original
Calories	120	120
Fat	2g	6g

• • • •

TOP SECRET RECIPES VERSION OF

MCDONALD'S ARCH DELUXE

☆ ✌ 💣 ✏ ☯ ✂ ☞

McDonald's introduced its new sandwich in 1996 with a $200 million marketing blitz aimed at winning over grown-ups. We watched Ronald McDonald golf, dance, and hang out with sophisticated human beings, rather than his usual gang of creepy dancing puppets. These messages were supposed to tug at the adult market lost to more inspired sandwich creations from chains like Wendy's and Arby's and Carl's Jr.

Did the campaign work? So far, the sales figures have been less than stellar for the burger with even more fat in it than a Big Mac. But the sandwich, with its specially developed Dijon mustard–mayo sauce, does have its share of devoted fans. Perhaps even more of us would get on the Arch Deluxe team if we could make a clone using reduced-fat ingredients to knock the fat down to nearly one-third that of the original, as I have here.

1 tablespoon fat-free mayonnaise
½ teaspoon brown mustard (French's Hearty Deli is good)
1 sesame seed hamburger bun
¼ pound super lean ground beef (7% fat)
salt and pepper
1 slice fat-free American cheese
1 large tomato slice
1 to 2 lettuce leaves, chopped
½ tablespoon ketchup
2 tablespoons chopped onion

1. In a small bowl, mix together the mayonnaise and the brown mustard. Set this mixture aside.
2. Grill the face of each of the buns on a griddle or frying pan over medium heat.

3. Roll the ground beef into a ball and pat it out until it's approximately the same diameter as the bun. You can freeze this patty before you cook it just like the restaurant chain does. This will also make it stay together better when it cooks.
4. Cook the meat on a hot griddle or frying pan for about 5 minutes per side until done. Be sure to lightly salt and pepper each side of the patty.
5. Build the burger in the following order, from the bottom up:

ON BOTTOM BUN

beef patty
American cheese slice
tomato slice
lettuce

ON TOP BUN

mayo/mustard
ketchup
onion

6. Slap the top of the sandwich onto the bottom and serve. Microwave sandwich on high for 15 seconds if you like the sandwich hotter.

- MAKES 1 SANDWICH.

TIDBITS

If you'd like to add bacon to the sandwich, as you can order with the original, just cook a piece of turkey bacon sprinkled with coarsely ground black pepper. Break the bacon in half and place each half of the bacon side by side onto the bottom bun before stacking on the beef patty.

Nutrition Facts *(per serving)*

SERVING SIZE—1 BURGER TOTAL SERVINGS—1

	LOW-FAT	ORIGINAL
CALORIES	430	550
FAT	11G	31G

WITH BACON:

Nutrition Facts *(per serving)*

SERVING SIZE—1 SANDWICH TOTAL SERVINGS—1

	LOW-FAT	ORIGINAL
CALORIES	450	590
FAT	13.5G	34G

• • • •

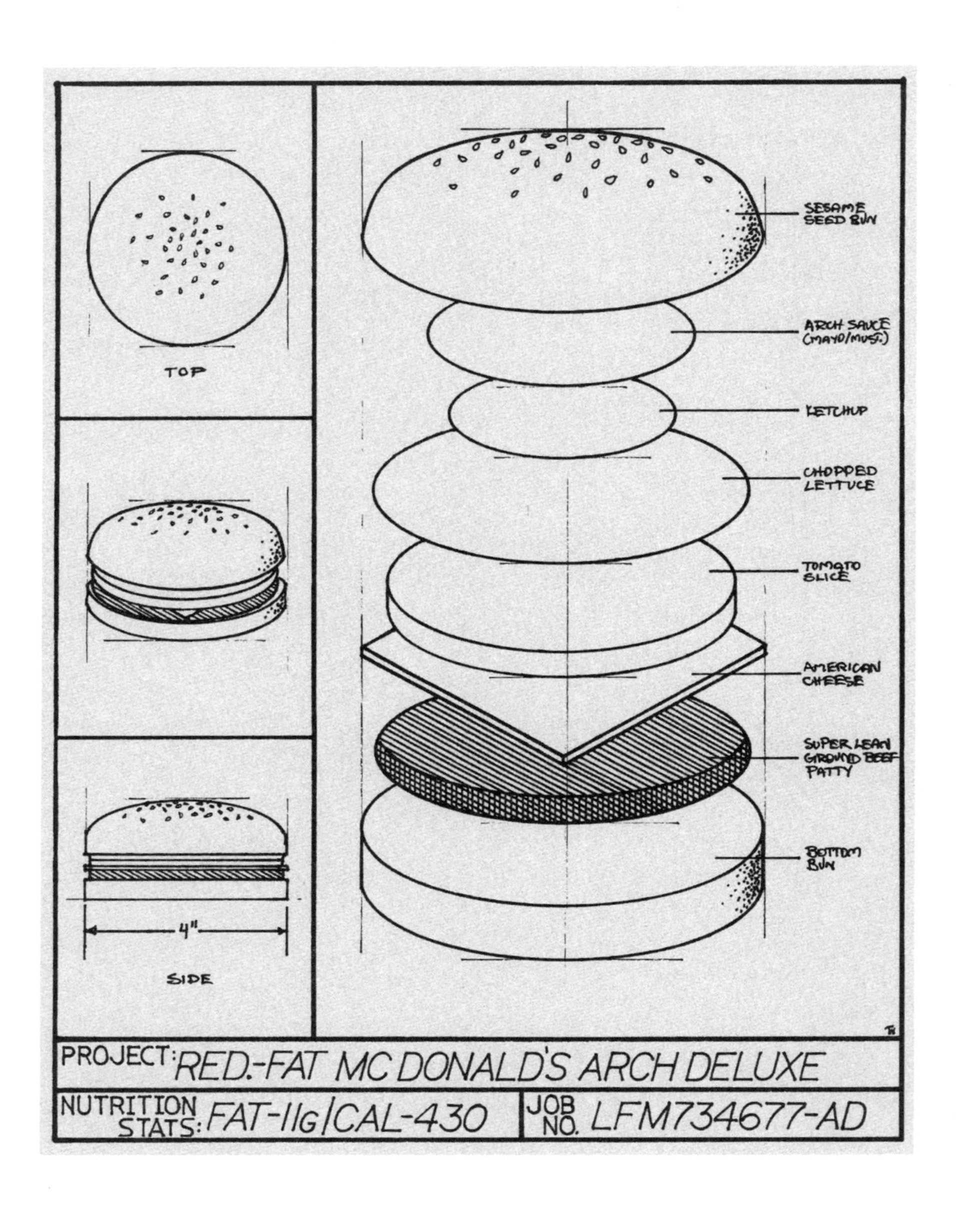
TOP
SIDE
4"
SESAME SEED BUN
ARCH SAUCE (MAYO/MUST.)
KETCHUP
CHOPPED LETTUCE
TOMATO SLICE
AMERICAN CHEESE
SUPER LEAN GROUND BEEF PATTY
BOTTOM BUN
PROJECT: RED.-FAT MC DONALD'S ARCH DELUXE
NUTRITION STATS: FAT-11G/CAL-430
JOB NO. LFM734677-AD

TOP SECRET RECIPES VERSION OF

MCDONALD'S EGG MCMUFFIN

☆ ✌ 💣 ✎ ☯ ✂ ☞

Like the Big Mac, the idea for this breakfast product came from an inspired McDonald's franchisee goofing around with ingredients in the kitchen—in this case, English muffins and a cylindrical egg mold. It was in 1977 that the world's largest burger chain unveiled the Egg McMuffin to a ravenous America on the go: the eat-breakfast-while-driving, morning rush hour workforce with the spill-proof coffee mugs.

Back then, concerns with fat intake were not big on our minds or in the news, so the 12 grams of fat per Egg McMuffin was disregarded. But if you've had your share of greasy breakfast sandwiches over the years and have a little extra time one morning, give this cool clone a test. Using egg substitute (egg whites) and fat-free American cheese, you can still create that signature Mickey D's taste while cutting the fat down to just 2.5 grams per sandwich. Now when you eat two of these you won't make such a dent in your daily fat allotment before the sun is barely up.

1 English muffin
¼ cup egg substitute
salt
1 slice Canadian bacon
1 slice fat-free American cheese

1. Split the English muffin and toast it or grill the faces until brown in a hot pan set over medium heat. Keep the pan hot.
2. Find a shallow can—such as an 8-ounce sliced pineapple can—that has the same diameter as the English muffin. Cut off both

ends of the can and thoroughly clean it. Spray a coating of nonstick spray on the inside of the can, and place it into the hot pan so that it heats up.
3. When the can is hot, spray more nonstick spray over the surface of the pan, and pour the egg substitute into the can. Salt the egg.
4. Place the slice of Canadian bacon into the same pan to heat up while the egg cooks.
5. When the egg seems to be firming up on top, use a knife to scrape around the edge of the can to help release the egg. Carefully pull the can off the egg, then flip the egg over and cook it for an additional minute or so.
6. Build the sandwich by first placing the slice of American cheese on the bottom half of the English muffin.
7. Place the egg on top of the cheese.
8. Stack the Canadian bacon on the egg.
9. Top the sandwich off with the top half of the English muffin.
10. Microwave the sandwich for 10 to 15 seconds until warm, and serve immediately.

- MAKES 1 SANDWICH.

TIDBITS

You can also purchase a device similar to what McDonald's uses to cook the eggs. It is a handle that has 2 to 4 circular molds at the end to hold the egg while it cooks. This can be used instead of a can, but it ain't as cheap!

Nutrition Facts *(per serving)*

SERVING SIZE—1 SANDWICH TOTAL SERVINGS—1

	LOW-FAT	ORIGINAL
CALORIES	217	290
FAT	2.5G	12G

• • • •

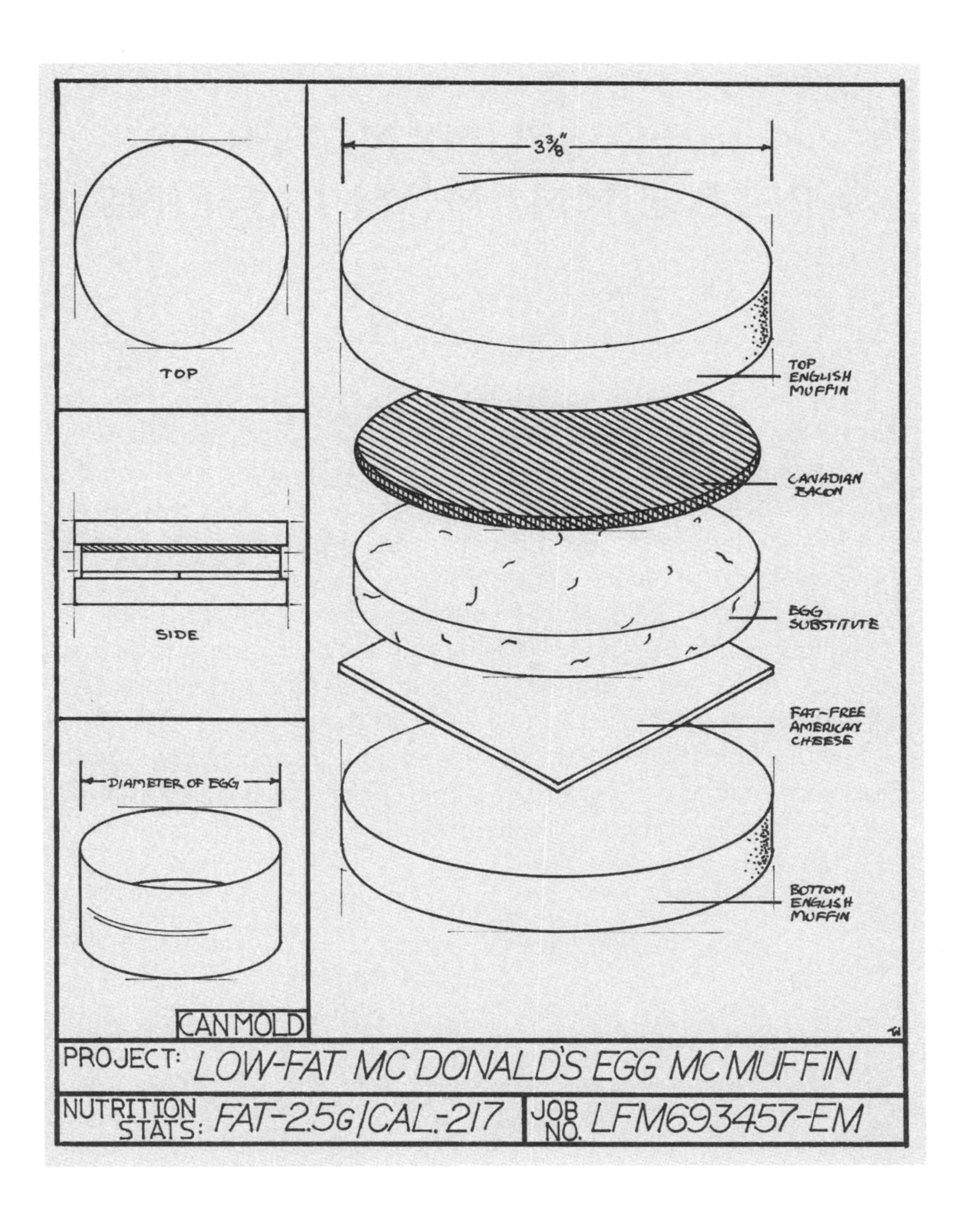
3⅜"
TOP
SIDE
DIAMETER OF EGG
CAN MOLD
TOP ENGLISH MUFFIN
CANADIAN BACON
EGG SUBSTITUTE
FAT-FREE AMERICAN CHEESE
BOTTOM ENGLISH MUFFIN
PROJECT: LOW-FAT MC DONALD'S EGG MC MUFFIN
NUTRITION STATS: FAT-2.5G/CAL.-217
JOB NO. LFM693457-EM

TOP SECRET RECIPES VERSION OF

OTIS SPUNKMEYER APPLE CINNAMON MUFFINS

☆ ✌ 💣 ✎ ☯ ✂ ☞

So who is this Otis Spunkmeyer guy, anyway? Actually, it's no one at all. The character who flies around in the plane that's pictured on the product labels, searching the world for premium ingredients for his line of baked goods, is just a catchy name dreamed up by founder Ken Rawlings's 12-year-old daughter.

The company offers low-fat versions of many of its 11 varieties of muffins, but they are more difficult to track down than the original versions. So we've got a clone here that uses some tricks to replace a lot of the fat.

While this reduced-fat conversion clone recipe of the famous Texas-size muffins has 4 grams of fat per serving, or 8 grams total, it's still quite a saving compared to the original muffins, which have a total of 22 grams of fat each.

¾ cup sugar
⅔ cup unsweetened applesauce
¼ cup egg substitute
¼ cup vegetable oil
¾ teaspoon salt
½ teaspoon vanilla
1 teaspoon baking soda
½ cup low-fat buttermilk (1 percent fat)
2 cups all-purpose flour
2 teaspoons baking powder
2 teaspoons cinnamon
fat-free butter-flavored spray
⅓ cup brown sugar

1. Preheat the oven to 325°F.
2. In a large bowl, mix together the sugar, applesauce, egg substitute, oil, salt, vanilla, and baking soda. Add the buttermilk and blend.
3. In a separate bowl sift together the flour, baking powder, and

cinnamon. Add the dry ingredients to the wet, and mix well with an electric mixer.

4. To bake the muffins, use a "Texas-size" muffin pan lined with large muffin cups. You may also bake the muffins without the cups, just be sure to grease the cups well with cooking spray. (If you use a regular-size muffin pan, which also works fine, your cooking time will be a few minutes less and your yield will double.) Fill the cups halfway with batter.
5. Spray a couple of squirts of fat-free butter-flavored spray over the top of each cup of batter. Follow that with a sprinkle of about 1 teaspoon of brown sugar.
6. Bake the muffins for 20 to 24 minutes or until brown on top (16 to 20 minutes for regular-size muffins). Remove the muffins from the oven and allow them to cool for about 30 minutes. Then put the muffins in a sealed container or resealable plastic bag.

- MAKES 8 TEXAS-SIZE MUFFINS (OR 16 REGULAR-SIZE MUFFINS).

Nutritional Facts *(per serving)*

SERVING SIZE—½ MUFFIN TOTAL SERVINGS—16

	LITE	ORIGINAL
CALORIES	142	220
FAT	4G	11G

• • • •

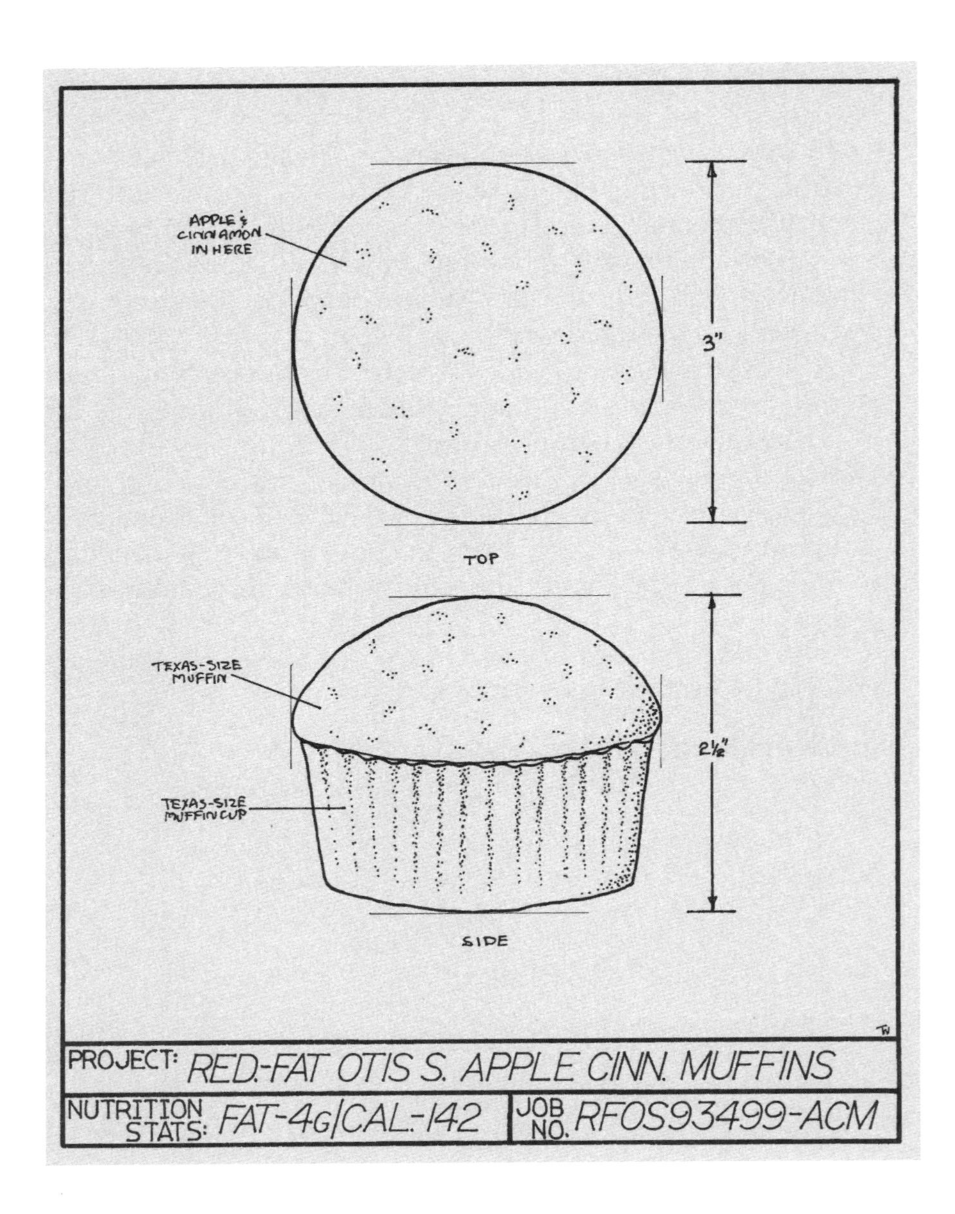
APPLE & CINNAMON IN HERE
3"
TOP
TEXAS-SIZE MUFFIN
TEXAS-SIZE MUFFIN CUP
2½"
SIDE
TW
PROJECT: RED.-FAT OTIS S. APPLE CINN. MUFFINS
NUTRITION STATS: FAT-4G|CAL.-142
JOB NO. RFOS93499-ACM

TOP SECRET RECIPES VERSION OF

OTIS SPUNKMEYER BANANA NUT MUFFINS

☆ ✌ 💣 ✎ ☯ ✂ ☞

Founder Ken Rawlings opened his first baked cookie store in San Francisco in 1977, and over the next five years the chain had grown to 22 stores throughout California. In 1990, after much success, Rawlings's Otis Spunkmeyer Company started selling Ready-to-Bake Cookie dough in grocery stores. That same year the company acquired a Modesto, California, muffin manufacturer, and Otis Spunkmeyer Muffins were born. Since then, the company has seen a 1200 percent increase in muffin sales, and today this is America's best-selling brand of muffins.

The banana-nut variety is my favorite, with 24 grams of fat per muffin. But we're in luck, because this product lends itself nicely to a reduced-fat clone. That banana is great for replacing the fat and helping to keep the muffin moist and flavorful. Even with a small amount of oil in there, and the walnuts on top, these tasty Texas-size dudes reduce the fat by more than one-half.

¾ cup sugar
⅔ cup mashed ripe banana (2 medium bananas)
¼ cup egg substitute
¼ cup vegetable oil
¾ teaspoon salt
½ teaspoon vanilla
¼ teaspoon banana extract
1 teaspoon baking soda
½ cup low-fat buttermilk (1 percent fat)
2 cups all-purpose flour
2 teaspoons baking powder
fat-free butter-flavored spray
¼ cup chopped walnuts

1. Preheat the oven to 325°F.
2. In a large bowl, mix together the sugar, mashed banana, egg substitute, oil, salt, vanilla, banana extract, and baking soda. Add the buttermilk and blend well.
3. In a separate bowl sift together the flour and baking powder. Add the dry ingredients to the wet and mix well with an electric mixer.
4. To bake the muffins, use a "Texas-size" muffin pan lined with large muffin cups. You may also bake the muffins without the cups, just be sure to grease the cups well with cooking spray. (If you use a regular size muffin pan, which also works fine, your cooking time will be a few minutes less and your yield will double.) Fill the cups halfway with batter.
5. Spray a couple of squirts of fat-free butter-flavored spray over the top of each cup of batter. Follow that with a sprinkle of about ½ tablespoon of chopped walnuts.
6. Bake the muffins for 20 to 24 minutes or until brown on top (16 to 20 minutes for regular-size muffins). Remove the muffins from the oven and allow them to cool for about 30 minutes. Then put the muffins in a sealed container or resealable plastic bag.

- MAKES 8 TEXAS-SIZE MUFFINS (OR 16 REGULAR-SIZE MUFFINS).

Nutritional Facts *(per serving)*

SERVING SIZE—½ MUFFIN TOTAL SERVINGS—16

	LITE	ORIGINAL
CALORIES	147	240
FAT	5G	12G

• • • •

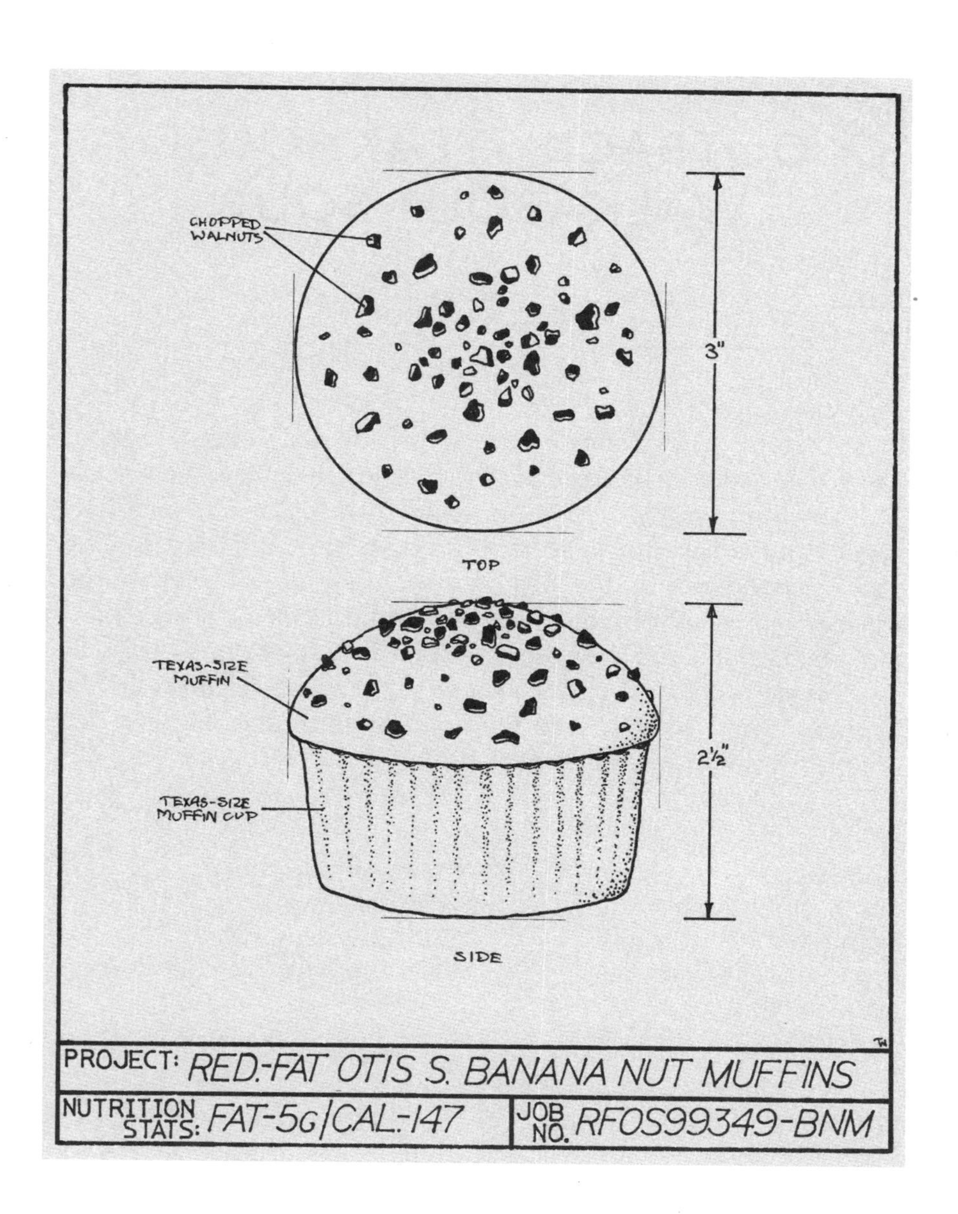
CHOPPED WALNUTS
3"
TOP
TEXAS-SIZE MUFFIN
TEXAS-SIZE MUFFIN CUP
2½"
SIDE
PROJECT: RED.-FAT OTIS S. BANANA NUT MUFFINS
NUTRITION STATS: FAT-5G/CAL.-147
JOB NO. RFOS99349-BNM

TOP SECRET RECIPES VERSION OF

OUTBACK STEAKHOUSE WALKABOUT SOUP

☆ ✌ 💣 ✏ ☯ ✂ ☞

Restaurateurs Chris Sullivan, Robert Basham, and Timothy Gannon knew they wanted an Australian theme for their new steakhouse and hunkered down to come up with a name. Robert's wife Beth pulled out her lipstick and started writing names on a mirror. "Outback" jumped out as the best name among the choices. When looking for Windex, the group later wondered if it wouldn't have been too much trouble to have just used a pen and a piece of paper.

This creamy onion soup has become a favorite item on the Outback menu. With this formula, you'll get all the flavor of the original with only one-third of the fat.

7 cups water
5 beef bouillon cubes
3 medium-size white onions
2 cups reduced-fat milk (2%)
1 ½ tablespoons sugar
1 teaspoon salt
½ teaspoon pepper
¾ cup all-purpose flour
1 cup reduced-fat shredded cheddar cheese

GARNISH

¼ cup reduced-fat shredded cheddar cheese
¼ cup Hormel Real Bacon Pieces
1 to 2 green onions, sliced

1. Combine 6 cups of water with the 5 beef bouillon cubes in a large saucepan over medium/high heat. Heat until bouillon cubes have dissolved.
2. Cut the onions into thin slices, then quarter the slices.

3. Add the onions to the broth, reduce heat, and simmer for 15 minutes.
4. Add milk to the pan. Add sugar, salt, and pepper.
5. Combine flour with 1 cup of water in a small bowl or cup, and stir until smooth. Stir the soup while adding this mixture to the pan.
6. Crank heat back up to high, add the reduced-fat cheddar cheese to the pan, and stir. Bring mixture back to boiling. Once the soup begins to boil, reduce heat and simmer for 15 to 20 minutes or until very thick.
7. Spoon 1 cup of soup into a bowl, and garnish with about ½ tablespoon each of cheddar cheese, bacon pieces, and chopped green onion.

- MAKES 8 SERVINGS.

Nutrition Facts *(per serving)*

SERVING SIZE—1 CUP TOTAL SERVINGS—8

	LOW-FAT	ORIGINAL
CALORIES (APPROX.)	144	230
FAT (APPROX.)	5.8G	17G

• • • •

TOP SECRET RECIPES VERSION OF

OUTBACK STEAKHOUSE CAESAR SALAD DRESSING

☆ ✌ 💣 ✏ ☯ ✂ ☞

The salad dressings are made fresh in each Outback Steakhouse from authentic ingredients, including olive oil from Italy's Tuscany region and Parmesan cheese that comes from eighty-pound wheels rolled in from Parma, Italy.

Salad dressings are usually one of the most fat-contributing components in your meal, but with a few tricks, we can clone Outback's delicious salad dressing with only two grams of fat per serving.

1 cup fat-free mayonnaise
1/3 cup water
1/4 cup egg substitute
1/4 cup grated Parmesan cheese
1 1/2 tablespoons lemon juice
1 tablespoon anchovy paste
2 cloves garlic, pressed
1/2 teaspoon salt
1/2 teaspoon coarsely ground pepper
1/4 teaspoon dried parsley flakes, crushed fine

1. Combine all ingredients in a medium bowl. Use an electric mixer to beat ingredients for about 1 minute.
2. Cover the dressing and chill it for several hours so that flavors can develop.

• MAKES 1 1/2 CUPS.

Nutrition Facts *(per serving)*

SERVING SIZE—¼ CUP TOTAL SERVINGS—6

	LOW-FAT	ORIGINAL
CALORIES (APPROX.)	51	331
FAT (APPROX.)	2G	35G

• • • •

TOP SECRET RECIPES VERSION OF

OUTBACK STEAKHOUSE ALICE SPRINGS CHICKEN

☆ ✌ 💣 ✎ ☯ ✂ ☞

Always a popular choice since the very beginning of this 517-unit steakhouse chain in 1988, the Alice Springs Chicken entrée would not likely be part of any low-fat diet. This marinated chicken breast is covered with honey mustard and bacon. Then the entrée is baked until the cheese on top is all melted and drippy. Add it up, and you've got yourself around forty-four grams of fat in just one serving.

We can cut the fat by more than half using fat-free and low-fat ingredients, plus some delicious-yet-low-fat turkey bacon (I recommend Butterball brand). Tastes just like the original without the guilt. Or the tip.

MARINADE

2 cups water
1 ½ teaspoons salt
½ teaspoon liquid smoke
¼ teaspoon ground black pepper
¼ teaspoon onion powder
¼ teaspoon garlic powder
¼ teaspoon paprika

4 skinless chicken breast fillets

FAT-FREE HONEY MUSTARD SAUCE

½ cup fat-free mayonnaise
½ cup honey
2 tablespoons Grey Poupon Dijon mustard
2 teaspoons white vinegar

1 tablespoon butter
8 slices turkey bacon
salt
ground black pepper
2 cups reduced-fat shredded Colby and Monterey Jack cheese

paprika
2 cups sliced mushrooms (10 to 12 mushrooms)
2 teaspoons minced fresh parsley

1. Combine the marinade ingredients in a medium bowl. Add all 4 chicken breasts to the marinade in a covered container or resealable plastic bag, and chill for 3 to 4 hours.
2. Combine the mayonnaise, honey, Dijon mustard, and vinegar in a small bowl. Stir well until smooth. Chill.
3. When chicken has marinated, preheat barbecue grill to high heat.
4. As barbecue preheats, prepare turkey bacon by frying it in a skillet over medium heat until done. Remove the bacon from the skillet to a plate lined with paper, which helps soak up excess fat. The bacon can sit here until it is time to assemble the dish.
5. Spray a light coating of nonstick oil cooking spray over the surface of each chicken breast. Sprinkle both sides of each chicken breast with salt, pepper, and paprika, and then grill for 7 to 10 minutes on each side. Preheat oven to 375°F.
6. As chicken grills, prepare mushrooms by heating up a medium skillet over medium/high heat. Add 1 tablespoon of butter to the pan. When the butter has melted, add the mushrooms, along with a little salt and pepper. Sauté the mushrooms for 10 to 15 minutes or until they become cooked through and light brown. If the mushrooms finish before the chicken, just turn the heat to the lowest setting until you are ready to assemble the dish.
7. When chicken is cooked, transfer the chicken breast fillets to a large baking dish. Slather the top surface of each breast with a generous portion of the honey mustard sauce. Stack two slices of bacon, crosswise, on top of each breast.
8. Quarter the mushrooms and stack a portion on top of the bacon on each chicken breast. Carefully pour about ½ cup of the Colby/Monterey Jack cheese blend over each of the chicken breasts.
9. Bake chicken in the preheated oven for 7 to 12 minutes or until cheese is melted.

10. Sprinkle each with about ½ teaspoon of fresh minced parsley. Serve with additional honey mustard sauce on the side.

- SERVES 4 AS AN ENTRÉE.

Nutrition Facts *(per serving)*

SERVING SIZE—1 PORTION TOTAL SERVINGS—4

	LOW-FAT	ORIGINAL
CALORIES (APPROX.)	603	838
FAT (APPROX.)	19G	44G

• • • •

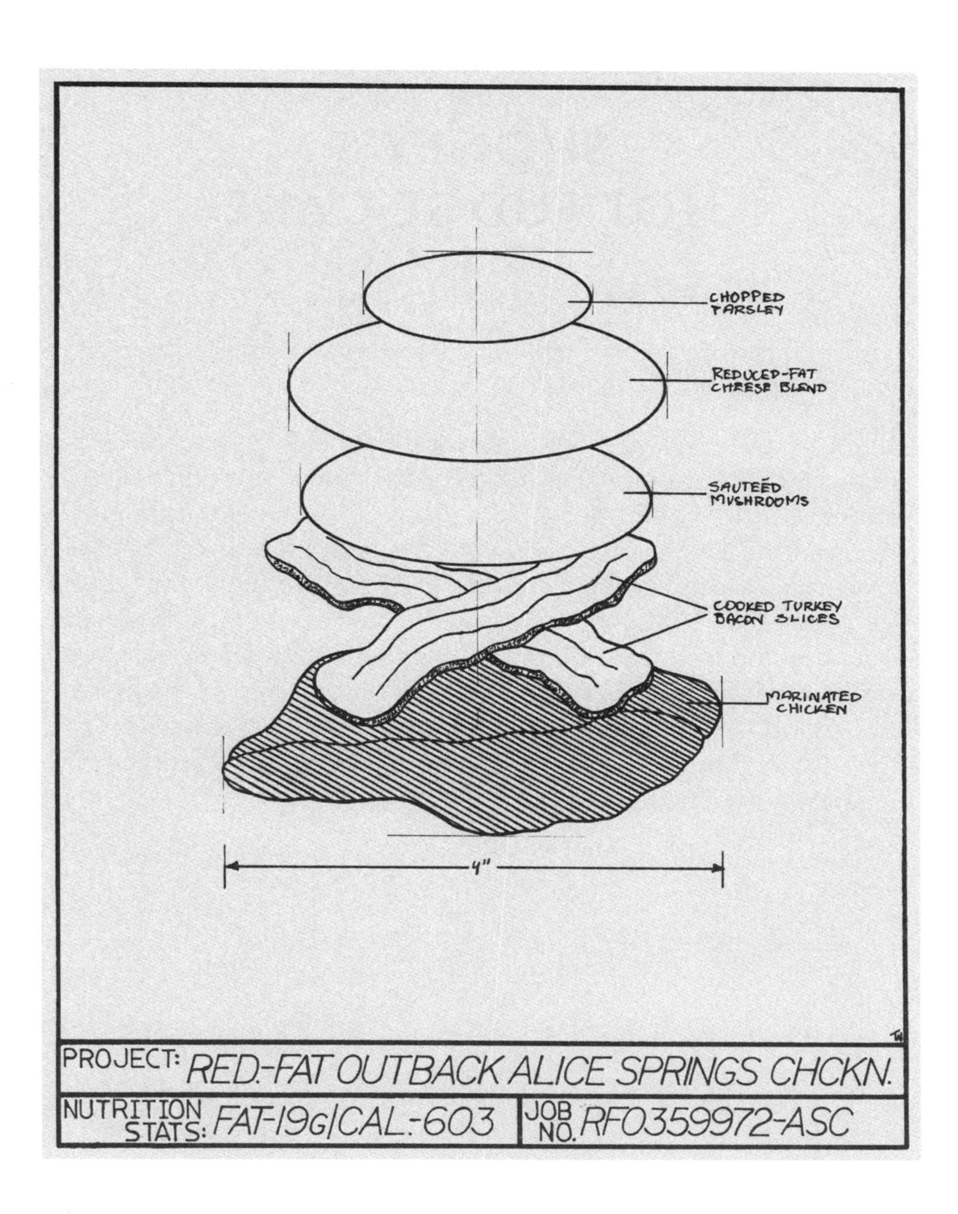
CHOPPED PARSLEY
REDUCED-FAT CHEESE BLEND
SAUTEÉD MUSHROOMS
COOKED TURKEY BACON SLICES
MARINATED CHICKEN
4"
PROJECT: RED.-FAT OUTBACK ALICE SPRINGS CHCKN.
NUTRITION STATS: FAT-19G/CAL.-603
JOB NO. RF0359972-ASC

TOP SECRET RECIPES VERSION OF

SHONEY'S HOT FUDGE CAKE

☆ ✌ 💣 ✎ ☯ ✂ ☞

If you've ever laid your fork into one of these babies, you know how tough it is to take only a bite or two. Now you don't have to stop just as it's getting good. TSR drastically reduces the fat in this clone of the Shoney's creation with the help of reduced-fat devil's food cake mix and fat-free ice cream. Just be sure to get the type of ice cream that comes in a rectangular container, so that slicing and arranging the ice cream on the cake is made easier. Breyer's makes excellent fat-free vanilla ice cream and the container works well for this recipe. You may have some ice cream left over, which you can then eat with the small cake or cupcakes you can bake with the cup of leftover cake batter.

1 18.25-ounce box reduced-fat devil's food cake mix
1 1⁄3 cups water
2 tablespoons vegetable oil
3⁄4 cup egg substitute
1 half-gallon box fat-free ice cream (Breyer's is good)
1 16-ounce jar chocolate fudge topping
1 can whipped cream
12 maraschino cherries

1. Preheat the oven to 350°F.
2. Mix the batter for the cake as instructed on the box of the cake mix by combining the mix with the water, oil, and eggs in a large mixing bowl.
3. Remove a scant 1 cup of the batter from the bowl and set it aside, then add the remaining batter to a well-greased

9 x 13-inch baking pan. We won't be using the extra batter that was set aside, so you can discard it or use it for another recipe, such as cupcakes.

4. Bake the cake according to the box instructions (about 30 minutes). Allow the cake to cool completely.
5. When the cake has cooled, carefully remove it from the pan and place it right side up onto a sheet of wax paper. With a long knife (a bread knife works great) slice the cake horizontally through the middle, and carefully remove the top. It helps to position the cake near the edge of your kitchen counter so that you can get a straight cut through the middle of the cake.
6. Pick up the wax paper with the bottom half of the cake still on it, and place it back into the baking pan.
7. Take the ice cream from the freezer and, working quickly, tear or cut the box open so that you can slice the ice cream like bread.
8. Make six ¾-inch slices of ice cream and arrange them side-by-side on the cake in the pan. Cover the entire surface of the cake with the ice cream slices. Fill in any gaps with additional ice cream. You may have about one-fifth of the ice cream left over in the box.
9. When you have covered the entire surface of the bottom cake half with ice cream slices, carefully place the top half of the cake, right side up, onto the ice cream in the pan. You should now have a layer of fat-free ice cream sandwiched between the two halves of reduced-fat cake. Cover the entire pan with plastic wrap or foil (trim the wax paper from the edges if necessary), and place the pan into your freezer for at least a couple of hours.
10. When you are ready to serve the dessert, slice the cake so that it will make 12 equal slices—that is, cut lengthwise twice and crosswise three times. If you will not be serving the entire desert, only slice what you will be using and save the rest, covered, in the freezer until you are ready to use it (it should keep for several weeks).
11. Heat up the fudge in the microwave or in a jar immersed in a saucepan of water over medium/low heat.

12. Pour about 2 tablespoons of fudge over the top of each slice of cake, and then add a small portion of whipped cream (about 2 tablespoons) on top of that.
13. Place a cherry onto the pile of whipped cream and serve immediately.

- SERVES 12.

Nutritional Facts *(per serving)*

SERVING SIZE—1 SLICE TOTAL SERVINGS—12

	LITE	ORIGINAL
CALORIES	328	522
FAT	9.5G	20G

• • • •

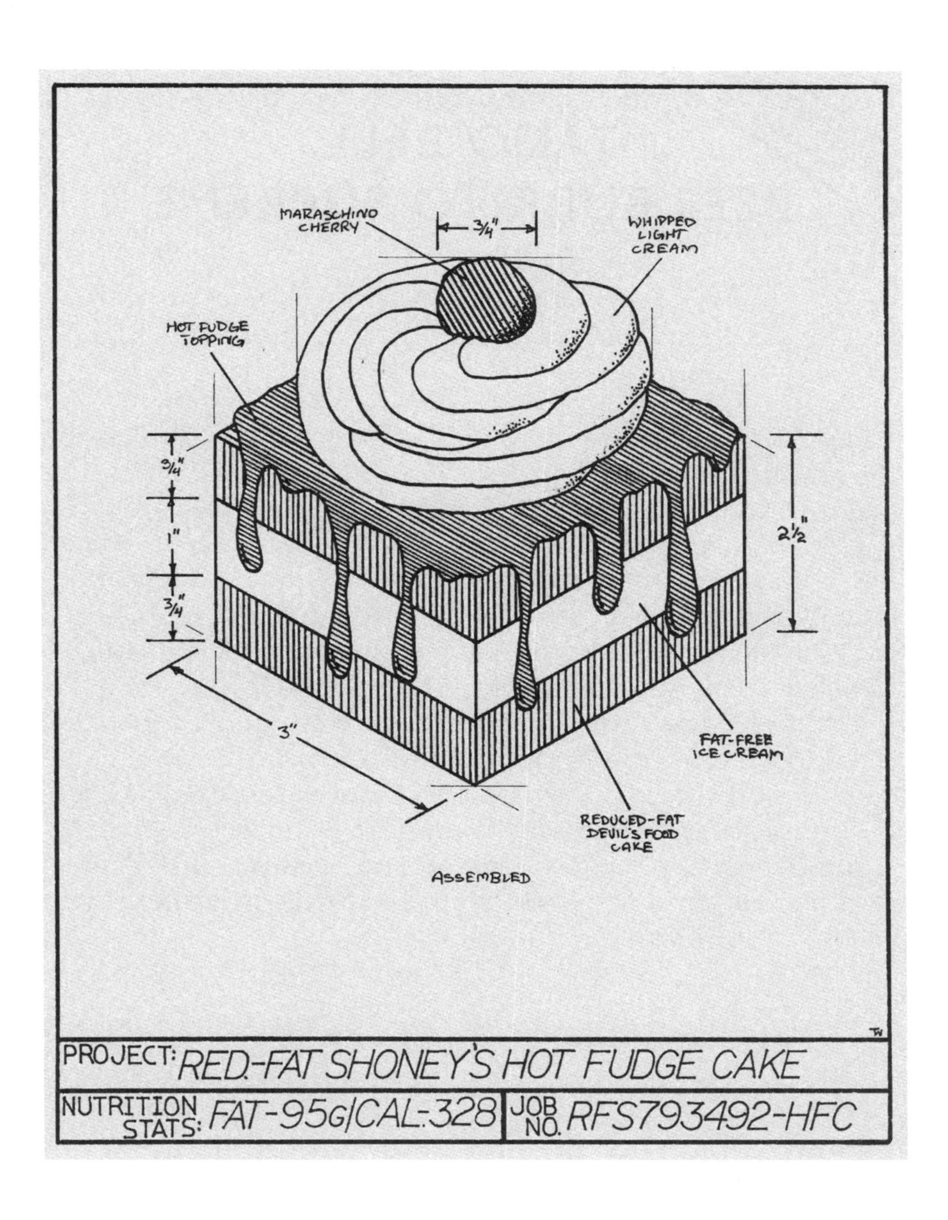
MARASCHINO CHERRY
3/4"
WHIPPED LIGHT CREAM
HOT FUDGE TOPPING
3/4"
1"
3/4"
2 1/2"
3"
FAT-FREE ICE CREAM
REDUCED-FAT DEVIL'S FOOD CAKE
ASSEMBLED
PROJECT: RED.-FAT SHONEY'S HOT FUDGE CAKE
NUTRITION STATS: FAT-95G/CAL.-328
JOB NO. RFS793492-HFC

TOP SECRET RECIPES VERSION OF

TACO BELL BEEF BURRITO SUPREME

☆ ✌ 💣 ✎ ☯ ✂ ☞

How's this for coincidence: Both McDonald's and Taco Bell got their start in San Bernardino, California, in the early '50s. Glen Bell opened a hamburger and hot dog stand called Bell's Drive-In, while the McDonald brothers, Dick and Mac, were just around the corner with their golden arches and speedy drive-up service. "The appearance of another hamburger stand worried me then," says Glen. "I just didn't think there was enough room in town for both of us." Turns out there was enough room—at least for a little while.

In 1962, Glen decided that it was time to offer an alternative to the hamburger stands that were saturating the area, so he opened the first Taco Bell and changed his menu to Mexican food.

Ten years and hundreds of new Taco Bell openings later, the Burrito Supreme hit the menu and became an instant hit. By making this clone version at home, we can reduce the fat to less than one-fifth that of the original.

½ pound super lean ground beef (7% fat)
2 tablespoons all-purpose flour
¾ teaspoon salt
¼ teaspoon dried, minced onion
¼ teaspoon paprika
1½ teaspoons chili powder
dash garlic powder
dash onion powder
¼ cup water
1 cup fat-free refried beans
4 10-inch fat-free flour tortillas
1 cup shredded iceberg lettuce
½ cup fat-free shredded cheddar cheese
1 medium tomato, diced
¼ cup fat-free sour cream

1. In a medium bowl, combine the super lean ground beef with the flour, salt, minced onion, paprika, chili powder, garlic powder, and onion powder. Use your hands to thoroughly incorporate everything into the ground beef.
2. Preheat a skillet over medium/low heat, and add the ground beef mixture to the pan along with the water. Brown the beef mixture for 5 to 6 minutes, using a wooden spoon or spatula to break up the meat as it cooks.
3. Put the refried beans into a microwave-safe container and cover. Heat on high for 2 to 3 minutes or until hot. You may also heat the beans in a small saucepan on the stove over medium/low heat. Stir occasionally, and heat until hot.
4. Using the microwave, heat up 4 10-inch fat-free flour tortillas in a tortilla steamer (or wrapped in a moist cloth or paper towels) for 25 to 30 seconds or until hot.
5. Spread about ¼ cup of refried beans in a 2-inch-wide strip down the center of one tortilla. Don't spread the beans all the way to the edge of the tortilla. Leave a margin of a couple inches so that you can later fold the tortilla.
6. Spread ¼ cup of the beef over the refried beans.
7. Sprinkle ¼ cup of lettuce onto the beef.
8. Sprinkle 2 tablespoons of the fat-free cheese onto the lettuce.
9. Sprinkle 2 tablespoons of diced tomato over the cheese.
10. Finish the burrito by dropping a tablespoon of fat-free sour cream over the other fillings.
11. Fold the left side of the tortilla over the fillings. Fold up the bottom, then fold the right side over, and serve hot. Repeat with the remaining ingredients.

- MAKES 4 BURRITOS.

Nutrition Facts *(per serving)*

SERVING SIZE—1 BURRITO TOTAL SERVINGS—4

	LOW-FAT	ORIGINAL
CALORIES	325	503
FAT	4G	22G

• • • •

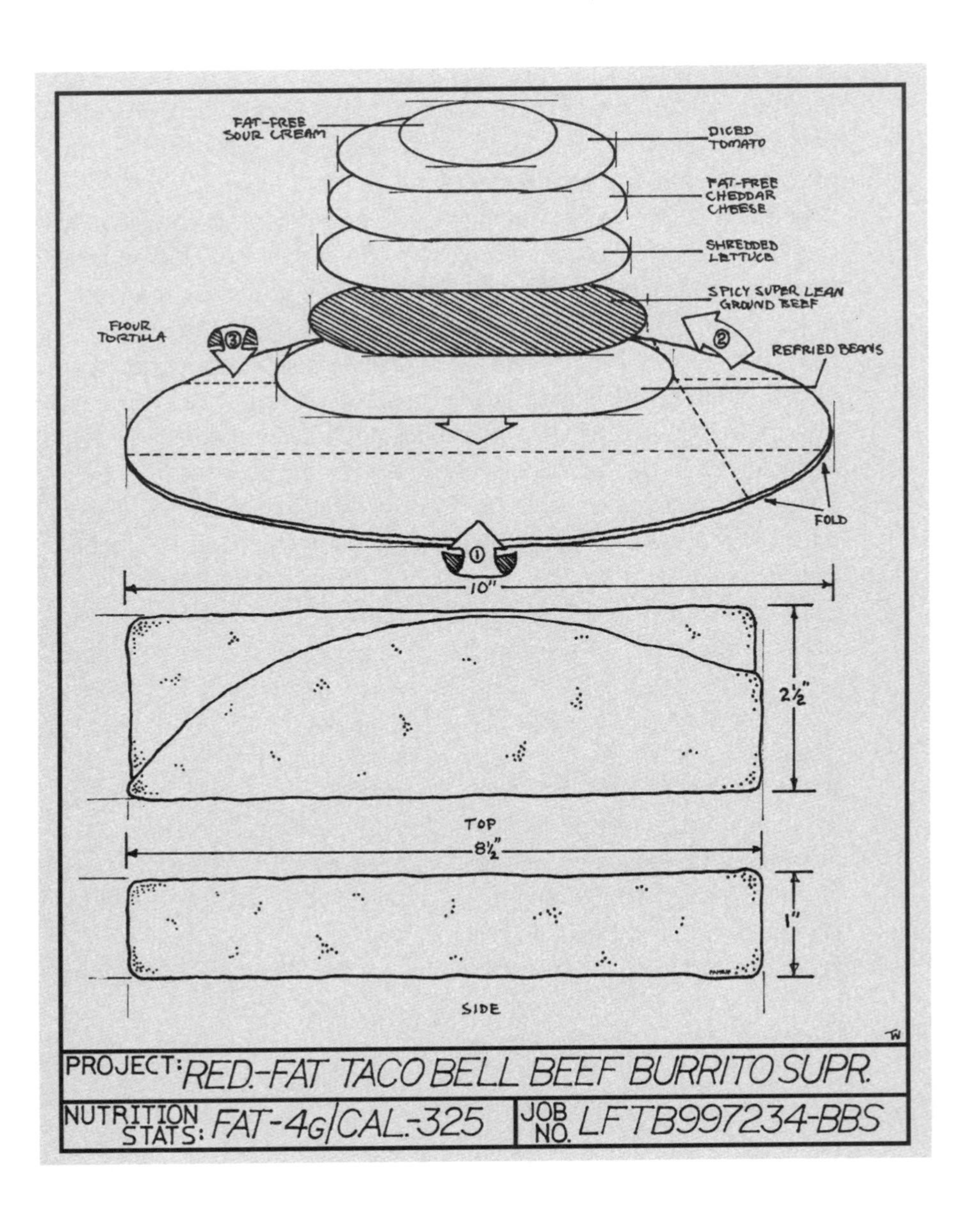
FAT-FREE SOUR CREAM
DICED TOMATO
FAT-FREE CHEDDAR CHEESE
SHREDDED LETTUCE
SPICY SUPER LEAN GROUND BEEF
FLOUR TORTILLA
REFRIED BEANS
FOLD
10"
2½"
TOP
8½"
1"
SIDE
PROJECT: RED.-FAT TACO BELL BEEF BURRITO SUPR.
NUTRITION STATS: FAT-4G/CAL.-325
JOB NO. LFTB997234-BBS

TOP SECRET RECIPES VERSION OF

TACO BELL CHICKEN SOFT TACO

☆ ✌ 💣 ✎ ☯ ✂ ☞

Taco Bell had very little luck with light menu items over the years. In 1983, the Mexican fast-food chain introduced Taco Light, a taco with a fried flour tortilla shell. But the fried flour tortilla that replaced the traditional corn tortilla only made the taco light in weight and color, not in fat or calories. The item was quickly discontinued. In 1995, the chain tried again with Light Line, a selection of several lower-fat menu items that also took a sales digger. Customers who frequented the drive-thru weren't there to lose weight; they were there to ingest some greasy taco meat and handfuls of shredded cheddar.

When we cook at home, though, we'd like to do what we can to make a meal better on the waistline, especially if it takes no extra effort and the food still tastes good. This recipe will show that you can do just that: knock the fat way down—from ten grams to just two grams—without compromising flavor. Check it out.

½ cup water
1 teaspoon soy sauce
1 teaspoon salt
1 teaspoon brown sugar
½ teaspoon onion powder
¼ teaspoon liquid smoke
¼ teaspoon ground black pepper
¼ teaspoon chili powder
2 skinless chicken breast fillets
6 6-inch fat-free flour tortillas
¾ cups shredded iceberg lettuce
½ cup fat-free shredded cheddar cheese
1 medium tomato, diced

1. In a small bowl combine water, soy sauce, salt, brown sugar, onion powder, liquid smoke, black pepper, and chili powder in a

small bowl. Pour the mixture over the chicken breasts and marinate overnight. You can marinate for less time if you wish, but overnight is best.

2. Cook chicken on barbecue or indoor grill over medium/high heat for 5 to 6 minutes per side or until done. Slice chicken into bite-size chunks.
3. Heat the tortillas in a steamer, or wrap them in a moist towel and heat for about 30 seconds in the microwave.
4. Spread about ¼ cup of chicken down the middle of one of the flour tortillas.
5. Sprinkle about 2 tablespoons of lettuce over the chicken.
6. Sprinkle a heaping tablespoon of cheese over the lettuce.
7. Finish the taco by stacking a heaping tablespoon of diced tomato on the cheese, then fold up the edges of the taco, and serve immediately. Repeat with the remaining ingredients.

- MAKES 6 TACOS.

Nutrition Facts *(per serving)*

SERVING SIZE—1 TACO TOTAL SERVINGS—6

	LOW-FAT	ORIGINAL
CALORIES	172	213
FAT	2G	10G

• • • •

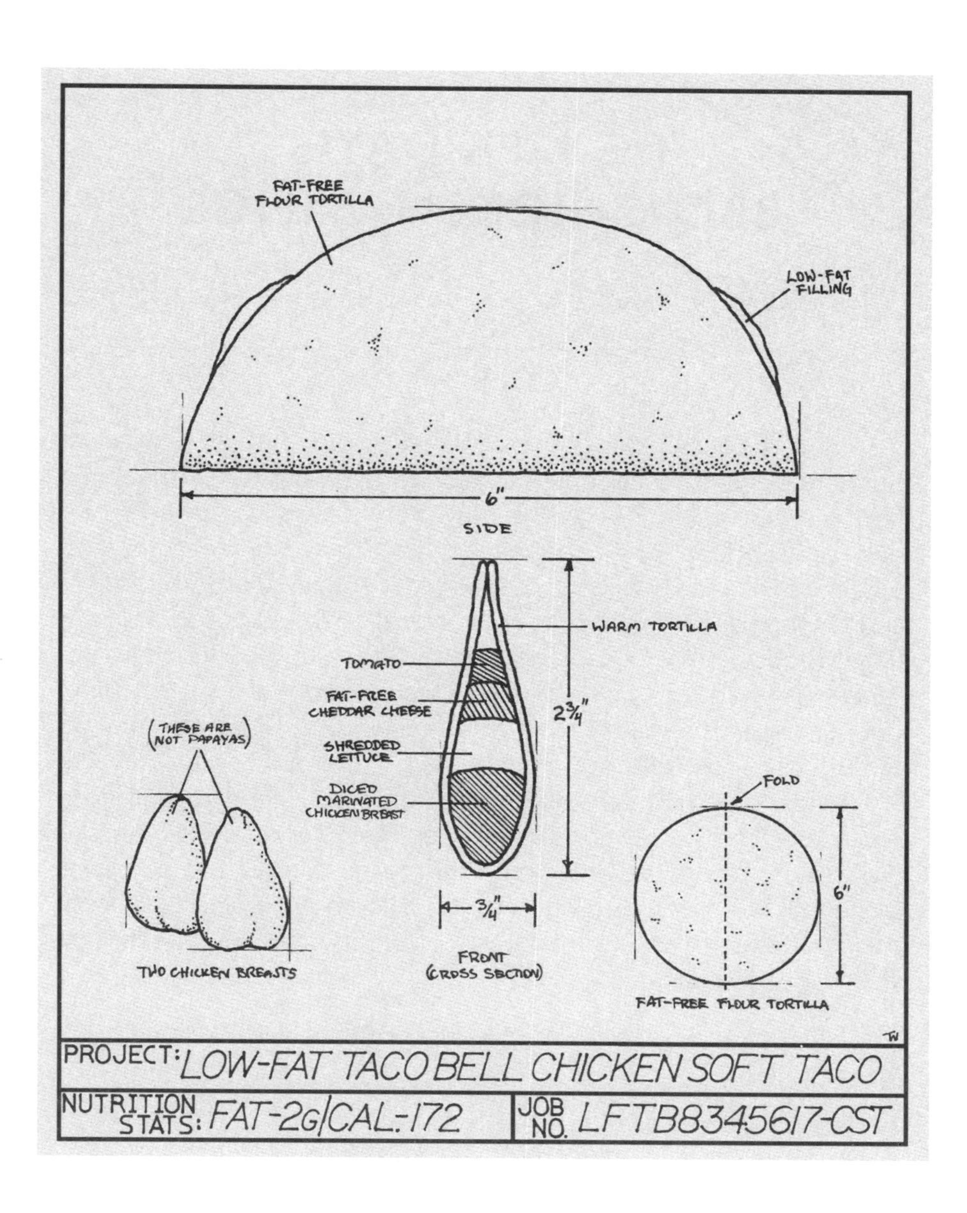

FAT-FREE FLOUR TORTILLA
LOW-FAT FILLING
6"
SIDE
WARM TORTILLA
TOMATO
FAT-FREE CHEDDAR CHEESE
SHREDDED LETTUCE
DICED MARINATED CHICKEN BREAST
2 3/4"
3/4"
FRONT (CROSS SECTION)
(THESE ARE NOT PAPAYAS)
TWO CHICKEN BREASTS
FOLD
6"
FAT-FREE FLOUR TORTILLA
TW
PROJECT: LOW-FAT TACO BELL CHICKEN SOFT TACO
NUTRITION STATS: FAT-2G/CAL-172
JOB NO. LFTB8345617-CST

TOP SECRET RECIPES VERSION OF

T.G.I. FRIDAY'S BBQ CHICKEN WINGS

☆ ✌ 💣 ✎ ☯ ✂ ☞

You've got to hand it to him. Alan Stillman thought that if he opened his own restaurant, it might be a great way to meet the flight attendants who lived in his New York City neighborhood. Not only did the dude follow through on his plan in 1965 with the first T.G.I. Friday's, but today the company is 387 units strong, Alan's rich, and his inspiration is still a popular casual dining spot for delicious finger foods, drinks, lunches, and dinners in an upbeat, festive atmosphere. Nowadays, the chain goes through more than five million chicken wings in a year, serving buffalo wings as well as this variation of the tasty appetizer.

Friday's kitchen came up with a delicious blend of barbecue sauce and apple butter to coat the deep-fried chicken wings. For our reduced-fat clone, we'll re-create the exact taste of the barbecue sauce, but we'll strip the skin from the chicken wings and use a cool baking process that'll cut the fat way down. By the way, I hear flight attendants love wings.

oil nonstick cooking spray
12 chicken wings with skin
½ cup Bull's-Eye or K.C. Masterpiece Barbecue Sauce (original flavor only)
2 tablespoons apple butter
½ cup flour
1 teaspoon salt
½ teaspoon ground pepper
1 cup milk

1. Preheat the oven on broil.
2. Line a cookie sheet or shallow baking pan with a sheet of aluminum foil. Spray the foil with nonstick spray.
3. Arrange each chicken wing on the foil with the side that has the

most skin on it facing up. Broil the wings for 12 to 14 minutes or until the skin begins to turn light brown and becomes crispy. Remove wings from the oven and let them cool. Turn the oven to 450°F.

4. While the wings are broiling, combine the barbecue sauce with the apple butter in a small bowl. Chill the sauce until the wings are ready.
5. Prepare the breading by combining the flour, salt, and pepper in a small bowl. Pour the milk into another small bowl.
6. When you can handle the chicken wings, remove the skin from each one. Throw the skin out.
7. Dip the wings, one at a time, into the breading, then into the milk, and finally back in the breading, so that each one is well coated.
8. Place the wings back onto the baking sheet. Spray a coating of oil spray over each wing so that the breading is completely moistened, and then bake the wings at 450°F for 12 minutes. Crank the oven up to broil for 3 to 5 minutes or until the wings begin to brown and become crispy.
9. Remove the wings from the oven. Let them rest for about a minute, then put them into a large plastic container or jar with a lid. Pour a generous amount of sauce over the wings, cover, and gently shake the wings up so that they are all well coated with the sauce. Be careful not to shake too hard or the breading may fall off. Serve immediately.

- SERVES 4 AS AN APPETIZER.

Nutrition Facts *(per serving)*

SERVING SIZE—3 PIECES   TOTAL SERVINGS—4

	LOW-FAT	ORIGINAL
CALORIES (APPROX.)	150	235
FAT (APPROX.)	6G	16G

• • • •

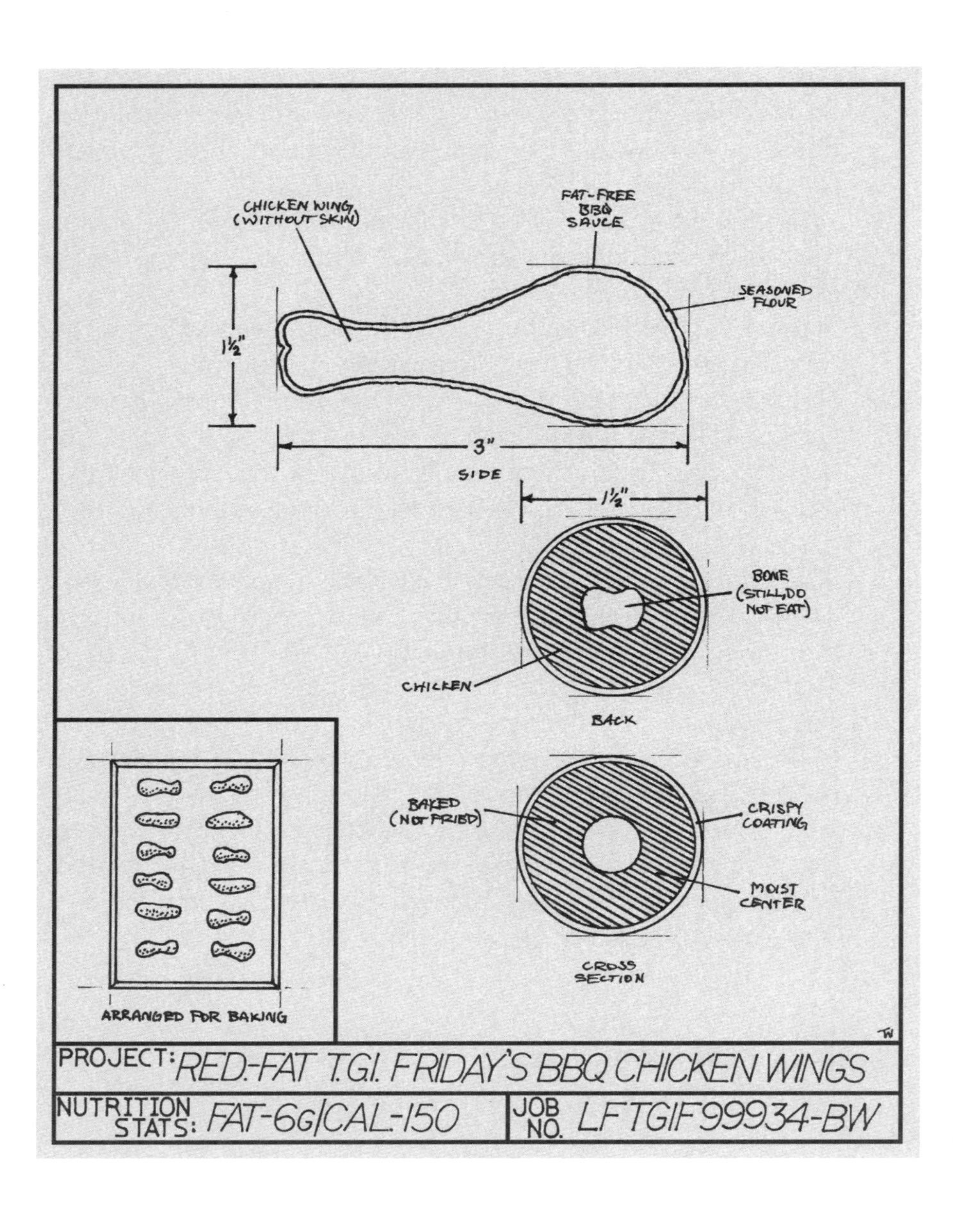
CHICKEN WING (WITHOUT SKIN)
FAT-FREE BBQ SAUCE
SEASONED FLOUR
1½"
3"
SIDE
1½"
BONE (STILL, DO NOT EAT)
CHICKEN
BACK
BAKED (NOT FRIED)
CRISPY COATING
MOIST CENTER
CROSS SECTION
ARRANGED FOR BAKING
TW
PROJECT: RED-FAT T.G.I. FRIDAY'S BBQ CHICKEN WINGS
NUTRITION STATS: FAT-6G/CAL-150
JOB NO. LFTGIF99934-BW

TOP SECRET RECIPES VERSION OF

T.G.I. FRIDAY'S DIJON CHICKEN PASTA

☆ ✌ 💣 ✏ ☯ ✂ ☞

That creamy, white Dijon sauce that smothers the original version of this delicious pasta is luscious indeed but cursed by oodles of flabby fat grams. This can be fixed in our reduced-fat clone by using strained fat-free yogurt—an ingredient apparently inspired by the ancient Mediterranean technique of straining yogurt through a cheesecloth—that adds a thick, creamy consistency to our sauce without adding fat.

DIJON PASTA SAUCE

1 clove garlic, pressed
½ teaspoon olive oil
*1 cup strained fat-free yogurt**
2 tablespoons cornstarch
1 cup evaporated skim milk
¼ cup fat-free milk
2 teaspoons Grey Poupon Dijon mustard
2 tablespoons grated Parmesan cheese
¼ teaspoon salt
dash ground black pepper
1½ tablespoons fresh parsley, chopped

CHICKEN SPICE BLEND

2 teaspoons salt
1 teaspoon paprika
½ teaspoon dried thyme
dash or two ground black pepper

fat-free butter-flavored spread or spray
4 skinless chicken breast fillets
1-pound package penne pasta
3 to 4 quarts water

* Make the strained yogurt by pouring a large container of plain yogurt into a coffee filter placed in a metal steamer basket or strainer. Overnight, the liquid whey will drain from the yogurt, leaving a thick, cheeselike substance in the strainer. Measure this thick stuff for the recipe and toss out the liquid.

GARNISH

1 small tomato, diced

fresh parsley, chopped

1. Preheat barbecue or stovetop grill to medium/high heat.
2. Prepare pasta sauce by first sautéing the pressed garlic in the olive oil in a medium saucepan. Sauté only for a minute or two over medium heat. Do not let the garlic brown or it will become bitter. Remove pan from heat.
3. Combine strained yogurt with cornstarch in a medium bowl. Add evaporated milk, fat-free milk, and mustard, and mix. Pour mixture into saucepan and place it back over heat. Add Parmesan cheese, salt, and pepper, and stir.
4. When sauce thickens, add parsley and turn heat to low, stirring often.
5. As sauce cooks, prepare the chicken by combining all of the spice blend ingredients in a small bowl. Rub a light coating of butter-flavored spread or spray over each breast, and sprinkle some of the spice blend over both sides of each chicken breast. Cook the chicken on the grill for 4 to 5 minutes per side. Turn the chicken at a 45-degree angle halfway through the cooking time on each side, so that you get crisscrossed grill marks on the surface.
6. While chicken is grilling, prepare pasta by bringing 3 to 4 cups of water to a boil in a large pan. Add pasta to the water and cook for 12 to 15 minutes or until pasta is tender. Strain.
7. Divide strained pasta into four portions on four plates, and pour a generous portion of the sauce over the pasta. Sprinkle some diced tomato over the pasta on each plate. Sprinkle some additional fresh parsley over the pasta.
8. Slice each chicken breast across the grain, and arrange each sliced breast on top of the pasta on each plate, being careful to retain the shape of the chicken breast as you position it.

- SERVES 4 AS AN ENTRÉE.

Nutrition Facts *(per serving)*

SERVING SIZE—1 ENTRÉE TOTAL SERVINGS—4

	LOW-FAT	ORIGINAL
CALORIES (APPROX.)	730	930
FAT (APPROX.)	8G	45G

• • • •

T.G.I. FRIDAY'S POTATO SKINS

Thousands of restaurants all over the world now serve this tasty finger food on their appetizer menu, but T.G.I. Friday's is the potato skin king. The restaurant introduced America to the little cheese- and bacon-covered spud boats back in 1974, and the dish quickly took off. As this recipe demonstrates, potato skins can be a great choice for the munchies and don't have to be filled with even half of the traditional fourteen grams of fat per serving.

4 medium russet potatoes
canola oil nonstick cooking spray
salt
1 cup reduced-fat cheddar cheese
8 teaspoons Hormel Real Bacon Pieces
1 tablespoon snipped fresh chives
⅓ cup sour cream

1. Preheat oven to 400°F.
2. Bake the potatoes for 1 hour or until tender.
3. When potatoes have cooled enough so that you can handle them, make two lengthwise cuts through each potato, resulting in three ½- to ¾-inch slices. Discard the middle slices or save them for a separate dish of mashed potatoes. This will leave you with two potato skins per potato.
4. With a spoon, scoop some of the potato out of each skin, being sure to leave about ¼ inch of potato inside of the skin.
5. Pop oven temperature up to 450°F.

6. Spray the entire surface of each potato skin, inside and out, with a light coating of the canola oil spray.
7. Place the skins on a baking sheet, open side up, salt each one, and then bake them for 12 to 15 minutes or until the edges begin to brown.
8. Spread about two tablespoons of cheese on each of the potato skins.
9. Sprinkle a teaspoon of bacon pieces on top of the cheese on each potato skin.
10. Bake the skins for another 2 to 4 minutes or until cheese is melted. Remove the skins from the oven and transfer them to a serving plate.
11. Combine the chives with the sour cream and serve in a small sauce cup in the center of the plate, with the skins arranged around the sour cream, like spokes on a wheel.

- SERVES 4 AS AN APPETIZER.

Nutrition Facts *(per serving)*

SERVING SIZE—3 PIECES TOTAL SERVINGS—4

	LOW-FAT	ORIGINAL
CALORIES (APPROX.)	302	420
FAT (APPROX.)	5G	14G

• • • •

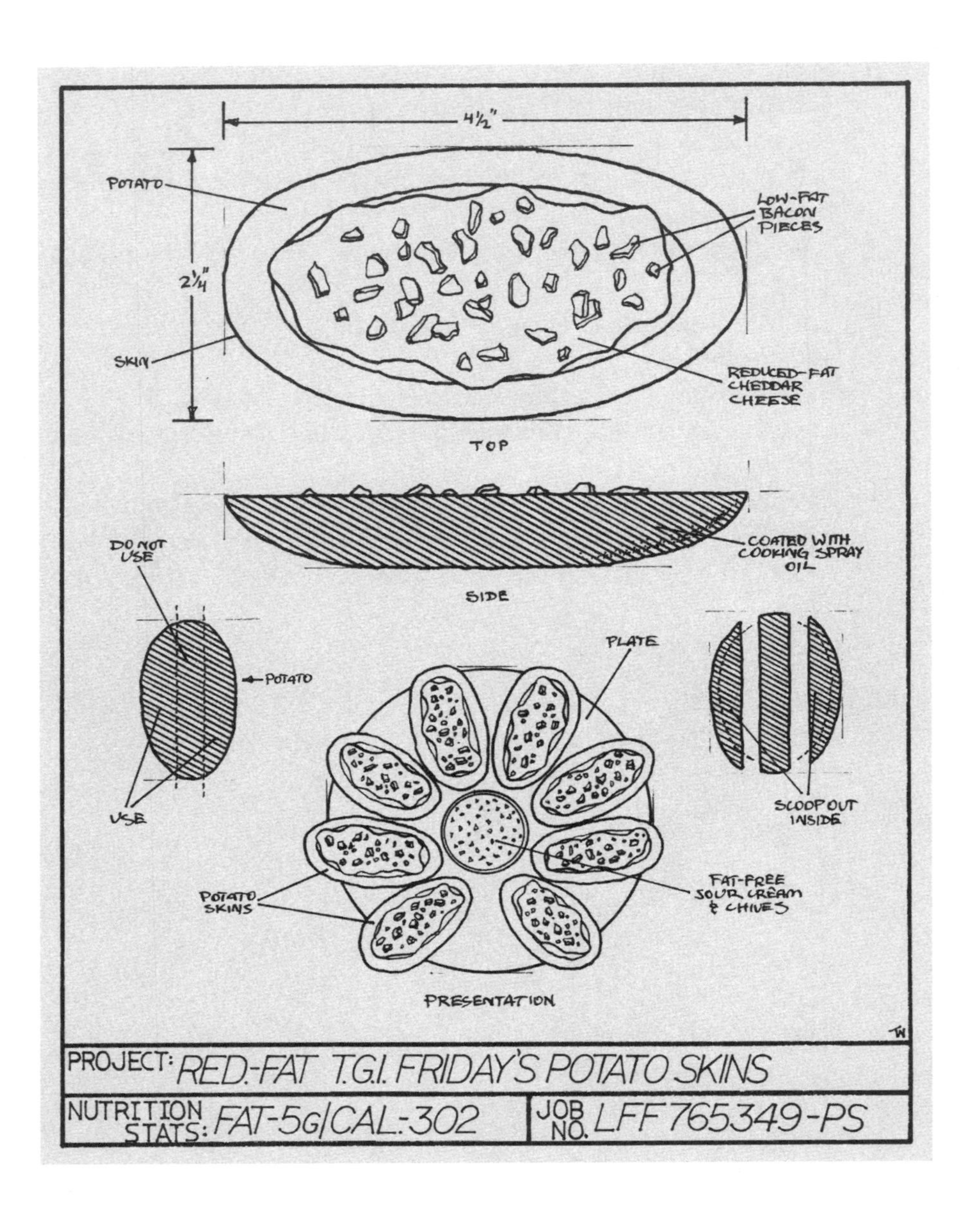
4½"
2¼"
POTATO
SKIN
LOW-FAT BACON PIECES
REDUCED-FAT CHEDDAR CHEESE
TOP
COATED WITH COOKING SPRAY OIL
SIDE
DO NOT USE
POTATO
USE
PLATE
SCOOP OUT INSIDE
POTATO SKINS
FAT-FREE SOUR CREAM & CHIVES
PRESENTATION
TW
PROJECT: RED.-FAT T.G.I. FRIDAY'S POTATO SKINS
NUTRITION STATS: FAT-5G/CAL.-302
JOB NO. LFF 765349-PS

TRADEMARKS

A&W, 7UP, Squirt, and Hawaiian Punch are registered trademarks of Dr Pepper/Seven Up, Inc.

Almond Roca and Brown and Haley are registered trademarks of Brown and Haley, Inc.

Applebee's, Low Fat & Fabulous, and Tijuana 'Philly' Steak Sandwich are registered trademarks of Applebee's International, Inc.

Arby's is a registered trademark of Arby's Inc.

AriZona is a registered trademark of AriZona Beverage Co.

Auntie Anne's is a registered trademark of Auntie Anne's, Inc.

Baskin-Robbins is a registered trademark of Baskin-Robbins, Inc.

Bennigan's and Cookie Mountain Sundae are registered trademarks of Metromedia Co.

Big Boy is a registered trademark of Elias Brothers Restaurants, Inc.

Big Mac, Egg McMuffin, Filet-O-Fish, and McDonald's Breakfast Burrito are registered trademarks of McDonald's Corporation.

Bisquick is a registered trademark of General Mills Inc.

Blizzard, Orange Julius, Pineapple, Strawberry Julius, Dairy Queen and Smoothie are registered trademarks of American Dairy Queen Corp.

Boston Market, are registered trademarks of McDonald's Corporation

Burger King and Whopper are registered trademarks of Burger King Corp.

Butterscotch Krimpets, Peanut Butter Kandy Kakes, and Tastykake are registered trademarks of Tasty Baking Company.

California Pizza Kitchen is a registered trademark of California Pizza Kitchen, Inc.

Carl's Jr. and Charbroiled Santa Fe Chicken Sandwich are registered trademarks of Carl Karcher Enterprises, Inc.

Carl's Jr., Sante Fe Chicken, Western Bacon Cheeseburger, Six Dollar Burger are registered trademarks of Carl Karcher Enterprises.

Carnegie Deli is a registered trademark of Carnegie Delicatessen and Restaurant.

The Cheesecake Factory is a registered trademark of The Cheesecake Factory, Inc.

Chevys is a registered trademark of Chevys, Inc.

Lone Star Steakhouse & Saloon and Amarillo Cheese Fries are registered trademarks of Lone Star Steakhouse & Saloon, Inc.
Long John Silver's is a registered trademark of Jerrico, Inc.
M&M/Mars, Snickers, and Munch are registered trademarks of Mars, Inc.
Maid-Rite is a registered trademark of Maid-Rite Inc.
Marie Callender's is a registered trademark of Marie Callender's Pie Shops, Inc.
Mounds, Almond Joy, and Peter Paul are registered trademarks of Cadbury U.S.A., Inc.
Nabisco, Nutter Butter, Oreo, Double Stuff, Big Stuff, SnackWell's, Fudge Brownie Bars, HoneyMaid Grahams, Apple Raisin Snack Bars, Banana Snack Bars, and General Foods International Coffees are registered trademarks of Nabisco, Inc.
Nestlé, and 100 Grand Bar are registered trademarks of Nestlé USA, Inc.
Old Bay is a registered trademark of McCormick & Co. Inc.
The Olive Garden is a registered trademark of Darden Restaurants, Inc.
Outback Steakhouse and Bloomin' Onion, are registered trademarks of Outback Steakhouse, Inc.
Pal's and Sauceburger are registered trademarks of Pal's Sudden Service.
Panda Express is a registered trademark of Panda Management Company, Inc.
Peanut Butter Dream Bar and Mrs. Fields are registered trademarks of Mrs. Fields, Inc.
Pizza Hut and Stuffed Crust Pizza are trademarks of Pizza Hut, Inc.
Planters and Fiddle Faddle are registered trademarks of Planters, Inc.
Popeye's Famous Fried Chicken is a registered trademark of AFC Enterprises, Inc.
Ragu is a registered trademark of Unilever Bestfoods.
Reese's, Hershey, and York are registered trademarks of Hershey Foods Corporation.
Ruby Tuesday and Strawberry Tallcake are registered trademarks of Morrison Restaurants, Inc.
Ruth's Chris Steak House is a registered trademark of Ruth's Chris Steak House, Inc.
Sara Lee is a registered trademark of Sara Lee Corporation.
7-Eleven and Slurpee are registered trademarks of Southland Corporation.
Shoney's is a registered trademark of Shoney's, Inc.
Skyline is a registered trademark of Skyline Chili Inc.
Snapple is a registered trademark of Quaker Oats Company.
Sonic Drive-In is a registered trademark of Sonic Corp.
Starbucks and Frappuccino are registered trademarks of Starbucks Corporation.
Subway is a registered trademark of Doctor's Associates Inc.
Swiss Miss is a registered trademark of Hunt-Wesson Foods, Inc.
T.G.I. Friday's and Jack Daniel's Grill are registered trademarks of T.G.I. Friday's, Inc.
Tony Roma's A Place for Ribs, Carolina Honeys, and Red Hots are registered trademarks of NPC International, Inc.

INDEX